To Think Like a Teacher

To Think Like a Teacher

Cases for Special Education Intern and Novice Teachers

Mark B. Goor
George Mason University

Karen E. Santos
James Madison University

Foreword by James M. Kauffman

Allyn and Bacon

Boston • London • Toronto • Sydney • Tokyo • Singapore

Executive Editor: *Virginia Lanigan*
Editorial Assistant: *Erin Liedel*
Executive Marketing Manager: *Amy Cronin*
Editorial-Production Service: *Matrix Productions*
Composition and Prepress Buyer: *Linda Cox*
Manufacturing Buyer: *Julie McNeill*
Cover Administrator: *Kristina Mose-Libon*
Electronic Composition: *Publishers' Design and Production Services, Inc.*

Between the time Website information is gathered and then published, it is not unusual for some sites to have closed. Also, the transcription of URLs can result in unintended typographical errors. The publisher would appreciate notification where these occur so that they may be corrected in subsequent editions.

Library of Congress Cataloging-in-Publication Data

Goor, Mark B.
    To think like a teacher : cases for special education intern and novice teachers /
Mark B. Goor, Karen E. Santos.
        p. cm.
    Includes bibliographical references.
    ISBN 0-205-28497-3
    1. First year teachers—Case studies.   2. Handicapped children—Education—Case
studies.   I. Santos, Karen E.   II. Title.

LB2844.1.N4 G65 2001
371.9—dc21

                                                                                2001035752

Printed in the United States of America
10 9 8 7 6 5 4 3 2   06 05 04

We dedicate this book to novice educators who persevere in the face of many challenges because they are passionate in their desire to make a difference in the lives of children with disabilities and their families.

CONTENTS

FOREWORD

Ideally, teacher education starts with recruiting intellectually capable college students or college graduates whose temperament and moral characteristics suit them to teaching. In the ideal world, these recruits have mastered or will obtain mastery of the content knowledge they are to teach. Furthermore, these recruits are prepared to teach many students who do not share either their high intelligence or their moral and temperamental characteristics. Those preparing to teach receive instruction in the science and art of teaching so that they know what to look for in teacher-student interactions and curriculum materials. They are beginning to think like teachers and to recognize familiar patterns in teaching and managing students; every classroom situation or student interaction no longer seems different from anything they have encountered before. Their preparation for teaching includes extensive experiences in clinical settings in which teacher educators first demonstrate how to instruct and manage a group of students expertly, subsequently give recruits practice in teaching and managing, and finally provide corrective feedback.

Most of us who prepare teachers recognize this as the ideal. However, we teacher educators always fall short in some ways, even if we're very good at what we do. The same is true of teachers. Learning to think like a teacher or a teacher educator requires that we acknowledge our shortcomings and strive to do better. We try to find ways around problems, to think up alternatives that might bring us closer to the ideal when we can't do something the ideal way. Ideally, all teachers in training will experience a great variety of problem situations, but for practical reasons we often can't provide all of these experiences. Teaching with cases lets us come closer to the ideal than we can get otherwise. Cases simulate the world in which teachers work and about which they need to learn to think. That's why I think they're useful.

We can, and we do, get better with practice—but if, and only if, we think about what we're doing. The thinking is critical; just following our intuition in teaching will not necessarily produce good results. That is, a good teacher is not just a bright person who intuitively knows how to teach. Being intellectually sharp helps someone become a better teacher (or better anything else), but good teachers are also prepared—educated about teaching. Preparation to be a teacher makes a difference; people trained to teach do better than those who haven't been trained (Berliner, 2000).

Recognizing the fact that teacher education needs improvement leaves us with this question: What can we do to improve it? Practice is a good idea, regardless of the performance to be acquired. But mere practice—just doing it—is not enough. The practice must be guided by precepts and feedback. Effective practice is guided by thinking about what we're doing using the wisdom of more highly skilled performers. This is true whether we're learning to fly a plane, play a sport, play an instrument, teach a concept, or manage a student's behavior. Here is one thing we can do to improve teacher education: We can help those who want to be teachers to think like teachers. Helping people learn to think like teachers is the primary objective of this book, and it is a worthy goal.

If learning to think like a teacher should be one of our objectives, then it is fair to ask at least these questions: How do good teachers think? How do we help people learn to think like that? A full response to these questions would require a substantial volume, but it is fair to expect some suggestions, even in a foreword. One thing a good teacher thinks about is clarity—whether the student knows exactly what to do. Another is the level of the task—whether the student is able to do the task with a high degree of accuracy yet still experience it as challenging. Another is whether the student has frequent opportunities to respond to and practice what's being taught. Another is whether the consequences of learning are positive—more specifically, whether the student receives meaningful rewards for desired performance. Still other things a good teacher thinks about are whether the tasks are being presented in a logical sequence so that the student gets the big idea, whether the task is relevant to the student's life, and whether the student is learning strategies for remembering and applying knowledge and skills to everyday problems. A good teacher also thinks about monitoring student progress. As we suggest in another volume using cases, thinking about all of these things and more is important for learning to teach academic, social, or behavioral skills (Kauffman et al., 2002).

Thinking like a teacher means being able to see recurrent patterns in academic tasks or social interactions so that an effective strategy can be used to deal with it. Notice that there are two parts to this statement: (1) seeing a recurrent pattern, and (2) selecting an effective strategy. Each is critical to learning to think like a teacher.

People who cannot see recurrent patterns are unsuccessful performers in any field; those who see the patterns have a distinct advantage. Consider sports, music, reading, mathematics, social interactions, or any other human endeavor. If people do not see the likenesses or samenesses—the commonalities—across plays, musical themes and chords, words, problems, or situations, then they can't become proficient. Each task is new and different, different from all the others in ways that defy analysis. They can't think, "Oh, right, I see, this is a problem of type ____, and I know how to deal with it." Teaching is not essentially different in this regard, though it is complex.

Effective strategies are those known to have a high probability of producing the desired outcome for a particular task. In teaching, no strategy is known to be unfailing in all cases (but this is true in all professions, including law and medicine). Some strategies for teaching particular things, however, have a much higher probability of success than others. Consequently, this is what we try to teach teachers to think: Go for the strategy with the highest chance of success based on carefully, repeatedly field-tested methods. In special education, we now know what many of these high-probability strategies are (see Forness et al., 1997; Lloyd et al., 1998).

I congratulate the authors of this book for their contribution to helping people think more like teachers. This means helping teachers *think about what they are doing and why and how they are doing it*, not thinking in the abstract. A widespread misimpression is that people who can think well about other things (science, math, or writing, for example) will intuitively know how to think about teaching, that their thinking skills in other domains will automatically generalize to thinking about instruction. We should disabuse ourselves of that notion in a hurry. Thinking like a teacher means thinking very specifically about what teachers do, and I'm glad to see a book like this one taking on that task.

James M. Kauffman
Charlottesville, Virginia
March 2001

References

Berliner, D. C. (2000). A personal response to those who bash teacher education. *Journal of Teacher Education, 51*, 358–371.

Forness, S. R., Kavale, K. A., Blum, I. M., & Lloyd, J. W. (1997). What works in special education and related services: Using meta-analysis to guide practice. *Teaching Exceptional Children, 29*(6), 4–9.

Kauffman, J. M., Mostert, M. P., Trent, S. C., & Hallahan, D. P. (2002). Managing classroom behavior: A reflective case-based approach (3rd ed.). Boston: Allyn & Bacon.

Lloyd, J. W., Forness, S. R., & Kavale, K. A. (1998). Some methods are more effective. *Intervention in School and Clinic, 33*(1), 195–200.

PREFACE

Students cite field experiences as the most important aspect of their teacher preparation program. These experiences provide the opportunity to observe and reflect on a variety of concepts and to practice skills presented in university courses. Fieldwork embedded in teacher preparation programs includes observations, structured practica, and student teaching. Not all courses are linked to field experiences with students with disabilities, however, and even the courses that are linked may not provide an effective transition to the world of practice. This critical linkage between coursework and fieldwork is often difficult to establish. One way to foster this linkage is through the use of cases. Cases offer an opportunity to examine genuine issues outside the real-life arena, thereby providing critical problem-solving experiences in a more relaxed time frame allowing deeper consideration. This book is designed to facilitate the development of reflective problem solving in preservice and novice special educators. The issues in this casebook are commonly experienced in practicum, student teaching, and beginning employment experiences in special education settings.

Rationale for Using Cases

The use of cases does not diminish the need for practical, school-based experiences. Rather, studying cases assists individuals in problem-solving a broader range of pertinent dilemmas likely to be experienced in the field and reflecting on potential solutions without being personally embroiled in the stresses and emotions of the true situation. By considering multiple perspectives of complex cases, teachers will be significantly more prepared to act in a purposeful, informed manner when they are actually confronted with problematic situations.

Cases serve the important function of preparing the reader for unexpected situations they may encounter during their induction into the teaching profession. Recognizing these situations as they arise and relying on a systematic problem-solving strategy may help teachers more effectively negotiate the terrain. The cases in this book are based on years of varied experiences in the field of special education. Both authors began as special education student teachers, served as cooperating teachers, and later as public school administrators. In addition, they have been university student teaching supervisors, coordinators of student teaching seminars that often accompany student teaching, and university administrators responsible for coordinating special education field placements. This broad range of experiences offers readers an in-depth understanding of dilemmas and needs of preservice and novice teachers. Each case was carefully constructed based on real-life situations of many intern and novice teachers with whom we have worked.

When we sit back and examine the career-long process of teaching, it is apparent that the latter portion of a teacher preparation program and the beginning years of teaching are crucial periods in an educator's development. Many puzzling experiences and ambiguous or confusing expectations bombard the novice. Successfully negotiating this critical period will depend on the teacher's ability to handle new situations and reflectively solve problems as issues arise.

Learning to teach is a lifelong journey that can be facilitated by a variety of training experiences and support (e.g., appropriate preservice courses, high-quality field experiences, mentorship programs, and continuous exposure to effective practices through staff development). Although no two situations will be identical, teachers who enter the field with a realistic understanding of what they may face, armed with a professional work ethic, prepared to reflect on their practice, and knowledgeable about ways to solve problems will be more likely to find satisfaction and success as teachers and therefore remain in the field. This book will reduce the number and severity of surprises preservice and novice teachers will face in the field. These teachers will be better prepared to deal with actual situations if they possess adequate background knowledge, are able to analyze a complex situation, and can envision a range of possible solutions. Although situations described in the cases in this book will not be identical to those that novice teachers will experience, common themes confront most special education professionals.

Content and Organization

This book is divided into eight chapters. Each chapter contains a brief introduction and multiple cases, each followed by "Consider This," a series of reflective questions that will help readers wrestle with issues and pose potential solutions. There is a blend of cases about student and novice teachers that address a wide range of typical experiences both groups face. The questions explore specifics in each case as well as broad issues applicable across settings. Chapter 1, "To Think Like a Teacher," consists of two longer cases and serves as an advance organizer for the book. The first case, "Can I Do This?" involves a novice teacher who marvels at the incredible talent demonstrated by a master teacher and questions whether she will ever be able to think and act with this level of skill. "First Solo Lesson," the second case, focuses on the thoughts of a student teacher preparing to teach his first lesson juxtaposed with the simultaneous feedback from the cooperating teacher watching the lesson. The next five chapters are organized by theme and contain cases of varying length. Chapters 2 through 6 consist of several shorter "single issue" cases followed by one longer, more involved case study. Shorter cases enable readers to focus on relatively few issues, whereas longer cases present more complex pictures for examination of competing demands and confusing expectations. Chapter 2 deals with issues of communication and collaboration as novice teachers learn the challenges of negotiating with adults to meet everyone's needs. Chapter 3 focuses on the impact of cultural/linguistic diversity as teachers struggle to communicate, understand, and serve an increasingly pluralistic society. Chapter 4 presents cases about discipline, motivation, and classroom management, the most prevalent concern of novice teachers. Chapter 5 examines dilemmas related to curriculum, instruction, and assessment of exceptional learners. Of critical importance are topics pertaining to special education law and procedures in Chapter 6 as special educators deal with competing pressure from parents, attorneys, and administrators. Chapter 7, "Induction," is a series of cases told by a first-year teacher encountering the surprises and challenges of the new job. Chapter 8 is devoted to helping novice teachers reflect on and systematically analyze their own experiences by writing cases; two cases illustrate issues related to case writing and teaching. An appendix provides a cross-reference for issues in each case with the Council for Exceptional Children Knowledge and Skills Standards for Beginning Special Educators.

Enhancing Case-Based Learning

Case-based instruction is enhanced when the instructor or discussion leader follows certain procedures and fosters a classroom climate that promotes open dialogue and higher-level thinking. We suggest that discussion participants take time to carefully read and reflect on the case before class to generate thoughtfully considered opinions. Instructors might provide questions to ponder before engaging in a class discussion. Participants should be encouraged to openly express their views and contribute to the discussion. After one opinion has been offered about the case, the instructor might solicit different interpretations, thus acknowledging the possibility of varying perspectives and explanations. Although differences in opinion should be valued and respected, it is important for instructors to recognize that not all interpretations or solutions are equally valid. While respecting feelings, instructors should give corrective feedback to ensure that no false perceptions are perpetuated. Instructors may need to refocus the discussion or restate main points when necessary. They may need to probe for clarification and encourage participants to cite evidence from the case to support their beliefs. Discussion participants benefit most when instructors promote the examination of values and beliefs underlying different interpretations. Instructors should summarize key points periodically throughout the discussion, possibly keeping a running list for reference. A visual format such as chart paper or a whiteboard will help to structure the discussion or frame the responses. Finally, in summative fashion, discussion leaders should examine the context for which certain decisions are made in order to assist participants in identifying when to apply similar principles in future situations. For more about how to use these cases, see the Allyn & Bacon website: www.ablongman.com/goor.

As preservice and novice teachers face daily complex situations in the field, they will rely on their ability to systematically analyze problems and make appropriate decisions based on the context. This book assists in bridging the gap between theory and practice. It provides a range of typical situations that will lessen the surprises and better prepare novice teachers for many situations they will face in the real world. Most important, these teachers will be empowered to act on the belief that they are capable of handling complex problems and can make a difference.

Using This Book

The broad range of issues addressed by the cases in *To Think Like a Teacher* facilitates multiple uses of the book. Instructors can use individual cases throughout a teacher preparation program. University supervisors can use this text as the central focus of practicum/student internship seminars. Mentors or staff developers will find that the cases stimulate collegial discussion and problem solving.

Acknowledgments

We are deeply indebted to all the professionals from whom we have learned so much. These include the educators who served as our own cooperating teachers and university supervisors many years ago. When we became classroom teachers and supervised student teachers, we learned from these enthusiastic novices. When we moved to new roles at James Madison University and George Mason University, we had the privilege of working jointly with classroom teachers to supervise practicum and student teaching experiences. The energy and enthusiasm of all these individuals were invigorating. In facilitating the student teaching seminar, we gained a unique understanding of the personal perspectives and fears of student teachers.

We especially want to thank the five talented special education teachers and five dedicated student teachers who participated in a research project using cases to promote reflection in student teaching. We appreciate the encouragement of James Kauffman at the University of Virginia, who initially supported this idea. In addition, we acknowledge the work of faculty at the University of South Florida in advancing the role of special education cases in teacher preparation.

At Allyn & Bacon, we want to thank Ray Short for promoting this manuscript and Virginia Lanigan for her patience as we completed it. We are grateful to the following reviewers who provided helpful feedback and insights that strengthened each chapter: Peggy L. Anderson, Metropolitan State College of Denver; Ann Boyer, Florida Atlantic University; Betty Epanchin, University of South Florida; Karyn Frank, Florida Atlantic University; Peggy A. Gallagher, Georgia State University; Mark P. Mostert, Old Dominion University; and Patricia Renick, Wright State University. Editorial assistants and editors offered valuable contributions.

We very much thank James Kauffman, a scholar in the field of case teaching, who graciously agreed to write the foreword.

1 · To Think Like a Teacher

After all the time and hard work invested in required courses, it's exciting to begin student teaching. New student teachers are usually anxious to implement those textbook theories and to test "best practices." However, the reality of schools, teachers, and students is often overwhelming. The following two cases highlight the observations of two new student teachers as they begin to realize how challenging it is to think and act like a master teacher. The first case, "Can I Do This?" examines the observations of a student teacher as she begins to see the complexities of instructing students with a wide range of needs. The second case, "First Solo Lesson," explores the experiences of a student teacher as he prepares and delivers his first lesson.

Can I Do This?

Caroline Altman had anticipated this day for months. From the moment she received her student teaching assignment, she could not wait to be in the school, see the teacher in action, and work with "her" students. The school had a wing for special programs with its own principal and support services. Mrs. Winslow, her cooperating teacher, had a reputation for being the most creative teacher anyone knew. And what an ideal situation: only nine third-grade students in a self-contained class.

Caroline arranged to be early on her first day. Arriving at the school at 7 a.m., she could not determine which door to enter. Eventually, she found a sign to the office. The secretary was already busy with phones ringing and teachers hurrying to get last-minute supplies. Caroline waited her turn and introduced herself. The secretary responded flatly, "Oh, Mrs. Winslow is in the Center. You need to walk to the other end of the building and ask in their office."

Not to be discouraged easily on this new adventure, Caroline navigated a labyrinth of halls and found the Center's office. This secretary welcomed her, indicated where to get a visitor's badge, and pointed in the direction of her new classroom. "She's expecting you . . . Room 3." The halls seemed quiet. Somehow Caroline had expected schools would be noisy all the time.

Caroline stepped into the classroom and was immediately drawn into the richness of the environment. She was so distracted by the posters, maps, carpeted areas, decorated bathtub, library, and computers that she didn't even see Mrs. Winslow approach. The teacher began enthusiastically, "Welcome to our class. Let me show you where to hang your coat and the best place to sit today to observe what we do. The schedule's on the chalkboard. Children arrive at 7:30. The opening activities are routines designed to help students enter the day gently and feel good about being here. Also, you can see most activities last 20 minutes or less. Consult the schedule throughout the day. I'm assuming you want to just observe today. Write your questions and we'll talk at lunch . . . that is, if we can talk over the cafeteria noise. Actually, the best time to discuss your observations will be at the end of the day."

Caroline began to realize why this teacher had such a great reputation. What a human dynamo! Another awareness was clearly emerging, however. This was going to be more complicated than she ever imagined.

Mrs. Winslow pointed at names taped to desks as she began describing the students, "Let me tell you about each student. Let's start with Jimmy. You'll find him interesting. Jimmy's diagnosed autistic. He can get violent if I don't monitor his anxiety level. If he gets agitated and starts patting his stomach and making noises, I give him a timer, and he walks around with it to regain his calm. But, don't worry, he's medicated . . . if his parents remembered. Next to him is Monty. He's our brightest student who spends most of the day in a general ed third-grade class. Monty needs lots of encouragement and a place to blow off steam if he becomes overwrought. He hates getting anything wrong. The desk next to him is for Brian, our new student. Brian has to stay in the general education third-grade class until we get his IEP from his former school. The next row starts with Eric, who doesn't finish anything willingly. I've got lists for him to check as he arrives to help focus his attention on tasks to complete. Let's see . . . Steve. Steve acts pretty normal until he doesn't understand something, then he quickly escalates into a tantrum and takes himself to time out. Leah, our only girl, has mild CP. She reads well but has trouble with written work. It can take her 45 minutes to write one illegible sentence. Our teacher's aide works with her on word processing." Mrs. Winslow pointed to four computers by the aide's desk. "Dante and Jerel prefer to sit together even though they are on completely different levels because they are the only African American students. Dante acts confident and easily engages adults, yet his records show a borderline retarded IQ. Jerel has the ability but sabotages himself. His current goal is to stay away from other students during work time. He loves to distract and annoy them until they blow up and get in trouble. Landon and Andrew sit together away from the others. Landon is the most ADD kid I have ever worked with. I've monitored him. During an average 20-minute work period, he is out of his seat six times for anywhere from 30 seconds to 4 minutes. Without an adult focusing him on his work, he gets nothing done. Finally, Andrew . . . who wants to do whatever we are not doing. If it's reading time, he takes out his math, and if it's math time, he gets up to finish his social studies report."

Mrs. Winslow stopped to take a breath and realized Caroline was on "overload." "It's a lot to remember; I know. As you get to know them, you'll see for yourself." Caroline had not imagined a small group of third-grade students could have so many differences and issues to consider.

At 7:25, there was an announcement to staff about the new bus behavior program. The teacher's aide arrived, and Mrs. Winslow introduced her, "Mrs. Hoffman, this is Caroline Altman, our new student teacher." The teacher's aide nodded, hung up her coat, and went to the back of the room to sit by a bulletin board with students' names and goals. Did Caroline detect a lack of warmth between the teacher and aide?

At 7:30, the teacher looked out the window and smiled, saying, "I see the buses. Get ready. Caroline, you can sit over there. I'll introduce you when they have all settled down. They're used to visitors."

Like one tornado after another, each student entered the room. Mrs. Winslow spoke to each with an individualized greeting as they began their established routines or approached her to show things. "Good morning, Eric. Glad you remembered where to put your coat. Good morning, Leah. I liked the way you used your words. Eric, good job checking your 'to do' list. Good morning, Andrew. Good morning, Jimmy. What do you need to do when you come in? Monty, I have some really cool news to tell you. Good morning, Steven. Good job going to get your points."

Students were filing to the back of the room for the teacher's aide to give them points. She was reminding each student of behavior goals and awarding points for yesterday's completed sheets.

Mrs. Winslow encouraged each student to hang up coats, get points, and go to his or her seat. Students were still arriving. The teacher prompted Eric to finish yesterday's math and Jimmy to sit in his seat quietly. Students wanted to talk about events from last night or this morning.

Caroline realized each student knew what to do to start the day. They were going to a board labeled "To Be Finished" with pouches that had their names printed on them. Students took unfinished assignments to their seats. Caroline consulted the schedule on the board: "Finish Work" from 7:40–7:55 and "Morning Message" at 8:00.

There were never more than three students working at any time. "I need help," said Landon. Mrs. Winslow gave a brief reminder of what to do. Steven raised his hand. But the teacher was getting Monty ready for his general ed class by asking him what materials he needed and affirming the positive day he would have. Once he was prepared, Monty worked at a computer until time to leave. Dante arrived. The teacher moved closer to greet him and quietly explain something. He looked angry. Mrs. Winslow encouraged him to get his points and return to his seat. Dante grumbled through the whole process. Mrs. Winslow saw Andrew was not working and encouraged him to get on task. She noticed Eric working and said, "Good job, working." She moved closer to Jimmy to quietly reinforce his on-task behavior. Finally, she had a moment to respond to Steven. "Yes, Steven?" "I can't figure out 3 'times' 2." Two students offered a way to think about the problem. "I remember that means the same as 3 'plus' 3," said Jerel. Mrs. Winslow commented, "That's a good strategy." The teacher noticed Landon out of his seat and assigned him a job stacking books in the class library. From his computer, Monty called out, "I found Godzilla on the Web." Two students started to jump up, but the teacher signaled them to stay at their desks and reminded Monty of his project topic and when to go to his general ed class. Leah wanted help, Eric had his hand up, Andrew was out of his seat, Monty asked a question about how to find something, and Landon said he couldn't find all the books on Egypt.

It was only 8 a.m. and Caroline felt exhausted just watching this large nest of chirping baby birds, all wanting attention, and the mother bird, feeding each one with love. The teacher seemed to know how to respond to each student so naturally.

Mrs. Winslow announced, "Time for Morning Message." Only two students were in their seat and ready. The teacher complimented them on being ready and the others quickly returned to their seats. Monty packed up and left for his class. A messenger from the office came to the door and asked to see Andrew. Apparently, he left for school with his mother's keys. Mrs. Winslow asked the teacher's aide to help Andrew look through his backpack.

"May I have your attention, please?" asked the teacher. "This is Miss Altman. She will be our new student teacher for the next eight weeks. Please introduce yourselves." Each student walked up and shook Caroline's hand. When the first student said his name, Caroline was unsure of how to introduce herself. Caroline? Ms. Altman? Leah asked, "Are you married?" Jerel wanted to know, "Are you a real teacher?" How should she answer? She thought she was better prepared than this.

"Eyes up here," said the teacher trying to refocus attention on the Morning Message displayed on the pull-down screen. A transparency on the overhead projector stated, "We have an assembly today at 8:15." "Dante, please read our message." Dante couldn't read "assembly," and others started calling out, "I know!" Dante finally figured it out and read aloud. "Nice reading, Dante," complimented the teacher. "Everyone please begin writing this on your 'message page,' and we'll finish after assembly." Mrs. Winslow explained to Caroline that students fill in a sheet daily to take home to inform their parents of special events.

Two students started talking about the pending assembly. Mrs. Winslow said, "Two people are talking . . ." Hands went up. The teacher realized assembly time was approaching rapidly, so she reminded students which papers went in the home folder, told them about the new "puzzle" center, and commented that some people had new goals.

"Okay, points before we line up for assembly." Mrs. Winslow asked each student to rate his or her performance for this time based on personal goals. Students reported point values from 7 to 10 and gave a reason they did not give themselves full points. For example, Steven said, "8, because I got frustrated and gave up on my math paper." Dante reported, "10, because I worked hard to read the Morning Message." As students reported their points, the teacher tallied points in her notebook, commented on their good work, or agreed with their assessment of why they did not earn full points. "Steven, you did get frustrated, but you stay calmer now when things get difficult for you." "Dante, that was good reading."

As the students lined up, Caroline wished she could sit there and process what she had just witnessed. But she decided she'd better stand up and join them cheerfully. She felt like she had been watching a master teacher in action with the neediest groups of children she could imagine. This short experience convinced her that a teacher has to be paying attention every second.

The class walked to the assembly without problems and behaved appropriately. About halfway through the assembly, Dante stood up and walked to Mrs. Winslow to say something. They talked for a minute, and he returned to his seat.

At the end of the assembly, as students from other classes sprang up to leave, Mrs. Winslow used sign language to communicate to her class, "Stay sitting." The students watched intently and waited for her hands to signal, "Line up." Walking back to the classroom, students began to get noisy and wander. The teacher stopped and just waited. It seemed the students knew the drill and quietly returned to line except for Landon, who appeared oblivious as he bounced against the wall. The teacher walked quietly to him and gently touched his shoulder. As if emerging from a dream, Landon looked at Mrs. Winslow and joined the line.

Upon returning to the room, the teacher announced, "Let's do points." Each student rated his or her behavior during assembly. When Dante said, "10 points," Mrs. Winslow replied, "Yes, and 2 bonus points for telling me the noise bothered you during the assembly instead of reacting!" The teacher reached out to touch Jimmy and signaled for him to be quiet. Andrew stood up to get his work. Mrs. Winslow remarked, "Andrew, I see you are anxious to get started, but it's not time now." The teacher reminded Landon to sit until everyone received points.

After all students declared their points, they returned to writing on their morning message sheets. While they completed this task, each stated his or her behavioral goal for the day to Mrs. Winslow. For example, Jerel said, "I will be kind to my friends." When a student started talking out of turn, the teacher noted, "I really appreciate people who can work quietly." "Landon," Mrs. Winslow said the student's name to bring his attention back to task. After Leah stated her goal, she went to a computer, where the teacher's aide assisted her in word processing.

After students finished writing and stating their behavioral goals, Mrs. Winslow walked to a poster called *Social Skills Strategies*. "Today's social skill is 'Accepting No.'" She briefly reminded students about the importance of learning to accept the answer "No." "Would anyone like to tell us about a time when he or she accepted the answer, 'No'?" Eric shared, "I asked to get a game, but you said, 'Not now, after lunch.' And I said 'Okay.'" Mrs. Winslow praised him, saying, "Eric accepted the answer 'No' even though he had to wait a long time. Nice job."

"Time for today's poem," announced the teacher. Mrs. Winslow turned on the overhead projector to show a poem. She looked at the assignment poster and voiced the name of the person who would lead the choral reading. Steven read and others tried to follow. Dante teased, "Leah's not reading." Leah started arguing. As if seizing the moment of chaos to cover his moves, Jerel walked to Jimmy's desk and started playing with things. Jimmy started to yell. Mrs. Winslow gave Jerel the "look" and he returned to his seat. As she walked around touching students and pointing to the screen to remind them where to look and to join in, she occasionally read aloud to keep students together. At the conclusion, Mrs. Winslow commented, "Nice reading," and walked to the assignment poster. She shuffled the name cards and revealed: "Tomorrow Andrew will read."

It was 9:10. Mrs. Winslow turned off the overhead projector and prepared to distribute papers. Caroline consulted the schedule and read, "Social studies." The teacher began the next lesson, "We have been studying about Egypt. Our activity today is writing postcards. Write to a friend describing something we have learned about Egypt and then draw a picture to show what it looks like. You may consult the vocabulary words on our Egypt wall."

Caroline focused on the wall with maps and lists of vocabulary words. Noticing that there was a sample postcard already taped in the center of the display, she realized how much planning had gone into just beginning this day. Would she ever be able to think so creatively and attend to so much at one time? What time did the teacher have to arrive this morning to be so well prepared?

The student teacher continued to observe as Mrs. Winslow moved from student to student, encouraging each to think and write. Andrew was working on yesterday's math. The teacher reminded him, "It's time for social studies."

Jimmy lifted his shirt and started patting his stomach and rocking. Mrs. Winslow made eye contact with Caroline to signal her to watch. The teacher moved quickly to get a timer for Jimmy. "You can have 3 minutes of space," she said matter-of-factly. Jimmy took the timer and left the room. The teacher quietly explained to Caroline that Jimmy walked around the halls watching the timer. When the time was up, he returned calmer.

In the meantime, Landon was out of his seat, wandering around the library area with his postcard, and Steve began calling out in an agitated tone, "I can't write all that. I don't know how to draw." Mrs. Winslow responded, "Let's look at the example on the wall. How can you start?" Steven escalated, "I don't know. I need time out." Mrs. Winslow agreed he could have time out if he needed it but asked, "Are you sure you need to leave, or can you use self-control?" The student responded, "I just need to calm down." He sprang up, took a pass from the board, and left. Mrs. Winslow explained to Caroline that he was going to the time-out area in the office where he would talk to a counselor and return when he was ready. Then the teacher turned her attention to Landon, who had been back to his seat and out again. Caroline observed that of the

Never a dead moment

Specific Positive reinforcement

"if it doesn't increase behavior it's not reinforcement.

nine students, no more than three were ever on task at any time and at least three seemed to need attention simultaneously.

After finishing postcards, the students placed their assignment in "Finished" folders in their desks. Then they walked to a box labeled "ZYLAR" and pulled out a Ziploc bag on which their names were printed. Some students took their books to the carpet, while others returned to their seats. Mrs. Winslow noticed Caroline watching and explained that ZYLAR meant "Zip Your Lip and Read." The bags were filled with books from a commercial series of books organized by reading levels. Students were assigned a bag with a book at their ability level. Students who achieved the highest behavior level earned the privilege of sitting on the carpet; other students read at their seats. Caroline realized there was yet another system in place, one in which students earned privileges. "How did the teacher keep all of this straight in her mind?" she wondered.

Steven returned from time out with a note about what had transpired. Mrs. Winslow helped him resume work on the postcard.

Someone came to the classroom door and handed the teacher a note. Mrs. Winslow announced that everyone got full points for bus behavior, eliciting cheers from the students. The teacher explained to Caroline that bus behavior had become an issue; so the center staff developed a program in which whole classes could earn a party for bus points.

Landon was wandering around. The teacher stated calmly, "Landon, you are not doing anything." He responded, "I don't want to do anything." Mrs. Winslow referred him to the "Needs to Be Finished" area of the board where each student had papers clipped. She directed him to the "Pyramid" worksheet from the previous day and instructed him to get a gluestick. He picked up the paper and gluestick and sat in his seat but did not begin working on the project. Mrs. Winslow asked the aide to help Landon get started. The pattern was now evident to Caroline; the aide did what was asked of her and what was clearly routine but took no initiative. Caroline wondered if it would be presumptuous to ask Mrs. Winslow about the teacher-aide relationship.

It was point time again for social studies. Landon was seated but hitting his desk, and Jimmy was walking around. Mrs. Winslow confirmed she would only give points to people who were ready and who raised their hands. She ignored students who called out and focused on Jerel, who had raised his hand. Students quickly quieted down.

Another teacher walked into the room, guided Jimmy back to his desk, and began working with him. Mrs. Winslow whispered to Caroline, "That's the itinerant teacher for autistic students. She comes twice weekly." This itinerant focused her attention exclusively on Jimmy and seemed not even to acknowledge the teacher or anyone else. Caroline made another note, about communication with staff, to ask about later.

At 10 a.m., students began taking out their lunches. "Lunch?" Caroline thought. Although it was too early to eat, she was certainly ready for a break. Then Mrs. Winslow reminded the student teacher that they ate with the students. Caroline wondered, "When do teachers have breaks and planning time?"

Andrew began yelling something about blood. Caroline spun around to see he had a bloody nose. Mrs. Winslow grabbed tissues, handed them to Andrew, and suggested he pinch his nose and sit calmly.

The class walked to the cafeteria and entered a huge room of noise and activity. The teacher and student teacher stood together watching the children eat, talk, and laugh. Her class didn't seem any noisier or more active than the rest of the elementary school. Mrs. Winslow suggested bringing a lunch and at least eating something at that time. Caroline was puzzled about how she could stay alert for any problems during lunch, think about getting ready for the next lesson, and digest food at the same time.

After lunch, students went directly to the game shelf. Those on "Level 1" sat on the carpet, and those on "Level 2" went to their seats. Monty came back from his general education class after lunch to inform Mrs. Winslow how his morning had gone and how well he was keeping to his behavioral goals. After 10 minutes, he gathered his books and returned to the third-grade general ed. class.

Mrs. Winslow sat in front and announced point time for lunch before they began handwriting. After points were assigned, the teacher turned on the overhead projector to show the handwriting lesson for the day. Mrs. Winslow reminded students that when they finished handwriting they could choose a learning center. Caroline looked around and began to see how many different areas of the room were set up with learning activities.

Landon announced, "I can't do a cursive *g*." He sprang out of his seat and walked away from his desk. Mrs. Winslow replied, "I can help people who are at their seat," and walked to his desk to wait for him. Students began calling out, "I'm done," "Mrs. Winslow, I'm done." The teacher modeled raising her hand and didn't acknowledge anyone until they followed suit.

During center time, two students chose to work at the computers. Whenever a student went to a computer, the aide seemed to automatically move over to help. Mrs. Winslow noticed Steven was crying. She started to walk in his direction when he blurted out, "I can't do this."

An alarm began ringing. Students jumped up and walked to the door. Caroline looked to the teacher, who rolled her eyes and said, "Fire drill."

Mrs. Winslow signaled to the teacher's aide to take the front of the line while she and Steven walked behind the others to talk about what was going on. Caroline stayed back to overhear the conversation, not wanting to eavesdrop but being too fascinated to miss this opportunity to listen. Steven cried and said he didn't feel well. Mrs. Winslow listened and encouraged him.

On the way back from the fire drill, Eric closed a door on Landon's fingers. Landon began crying. Mrs. Winslow asked the aide to get ice. Landon paced around the room with ice on his hand, pouting. "Unbelievable!" thought Caroline.

Math and health lessons proceeded without any new calamities. The health lesson focused on the food pyramid. Mrs. Winslow related the pyramid shape to their social studies unit on Egypt. Caroline was struck by the teacher's "big picture" conceptualization of curriculum. It occurred to the student teacher that up until this moment she had thought of curriculum as a collection of subjects prescribed for each grade. Not only did the teacher have a handle on multiple student needs, but at the same time she kept in mind everything she taught.

After the social studies lesson, points were given. The final activity of the day was a self-appraisal for each student about whether they had behaved appropriately during the day according to their goals. Each student stated his or her goals and then commented, "Yes," "No," or "Most of the day." Mrs. Winslow followed each student's self-assessment with a concrete example of when the student did or did not adhere to the goal. For example, when Landon said, "No, I didn't," the teacher replied, "Landon, you had trouble staying seated today, especially during social studies."

After reviewing daily goals, students got their coats and lined up to go home. As she watched Mrs. Winslow put on her coat to walk the students to the bus, Caroline mused, "What made me think this would be so great? The kids are so needy. I don't have a clue how to respond to all those different behaviors. This teacher has a bottomless bag of tricks to teach skills. The schedule is relentless. There is so much going on; it feels like chaos. But I better compose myself. Mrs. Winslow will expect me to have questions when she returns. Where do I start?"

Caroline began to write questions in a stream of consciousness. How do you know when to ignore and when to insist? Why do you give points so often? Where do you get all your ideas? How much time does it take you to plan? Aren't you exhausted? Is it okay to ask about the teacher's aide? What about that itinerant teacher; does she say anything to you? Andrew's bloody nose. . . . What about universal precautions? How long did it take you to get this good? Will I ever be able to do this?

Consider This

1. What realizations made Caroline feel so overwhelmed?
2. What do you think is most challenging for new student teachers?
3. How might Mrs. Winslow respond to some of Caroline's questions?
4. What other questions would you have for Mrs.Winslow, Caroline, or the teacher's aide?
5. Identify features of the physical environment designed for effective instruction. Speculate the teacher's rationale for each.
6. Identify challenging behaviors and how the teacher created routines to prevent problems or responded to problems as they arose.
7. List the scheduling issues that Mrs. Winslow had to consider when planning.

Observing a talented teacher respond to multiple demands and provide seemingly effortless instruction is intimidating to many student and novice teachers. It is a shock for preservice teachers to arrive at the true realization that teaching is a complex act and that master teachers have talents preservice teachers have previously taken for granted. However, there is a quantum leap in awareness when student teachers implement their first lesson. The following case illustrates the experiences of one student teacher as he prepares for and delivers his first solo lesson.

First Solo Lesson

On Monday morning of his third week of student teaching, Roger woke up thinking about the math and language arts lessons he was to teach that day. The math lesson on liquid measurement would be easier because it was based on plans and materials from Mrs. Norr, his cooperating teacher, but the poetry lesson was the beginning of his own unit and his first solo teaching experience. He was not quite sure how he felt. On one hand, the beginning of this student teaching assignment had gone fairly smoothly; on the other hand, he had been taken by surprise with the overall complexity of the experience. "They never told us it would be this complicated. It is so multidimensional," he had thought at the end of the first week. Roger was confident that he was capable of handling the variety of individual daily responsibilities of a teacher. Within a short period of time, he mastered the routines of the classroom and figured out the distribution of points for managing behavior and reinforcing homework. He successfully implemented lessons based on his cooperating teacher's detailed plans. Mrs. Norr seemed pleased with the assistance he provided in the classroom, and he had overheard her mention several times that she wished she had an extra pair of hands like this all the time.

Moving to get out of bed, Roger thought of the upcoming lesson and coached himself by thinking, "Just focus on teaching the lesson and everything will be great." But doubt kept creeping back in.

At 7:45, Roger entered Harris Middle School and headed down the main hall toward the seventh-grade wing where the Stars Team was located. As he approached the special education resource room, he passed Mrs. Norr and the assistant principal discussing the previous day's discipline referrals received by some of the special education students. The Stars Team's rooms were on an inside hallway without windows. There was Mrs. Norr's room, the team office, and then two other rooms, divided by a movable wall, for the general education teachers, Mr. Brent and Mrs. Wilfong. The resource room was arranged with a combination of round and rectangular tables rather than individual student desks.

Months ago, when Roger received notification of his placement, he felt very lucky to be placed on the Stars Team with his cooperating teacher, Mrs. Norr, and the two general education teachers. He had heard about their exemplary collaboration from professors during his special education classes. Oddly enough, he had even noticed a car around town with the license plate "LV TCH-ING" and it turned out to be Mrs. Norr's. The inclusion of Mrs. Norr as an integral member of the middle school team and her daily co-teaching in social studies presented a textbook case of effective collaboration. These teachers were professional colleagues and had grown to be personal friends. Roger only hoped that someday he would be fortunate enough to teach in a similar situation.

Roger entered the room and found some students had already arrived. He greeted several students, asking how they were doing. Doris, the teaching assistant (TA) who for all practical purposes fulfilled the role of an additional teacher, returned with Nathan from a meeting about his discipline referral from the science teacher. Everyone turned to look at Nathan as he loudly exclaimed, "I got it for a stupid reason." The language arts and social studies teachers arrived to discuss with Mrs. Norr the problem of too many Star Team discipline referrals. One student was working on the computer while others wandered in, sat down, and took out their materials. Roger used this time before the 8 o'clock bell rang to make connections with individual students. He wanted the students to like him.

Roger was pleased with the student diversity in this school because his other field experiences had been much more homogeneous. In first period there were a total of eight students: Demarcus and Keesha were African American, Miguel was bilingual and spoke Spanish at home, and Hyon was Asian. In addition, there were four Caucasian students, Tara, Mark, Nathan, and Noah. Despite their differences, this was a fun bunch of kids who got along pretty well together.

From 8:00 to 8:20, students were assigned to a homeroom and remained there for their first-period class. Typical activities, such as attendance and announcements, took place during this time, but in addition students were able to work on homework, study for tests, or receive extra help if needed. Three girls at the back table were studying for a music test by completing a study guide. Roger realized the reading level and vocabulary would challenge most people as he referred to the materials to try to explain the meanings of "monophonic" and "syncopated." Other students were either working on computers, studying spelling words, or completing math word problems. Mrs. Norr and Roger were both involved with keeping students on task, monitoring progress, or helping with reading. For a while, there was relative quiet except for the low tones of the girls working together, the click of computer keys, and Miguel orally reading a math problem. With a well-understood look or a hand signal, Mrs. Norr was able to effectively communicate a variety of commands (think, work quietly, come here, get to work) from across the room as she sat next to Demarcus. Roger, however, had a little more difficulty. He moved about the room, assisting or prodding as necessary, but as he became involved with a student his concentration was so intense he was often unaware of what others in the room were doing. He knew he needed to work on developing what Mrs. Norr called "eyes in the back of his head." "How will I keep track of everyone when it is just me in the room?" he wondered.

At 8:15, Roger took a few minutes to prepare for his first-period math lesson, which would begin at 8:20. Working from Mrs. Norr's plans, he was going to have the students sit in their present groups at the tables. Each group would have plastic containers of various sizes, colored water, and a worksheet. Mrs. Norr had successfully taught this same lesson before and Roger was looking forward to seeing the students learn through an active, hands-on activity. He knew his professors would approve of this well-designed lesson.

Mrs. Norr moved to the side of the room to allow Roger to take over. At 8:20, Roger began the transition to first period by saying, "Put away your materials so we can do math." Doris, the teaching assistant, left to assist in a general education math class where several students with disabilities, as well as other students, needed help. As the students complied with the request to get ready, Roger asked them all to sit around the front table. "The first thing I want to do is review yesterday's work. What did we do?" Tara called out a variety of answers, mentioning pints, quarts, gallons, and cups. Roger went on to ask about relative capacity of several of the containers. "Who wants to show us?" All students began waving their hands and calling out, "Me, me, me." When Mark made an off-task remark about baseball, from across the room, Roger's cooperating teacher signaled Mark to attend to the lesson. Students took turns pouring water into containers to illustrate various equivalent amounts. "So far, so good," thought Roger. The classroom door opened, and Roger was pleased to see a small student enter. Noah had already accumulated seventy-two absences this year and had been transported to school by a truancy officer. When Noah was in school, he was an active participant; it was just a matter of getting him there. Promptly and without fanfare, Noah sat down and jumped into the lesson.

At 8:40, when Roger was satisfied the students knew what to do, he grouped them in pairs and sent them back to their tables with measuring equipment, colored water, a large baking pan to catch the water, paper towels, and an activity sheet. The students became actively involved in measuring, discussing, reading, and writing. Knowing the students were totally on task and engaged in the lesson gave Roger an exhilarating feeling. He moved around the room, monitoring their performance and giving several reminders to be very careful when measuring. He related the importance of being precise to measuring Tabasco sauce in a recipe. Roger felt positive about how things were going and on several occasions received visible signs of approval from Mrs. Norr.

Close to the end of the period, Mrs. Norr left the room and Roger announced they had 5 minutes left to finish. Some groaned that they were not done and others avoided cleaning up by wandering around the room. Mark chewed on a pen top and poked himself with a tack. As Roger tried to close up the activity, he realized things were falling apart. It was a challenge to keep students who were finished under control while prodding others to clean up. Finally, Roger picked up the timer and waved it as a warning. He requested three times for Mark to take his seat and finally wrote Mark's name in the corner of the board. Mark replied, "That sucks." Tara walked out of the room. Minutes later, Roger looked around the room and asked who was missing.

At 9:28, the bell rang and students hurriedly exited from both sides of the classroom into the crowded hallways. During the 4-minute break, Roger, who still felt somewhat frantic from the math lesson, rushed to finish cleaning up and get organized for the upcoming language arts lesson. Before he knew it, students began drifting into the room, dropping piles of books noisily on the tables.

At 9:32, the bell rang for second period and all ten students were on time, although not necessarily settled down. Doris returned from the general education math class, which reminded Roger that he had not thought ahead about what role she should take in the lesson or the classroom. Working with Doris was somewhat awkward for Roger. She appeared very competent and was the age of his mother. Now not only was Mrs. Norr watching, but so was Doris. Roger felt doubly nervous and hoped he could remember all the students' first names. Two of the students from first period returned, while the other eight were new. Although Roger had carefully read all their files at the beginning of student teaching, he didn't yet feel he knew these students as individuals.

The language arts time was divided into 10 minutes of word study and 38 minutes devoted to a specific instructional unit based on IEP objectives and state curriculum standards. "I want everyone to get out their word-study materials now," requested Roger. As he passed out sheets of paper, he asked, "Do you know what you are supposed to do with the words?" One student pointedly replied, "No." Some students began working immediately, while others noisily leafed through their notebooks trying to locate words that were written on small pieces of paper stored in Ziploc sandwich bags. Scott complained, "I can't find my words. I don't remember putting them in my binder." He searched through a notebook that clearly showed evidence of teachers' efforts to keep him organized. Roger suggested that Scott try his locker and then complimented Heather on her word sort, which was almost finished. In a few minutes Scott returned, shaking his head as a signal he couldn't find the words. Eventually the bag was located on a table in the back of the room. "I need an eraser," "I need a pencil," and "My pencil needs sharpening" were comments dotted throughout the work time. Adam was off task and literally in midair with his chair tilted back, kicking his feet. Roger tried to imitate a look Mrs. Norr might give, but each time Roger turned around, Adam started again. Adam said to another student just loudly enough for Roger to hear, "There is one teacher in the whole school I do not like," and he pointed to the student teacher. "If he comes over, I just stop what I am doing. I pretend to listen but he can't tell me what to do." Roger felt his spirits sinking.

Mrs. Norr made timing and balancing students' needs seem effortless. But Roger found himself in a predicament. Anna came up to show Roger her finished work while Scott had barely started. Up to this point, Mrs. Norr had identified each student's words and Roger began to realize he didn't know how to select words to keep the students moving forward on their individual skills. He made a mental note to look back at his course text to refresh his memory on word study. Abruptly, Roger realized it had been more than 10 minutes, and it was time to begin the poetry unit.

Mrs. Norr returned, commenting that she was always cornered by someone when she left the room. She was talking with the guidance counselor about the discipline referrals. At this point, the physical education teacher and assistant for a special education class came in to ask Mrs. Norr about dates for several upcoming school events.

"If you are not finished, take your words home to study," Roger directed. "Please put away your materials so we can begin the lesson," Roger stated, making a concerted effort to be positive yet maintain control. He continued with several attempts to be firm. "Clean up and get your desk ready for the next subject," he directed as confidently as he could, even though he didn't know what else to do when the students' work was in different stages of completion. He knew Mrs. Norr would say something about this later and ask him to provide some solutions. "Oh, well," he thought, "I can't be concerned about this now, I need to get started with poetry."

Roger put a copy of his lesson plan as well as the detailed outline of his unit in front of Mrs. Norr, who smiled encouragement. He kept a copy near the overhead projector for his own reference. Since he had not been able to go over the lesson with Mrs. Norr before now, he hoped she liked what he had planned. It had taken a lot of hard work last weekend to prepare the overall poetry unit. Roger remembered not liking poetry when he had studied it in middle school, which might explain why he really did not remember much about it. It was difficult to determine what to include in the unit. He had spent a lot of time in the university library and on the World Wide Web to find appropriate middle school objectives, materials, and activities, particularly seeking ideas relating to these students' diverse backgrounds. It was significantly more difficult than the magnetism unit he had written for one of his courses. This might have been because science was an area of interest for him, and he knew he could incorporate fun activities with actual magnets. Another difference was that he didn't ever have to actually teach the science unit. This poetry unit, however, was another story.

Roger took a deep breath, gathering all the confidence he could muster, and began the lesson. Out of the corner of his eye he noticed Mrs. Norr pick up his papers and carefully start to review the written plan. Last Friday at their scheduled conference, she had expressed disappointment that he had not brought either an outline of the ten-day unit or the first three lesson plans. Mrs. Norr lectured him that from previous experience with many student teachers, she knew, "Careful communication and troubleshooting in the beginning usually prevents a lot of problems. Some student teachers do not fully appreciate the necessity of having well-developed, detailed plans, even those who come from your university, where I know effective planning is stressed." Today, Roger could tell from her smile that she was pleased with the in-depth written lesson plans he had labored over the entire weekend. He had made sure to include all components: a date, instructional period, subject, objectives, time frames, and descriptions of what he planned to do.

Once the students were all seated quietly, Roger began by stating, "Today we are going to begin a unit on poetry." Loud groans immediately ensued. Roger inhaled deeply and countered defensively, "No, really, this will be fun."

His shaky voice barely convinced himself. "Let's start by writing some easy poems called paired couplets." He could tell by the looks on their faces that this was going to be an uphill battle.

Fearfully, he glanced at Mrs. Norr, hoping she was not seeing his mounting frustration but realizing she had predicted this uncomfortable moment. Roger remembered Mrs. Norr saying that student teachers need to learn from experience and that sometimes it was difficult to watch these first lessons. Although she knew in her heart the student teacher needed to learn by experience and her students needed time to adjust to a new instructor, her "teacher mind" was constantly judging and modifying how she would have taught the lesson. She had told Roger, "It is unrealistic to expect perfection from student teachers, yet my first priority is to my middle school students, who deserve quality instruction."

Mrs. Norr had carefully and gradually guided Roger through several steps leading up to this moment. First, he had observed her and discussed his insights. Second, he implemented one of her lessons. Finally, he was asked to develop and implement his own lessons. The first transition from observing to implementing one of the teacher's lesson plans had gone fairly smoothly. However, this next transition to independently planning and teaching a solo lesson was much harder than Roger had imagined it would be.

It was clear from the looks on the students' faces that they had no idea where he was going with the unit or specifically with directions for the paired couplet. Roger showed a handwritten example of a paired couplet on the overhead projector. He read it aloud and pointed out the rhyming words at the end of the lines. Then getting out a blank transparency, he stated that they would write one together.

Roger asked the students for two words to use in the couplet. One student chimed in, "Hotdog," but Roger didn't think it would work very well, so he changed it to dog. Another student suggested, "Peninsula," but Roger said that word was too complicated. He ended up with "dog" and "cat." Using these words, Roger led the group through the steps of writing a couplet.

Next, Roger told the students they would each write a paired couplet. "First write two words on your paper to use in your poem. When you are finished, raise your hand," he directed. Roger had allotted 3 minutes for this activity. Some students had their paper and pencil ready; others did not. They couldn't think of words without talking out loud, and the noise level quickly rose. As students shared their words, Roger had to help them revise or spell the words. "This is chaos," he thought as he tried to suppress his panic. The supposedly simple process of identifying two words took much more time than Roger ever dreamed. He was shocked as the bell rang and several students had not even identified two appropriate words. He looked at his watch in amazement, realizing he had made a serious timing error. "What a disaster my first solo lesson has been."

Roger was confused and exhausted. Once the last student had bolted out of the door, Mrs. Norr walked calmly to Roger, and said, "This lesson is going to give us a good opportunity to talk about what works with these students and what could have been done better. Let's sit over here." Mrs. Norr motioned toward two chairs beside her desk.

When they were seated, Mrs. Norr asked, "How do you think the lesson went?"

Roger could barely look at her and replied, "I lost them as soon as I said the word 'poetry' and I never recovered."

Mrs. Norr replied, "I could have predicted how these students would respond. These are basically good kids who have experienced a lot of school failure. They were scheduled into the language arts resource period because of significant weaknesses in reading and writing. Writing poetry would not be their first choice of fun activities. That's why you needed an advance organizer or anticipatory set. How could you have captured their interest in poetry, possibly without even using the word?"

Roger admitted, "I wish I knew."

Mrs. Norr smiled and offered, "I know you are feeling tired and frustrated. Instead of asking you questions, why don't I just tell you what might have helped?"

Roger nodded.

Mrs. Norr continued, "Without even using the word 'poetry,' you might have begun with a simple cooperative learning activity to intrigue the students and show each of them they were capable of writing interesting poetry. For example, you could have given each group a topic and each student a piece of paper to write one line of poetry. The papers are passed clockwise and the next person writes another line and then folds over the first line so that only one line is visible at a time before passing the paper again. Once the paper has been passed around the group, the students unfold the papers and read their poems. The resulting poems can be amazingly clever and students often enjoy sharing with the class."

She paused and then continued: "Jumping into paired couplets seemed a little premature as the students need an overview or a 'big picture' of the unit first. I would have liked for you to use a graphic organizer clearly showing students the relationship of the subtopics to the overall unit theme. Although I was glad to see you had a concrete example ready to show the students a couplet, these students depend on the right mix of auditory and visual information in order to learn best. I wish you had taken the visual part of the lesson one step further by using a colored marker to highlight the rhyming words and show how they were placed on alternating lines. Underlining one set in red and the other set in green would have helped the students visualize the relationship of the rhyming words to each other."

Observing his downcast expression, Mrs. Norr smiled. "I thought that it was a good idea for you to model the writing of a couplet and request input from the students, although it would clearly have been better to identify the type of words that would work best. If you wanted to do something like that—provide some baseline criteria, such as one-syllable words that do not rhyme—

then you might not have had to reject or modify the students' suggestions. Or I would have had word pairs written on cards for the students to pick from a hat. This would have taken less than 2 minutes."

Finally, she said, "The next thing that was desperately needed was additional structure to the lesson and written directions for reference. It might have been advantageous to let the students work in pairs. Knowing my kids, I probably would have assigned roles for each student. The directions for writing a couplet could have been typed at the top of an activity sheet along with a place for the students to self-monitor each step of the way. An organized worksheet with places to write would have helped to keep the students on track. The first section might include a place to write the two words and then a place to write words that rhymed with the two words, and so on. Judging from your written plan, I know you had expected to cover more."

Roger finally spoke: "How will I ever be able to juggle objectives, timing, materials, activities, and behavior?"

Mrs. Norr smiled knowingly. "Learning how much students can do in a period of time comes with experience. And balancing all those considerations is an art. You thought it would be easier, didn't you?"

Roger nodded. The bell rang and they stood up to walk to the next class. Roger was thankful that in this next class he only had to follow the lead of the other teachers and chip in when needed. Next week, he was scheduled to begin co-teaching, although he was not sure what exactly he was supposed to do. Mrs. Norr and Mr. Brent made it look easy, but something told him this was as deceiving as the effortless way Mrs. Norr balanced disparate students' needs. Nothing, so far, was turning out to be easy.

Together, Roger and Mrs. Norr quickly moved toward the social studies classroom. Roger was hopeful Mrs. Norr would say something encouraging, but the silence spoke volumes. The bell was about to ring and they wanted to model promptness. As in Mrs. Norr's room, the furniture consisted of mainly tables where the students were seated in groups of four to six. He had already observed that the students were assigned to cooperative groups and that students with disabilities had been carefully distributed among the groups. In the center of each table was a colorful plastic box containing various supplies and any specific materials needed for that day's lesson. Mr. Brent was the epitome of organization, and Roger knew he could use a few lessons in this arena.

The previous day the two teachers had spent over 45 minutes during the team planning time working on social studies, and Roger expected the lesson would be carefully orchestrated. He had observed them carefully weave several objectives from the state social studies standards into each lesson. Their knowledge of the curriculum content was awesome. Roger had expected this from the social studies teacher but observed Mrs. Norr was equally on top of things. During his first week, he remembered Mrs. Norr sharing her belief about the importance of having adequate knowledge of the general education curriculum in order to teach in both special and general education classes. These two teachers made coming to social studies enjoyable for the students. Roger looked forward to it every day as well. The enthusiasm of the teachers, both for the subject matter and also for working with each other, was contagious. Roger had taken a class on consultation and collaboration at the university in which the professor had been pessimistic about actual collaborative practices in some of the schools. It was exciting to see these teachers actually doing many of the things he had learned about. He knew experience in this area would be beneficial when he was interviewing for a teaching job.

Today, Mrs. Norr and Mr. Brent began with current events. Two days a week, students received points for bringing in timely articles about international events and showing the class where the country was located on the globe. A lively discussion always ensued about the various topics, and Roger was amazed that the teachers were so knowledgeable about both the event and geography. These teachers must read every word in the newspaper, he thought to himself. Previously, Roger had not kept up with the news very well but starting last week he made a concerted effort to watch the evening news. This would hardly be enough if he was to fill Mrs. Norr's shoes in these discussions. Next, they showed the news broadcast, a short program made for schools. This was the basis for an interesting lesson that involved a combination of history, geography, civics, and economics.

The teachers had explained to him how their present teaching strategies gradually developed over a period of two years. They wanted Roger to understand that a lot of reflection and hard work went into providing appropriate instruction for the diverse range of the students in this class. Two years ago, they had just shown the program and expected students to take notes. This was followed by a teacher-led discussion, the assignment of a follow-up activity for homework, and the eventual inclusion of current event questions on their tests. Unfortunately, as Roger would have been able to predict, this only worked for a handful of students. Some students had not been interested in the news or had such a limited background of experiences that they got very little out of the broadcast. Others paid attention but either were not capable or chose not to take notes. As a result, students were often not able to complete the assignment or did poorly on test questions related to current events. Mr. Brent and Mrs. Norr wanted everyone to be as excited about national and international news as they were and wanted to differentiate instruction so each student was able to participate and benefit. They gradually changed the procedures to what they were now, and from the first day of student teaching Roger had been impressed with the enthusiasm as well as accomplishments of all the students. If he could keep abreast of the news he knew this would be a fun co-teaching experience.

The collaborative lesson was awesome to observe. Both teachers took turns presenting and adding to each other's comments. During several brief activities, the teachers seemed to intuitively know who would lead while the other moved around the room supporting students. The teachers seemed to respect each other and stimulated more dialogue than Roger believed possible with middle school students. With 10 minutes remaining in the class period, the teachers divided students into groups Roger guessed were assigned by ability level. But to his amazement, the special education teacher went with the more able group.

The bell rang and, as before, Roger was surprised the period was over. There was so much to accomplish, but time went by so quickly in school! He had entered the room keyed up from his two lessons this morning but had quickly forgotten about them as he became involved in the social studies lesson. Now his thoughts returned to the earlier periods, knowing Mrs. Norr would want to talk more about the lessons over lunch.

Consider This

1. Describe the excitement a student teacher might feel preparing for a first solo lesson.
2. What fears might a student teacher experience before teaching a lesson?
3. What might help a student teacher be ready for this solo experience?
4. What might Roger say to Mrs. Norr about his own reflection on the lesson?
5. What feedback would be helpful to Roger at this time?
6. What do you think Roger should learn from this experience?
7. How did Roger view the collaborative teaching experience?
8. To plan individual lessons, what does a teacher need to know about IEP goals and unit objectives?
9. How does a special education teacher balance the need to advocate for the best possible instruction for students while assisting the preservice teacher to develop professionally?

CHAPTER

2 Communication and Collaboration

Individuals who choose to teach will generally tell you they love children or they want to make a difference in the lives of youth and their families. It is a rare pre-service teacher who says, "I like working with other teachers, parents, and administrators. I love the challenge of collaborating with reluctant adults." Yet the modern reality of special education success is founded on the ability to inform general educators of the needs of exceptional students, to negotiate for resources, to develop partnerships with parents and other professionals, and to resolve conflicts over most appropriate services.

Cases in this chapter will present dilemmas of student teachers who are confronted with adults who do things the student teachers do not appreciate or agree with. Student teachers will examine the difficulty and challenges of communication with adults who have different opinions and priorities. Other adults include cooperating teachers, university supervisors, paraprofessionals, parents, and co-teachers.

A Mismatch with the Cooperating Teacher

Most student teachers assume they will be placed with a cooperating teacher who will provide a good model for effective teaching. Unfortunately, the selection process for cooperating teachers is often out of the hands of the university and sometimes results in situations that are less than ideal for the student teacher. In the first case, a student teacher who is uncomfortable with the way her cooperating teacher manages and instructs children wonders about expressing a difference of opinion.

What Did I Get Myself Into?

"That's it, James! No recess today. Does anyone else want to stay in this morning? How many times do I have to tell you to sit down and do your work?" Mr. Nelson stood glaring at his nine special education students. They were quiet, but Audrey could see they were angry. Audrey had been told these were the most challenging students in the school; teachers talked of how disruptive these students had been in their classrooms (and, confidentially, how glad they were to have the students out of their rooms). At the same time, the principal had bragged to Audrey that she would be seeing a master of classroom management; Mr. Nelson had *no* discipline problems! Audrey had eagerly anticipated observing what techniques were so effective with such challenging students. But now, after two weeks of student teaching, Audrey had begun to refer to her cooperating teacher as "Mister Negative."

The student teacher returned her attention to Sally, the student she read with each morning. Sally stared at Mr. Nelson and whispered through clenched teeth, "I hate him." Audrey was afraid to respond because her own feelings might be apparent. Regaining her composure, Audrey asked genuinely, "Well, Sally, how would you get those boys to settle down and do their work?" Sally shrugged her shoulders and commented, "He never says anything nice to them. They don't think he likes them, so they won't try." Audrey responded, "That's good insight. You have helped me to be a better teacher." Sally softened and declared, "But I like you."

Reflecting on her student's simple but profound insight, Audrey glanced around the room. The picture was clear: there was no evidence of student success or progress displayed, the classroom rules were twelve "DO NOTs," students' names were written on the board for every infraction, and there was a perpetual unhappy expression on Mr. Nelson's face. At 10:00, it was math time, which meant work sheets and flash cards. Students were supposed to get work sheets from their folders to complete while they waited for Mr. Nelson to drill them on their facts and correct work sheets in their folders. As the teacher entered marks in his gradebook, he commented in succession, "You're not thinking today. . . . Earth calling Brian. . . . That's all you did? . . . It's about time you remembered that one. . . . Didn't you say you wanted to go to math back in Mrs. Pataki's room? Not at the rate you're going."

Audrey had to say something. Not only was she observing poor teaching, but she felt sorry for the kids as their low self-esteem was reaffirmed time after time. Although Audrey felt the need to say something, she wondered if it was her place to question her cooperating teacher. "Who decided this guy should have a student teacher?" she thought. Then a more personal fear struck. "How can I teach the way I believe is best with Mr. Nelson evaluating me? He'll tell me to do it his way, and I can't." Audrey felt sick to her stomach as she ruminated, "Should a student teacher openly disagree with her cooperating teacher? I care too much about these students to be silent. How do you tell a teacher his negativity is hurting children?"

Consider This

1. About what issues might a student teacher disagree with a cooperating teacher?
2. What communication strategy could a student teacher use to address concerns with a cooperating teacher?
3. What might the student teacher be missing by focusing exclusively on points of disagreement?

4. If you were Audrey, what would you do in this situation?
5. If this were your classroom what would you do to establish a positive climate?
6. How would you develop classroom rules?

Disagreements between University Supervisors and Cooperating Teachers

Student teachers sometimes find themselves between two strongly opinionated professionals. Cooperating teachers are ultimately responsible for their students and have clear beliefs about managing their students and delivering instruction. On the other hand, university supervisors feel responsible for linking their teacher preparation program with the school setting and ensuring student teachers practice research-based, effective instruction. In the following case, a student teacher has to handle a situation in which the beliefs and practices of the cooperating teacher are not compatible with the expectations of the university supervisor. What communication and negotiation skills might be necessary?

Caught in the Middle

On the first night of the student teaching seminar, Dr. Hindamin, the university supervisor, reviewed the syllabus that outlined course requirements. Evidence of progress in all areas would be developed into a portfolio including journal writing, videotaping, and plans and reflections on a variety of lesson formats the student teachers would implement. Dr. Hindamin recommended that student teachers show the syllabus to their cooperating teachers. Mindy, her student, agreed that immediately informing her cooperating teacher of these expectations would enable her to schedule all the requirements.

Dr. Hindamin highlighted her particular interest in observing a lesson that used a cooperative learning format, as taught in their methods class. Mindy was excited by the prospect of teaching middle school students in small groups. "I'm sure it's a challenge, but at their age those kids like talking with each other better than listening to me," she thought.

Colleen Kane, the cooperating teacher, was an experienced middle school special educator. On her first day, Mindy was pleased to see how smoothly classes ran. Mrs. Kane was fun but firm. As long as students complied, everyone had a good time. Students knew the routines, stayed on task, and seemed to genuinely like Mrs. Kane. After school on the second day of observation, Mindy showed Colleen the syllabus. The cooperating teacher laughed empathetically, "I remember all those requirements." Then Colleen leaned forward for emphasis and declared, "But let me tell you, I know how to teach these kids, and you're here to learn from me. So when you're in my class, you do it my way." Mindy was in awe of a confident, competent teacher, but at the same time she felt uneasy about Colleen's potential inflexibility. As Colleen looked down the list, she stopped, pointed at "cooperative learning" and said, "I can tell you one thing for sure, small group stuff with these students is a waste of time. Trust me; I know." Mindy was surprised and began to question, "Yes, but . . ." Colleen interrupted, "My class, my way. You won't regret it. . . . Now, let me tell you about the kids." There was no doubt this was the end of the discussion.

When Mindy reported to her supervisor that she had hit a stone wall with Mrs. Kane about cooperative learning, Mindy expected the supervisor to offer to intercede on the first visit. Instead, Dr. Hindamin responded excitedly, "What an ideal opportunity to try out the conflict resolution skills you've learned in the consultation course. This is the beginning of your professional experience collaborating with educators." For Mindy, the initial enthusiasm for working with an excellent teacher had been replaced with a dread of confrontation.

The next day, instead of excitement about observing excellent teaching, Mindy could hardly pay attention throughout the day. She was preoccupied with a variety of imaginary scenarios in which she brought up the subject of cooperative learning but hit a brick wall each time. As the students were leaving the final class, Colleen commented to Mindy, "You seem less enthusiastic today than yesterday. Maybe seeing the little darlings in action for another day has changed your mind about the reality of this job?" Mindy thought to herself, "Oh, no. It's even worse, she thinks I don't like the kids or I'm afraid of teaching." Mindy could not speak.

Consider This

1. Describe the situation from the viewpoint of student teacher, cooperating teacher, and university supervisor.
2. What would you say if you were Mindy?
3. What conflicts may arise between teachers who are responsible for and in charge of their classes and the expectations of university teacher preparation programs?
4. Who do you think should attempt to resolve this conflict?

Supervision Can Be Anxiety Producing

University supervisors are in the position of supporting student teachers but also upholding university standards. No matter how much students are assured that supervisors can provide helpful feedback and support them through difficult challenges, student teachers know that their supervisor decides grades and signs legal documents for licensure and graduation. So even under the best of circumstances, it is natural that student teachers feel anxiety about their supervisor's visits. In this case, the student teacher feels confident after a week of teaching but is surprised by her response to the supervisor's visit.

She Makes Me Nervous

Marsha observed her cooperating teacher, Mr. Ishii, in the high school special education resource room. Mr. Ishii was a good teacher with an encouraging manner. His routines were simple; students seemed to know what to do from the time they entered the room until they left when the bell rang. If students challenged his authority, the teacher had a way of diffusing the threat and quietly redirecting students back to the task. Mr. Ishii had the same gentle way with Marsha. He guided her easily, introducing her to the plans and materials gradually over the first week. On the first Friday, Mr. Ishii asked Marsha, "Would you like to plan to teach third period next week? You know there are only five students, and Barbara, the only girl, would be thrilled. They're all working on basic writing skills, and there's a workbook I use for lesson ideas. What do you say?" Marsha was anxious to get started and leaped at the opportunity. So beginning the second week of student teaching, Marsha was responsible for one period each day and enjoyed it.

Mr. Ishii encouraged Marsha's ideas and complimented her on the rapport that developed so quickly between her and the students. On Thursday afternoon, Marsha was feeling confident and talking about taking more responsibility the following week. This was good timing for the supervisor's first visit the next day. Although Marsha had met with success up until now, when Dr. Jones walked into the room Friday before third period she felt unnerved. Pretending to be confident, Marsha began explaining her plans for teaching the writing group, but she knew the presence of her supervisor made her anxious. As students arrived, things went from bad to worse. The normally compliant group was tired and grumpy, and Barbara was late. When Barbara finally arrived after the bell, Marsha inquired, "What's going on?" Barbara fired back, "None of your damn business." Marsha felt like the wind had been knocked out of her and did not know what to do. Mr. Ishii was torn between stepping in, which would make Marsha look incapable, or holding back and letting Marsha handle it as he believed she could. Dr. Jones was reassessing her initial impression of Marsha as a strong student.

Marsha decided to move into the lesson with what had seemed last night to be an engaging beginning. Unfortunately, the students whined and moaned, "Do we have to work? It's Friday. C'mon, Miss Roth. . . ." Marsha persisted, but when the planned activity did not work and Barbara sat fuming, Marsha turned to Mr. Ishii with tears in her eyes and shrugged her shoulders. The teacher stepped in and quietly nudged each student to get out materials and "show our visitor what a great class we have." Marsha and Mr. Ishii worked together until the end of the period.

When students left, Dr. Jones asked, "Is there a place we can talk?" Marsha wondered how she could have felt so confident yesterday but so incompetent now. As Dr. Jones began asking how things were going, Marsha felt herself become increasingly defensive.

1. What might have happened during third period if the supervisor had not been there?
2. What impression do you think the supervisor received?
3. How could Marsha represent herself without feeling defensive?
4. Is anxiety about supervision avoidable?

Working with Paraeducators

Paraeducators, also known as paraprofessionals and teacher's aides, are employed in special education programs to provide more individualized attention and to allow teachers to offer more direct instruction to students. Paraeducators perform a wide range of tasks, from nonspecific, all-around support for a whole class to implementing carefully designed plans based on IEP objectives with one child. Many paraeducators learn skills on the job and become valued assets. At the same time, paraeducators are adults with beliefs, idiosyncrasies, and personal needs. Working effectively with a paraeducator requires understanding how to collaborate with another adult—that is, communicating clearly, mutually respecting each other, sharing responsibilities, and giving and receiving helpful feedback. This is a challenge for mature, experienced teachers, but often confusing or overwhelming for the novice, as in the following case.

Old Enough to Be My Mother

Hillary Williams saw the tension building over the previous two weeks but hoped the two parties involved would work it out themselves. Her paraeducator, Janice Winters, had twenty-five years of experience with elementary students with disabilities. Hillary and Janice had worked together for the last five years at Canterbury Elementary. Although they were not friends, they appreciated and respected each other. Janice had no college education but her experience raising four children and working alongside excellent special educators resulted in an effective albeit opinionated assistant.

The student teacher, Linda Kohler, had been described to her cooperating teacher as possibly the brightest student the special education professors could remember. She was creative and hardworking; her lesson plans were of publishable quality. On the first day, Linda's enthusiasm was immediately apparent when she asked, "Can I start teaching tomorrow?" Hillary took an amused "wait and see" approach on Thursday when Linda confidently directed the teacher's aide to "finish up with Alex while I help Belinda." Janice glared at the young novice, commenting sarcastically, "Whatever you say, Boss." Three weeks later there was a standoff with both women firm in their attitude about the other.

As soon as the students left, Linda went to the office and Janice lingered until the student teacher was gone. Janice paced as she blurted, "Who does she think she is, ordering me around? I don't take that from my kids, and I won't take it from her. Do you know what she said? She told me I need to 'be more positive with Jimmy.' I know how to work with Jimmy. He loves me. As a matter of fact, after twenty-five years, I know what works. What's this tapping on desks phonemic thing and calculators for math when they don't know their facts? And, how politically correct to say 'culturally acceptable behavior'? Bah! Kaela's too loud. I don't need this job; I do it for the kids." It took Hillary an hour to calm Janice to the point she would agree to return tomorrow "for the kids."

Afterward, Hillary found Linda in the media center gathering materials for the next social studies unit. "Can we talk?" asked Hillary. Linda launched into her monologue: "If it's about Mrs. Twenty-Five-Years of Experience, I have a few things to report." When Hillary nodded, Linda continued, "She tells the kids, 'That's wrong, pay attention to the right way.' She contradicts me in front of the students. During my calculator math lesson, she told Alice to follow her to the back of the room to practice multiplication facts. And I don't even want to start about her lack of cultural sensitivity. Frankly, I'd rather not have a teacher's aide if this is what I have to work with."

Hillary knew that both paraeducator and student teacher had good points. Yet the teacher realized that after Linda finished her internship in four weeks, Janice would continue to be Hillary's instructional partner. Janice had strengths, and Hillary did not want to lose her. At the same time, the teacher felt strongly that educators have to learn to collaborate with adults who are different. Hillary had only four weeks to influence the student teacher on this critical point.

Consider This

1. What do you think Hillary said to her aide to get Janice to promise to return?
2. Hillary realizes that Linda must learn to work with other adults. What should she say to Linda?
3. Would you rather work alone than with someone with whom you disagree?
4. Janice is as old as Linda's mother. What suggestions do you have for supervising adults older than you?

Joys and Challenges of Parent Partnerships

Parent partnerships enable teachers to understand their students better and increase the likelihood that school programs may be enforced at home. However, there are many challenges to creating successful partnerships between parents and educators. Parents may have logistical problems in attending meetings, such as transportation, schedule, or child care. There may be language barriers, different communication styles, and conflicting beliefs about authority that impede understanding. Many parents are overwhelmed by the school bureaucracy or by lack of knowledge of the system. On the other hand, educators may label parents' lack of participation as apathy and reduce efforts to develop partnerships. Educators are busy professionals with family and community responsibilities; extended hours to accommodate parents' schedules may be a hardship for them. Finally, schools often create systems to retain power because of an underlying belief that educators have the knowledge and should therefore be primary decision makers. Sometimes student teachers have the opportunity to participate in the development, maintenance, or challenge of parent partnerships, as the following case describes.

New View

Although I love working with my ninth graders, I've looked forward to the experience of this teacher workday because my cooperating teacher, Elizabeth Cook, has scheduled parent conferences and an IEP meeting. Mrs. Gomez was scheduled for 9 a.m.. At 10:15, she arrived with two young children, explaining in accented English, "I try to find my mother to watch the kids but many times she has to take care of Abuela [grandmother]. Gerardo, he is trouble again, no?"

I introduced myself and said, "I'm the student teacher. I really enjoy working with Gerardo. His reading is improving." Mrs. Gomez looked surprised and asked, "Really? Why you ask me to come here?" My cooperating teacher took over, "Gerardo is making excellent progress now, and it would help if you would encourage him to practice at home. He doesn't always bring his homework back to school completed." Mrs. Gomez admitted sadly, "I can't help. My English is no good. And Gerardo, he works at night. He loves to buy $100 shoes and go with girls." Mrs. Cook listened empathetically to the mother who shared her frustrations while holding both children, rocking and kissing them as she talked. I had prepared a list of suggestions for parents to encourage homework completion which I discreetly slipped back into my folder. Maybe next time?

At 11:00, Mrs. Alred arrived looking like a fashion plate. I saw my cooperating teacher stiffen and was puzzled about what to expect. "Have you seen Brandon's grades?" Mrs. Alred asked. She waved the report card and continued, "History D, Algebra C, English D minus. When I agreed to let Brandon go back to the mainstream, I expected he'd get a little support from you." Mrs. Cook began to explain, "Brandon wanted to try it on his own and ask for help when he needed it." Mrs. Alred interrupted, "Obviously, that was a failure. I want him back in LD classes." Mrs. Cook was trying to remain calm, but I heard her voice cracking, "I think Brandon would consider coming back to LD classes as a failure." Mrs. Alred reached into her large pocketbook and pulled out Brandon's IEP. It looked like more than twenty pages. The mother asked sternly, "When can we reconvene an IEP meeting to correct this mess?"

I could see my cooperating teacher struggling. I thought back to my consultation class and the negotiating skills we had learned. Summoning all my courage, I spoke up, "That's your right, Mrs. Alred. But, I wonder if first we could agree that we all want what's best for Brandon?" I thought I detected a smile on the teacher's face, and it caught the mother off guard. I felt proud. I continued, "It's only been four and a half weeks since Brandon has been in these new classes. He really wants to succeed. Maybe we can think of ways we all can help." Even though my heart was beating fast, I was feeling excited about my apparent successful intervention. But nothing could have prepared me for Mrs. Alred's response. "Who is she?" the mother demanded of my teacher. "What do you know about my son?" she said to me. Mrs. Alred stood, gathered her things and said, "IEP meeting. Thursday? Friday? Call me. I'll be available." Mrs. Cook looked at her and nodded. After the mother left, the teacher offered, "Thanks. That was smooth; you'll be good at this. But I'm not sure anything would have helped with her. Nice try, though."

At noon, there was an IEP meeting for Sean, a student who was new to the district. I got to see the whole process and was pleased to see how well Sean, his mother, his stepfather, and Mrs. Cook worked together. The English and World History teachers also stopped by for a little while. They developed mutually agreed-upon goals and objectives. The parents seemed comfortable and concerned about a good transition to the new school. Sean liked having input into his IEP and agreed to all (although begrudgingly to some) objectives. I wondered why they all couldn't be like that. After the meeting, Mrs. Cook asked me, "What do you think of parent partnerships now?"

Consider This
1. What motivated each parent?
2. How might each parent describe the meetings?
3. Is a partnership with all parents possible?
4. What role could a student teacher play in each of these meetings with parents?
5. Comment on the student teacher's attempt to resolve conflict with Mrs. Alred.

Challenges of Co-Teaching

More than ever, parents, special educators, and administrators expect students with disabilities to be included in general education settings. Yet everyone involved has both hopes and fears. Parents want their children treated as normally as is possible, but at the same time they want individualized, intensive instruction. Special educators see that their students can rise to the level of higher expectations but then find the students have gaping holes in their skills. Many administrators seek communities of learning and positive collegiality among general and special educators but then realize there is a price to pay in resources and conflict management. General educators have various responses depending on their philosophy, experiences, skills, time, and perceived level of support.

Most special educators find they must collaborate with general educators to provide appropriate instructional experiences for their students. Some special educators and general educators report that collaborative teaching has been the most stimulating and powerful professional experience imaginable. Yet special educators are often surprised how much more challenging working with adults is than teaching children. General educators frequently express a preference for working alone. They have developed philosophies of education that may not be compatible with teaching diverse groups of children, and they have strong territorial feelings about their classrooms. In the following case study, a special education teacher describes the positive and negative experiences of beginning a co-teaching program in an elementary school.

She's Not Your Teacher!

We're here for the kids, right? We do what is best for all children, don't we? What I thought was going to be one of the most exciting opportunities in my professional career has degenerated, in part, into the most frustrating experience of my life. Teaching difficult kids is simple compared to collaborating with some adults. Let me tell you what happened last week to give you a flavor of what I mean.

On Monday morning at 10, I entered Bonnie's fourth-grade class in time to set up for reading groups. Four of my students received most of their instruction in this room. Bonnie was finishing a math lesson as I walked in. She didn't look up at me. Bonnie barely acknowledges when I join the class. Bernardo, one of the fourth-grade students I often help along with the special needs students, raised his hand when he saw me. Bonnie snapped, "Put your hand down." Bernardo quietly pleaded, "Can't she help me?" Bonnie walked to the board and wrote Bernardo's name where she put names of students who did not follow the rules. Then Bonnie stated, "You follow my directions. She is not your teacher! She has plenty to do. Her kids don't have a clue what's going on." Even though this co-teaching situation had gone from bad to worse, I was unprepared for today's attack. Fighting back the tears, I looked at Bernardo and mouthed the word, "Sorry." Then I signaled my four assigned students to move to the back table. Sadly, Bonnie was correct; these students didn't have a clue. One hadn't started the work, one had done the three he knew how to do, and the other two students had done them all wrong. I knew they needed help, but it was hard to concentrate. I didn't want to return to a resource room model. However, the current situation was intolerable.

It started last spring when our principal, Gary Martin, planned a meeting with a fourth-, fifth-, and sixth-grade teacher along with me to propose an experiment in co-teaching. Gary outlined his idea for me before the meeting. Starting this next year, my thirteen students would join three classes and I would divide my time among them. Gary had selected three teachers with excellent reputations for effective instruction. I was so enthusiastic I could hardly wait for the meeting. I prepared by writing brief descriptions of each student and copying their IEPs. I had reread an article about co-teaching to suggest several ways we could work together.

Elena, the sixth-grade teacher, was young and interested in innovative approaches to teaching. She was open and had lots of ideas of her own. Shirley, the fifth-grade teacher, was the veteran of the group. She had a reputation for setting high standards for students and helping students to achieve. Shirley was curious to see if the co-teaching arrangement could provide assistance for the students who did not meet her expectations. On the other hand, Shirley did not want to shift her focus so that the gifted students lost out. Bonnie, the fourth-grade teacher, was negative from the beginning. Even though she was as young as Elena, she acted stodgy and unwilling to stretch.

Mr. Martin led the meeting, explaining the districtwide emphasis on including students with special needs in the general education classroom. One model successfully used in a neighboring school district was co-teaching. The principal wanted to develop an exemplary program in our school. He was counting on us to collaborate in creating an effective system of education for all. I felt like the cheerleader, describing how many teachers nationwide have reported using co-teaching approaches for the benefit of a wide range of students. I thought I'd have the opportunity to talk a little about what I knew and describe my kids. Instead, Bonnie launched into a diatribe that could have been titled, "Don't we have enough to attend to?" She was overwhelmed by the assessment of the state standards of learning. I was offended when she contended that my students would probably bring her class score down. Bonnie questioned how two teachers could work in the same room: "Who is responsible for planning, teaching, and grading?" At one point, Bonnie even turned on me and asked, "What do I do with your students when you're not there?" I thought they were all good points but presented so negatively that everyone seemed discouraged. Shirley rescued the meeting by declaring, "Gary, I think we should try it. There are a lot of questions to be answered, but we're a hard-working, talented group who have overcome many challenges, and we're here for the kids." Bonnie looked down. Elena offered, "Let's talk next week about your ideas. I can already imagine some fun ways to work together." Thank goodness for Elena; she gave me hope, again.

Despite the fact that the principal initiated the change, it became my responsibility to invite the general education teachers to plan for next year. Although it was the principal's idea and initiative, I clearly felt the responsibility for the program's success was on my shoulders. I didn't know what to expect at the first meeting. After meeting once together, however, I realized I would have to "divide and conquer." Bonnie poisoned the first meeting with such comments as, "More work for us, less for you," and "I don't have time for anything else." Since Shirley had the potential to evaluate the impact on her students independently of the others, I thought it best to remove the possibility of Bonnie's negatively influencing perceptions. And no matter what, Elena and I would have fun; so I might as well enjoy that part without the stubborn pessimism.

As surely as there were three completely different teachers, there were three completely different approaches to planning and three distinct models for co-teaching proposed. Elena and I met for an hour every other week to discuss assigning students to groups, alternative teaching approaches, and ways to support each other's goals. We planned that when I was with the sixth-grade class there would be two simultaneous activities either dividing up the content, providing two levels of presentation, or approaching learning from a variety of modalities. Each time we met, we grew more excited.

Shirley appreciated my enthusiasm and dedication to children with special needs. She wondered if others in the class who were not labeled could get help and benefit from different approaches to a topic. Shirley preferred to plan and present the lesson while I checked if students needed individual help or small-group remedial instruction. She was interested in learning about the students, but she stated explicitly that when I was there, it was my responsibility to respond to their needs.

Bonnie was another story. Once she was away from the others, she really spoke her mind: "I only agreed to do this because I'm a new teacher and the principal asked me to do it. What am I going to say, 'No'? Don't go telling him I said that. Look, you take care of your kids and stay out of my way. I didn't get a degree to work with adults; I got a degree to teach children. It's my room . . . just remember that. And don't make trouble by talking to the principal about everything that happens in my class. Understood?" I replied, "I'm sorry this seems like such a hardship. I'll try to be as helpful to you and your students as possible." My willingness to listen and support took the edge off of her tirade, but she was not finished. "My responsibility is to the average and above-average kids," Bonnie stated. I had been so patient, but this pushed me over the edge. "Aren't you responsible for all the children in your class?" I questioned. Bonnie stood up and ended with, "Do what you want. Just don't expect me to change for you or your students."

So I began the school year excited about teaching in the sixth grade, prepared to work hard to win the trust of the fifth-grade teacher, and in full armor for coexisting with "stay-out-of-my-way Bonnie." The first time most of the other teachers in our school heard about the co-teaching experiment was at the teachers' meeting in August. Mr. Martin briefly explained that I was co-teaching with the three teachers and we would create a model for other grades and schools. After the meeting, several teachers sought me out to express their support and interest in future experiments in co-teaching. Some other teachers were less positive, saying, "Glad it's not me," or "You really think that will work?" It occurred to me how unprepared the principal, the faculty, my co-teachers, and I were for this new year.

Working in the sixth grade was a joy. Although we were making it up as we went along, we planned every week, and every week got better. Elena would stop me in the hall with a new idea and call me at night to change plans because she had read something or learned about something to enhance the lesson. She would leave me notes about how well a certain student had done when I was not in the room. The classroom was rich with projects, portfolios, learning centers, and activities. Kids were happy, parents were pleased, and the principal had a model to brag about. For the most part, the five special needs students were doing well, although I had concerns about one. Jared read on a second-grade level and required a lot of modifications to keep up with the class.

Elena and I took turns presenting new material. I felt comfortable letting her know when I didn't think students were following. She could signal me to help someone or move between potentially boisterous boys as tempers flared. It was also fun for me to teach science and let Elena work with the students who needed extra help. When I made a mistake, Elena lightheartedly whispered the correct page or a more accurate answer. I never felt put down. She told everyone that co-teaching with me was the best thing that ever happened to her teaching.

In the fifth grade, Shirley was more formal. She was polite with me and was professional in the way she interacted with children and conducted lessons. After the first week of school, Shirley made excuses about meeting to plan: "Sorry, I have got to get the room ready," "The fifth-grade teachers are meeting this week and that doesn't leave much time for me to write that test," or "I have to call several parents." My offers to help were gently declined. When I arrived in her classroom, children were on task. I just slipped in and glided around the room looking for students to help. Shirley was happy for me to work with students who needed extra repetition or another explanation. However, whenever I would make a suggestion about a way we might approach a specific topic, Shirley generally replied, "We have too much to cover to take time for that," or my least favorite, "That's dumbing down the content, don't you think? The parents of the gifted kids complain when we water down the curriculum."

In spite of being discouraged from more active co-teaching with Shirley, three of the students with special needs were keeping up with the class. The fourth special student required special parallel lessons I developed, and Shirley was willing to concede that this was best. Once, she even asked if another student might do better with those lessons as well. I leaped at the opportunity and always made an extra copy. However, there was no doubt that in this classroom Shirley was the teacher and I was the assistant. On the other hand, I began to notice that Shirley was now more likely to do things that helped students with learning problems. She posted assignments on the board, glanced around to make sure everyone opened their book to the correct page before beginning, and requested a peer to help one of the special students get started. One day after school, Shirley surprised me by asking, "Tomorrow would you observe Alice? I wonder if she has a learning disability. Maybe if you worked with her, you could see if this is worth pursuing. Oh, and would you like to see the social studies test? I'd be interested to see if you think the directions are clear enough for students like Alice." Wonders never cease. Possibly she might ask for my input on student grades for the next report card, but that's a lot to hope for.

With all the excitement in the sixth grade and slow but steady progress in the fifth grade, you might think I could just "bite the bullet" and live through a year with Bonnie. Unfortunately, it grew worse all the time. Yesterday, I found that Bonnie had begun sorting "her" students' work from "my" students' work. When I arrived, Bonnie was returning papers to the students. That is, she returned papers to her students. When the special needs students didn't get their papers back, I asked in my practiced cheerful voice, "Can I help find the rest of papers?" Bonnie coldly announced, "They're in that box over there with your name on it. You'll need to grade them. Since you need to know how your students are doing, you might as well grade all their papers." I knew there was no reason to point out the importance of informing our colleagues when we changed the rules. I looked at my students and said, "I'll take care of that right now." As I was grading Eva's paper, I came upon a word I couldn't read. I went to the student's desk, pointed at her paper, and quietly asked, "What is this word here?" Bonnie murmured, "If she can't write, she doesn't belong here." I stared daggers at her before I caught myself. Bonnie continued despite my discouragement, "In my class, if I can't read it, it's wrong. None of the other children get to tell the teacher what they wrote, why should yours?" I tried to respond professionally, but I'm sure my tone was challenging when I suggested, "That will be an excellent place to begin a discussion later."

Unfortunately, the discussion later revealed a situation worse than I had realized. Rather than being apologetic about her public confrontation and lack of sensitivity, Bonnie was angry. She verbally assaulted me, "So, you think everyone wants your students in our classes? Lots of the teachers I talk to think you should take your students back to your room and teach them what they can understand. Even the principal agrees it's not working out in the fourth grade. When I told him about your attitude, he wasn't surprised. My other parents are complaining about how much time I have to spend on your students. Even your students' parents are opposed to this arrangement. Alex's mother stopped by last week to see how he was doing, and when I told her he was not keeping up with the class, she said the old way was better." I could not believe my ears. She had talked to the principal, other teachers, and parents of special students while I had stoically resisted every opportunity to complain or report her abuses. I stood up and said, "You are right. It is not working."

Consider This

1. What was the principal's motivation to "develop a model of co-teaching?"
2. How might the faculty have been better prepared for this new co-teaching model?
3. What characteristics would you look for when selecting general education teachers for collaboration?
4. What ideas would you propose to enhance the co-teaching arrangement with Elena in the sixth grade?
5. Should the special educator be content with the "slow but steady progress" with Shirley in the fifth grade? Why?
6. What are the most important considerations at this time in the fourth grade?
7. What should the special educator do now?

3 Diversity

As the school-age population becomes increasingly diverse, the demographics of teachers remain disturbingly unchanged. That is, one-third of U.S. students are from a broad range of culturally and linguistically different backgrounds. Schools in growing numbers of states and large cities have majority populations of formerly "minority-status" students. In contrast, most teachers are white from a European heritage, with no foreseeable change in the near future because the vast majority of teacher education students still come from this background.

More than ever, teachers will be instructing students who have grown up with different languages and customs than their own. Many student teachers will feel the anxiety of learning to work with children and parents who see the world through different lenses. Teachers will be confronted by differing community cultural values and expectations. Educators will be challenged by issues of behavior, learning style, and language acquisition. To be more effective, new teachers must have increased awareness of the needs of a diverse population and better skills to educate culturally and linguistically diverse students. The following cases and questions highlight major issues in the teaching of this changing population.

Apprehension before Student Teaching

Many students approach teaching with an idealized notion of working with children and a mission to change the world that is often not based on real-life experience. In many cases, student teachers attended majority-white, European culture–based public schools and grew up with educated, English-speaking parents. As the reality of student teaching approaches, students' fears begin to surface, especially if the anticipated settings are dramatically different from their own. The first case explores a student teacher's feelings prior to teaching in a diverse school setting.

Not like Me

How can I tell my advisor, without sounding childish or ridiculous, that I am scared to go to Madison Middle School? Four years ago, I was thrilled to receive the acceptance letter from the university that would enable me to fulfill my dream of becoming a special education teacher. At that time, I only had thoughts about campus life, my friends who were also attending the university, and new friends I would meet. I had not even considered the eventual reality of student teaching.

My education courses addressed all aspects of teaching. In my management class, when we discussed students from "other backgrounds," I was a champion of liberal thinking, examining multiple meanings for behaviors. In curriculum, I developed many alternative ways to teach in order to ensure motivation and relevance. I felt confident of my beliefs and the importance of my mission. While conversing with my peers, I even ridiculed teachers who were stuck in their ways or who didn't understand the importance of considering cultural and linguistic backgrounds when assessing behavior or learning needs.

Now I stand outside Dr. Martin's university office debating whether to share my fears. Will she understand? In some ways I feel foolish, while deep down I know how anxious I am about what seems to me a very real problem. I am not like the students at Madison, and they are not like me. I did not grow up in an area like this, and I am totally unfamiliar with the cultural norms and values.

Why is there no place on a student teaching application form to identify concerns about placement? One just hopes for the best. The placement office was late in locating my student teaching assignment, and I was notified at the last minute of the school and school division. Now I feel stuck with the results. With student teaching starting in less than two weeks, it seems as if there will not be enough time to change the situation even if someone sympathizes with my concerns.

Since my special education program emphasizes multicultural aspects of instruction and preparation for diversity, the placement office seeks to assign us to settings that are culturally and linguistically diverse. Well, they certainly achieved that goal! Almost every student at Madison Middle School is from a different background than mine. I am especially worried about whether the students in the ED class will accept me. How will I relate to them or their life problems? Will I be able to develop a rapport with them? Will I be able to communicate effectively with their parents? This is supposed to be a time when I can practice what I learned in my courses, but I am haunted by the fear that I will not be able to span the gap between who I am and who they are. Wouldn't I learn more from teaching students like me without having to cope with all the differences?

The office door opens, I walk in, sit down, and proceed to explain to Dr. Martin why I do not think this placement is going to work for me.

Consider This

1. Which of the student teacher's fears do you relate to most?
2. Would this student teacher learn more from practicing with students from similar backgrounds?

3. Can you describe placement situations in which the student teacher might have legitimate concerns about his or her ability to handle such a different cultural environment?
4. What might be the advantages for students in the class if the student teacher is placed in their classroom?
5. How do you think Dr. Martin will respond?

Influence of Culture on Expectations

Effective teachers understand the impact of culture on students' learning and behavior. The first step in developing sensitivity to the influence of culture is to examine how culture influences oneself. In the following case, a new teacher must examine her own assumptions about learning and behavior as the result of an interesting cultural experience.

No Response

Elementary teaching positions were scarce in Laurie's home state of Pennsylvania. When a friend encouraged Laurie to apply for a teaching position on a Native American reservation, it seemed like a real adventure. Now, after three weeks, the excitement of moving to New Mexico had fizzled with the reality of unrelenting heat and being 100 miles from anything fun to do. But more disturbing was the lack of connection Laurie felt with these children and their community.

Laurie had spent days setting up her new classroom. Her enthusiasm provided boundless energy for putting up colorful bulletin boards, creating learning centers, and planning fun activities. She could not wait to meet her new students and get to know them. Laurie was excited to join a community that was different from her own. Certainly they would welcome a dedicated teacher who had come to help them. She could hardly wait for the adventure to begin.

On the first day of school, students filed into the room without looking at Laurie. She felt a disappointing lack of connection. Not to be dissuaded, and in an attempt to set an excited tone for the new year, Laurie enthusiastically directed, "I'd like each of you to stand, say your name, and tell us something you like to do." The children looked down. No one volunteered. "Who would like to go first?" No hands were raised. Laurie walked to one of the girls and asked, "Would you start?" The girl would not make eye contact and quietly, almost imperceptibly, shook her head, "No." Assuming the students were shy, Laurie offered, "Maybe you'd be more comfortable introducing yourself sitting down." The awkward scene degenerated until finally Laurie called attendance from her class roster and feigned an enthusiastic, "Nice to meet you."

Puzzled but undaunted, Laurie planned daily for active approaches to learning. However, she experienced repeated "lack of cooperation," with no volunteers to answer questions and outright refusal to go to the chalkboard to write an answer. Yet on the playground the students were active and animated.

When Laurie assigned seatwork, students worked slowly and looked at each other's papers. Laurie observed that during math one female student seemed to complete each problem, then leaned back for others to copy or check their own answers. Instead of turning in her completed work, she moved her paper to the corner of her desk to ensure that any student who needed an answer would have access. "Do your own work," was all Laurie could think to say without accusing anyone or offending her new students.

In an attempt to encourage faster task completion, Laurie asked, "Who will finish first? Let's see who can get the assignment on my desk first." Instead, as if signaled by telepathy, all the students rose simultaneously to hand in their papers together.

As the students filed past, Laurie stopped the girl who seemed to finish before the others. "You could be the best," Laurie explored, "don't you want to be the first to hand things in?" Without looking up, the student responded quietly, "Teacher, that's not our way."

Consider This

1. What assumptions is Laurie making?
2. How does her teaching approach reflect her culture?
3. What pattern is evident in this group behavior?
4. Suggest other approaches to working with these students.
5. How might a teacher learn more about cultural factors that impact students' behavior and learning?

Perseverance in Challenging Settings

New teachers quickly realize the challenges of educating a diverse population can be overwhelming. In these settings, traditional assessment and instructional methodologies are frequently ineffective. Yet many educators choose to work in schools with students from different cultures whose language, values, expectations, levels of motivation for school, and educational expectations differ. Successful educators in these schools must learn new strategies as well as find sources of inspiration and comfort. What motivates some to work in these environments and what enables some educators to persevere when many give up?

How Do You Keep Going?

Jim arrived in September eager to begin his first special education job in what he imagined to be an exciting multicultural environment. Before winter break, however, Jim told the principal he would not be returning. Sally was hired as a full-time substitute teacher in January. At the end of the month, she informed the secretary they would need to find someone else. Molly had just completed her master's in special education in December and was thrilled to receive a phone call about a midyear teaching position. She was so excited she neglected to question why there was an opening in February, and the principal did not offer an explanation.

Molly had never quit anything in her whole life, but after three weeks with her new class she was more discouraged than she could remember. It had been a particularly difficult day, and she needed someone to talk to. As she wandered dejectedly toward the copy room, Molly noticed Sylvia, a veteran teacher who appeared to be whistling as she posted papers and wrote assignments on the board.

The new teacher stood in the doorway and asked Sylvia, "Do you have a few minutes?"

Sylvia offered a welcoming smile, invited Molly in, and queried: "How's it going?"

Molly felt the floodgate open and poured out her frustrations: "Sam and Juan can't read and don't seem to care. I don't know what I did to Alice, but I'm sure she hates me. Mei-Shu and Ly-Ching speak Chinese about me and laugh. Larry steals, Sean bullies, and Mikala arrives whenever she pleases. It doesn't do any good to call their parents. Either they don't have a phone, don't speak English, or act like I'm accusing them of something. William, Lauren, and Ogan desperately want to learn, but I am so overwhelmed by the chaos that it feels like I never actually get to instruction."

Molly stopped and looked into Sylvia's empathetic eyes. Then Molly pleaded, "You've been here a long time, yet you don't appear discouraged. As a matter of fact, you seem quite happy. In the face of such demands, how do you keep going?"

Consider This

1. Identify the possible sources of Molly's frustration.
2. How might Sylvia answer the question about what keeps her going?
3. What help might Sylvia offer Molly concerning awareness of other cultures, management, strategies, support, or sources of information?
4. What additional supports could the school division offer to help Molly adjust?

Differentiating Diversity from Disability

One response to the challenges of educating a diverse student population is for each school to develop building-level teacher support systems. One example is a Teacher Assistance Team (TAT), in which a group of educators meet regularly to help individual teachers with concerns and requests for ideas for instructing specific students. Many TATs require teachers to complete referral forms describing the current instructional challenge and documenting what course of action has already been taken. Members of the team read the referrals before the meeting so they are prepared to spend time efficiently in clearly identifying the problem, brainstorming solutions, planning a course of action, and determining appropriate follow-up procedures. Special educators find they are called regularly to clarify which students truly qualify for their services. As experts in instructional methodology for students who do not succeed with traditional approaches, special educators are also asked to offer suggestions for at-risk students.

The following case is from a school in which teachers are learning to instruct a rapidly changing student population. The Teacher Assistance Team received four requests concerning students who were not born in the United States. In each instance, there were questions regarding learning ability, emotional health, or appropriate behavior. Consequently, members of the TAT asked the special education teacher to attend in order to offer guidance and helpful suggestions.

Different or Disabled?

Ten years ago, this was a sleepy bedroom community for a rapidly growing nearby city. Teachers taught successfully using traditional methods with middle-class students of well-educated, English-speaking parents. The city grew and attracted big industry, resulting in a student population of 28 percent from diverse backgrounds, including fourteen ethnic groups and sixty languages or dialects. As the schools became increasingly more diverse, veterans formerly praised as model teachers more frequently sought help for their new students. This emerging population presented cultural and linguistic challenges. In response, frustrated and confused general educators asked if certain behaviors or difficulty learning would qualify students for special education services.

Tyler Elementary School developed a system called Teachers Supporting Teachers (TST) Team that met weekly to offer help for working with challenging students. The docket was full today, with four teachers seeking assistance. John, the special education teacher, was a regular member of this team. He felt defensive, even before the meeting began, because all four of the teachers who had completed a referral had said to him this week, "I've got a new one for you." Over the last two years, John had learned to encourage teachers to take their concerns to the TST team rather than engage in a fruitless dialogue about "Why can't you take just this one?"

The four teachers were given 15 minutes each. During that time, the teacher described the challenge he or she faced teaching the student, and the team responded with questions and suggestions to improve instruction. At this point, even though a teacher might request consideration for special education assessment, the team explained that the purpose of the process was to provide suggestions for modification or accommodation. The following are excerpts from the four teachers' presentations.

Alice Kominsky, the first teacher, described a third-grade student named Esteban. According to the teacher, "Esteban does not speak in class, nor does he seem to respond to my class instructions. He stays by himself on the playground despite offers from peers to join them." During the ensuing discussion, Esteban's records revealed that this year was his first full-time school experience. In his native El Salvador, he received weekly lessons from an itinerant teacher who had no materials for students. Alice asked, "Couldn't the LD teacher provide some one-on-one instruction to catch him up?"

The second teacher, Mary Ann Ford, seemed angry as she described Murat, a sixth-grader from Turkey. "Murat is defiant! He gets up out of his seat whenever he pleases and thinks nothing of grabbing things from other students. When I called home, his mother said the father was *the* disciplinarian, and when he's gone Murat can't be controlled. The mother threatens Murat with beatings, but it has no effect." Mary Ann paused for effect and continued, "Clearly, this child has behavior problems! On top of that, he is failing because his attention span is so short he barely completes any task before popping up and walking around. I don't know whether he needs an ED or an LD program."

The third teacher, Pam Welter, presented concerns for a fearful child in her fifth-grade class. Pam explained, "Tran learned English well from missionaries in Vietnam and in refugee camps as her family traveled through several countries on the way to the United States. Here a church sponsored the family's travel and initial settling into the community. Schoolwork is no problem for this child. The family's standards for education are high, and Tran works very hard to achieve." Pam looked sad when she said, "I just feel so bad for her. She could really use some special attention from an ED teacher. Tran's a scared little bird who shrinks from my touch and avoids the other children when there is a lot of movement."

The fourth teacher, Al Klein, said he was perplexed and wanted some expert advice about teaching reading to one of his second graders. Al said, "Mi-Hwa is not learning to read. She is so alert and friendly. When I teach, I look around to see who is getting it, and Mi-Hwa is the first to smile at me. She learned to converse in English during her first two years of school in a Korean bilingual school. She speaks clearly and can read words, but she cannot read sentences. It seems the words have no connection to each other. She reads every word individually, proud to be correct each time. It seems like a processing problem a student of mine had last year when she was identified as needing LD services."

Consider This

1. What cultural/linguistic issues are evident in each situation?
2. What suggestions could the TST team offer to each teacher?
3. Why might teachers think these are special education issues?
4. How can special educators respond to the many teachers who think any child who is experiencing problems in school should be the responsibility of special education?
5. What other support services might be available in the school division to help these teachers?

Parent Involvement

There is widespread agreement that involved parents powerfully affect the outcome of their children's education. To be effective, however, partnerships between schools and parents will require educators and parents to rethink their roles. Traditional schools are based on majority-culture assumptions, including the assumption that educators hold the authority and parents need to follow rules, adhere to schedules, and learn from school personnel. Most schools that made strides in parent involvement began by working to understand the needs and realities of their parents' lives as well as how, when, and why parents were hard to involve. No one design or single method of communication will always be successful with all parents. Effective involvement programs report they have actively sought to understand their constituent communities, respond to specific needs, encourage two-way communication, and include parents in program development. In some cases, the greatest barrier to effective parent partnerships is lack of awareness that educators and parents need to reevaluate their roles.

Back-to-School Night

Lee Ann Gomez began her student teaching assignment the last week of August at Thomas Jefferson Middle School. On the first Monday afternoon of September, there was a teachers' meeting scheduled. It would be Lee Ann's first teachers' meeting, and she was secretly intrigued about what really happened at these meetings, having heard from teachers and student teachers everything from "boring" to "down-right rude behavior." Lee Ann walked with her cooperating teacher, Janet Gordon, to the Library/Media Center with great anticipation. They entered the room to a noisy greeting, and Lee Ann was informally introduced to at least twenty teachers.

As the meeting began, Janet Gordon officially introduced Lee Ann as her "wonderful student teacher who has youthful enthusiasm and all the latest ideas." Lee Ann felt proud of the introduction but also a little intimidated. As the student teacher looked around the room, she saw a sea of mature faces, tired at the end of a long day.

The principal, Carl Lepky, led the meeting. After welcomes and introductions, he began to discuss the meeting topic, "Back-to-School Night." Carl planned to state his concerns, lead a general discussion, and assign a committee to propose some quick suggestions for the upcoming event. The principal stated, "Back-to-School Night has always been the third Thursday in September from 7 to 9 p.m. I'm assuming you all have begun to think about how you will share your curriculum and management procedures with parents." Becoming perceptibly anxious, the principal added "It used to be a major event. A notice sent home with students was sufficient to pack the house. But, attendance has been declining steadily over the last five years. Last year, less than a third of our students had representation at Back-to-School Night." Carl asked rhetorically,

"Do you think Back-to-School Night is a valuable activity?" There seemed to be general agreement until an eighth-grade Civics teacher spoke up, "I don't think the current format serves our community any longer." There was a lot of murmuring among the teachers. Carl asked the teacher to continue. The teacher observed, "As I see it, the parents have voted with their feet. They're not showing up because they can't get here or they don't get anything out of it." Another teacher blurted out, "They're not showing up because they don't care!" That comment elicited a loud reaction as everyone spoke out at once either agreeing vehemently or disagreeing in amazement.

Lee Ann was surprised by the teachers' reactions. She had learned about the importance of parent partnerships, the barriers to parent involvement, and solutions schools had implemented successfully. However, she hardly felt prepared or confident enough to speak up in this setting.

The principal was equally astonished. He had not expected the level of emotion this topic would generate. It was clear there would not be a resolution at this meeting.

Consider This

1. Why is parent involvement important?
2. What changed in this community?
3. What issues must the principal and teachers consider?
4. What options might there be for parent connection early in the school year?
5. Why do teachers have such strong feelings about parents and parent involvement?

Culturally Responsive Curriculum and Sensitive Management

As classrooms become more diverse, teachers must learn to use culturally responsive curriculum and culturally sensitive management approaches. Culturally responsive curriculum improves academic performance, enhances self-esteem, promotes harmony, and increases knowledge of all students about our combined heritage. Culturally responsive curriculum also involves awareness of language ability and accommodations for language acquisition. Culturally sensitive management is based on being aware of one's own culturally linked expectations, reducing misperceptions, and teaching self-control as well as empowering students. In the following case, the new student teacher anticipates learning many new skills but instead learns by observing the results of ineffective techniques.

It's All Yours!

On Friday afternoon before student teaching was scheduled to begin, Jack Thompson was finally able to arrange a meeting with his cooperating teacher,

Don Wallace. Jack arrived at 2:30 as 1,500 high school students came bursting through the doors, loudly cheering themselves on to the weekend. Jack marveled at the diversity of the student body, where white faces were in the minority.

Jack had hoped to meet earlier, but Mr. Wallace was so busy it was difficult to arrange a time to see him. On the phone, Mr. Wallace had briefly explained he was the learning disabilities resource teacher. That meant he taught four periods of LD and one period of an "experiment in co-teaching which was not my idea." And what did the cooperating teacher mean when he said, "Thank God, they finally gave me a student teacher; there's so much to do"? At first, Jack optimistically hoped Mr. Wallace meant he was looking forward to the stimulation of having an apprentice and the increased potential of two teachers addressing the needs of his special education students. Secretly, Jack imagined that the cooperating teacher was responding positively to him because he was young and "cool," someone the kids could really relate to. But an uncomfortable suspicion immediately replaced his optimism: Mr. Wallace was looking forward to time away from class. Jack got the real picture quickly when his cooperating teacher complained, "I am the president of Nelson County Teachers' Union and we are deadlocked in unresolved negotiations with those stuffed shirts in central administration. I have phone calls to make and meetings to attend. You're gonna get a real experience here. I hope you are ready!"

Friday's meeting was brief. Mr. Wallace greeted Jack at the office and walked him to his room. The LD resource room was small with a table, ten desks, and bookcases stacked with reading and math books. Posters on the wall were old and faded. The bulletin board had students' papers stapled in what appeared to be an attempt to showcase good work, but it lacked visual appeal and had not been updated for several months. Jack and Mr. Wallace sat at the table. In a matter of moments, the cooperating teacher dropped the bomb, "On Monday, you watch me. On Tuesday, it's all yours. I'll be around if you have any questions. Do you want to look at the students' folders?" Jack was too flabbergasted to speak. He thought, "Having my own class has always been a dream, but I thought student teaching was about easing into this thing?"

Mr. Wallace stood up and said, "Let's go back to the office. I'll introduce you and show you where the special ed files are." As they walked to the office, Mr. Wallace was so busy making comments to teachers as they walked past, it seemed he forgot Jack was there. In the office, Jack was introduced to the secretary and directed to the file room. "See you Monday at 7," the cooperating teacher said as he left and the secretary took over. "He's a piece of work, isn't he?" she commented, shaking her head. Jack did not know how to respond, but he was grateful for the secretary's attention. The files were thick with imposing forms and reports and unfamiliar immigration documents; Jack was not sure what he was supposed to get from them, but he read attentively as many as he could before the office staff announced closing time at 4:30.

Monday at 7:00, Jack found himself alone in the room trying to make sense of the available materials and lack of apparent preparation for the day. Mr. Wallace blew in about the same time as the students arrived for homeroom at 7:30. Ten students milled around the room and eyed Jack suspiciously. Initially, Jack felt intimidated by the student mix of mostly African-American and Hispanic students with only one white student. "Sit down and finish your homework you no doubt didn't think about over the weekend. Oh, this is Mr. Thompson, our new student teacher," barked Mr. Wallace. The students turned to stare at Jack. "Don't you have work to do?" said the teacher, less a question than a command. Students reluctantly opened books and notebooks, but no one really did anything.

When the bell rang at 7:40, the teacher turned to Jack, saying, "First period, English." To the class, he said, "Everyone get an American Literature book. . . . Not tomorrow, now." All but one student slowly got out of their seats and walked to a bookcase to pick up huge literature books. The students glared at their teacher and made faces to each other, mumbling about "who's in a bad mood as usual" and then laughing. The one student remaining seated, Jamal, just stared angrily at the teacher. Mr. Wallace looked at Jack and rolled his eyes about the noncompliant student. The next half-hour consisted of Mr. Wallace calling on students to read aloud a story about early settlers in New England. Students could only read half the words, and no one seemed to attend when someone else was reading. When the teacher asked a question, students looked down and just shrugged if called on by name. So Mr. Wallace would recap the story every 5 minutes, commenting, "A person could learn something about the founding fathers of this country if he paid attention." After reading aloud, the teacher instructed students to put away their books and take out their journals to write about the topic, "The dilemma faced by these early settlers." Everyone knew the drill: open up your notebook and write something. Mr. Wallace never checked, anyway.

The bell rang and students grabbed their books and left without saying anything to Mr. Wallace. As the next group entered, the teacher said to Jack, "If you think those guys couldn't read, wait until you hear this group. Second period is Basic Reading." As the six students walked through the door, Jack noticed several students whose ethnic origin he could not determine. Mr. Wallace said to each, "Folders." After one or two reminders, students picked up their folders from the white plastic bin on the floor next to the teacher's desk. Mr. Wallace pointed to a stack of workbooks on the bookshelf closest to the desk and explained to Jack, "Students are all working individually on basic skills. I copy work sheets from these elementary workbooks depending on what grade level they tested at." Second period consisted of students doing individual work sheets and the teacher working with one student at a time. Jack observed that two of the six spoke with an accent and appeared to have difficulty with English. Throughout the period, only the students who were working with the teacher and one or two others would be on task. The rest slept or just stared blankly. Jack asked, "Can I help anyone?" One student seemed eager, so Jack sat with him. It was obvious from the beginning that this student did not understand directions in English. Jack looked at previous pages in the folder and found half-completed pages and many errors. The student teacher was feeling discouraged and overwhelmed. When the bell rang, students put their folders back in the bin and left.

Third period was math. A teacher's aide showed up and introduced herself as the special ed assistant who worked in all the rooms. "Third period I help Mr. Wallace." The teacher had divided the students into two groups: "basic skills" and "pre-algebra." The aide sat with six "basic skills" students at desks at one end of the room, working in folders on arithmetic skills, while the teacher sat at the table with four students, working out of a pre-algebra book. Jack observed the aide helping each student complete work sheets. Some worked on basic two-column addition, some on subtraction with zeros, and others tackled long division. Over and over students complained they couldn't remember the steps. At the same time, tension was building at the pre-algebra table between a white student and an African-American student. When the white student gave a wrong answer, the African-American student laughed. The white student got up ostensibly to sharpen his pencil and bumped into the laughing student. In an instant, they were standing facing each other and shouting racial epithets. Mr. Wallace stood up and announced, "To the office, the both of you." The teacher walked to the door, told the aide to take over, and escorted the students out of the room. There were 15 minutes left in the period. Jack walked over to the table, introduced himself and asked if he could join them. "Whatever," they replied. Mr. Wallace did not return that period.

Students arrived for fourth period and did not see their teacher. Jack explained that Mr. Wallace had to go to the office with two students. One student responded, "Probably Dex and Andre . . . happens every week," and laughed. Jack looked around the room for any indication of a schedule, but none was evident. So, Jack asked the eight students who had just arrived what subject was taught fourth period. Tanya offered, "This is for people who failed their classes, so we get a study hall." Jack asked, "Can I help anyone with assignments from other classes?" "Yeah, write my report for science," kidded Jacob. Jack replied, "I can help. What do we need?" Jacob answered, "I don't know." Everyone laughed. Jack instructed, "Let's take out something to work on that I can help you with this period." Students exchanged disbelieving glances. Jack asked, "What do you usually do?" Sharon responded, "As long as we don't make trouble, we can talk or write notes." Jack suggested, "This would be a good time to get help." Students began ignoring him.

When no one showed up fifth period, Jack figured it was lunchtime. He went to the cafeteria, where he saw Mr. Wallace talking with another teacher. Mr. Wallace looked sheepish and apologized "Sorry, it took a long time to get those two suspended. I figured since fourth period is a study hall, you could handle it without me. But I did mean to come get you for lunch." They ate together. Mr. Wallace explained that sixth period was the experiment in co-teaching in a ninth-grade English class. "Follow me to the classroom. We just sit there until a kid needs something."

Just as Mr. Wallace had described, he sat watching the lesson until the teacher assigned deskwork. Once seatwork was assigned, Mr. Wallace waited to see if students raised their hands and if the English teacher responded; if not, he got up and answered the question. Mr. Wallace pointed to four students in the class and whispered that they were "our LD students." Jack watched to see if they were on task and wondered if he should walk around monitoring. Many of the other students were obviously not working on the assignment as they laughed and "high-fived" each other. But with neither teacher moving, it felt presumptuous for the student teacher to get up and walk around.

After class, Mr. Wallace said he thought this co-teaching was a waste of time for two teachers. "Somebody must have read a new article or something, but they weren't writing about these kids. But, hey, that's what we were told to do, so. . . ." Mr. Wallace commented sarcastically. Jack was reeling from the total mismatch between what he had experienced that day and everything he had been taught as well as his personal mission to make a difference in children's lives. Mr. Wallace said, "I'm not assigned students during seventh period so I can test kids or do paperwork. Nothing needs to be done today. So, I suppose you can go to the room and get ready for tomorrow. If you have any questions, I'll be in the office making some calls." As Mr. Wallace walked away, Jack had a fleeting thought run through his mind, "Get out now. You'll never learn to be a good teacher from this guy." Then, another thought came to him, "Even for a little while, I could make a difference in these kids' lives." With that last thought, he headed for the classroom with his mind buzzing about relationships; appropriate, relevant materials; motivational systems; social skills; and co-teaching. What should he tackle first?

Consider This

1. For each class period, identify some core issues and how they might be related to diversity issues.
2. Describe professional behaviors that enhance a special education teacher's reputation and credibility within the school.
3. Identify some instructional materials or activities that might be more effective than work sheets for these students.
4. What recommendations might you have for each period?
5. Where would you begin?

4 Classroom Management

New special education teachers, despite their coursework, often question their abilities to motivate students and manage behaviors. They worry that students will not follow directions or demonstrate respect. They struggle to facilitate lasting changes in social skills and they cope with defiant attitudes, work refusal, and even violent tendencies. Accountability for academic progress can clash with their desires to accommodate for students' emotional difficulties or home lives. Finally, because of trends in inclusion, team teaching, and student service models, many special educators consult with regular education teachers and other professionals regarding student behavior, acting as either expert, colleague, or advocate.

Ignore or Intervene?

Students misbehave for various reasons, which include distrusting others, needing attention, gaining control, and concealing inadequacy. Some students with disabilities present multiple behavioral issues, and teachers need to identify and prioritize these behaviors requiring intervention. Problems also occur when students are not productively engaged in instructional activities. Thus special educators need to be prepared, develop lessons at appropriate levels of difficulty, and maintain high expectations for student performance. This case describes a novice teacher trying to balance instruction and management while planning a lesson.

They Won't Listen

It's my third week of student teaching in a class for students with learning disabilities and behavior disorders. As I sit on the living room floor planning my lessons, I'm excited, yet secretly anxious, about the upcoming days. I'm excited because English is my favorite subject, and I've taken over the two language arts groups in Erin Fitzgerald's class. I dug up the notes from my methods class and spent a lot of time this weekend reviewing the curriculum objectives, cruising the Internet for interesting teaching ideas, and making some fun games to reinforce new vocabulary. Once I'm comfortable, I'll use some cooperative learning techniques to get the students really involved.

Although I feel prepared to use the writing process to teach or reinforce skills in writing, vocabulary, punctuation/capitalization, grammar, and spelling, I'm anxious about managing the students' behavior. I feel inadequate and inexperienced with classroom management, and I don't know what to do about it. My cooperating teacher, on the other hand, is fantastic. I know how lucky I am to have landed such a great role model. Mrs. Fitzgerald has high expectations for her students, and she definitely has this class under control. She knows the students so well that she is able to predict most of their actions and almost effortlessly prevents potential problems. One stern look from her draws students back into their lessons. I wonder how she accomplished this?

Last week, I had difficulty getting the students to listen to me. . . . A couple of times I felt like I was totally invisible. As soon as I stepped up to the plate to take over Friday's lesson from Ms. Fitzgerald, James began to entertain himself and those around him with something that squeaked, bounced, spun, and was far more attractive to the students than my lesson. Although Clark refused to open a book during Sustained Silent Reading, he became totally immersed in his novel as soon as I said it was time to write. Then, there's Michael, the artist. He decorated the edges of every work sheet but chose not to attempt finding and correcting the sentences with punctuation errors. And it's a mystery to me what I did to deserve the way Evelyn glared at me over her text, refusing to be involved in spite of my enthusiasm.

As I plan for this coming week, I can't help but picture a classroom in total chaos while I try to teach one group about antonyms/synonyms and continue working with the other group on capitalization. The fun part has been finding language arts ideas and making materials, but all my great planning will be a total waste if the kids don't pay attention or try. Although Mrs. Fitzgerald doesn't seem to have any formal classroom rules or reward system, it just seems to work for her. We learned in our management class about developing rules and posting them. "Should I develop rules? Should I write the rules on the board? Do I need to ask my cooperating teacher's permission and why doesn't she have posted rules? I think I need some kind of reward system like we learned about . . . maybe a point system? Should I put consequences for noncompliance on the board? Is this part of planning too? I know how to plan the lesson content, but how do I plan so that the students will listen to me?"

Consider This

1. What are some possible reasons the student teacher is having difficulty establishing her authority?
2. Why might the students be engaging in the behaviors mentioned in the scenario? Are any of the behaviors a direct result of the students' disabilities?
3. What proactive steps can teachers take to prevent misbehavior?
4. Identify situations in which teachers can use planned ignoring or nonverbal redirection strategies rather than intervening verbally or with consequences.
5. How should the teacher decide which behaviors require intervention?

Explain what you want with a student, proximity)

Anticipate bouncing - Problem kid removed and sent to the classroom.

Do not argue with children

Send victim to the office not the perpitrator.

6. What is the relationship between effective instruction and behavior management, and how do both relate to lesson planning?
7. What types of cooperative learning strategies might the student teacher use, and how might she set them up so the students will successfully participate?

Changing Roles from Student to Teacher

Reinforcement first.

Do not argue

As novice professionals assume teaching responsibilities, they often find it can be challenging to "look the part," especially in high school settings. Despite having prerequisite knowledge and skills, students may not perceive novices as official teachers, not finding them credible and thus failing to treat them with respect. The thought of handling direct confrontations causes anxiety. Teachers who are effective managers have a strong presence in the classroom. They convey authority in subtle ways that often take practice to develop. These teachers remain calm, clearly state expectations and directions, use nonverbal communication and proximity control, and confidently follow through with consequences. In this case the student teacher struggles to assume a teacher image.

Is This Instruction?

Moving from my previous placement, in an elementary class for students with mental retardation, to this final student teaching experience, in a high school resource program for students with learning and emotional disabilities, was a shock. For one thing, my petite stature caused students and faculty alike to tell me that I looked like one of the kids. When walking back from the office on the first day, one teacher even asked to see my hall pass! A youthful appearance wasn't a problem when I taught seven- to ten-year-olds, but high school was a different story. In my first placement I practiced many of the skills taught in our university courses . . . improving my lesson plans, teaching lessons using direct instruction, and keeping track of my students' progress on their IEP goals. But here, I couldn't imagine myself demonstrating any of the required teaching skills outlined in the student teaching syllabus.

From the first minute of the first period of my first day, I was just thrown in to either sink or swim. We had students for three out of four 90-minute block periods and anywhere from eight to ten students arrived with homework/projects, class assignments, or tests to study for from their general education classes. I helped students with their algebra, biology, eleventh-grade English, or American government. Mr. Black and I jumped like grasshoppers from one student to another, helping them as best we could with the incredibly diverse content and requirements. The small classroom size, more like a large closet, didn't help either. Students were seated so close to one another that we could barely circulate to help them with their work.

I assessed quickly that we were supposed to know everything about all their subjects, and from memory! Soon I took on one of the characteristics of my students, work avoidance to prevent embarrassment and frustration. I steered away from students who had their hands raised with questions about science because I knew my own weakness would become public knowledge, and students would laugh that I couldn't do their level of work. Once in a blue moon, a note from the classroom teacher briefly explained an assignment or highlighted specific expectations for the students, but that didn't necessarily mean we had the materials or time to be able to effectively help them.

In addition to the fast pace and loose academic structure, critical instructional time was spent dealing with behavior issues that arose as students waited, not so patiently, for our help. Thinking I was being proactive, I approached Andre, one of the students that Mr. Black teaches for two different subjects in first and fourth periods. Andre unexpectedly stood up, towering over me. I felt instantly intimidated, possibly even threatened. I tried to manage my body language so that I wouldn't appear afraid, but I'm not sure it worked. Andre, on the other hand, successfully conveyed with one menacing look that he was not interested in working, wouldn't take any teacher or peer assistance, and could easily stir up enough trouble to derail the whole class if I wanted to engage him any further. I retreated quickly, thinking I'd find a time later to ask Mr. Black about some strategies to use with Andre.

By the end of that first day, I wondered how Mr. Black even came close to meeting the needs of all these students by himself. One nice thing, however, in direct contrast to my previous placement, was that Mr. Black left in the afternoon shortly after the students and didn't have to bring any work home with him. This would be great because I would get back my sorely missed social life and sleep.

On my fifth day in the classroom, Mr. Black called in sick and had been unable to secure his own replacement. Although the secretary tried, she was, as is often the case, unsuccessful in finding a substitute for this special education position. If a special education teacher was absent without a substitute, an announcement was typically made over the intercom that students were to report to the library for a study hall. Instead, to my surprise, the assistant principal came down to the room. He explained, "You will be in charge today. Send a student to the office if you have an emergency." Before I could digest this news and respond, he exited. I knew I wasn't supposed to have sole responsibility, but what could I possibly do, especially when it was the principal who told me to take the class?

Students began entering the room, asking, "Where is the teacher?" I took a deep breath and said, "I'm the teacher today." Unfortunately, Andre was walking in just as I tenuously announced my role. He laughed and provoked the whole group by saying sarcastically, "Right, like you could handle us."

Consider This

1. Some high school special education positions, like those based on teaching study skills or providing resource time, seem to require teachers to have extensive content knowledge across the curriculum and several grade levels.

How might you handle times when you don't know something related to the curriculum? How responsible are you for the content knowledge?

2. How might the student teacher establish effective communication with the general education teachers whose assignments the students are attempting?

3. What are the classroom management challenges of block scheduling for this population?

4. How can young teachers establish presence and authority in a high school classroom? What are some other characteristics of teachers that might produce a less than respectful reaction in students?

5. Why must this student teacher find out more about Andre's life, his disability, and his learning needs? How would you go about obtaining this information?

6. What would you do if Andre misbehaved during your first-period class?

7. Can you envision ways the student teacher might effectively use humor in her dealings with Andre and the other students?

8. The special education program in this case is based on a tutorial model in which the special education teacher assists students with work they bring from their general education classes. What are the strengths and weaknesses of this approach? How could you change the schedule and focus of instruction to better meet students' needs?

9. Does your university program have a policy regarding student teachers acting as substitutes for classroom teachers who are out of the building? What is the purpose of this policy?

10. What are some ways the student teacher might handle the assistant principal's request?

Impact of Students' Lives on School Performance

In addition to diagnosed disabilities, there are many reasons students may have difficulty in school. While teachers arrive to school prepared to teach, some students arrive not prepared to learn. Cultural and linguistic differences may contribute to problems learning or adjusting to school. The impact of homes with violence, abuse, or poverty can be significant. Students may be involved in communities with gangs or drugs. Teachers must know about, empathize with, and sometimes deal with these challenges before they can expect students to focus on instruction. In the following case, a student teacher is challenged to respond to behaviors and work habits that may or may not be related to circumstances at home.

So Much Baggage

Finally! It's the beginning of my last two weeks of student teaching and, as suggested in the university handbook, I am now fully in charge. Mrs. Gilka, my cooperating teacher, was a wonderful model, and we jointly agreed when I seemed ready to take over each period. Since third period was her most challenging class, we wisely saved it for last. I vividly remember her comment when I came for orientation. "It is not so much their behavior. I can handle that. It is all their other problems that frustrate me, the ones I can't control."

Today, Mrs. Gilka told me she'd be just in the conference room down the hall working on Child Study Team paperwork, a huge responsibility that she takes very seriously. I also know, without her saying it, that she wants me to experience the full flavor of teaching the six math students who make third period feel like the last period of the day. They can be truly energy zapping. I can anticipate some of the "same old stuff" that will make it challenging, but I also expect some new issues to jump up and demand my attention since they're bound to react to my teaching alone for the first time.

Unbelievably, all are here today, staggering in past me as I offer doorway greetings, and sitting down to groan at the full schedule of activities I've written on the blackboard. Mike enters saying, "Why do we hafta do this crap? This stuff sucks." He is a tall, angular boy and the class clown. He's always good for getting a laugh, especially when instruction begins. Half the time the other students do not even know why they are laughing, except that they have been laughing with or at Mike for three years now. Thanks to Mrs. Gilka's persistence earlier in the year, Mike's truancy officer brings him to school when he refuses to get out of bed.

Next comes Ken. Some days, because he is so physically and emotionally restless, he gets permission to pace, run short errands to the office or library, or to do small classroom chores. When seated, he puts his head down, props it on his upturned palms, rests it on his arms, or stretches back looking almost upside down. Today, as I stand next to him he says, "I'm trying, Ms. Pattell. Do you have anything to eat? My grandmother is in the hospital and there's not enough food for the six of us." I scrounge up a granola bar from the closet where Mrs. Gilka keeps a stash for just this purpose.

Norman's demeanor changes from day to day; so I never know which Norman is going to walk through the door. "This is too hard. . . . This is too easy. . . . We did this yesterday. . . . How do you expect me to do this?" He has weathered many court battles over the past twelve years and is currently being pulled from both sides in a custody dispute. Mrs. Gilka was subpoenaed to testify, but the trial was postponed, making life at home and at school more difficult for him. I think "angry Norman" is here this time.

Geraldo and Bijan noisily slide in seconds before I close the door. They announce their presence by reporting a fight they've just witnessed and laughing about who just broke up with whom. Geraldo is in his fifth foster home in his short fourteen years and Bijan has only been in the states a year since his move from Iran. The last thing on their minds? Math.

Janel, late again without a pass, is actually a welcome change. She is academically capable and very cooperative, but even Janel has her suitcases loaded.

She is one of those students who's "too quiet." She dresses provocatively, a direct contrast to her immature social skills, yet doesn't have much to do with the boys in the room. She is another one who misses a lot of school, making teachers question and talk about what kind of double life she could be leading. When I asked her why she was absent yesterday, she made a comment about her stepfather in a tone that made me wonder and worry.

With all six present, and after an extensive "settling-in" time, I began the same routines that structure each class. We began with "Mad Minute," a timed math drill. Next, each student completed a work sheet with a couple of math problems to review concepts presented the day before. Keeping an eye out for off-task behaviors, I darted around the room encouraging them to work, quickly evaluating each student's drill page and discussing any error patterns.

Working in small groups starts with a quick hand signal indicating the transition. I gave directions with both my voice and arms, moving students to locations in the classroom where I predicted each would be most likely to stay on task and avoid conflicting or socializing with peers. Finally, after all the orchestration, and disruption, they were in their places. I set the timer, and we were off.

I started working with the "fractions" group, using plastic fraction parts to illustrate the concept of equivalence. While I focused on these three students, the voices of the others, who were supposed to be jointly solving word problems, gradually got louder. Momentarily distracted, my eyes darted across to the other group just in time to witness Geraldo stand up and move toward the window while Norman and Janel argued heatedly over the answer. "At least two of them are working on math," I think to myself. But just at that moment Norman quickly reached over and grabbed a handful of hair, resulting in an ear-piercing screech from a terrified Janel. I jumped up, shouting, "Norman, let go of her!" By the time I reached the other table, Janel was crying and Norman had his arms crossed, looking defiant. Geraldo seemed oblivious to the commotion as he frowned at the police car that just drove up to the front of the building. "Norman, apologize to Janel this minute," I said as I signaled Geraldo to move back to the table. Under his breath he muttered something that I took to be his apology. At this point I lowered my voice and tried desperately to refocus their attention on the task at hand, which, thank heavens, they reluctantly started to do. I returned to the group, trying to finish up before anything else breaks loose. The first group seemed to catch on to the concept of equivalence, so once I saw each student independently complete a problem with manipulatives, I quickly said, "Finish the last six problems on your sheet while I work with the other group."

But then . . . this short spell of concentration was broken and a large chain of commotion ensued. Just as I glanced at my watch, realizing there were still 15 minutes left, Mike loudly exclaimed, "It's time for lunch!" Everyone looked at the clock only to realize that the period was *not* over and, because Mike initiated the trick, they laughed. Norman, willing to play along with the joke, stood and walked toward the door, as if to leave. Janel quietly asked to go to the bathroom. Bijan noisily slammed shut his notebook and exclaimed, "I hate tech school. It's full of retards. " Geraldo matched the mood, boldly blurting out, "I have a geography test, so I'm skipping." Oh, what a mess. All of a sudden class felt more chaotic than usual and I felt totally helpless. I estimated the students had been on task for only about 15 minutes of the possible 50, and I'm glad Mrs. Gilka was not here to witness my ineffectiveness.

Consider This

1. Categorize the students' behaviors. Which would you call disrespectful? Which would you label as work avoidant? Which seem most closely related to "issues at home"?
2. Why might the novice, Ms. Pattell, experience more disruptions and off-task behaviors than Mrs. Gilka?
3. Identify the possible multicultural or socioeconomic factors affecting these students' availability for schoolwork.
4. What strategies would you use to meet diverse achievement and behavioral levels of students and increase their on-task performance? Are there routines you would modify or rules you would enforce to help Ms. Pattell and her students be more successful?
5. What consequences, if any, would you apply?
6. Recommend to Ms. Pattell some helpful attitudes or strategies for balancing academic accountability with demonstrating consideration for students' "problems." How can teachers encourage students to focus on success despite the negative impacts of their family and home situations?
7. What is the teacher's role in relation to chronically absent students?
8. What are signs of physical or sexual abuse, and what steps must teachers take when abuse is suspected?
9. Describe ways that teachers and other school staff can share the responsibilities for assessing and providing for the emotional and physical needs of students.

School Violence and/or Disability

Our society is bombarded with media reports of the shockingly violent plans and actions of school-age students. Many of these students have not been found eligible for special education services, although some have identified disabilities. Although school plans and teacher handbooks often provide guidelines for emergencies, teachers may lack practical training and experience for dealing with crisis situations. How can teachers be prepared to discern between benign problems and real threats, to handle the ultimate crisis when it arises? The novice teacher in the following case is faced with some very disturbing evidence and must decide what to do.

Russian Roulette

The bottom line was that I was expected to handle problems with my students and keep them out of the principal's office. In return, the administration was supportive of my special education program in tangible ways, such as defending my need for a full-time assistant, ordering copies of classroom texts, providing money to purchase behavior reinforcers, and allowing me to visit other programs for students with behavior disorders.

As a new teacher, I appreciated these efforts and wanted to demonstrate my ability to meet the expectations for managing my students' behavior as well as meeting instructional goals. In some ways, I was amazed that I was even teaching these students, because before I entered student teaching I thought I wanted to be a learning disabilities teacher. I couldn't imagine having the guts to try ED. In one of my student teaching placements I was exposed to an incredible teacher who loved her job and her kids. I, too, came to love the challenges and the rewards, and thus at the last minute put a different spin on my career goals.

So far, I was surviving this first-year teaching experience. My current students, all boys, were an extremely needy bunch, but in a short time I had grown to really like each of them and admire their tenacity. For a high school class, the students were relatively young, mainly ninth- and tenth-graders. I knew that I needed to establish rapport, keep them in school, and help them stay out of problems with the law. After reading their school files, I made a concerted effort over the first few weeks to get to know each student individually, both at school and in terms of their family situation.

Terrence, Seth, and J.R. responded to this attention and interest and several others were slowly coming around, but I didn't seem to be able to break through or even chip away at Allen's exterior. He wasn't difficult to get along with, but he never smiled and just didn't seem to take any pleasure from personal interactions with me or anyone else. In a report one psychologist described Allen as quiet, withdrawn, and somewhat robotlike in his responses. His self-ascribed name, the "Lone Wolf," seemed to fit well. On the whole, though, it was surprising that these boys even functioned as well as they did given the events and circumstances of their lives. Although the daily challenges posed by this rowdy group were inevitable, for the most part these were situations for which I was basically prepared. Not to say that these boys didn't create frequent problems for me to handle, but gradually I earned the trust and respect of most of them. They knew that I cared and that I would advocate for them when I could. Allen, however, was a puzzling young man whom I wasn't reaching.

I sat at my desk wondering what being an advocate for Allen really meant. He was an extremely bright fourteen-year-old, but the complexity of his emotional needs was slowly revealing itself. One or another of my students had already gotten into fights, pulled the fire alarm, left the school grounds at lunch, stomped out of a class swearing at the teacher for a failing grade, and been kicked out of a football game for smelling like alcohol. I consistently tried to apply our classroom and school rules, implement our established point/level behavior program, actively use preventative strategies, and provide as much positive reinforcement as possible. Collaborating with the high school resource officer was especially helpful in resolving these problems as we tried to deal with the manifestations of their emotional disabilities.

An unwritten part of my job description involved keeping my ears and eyes open, constantly on the lookout for potential problems involving my students. Their difficulties in school and desperate desire to be accepted made them prime targets for involvement in unwholesome activities, and they surely didn't need any more problems in their lives. I was surprised to realize the level of gang activity in this nonurban school district, but as far as I knew none of my students was involved at this point. Since this kind of situation was totally unfamiliar to me, I made it my business to learn as much as I could. I diligently tried to prevent problems or at least attempted to nip them in the bud before they escalated to bigger issues.

Two weeks before, I had heard a rumor regarding Allen that had greatly disturbed me. I knew I needed to take it with a grain of salt because uninformed faculty, administrators, or even other students too often jumped to the conclusion that my students would naturally be involved in any trouble that arose. In this instance, another ninth-grader supposedly witnessed Allen at home playing Russian roulette with his father's handgun. The gun had only one bullet in it, and the student said that Allen had fired it twice. When I asked Allen about this, he denied both the story and the fact that he had access to a gun. I couldn't tell if he was telling the truth, but I certainly didn't have any concrete proof otherwise.

Now, only a week later, I was shocked by some new information. When I entered the classroom, I was immediately aware of four of my students huddled around a desk looking at something. Rather than approaching directly in an accusing manner, a move certain to set someone off, I continued to observe out of the corner of my eye. They tried to be quiet and inconspicuous, but it was evident that they were getting increasingly worked up. When one boy grabbed the paper it became clear that a problem was going to erupt. I jumped up, inserting myself between the two boys and asked what they were arguing over. A resounding "Nothing" was the quick reply. I asked to see the paper, but Terrence quickly stuffed it in his pocket. "Give me the paper, please," I calmly yet forcefully demanded. It was obvious that he was torn between trying to protect the paper and following my directions. I waited patiently with my hand outstretched, trying not to box him into a corner. "Think about the choice you are making, Terrence," I added. He looked furtively around and then, amid stares of disbelief, he handed it over. I took the paper but immediately redirected the boys' attention to returning to their seats and filling in points earned during third period on their behavior cards. We then began our daily analysis of a recent problematic school situation. Together we discussed needed social skills, and then the boys role-played alternative responses to the situation.

Lunch was my first opportunity to look at the confiscated paper. Settling into my desk chair and opening the thermos with soup brought from home, I leisurely began to read the five typed pages. Almost immediately however my attention was fully riveted on what appeared to be a printout from a website containing the name "Lone Wolf." The message was long and convoluted but goose bumps rose on my neck and my stomach felt nauseous as I read what I only hoped was a huge joke. The author, Lone Wolf, ranted in a somewhat incoherent yet very intense way about his hatred of humankind, made threats against the high school, and displayed intense anger at staff. When I saw my name in print, I gasped. These were the ramblings of a crazy person. Could one of my students be plotting what could only be another Columbine school incident?

Consider This

1. Why would an administrator send the signal that the special education teacher was responsible for keeping the students out of the office?
2. What should the teacher do with the printout and her suspicions?
3. How can Ms. Deeds determine if the contents of the paper are real or fictional?
4. How can she balance her desire to build trust with her students while performing her professional responsibility to intervene in a potential crisis situation?
5. Students with emotional problems do not always exhibit externalizing or acting-out behaviors. How can teachers identify the needs of students with internalizing behaviors?
6. What are some of the more obvious, frequently displayed behaviors exhibited by students with emotional or behavior disorders? How is Allen's manifestation different? How does that fact relate to your approach to behavior management?
7. Describe the methods a teacher might use in assessing a potential crisis situation in order to determine the appropriate level or intensity of intervention. Describe times when you might recommend the teacher hand off the issue to other staff members.
8. How do school faculty and administrators adhere to policy while still taking into account the impact of disability on student behavior? Can consequences be reduced or changed as a result?
9. Describe what might be an ideal relationship among the special education teacher, principal, and school resource officer.

Collaborating to Identify Solutions and Implement Interventions

Schools that are effective at providing and implementing teamed classes have usually followed a formula for success, such as ensuring common planning time for teams, offering staff development opportunities for regular education teachers to learn special education strategies, issuing guidelines for effective teaming relationships, developing resource libraries to assist with accommodating and modifying curriculum, giving advance notice when new teaming arrangements are going to be implemented, and offering teachers choices.

Despite what we know about the work it takes to collaborate well, special education teachers often find themselves in the position of being advocates for their students and themselves in the general education classroom. The following scenario highlights some of the issues that can arise in a poorly supervised team teaching situation.

Throwing in the Towel

The tears just wouldn't stop flowing. Although Marie had been dealing with these behavior problems for a while, it all came to a head today when the fifth-grade teacher slammed the door, practically in her face. Maybe it wasn't meant personally, but Marie took it that way. Despite the valiant efforts of her mentor and former professor, Dr. Watson, Marie couldn't be consoled. She was devastated and now committed to leaving her teaching job. It wasn't just these new kids or even working with the two teachers; coupled with all the other demands, this was the last straw. Although teaching was what she wanted to do with her life, this wasn't how she wanted to be doing it. "I just can't take it anymore," she cried. Dr. Watson listened empathetically.

Marie could not help thinking that her two new students were a major source of the problem. As she sat in Dr. Watson's office lamenting the situation, Marie gave a rapid, breathless description of them: "Sophie's a year older than the typical fifth grader . . . slightly overweight but pretty, with beautiful sad blue eyes. She's labeled OHI (Other Health Impairment) and ADHD (attention deficit with hyperactivity disorder) and takes Lithium as a mood stabilizer, but her parents adamantly refuse to allow her to take the Aderol she needs to focus her attention and control her impulsivity. Sophie is smart, so she's acutely aware of her difficulties, staying focused and quiet. If I rank her impulsivity on a scale from 1 to 10, it would be an $11\frac{1}{2}$! Besides constant talking in class, she is in a whirlwind of repetitive small motor motion . . . picking at scabs, pulling at her clothing, fidgeting and playing with anything in sight. The motion and noise are distracting to everyone in the room, including Sophie herself. This energy level and animation might make her a fun companion at an amusement park or on a shopping trip, but not sitting in a school desk!"

Dr. Watson began to speak, but Marie continued as if she couldn't stop. "Last year's teacher told me over the phone that Sophie responds best to the type and tone of commands that you would use with a dog. At the time, I thought this was bizarre and unprofessional, never mind unkind to say. But I now know what she means, and I hate to admit it, but I agree. Sophie so desperately wants to have friends but yikes—she's always in everyone's personal space and tries way too hard! The cliques of fifth-grade girls shun her. Not wanting to provide an incomplete picture, Marie describes Sophie's other side. "At times Sophie is lethargic, laying her head on her desk, unable even to keep her eyes open." Marie hurries on, posing a series of questions without allowing time for a response. "Do you think she is intentionally trying to avoid work? Maybe she's frightened of not succeeding? Is being tired a result of her medication?" Remembering to insert information about academic performance, Marie adds, "On individualized testing Sophie's scores are close to grade level but her daily performance is a disaster. She can't seem to complete tasks or work cooperatively in any group."

Dr. Watson asked, "Is all of this frustration about Sophie?"

Although Marie could hear the negativity in her voice and knew how she must sound to Dr. Watson, she couldn't help herself and went on. "Damien, my second challenge, is entirely different. He has learning disabilities in reading and writing. Like a raincoat is water resistant, he is schoolwork resistant. Damien doesn't seem to understand or be interested in much of the fifth-grade curriculum except the muskets used in Jamestown. I know this is at least partially because of his second-grade reading skills and unbelievably bad spelling, but it is also because he loudly bemoans his hatred of social studies, refuses to do the assigned work, and repeatedly whines about wanting to go home. Thank heavens his math skills are fine." Another breath and Marie starts again. "When Damien doesn't behave, everyone knows it. I'm getting more and more concerned about his disturbing preoccupation with violence. In the mildest form, he walks around the classroom making loud noises and exaggerated kung fu movements with his arms and legs, often knocking over or bumping into things with his adolescent clumsiness. He draws weapons all over his papers, and his writing topics always involve attacks and killing. Is this normal 'boy behavior' resulting from hours in front of the TV and playing video games? Or do you think it's something more serious that I should try to do something about? I already know I have to work on his swearing, hitting, kicking, and bolting out of the classroom. The teachers just love these episodes!"

When she had finished this tirade, Marie couldn't believe that had been her talking. She was usually an optimistic person who thought she could make a difference. Why had she so quickly given up on these two youngsters? Her own students! With her professor still listening and shifting facial expressions back and forth from empathetic to distressed, Marie thought back two years before to her first day as a special education teacher. "I was overjoyed to land this placement in what I thought was the best elementary school in the district, and I even got my first choice of positions, teaching upper elementary students with mild disabilities." She remembered the graduate courses in behavior management and collaboration and still vividly recalled the two energetic schoolteachers who shared their insights about the time and energy needed to manage a classroom of diverse students and make professional collaborative relationships actually work. She said out loud, "I knew it wasn't going to be easy, but I never dreamed it would be this difficult. Maybe this inclusion situation is impossible, or maybe I am just not cut out to work in general education classes."

Dr. Watson probed, "So this is about more than Sophie and Damien?"

Marie responded, "I'm so disappointed that I won't be working with Mrs. Short because she has the reputation of being the best in the school. Nothing seems to be going well." As she reflected aloud, Marie named at least three possible reasons for her frustration, not the least of which was the behavior of her two students.

Marie said, "I know one reason involves class size. They are way up this year. Each of the three fifth grades has twenty-seven students rather than the typical eighteen. Boy, are the teachers hot about this! They've even complained to the superintendent. Although only six out of the seventeen students on my caseload are in fifth grade, their learning needs are substantial and their behavioral problems are pervasive, especially Sophie's and Damien's."

Not only that, Marie continued, "Another factor that is definitely out of my control is our school division directive not to pull students from science or social studies classes because of the end-of-year mandatory state standards tests. Unless they are mentally retarded, all fifth-grade students must take these assessments. How can they acquire this knowledge if they aren't exposed to the material?" Marie knew that the administration of the fifth-grade high stakes tests on the curriculum standards in May were going to be a disaster for Sophie and Damien but also for the teachers and even the school and division if enough students didn't pass. The newspapers were having a field day reporting the scores and criticizing the local schools and the educational system. Mr. Howard, the principal, seemed especially neurotic about scores and could hardly have a meeting without harping on the upcoming tests.

"I know classroom teachers are frustrated trying to meet everyone's needs, but they're taking it out on me and my kids. This year my sole purpose in fifth grade seems to be limited to helping Sophie pay attention and keeping Damien out of trouble. The teachers made it abundantly clear that the behavior problems are my responsibility. Why did I bother getting a master's degree if all I do is babysit?" Almost in tears, Marie said, "I don't deserve this treatment and I've had enough of it!"

Thinking Marie was finished, the professor started to open his mouth in response, but before he could get a word in Marie quickly interrupted by saying, "Just let me explain one more thing to you. It's important for you to know about the two-person team I work with." Marie had been frustrated with her relationships with the two women but for very different reasons. She hoped she could describe them objectively. "Mrs. Short is highly organized and a control freak about her classroom, especially behavior. She loves her reputation of being the strict teacher and is determined to have the most well-behaved class with the highest test scores. Even though she has fifteen years' experience, a great reputation, and an enormous bag of teaching tricks, things just don't seem to be going her way this year. Unfortunately she blames me and my students and basically wants all three of us out."

Now Marie described the second teacher. "Mrs. Poole, on the other hand, is not nearly as competitive. Her classroom style is much more laid back, which seems to help her get along well with the students, but she certainly has a snappy, somewhat defensive approach with teachers and parents." Exhausted, Marie concluded by saying, "I don't feel at all welcome in Mrs. Short's classroom, and I feel as if I have a personality conflict with Mrs. Poole. Last week, when I mustered the nerve to stand up to Mrs. Short and tell her what I thought, she slammed the door and walked away, just leaving me standing there!"

Waiting to see if Marie was truly finished, Dr. Watson thought about what he could or should say to one of his favorite, most promising students. This wasn't the Marie that he remembered. She didn't even sound the same. He knew that what she described was real, at least from her perspective, but what concerned him most was her apparent inability to see any solutions. It seemed as if she was immobilized, not able to demonstrate or even recall the knowledge and skills she had learned only two years ago. Hundreds of thoughts came to mind. . . . IEP meetings, pinpointing observable and measurable behaviors, collecting baseline data, reducing negative behaviors and increasing positive replacement behaviors, point-level systems, token economies, contingency contracts, social skills instruction, task analysis and direct instruction of behaviors, goal setting, self-recording and monitoring, preventative techniques, continuous versus intermittent reinforcement schedules, conflict resolution. . . . He looked up at a tearful Marie, knowing that he needed to help her use the knowledge she had to find realistic solutions. This was one teacher who was not meant to leave the teaching field.

Consider This

1. If you were Marie, what comments, questions, or suggestions from Dr. Watson would be helpful?
2. Is the pressure on teachers in a standards-based environment real? What impact might this pressure have on tolerance of students with behavior and learning problems as well as the professional relationships between general and special education teachers?
3. Why might classroom teachers resent having Sophie and Damien in their classes? How might Marie improve the situation?
4. Should Marie pull her students with behavior problems out of the fifth-grade classrooms and try to meet all their needs in the special education setting? What variables should she consider, and whom should she involve in making this decision?
5. Describe what Marie might do to improve Sophie's attention and reduce her impulsivity. Include specific strategies for extinguishing undesirable behaviors.
6. Since social skills are not assessed on state tests, should working on Sophie's social skills be a priority? How would you improve her social interactions with peers?
7. Describe a behavioral intervention you might try to extinguish Damien's hitting or swearing.
8. What are the variables impacting on the collaborative relationship between Marie and the fifth-grade teachers? Which factors does Marie have any control over?
9. What suggestions can you provide Marie for changing the nature of this collaboration?

10. Although novice teachers should be able to ask for help, how might this request be perceived by others? Who might be available and a safe source of assistance?

11. If you were her mentor, how would you counsel Marie regarding her desire to leave teaching?

5 Instruction

With the emphasis on higher standards as well as the impetus to provide students with disabilities increased access to the general education curriculum and accompanying assessments, the instructional responsibilities of special education teachers are immense. Not only are special educators expected to remediate students' academic and behavior skills, but they must also work with a range of other professionals to provide effective instruction for students with disabilities in a variety of school settings.

The complex act of teaching requires knowledge of curriculum as well as pedagogical skills. Effective instruction is a multiphase process involving planning, implementing, assessing, and reflecting. New teachers are expected to be able to provide appropriate instruction for individual students, small groups, and whole classes. In addition, special education teachers may have multiple endorsements for teaching students with different disabilities and needs across a wide range of grade levels. The responsibilities are broad and the emphasis on accountability can be daunting. Cases in this chapter highlight the myriad of instructional demands that novice teachers face in today's schools.

Stages of Professional Growth and Development

Teaching has been described as an unstaged career in which beginning professionals are expected to have the same knowledge and skills as those who have been teaching for years. With the basic job requirements the same, how does a novice teacher fulfill the expectation of competence yet acknowledge the need for ongoing professional development and time to grow as a professional? In addition, the clash between personal and professional life often comes to a head during the initial teaching years, and finding an appropriate balance is not always easy. The first case highlights the skills of a competent, experienced teacher and raises issues regarding realistic expectations for a novice or student teacher.

The Perfect Placement

Karen lived with several other university students in an apartment, but she was the only one of them in teacher education. Her spring semester of practice teaching was going to be much different than that of her friends. This was all right because Karen had always known she wanted to be a teacher, and this final step brought her closer to her goal. Karen approached her student teaching placement in an LD class with much anticipation. She knew she wanted to be an elementary LD teacher and had been told that the teacher she would be working with, Mrs. Harmon, was the best. Once she received notification of her placement, Karen called Mrs. Harmon, and arranged to visit the classroom. Over the holidays she bought "teacher clothes" so she would look the part and had her car worked on so that she wouldn't have unexpected transportation problems, even though it was only a 15-minute drive. Karen quit her part-time job as a waitress to devote her full attention to teaching. She scoured the discount and teacher stores for inexpensive resources and reinforcers. Because she knew that Mrs. Harmon was a renowned reading teacher, Karen reread her notes and portions of the textbook from her reading course. Before setting foot in the classroom, Karen didn't know what else she could do to prepare for her upcoming experience.

It was obvious from the start that Mrs. Harmon and Karen had a lot in common. They were both hardworking, detail-oriented people. Mrs. Harmon arrived to begin her day between 5:30 and 6:00 a.m. Karen was amazed to see that Mrs. Harmon's lesson plans were like textbook examples, even better. She was a master at using curriculum-based assessment to pinpoint at exactly what level each child was functioning and created individual lesson plans in reading for all ten students. Karen hoped she would still to have this much energy and dedication after eighteen years of teaching! She actually hoped she had it now. Mrs. Harmon even went the extra step to write backup plans in case her first teaching strategy failed. She used an eclectic mixture of commercial and teacher-made materials, and the kids seemed to especially enjoy the file-folder learning games she created for phonemic awareness and phonics activities. The classroom was aesthetically pleasing, highly structured, and always ran on schedule. In addition to her incredible instructional strengths, Mrs. Harmon showed a sense of humor and sensitivity to her students. She knew their strengths and weaknesses, their home lives, their interests, and their frustration limits.

Karen couldn't have been more thrilled with her placement. Everything was just as she had learned, and here it was in real life. She knew in her heart that she was going to become a great teacher as a result of this experience, but she had a nagging worry about being able to keep the same pace as Mrs. Harmon, meeting the high expectations that Mrs. Harmon not only set for herself but would certainly expect of her student teacher as well. Another wonderful advantage was that Karen's favorite professor, Dr. Frend, was her university supervisor. It was in Dr. Frend's class that the multiple aspects of teaching had come alive and connected for Karen. Dr. Frend was one of those professors who obviously had been a great teacher herself and now transferred these skills to teaching preservice teachers. She was an inspiration to all her students, and Karen would never forget the excitement of that semester. It would be great to have the support of her favorite teacher, and Karen was determined to demonstrate her best teaching skills.

The first two weeks went beautifully as Karen gradually became acclimated to the classroom, students, paraprofessional, and Mrs. Harmon's style of teaching. Dr. Frend's first visit showed the close professional relationship and respect between professor and cooperating teacher. Both were complimentary and thoroughly supportive of Karen. Their questions made her think, their expectations motivated her to strive, and their work ethic led her to work incredibly hard. She didn't want to let anyone down, especially these two first-class professionals. As she took on more management and instructional responsibilities, Karen found herself working increasingly hard. She stayed up later and later each night to prepare lessons and materials for the next day and then went in early to work with Mrs. Harmon. The first two individualized reading lessons went quite well, and Mrs. Harmon was amazed at Karen's ability to plan and implement in this area. So many of her previous student teachers did not feel prepared to teach reading and were not able to meet each child at his or her individual level. Mrs. Harmon was pleased to see that this young woman thought the same way she did. It was often difficult for her to give up control of her students because she couldn't bear to sacrifice their instruction to a novice who was learning by trial and error. In this case, however, Mrs. Harmon willingly gave Karen more and more responsibility.

Karen was proud of her accomplishments so far, and each week during the student teaching seminar she was secretly thankful that she seemed to be learning more and struggling less than her peers. As the end of the fourth week arrived, Karen was exhausted. On and off all day, she found herself thinking "Thank God it's Friday" and wondering what she might do that evening to relax.

Unfortunately the weekend didn't seem to refuel her energy, partially because she worked on lesson plans and materials for much of the time but also because she was getting too run down with the increasing lack of sleep. Karen knew that being tired would lower her resistance to the many colds the students had and that she would get sick if she kept this up. But what could she do? If anything, the pressure was getting worse as she continued to take on additional responsibilities. In one more week she'd be handling the full load, which included planning for the paraprofessional also. She couldn't let on to Mrs. Harmon or Dr. Frend that this was too much for her to handle. With pages of written plans, new creative teacher-made materials each day, and the demand to be accountable for all student learning, Karen felt as if she were drowning. What would it be like when she was totally responsible for the class, and how could she possibly do it all just right? As she drove into the parking lot on Monday, she burst into tears.

Consider This

1. How could Karen be more honest with Mrs. Harmon and Dr. Frend about the pressures she feels? Do you think they would be receptive?
2. What could the three of them do to help Karen's increasing fear and anxiety?
3. Is it necessary for teachers and student teachers to spend all night and every weekend working on lesson plans and materials to provide effective instruction for students?
4. Is it reasonable for Karen to expect herself to perform at the same level as Mrs. Harmon?
5. What support do beginning teachers need in the first years of teaching, and how can they seek this support?
6. How can teachers, especially novice teachers, attain a good balance between their personal and professional lives?
7. Does a good teacher need to spend the amount of time and energy that Mrs. Harmon does?

Young Novice versus Experienced Professional

Instruction in special education is provided by an array of professionals and paraprofessionals. For student teachers, this often means taking on roles for which they have not been adequately prepared. They may be expected to collaborate with, schedule, plan for, and supervise other service providers. In this next case, a novice teacher faces challenges she had not previously considered.

Been There Forever

Karla was excited to begin her next placement in an elementary self-contained special education class. The previous week she had successfully completed an eight-week placement in a high school resource program, and although Karla really enjoyed the older students, she had always wanted to work with younger kids and was looking forward to this change. Karla had not yet seen the classroom but knew it would more closely resemble how she imagined teaching would be than her first placement. In this new self-contained setting, she hoped to feel more stability and ownership. A secondary resource teacher's job seemed to involve a lot of floating from place to place, even though there had been a designated "closet" called a resource room.

On Monday morning, Karla arrived early to meet Mrs. Summers. She had spoken with this teacher on the phone two weeks earlier, but it had been difficult at the time to focus on the details of the upcoming placement. Now she eagerly anticipated learning about a new school, students, and curriculum. Mrs. Summers greeted Karla warmly, and she immediately felt welcome. The room had a friendly, casual, somewhat cluttered atmosphere. The class consisted of nine students with extremely diverse academic, social, and physical needs. In addition, there were two paraprofessionals, which added up to a dreamy student-teacher ratio of three to one! It was immediately evident that without the paras, Mrs. Spencer and Mrs. Gonzalez, it would be impossible to manage everyone, never mind teach them.

Mrs. Summers, a talented teacher by reputation, had a very laid-back approach to managing her classroom. There was a posted schedule, but it quickly became clear that this was not adhered to very closely, and sometimes not at all. As Karla observed the first day, she was often unable to determine what was going on or what each of the adults was doing. Sometimes they looked busy, but it seemed like they spent a lot of time talking with each other or with Mrs. Summers. To confuse things even further, several children received related services, so the occupational therapist and speech-language pathologist came and went at various times. One child even had an itinerant vision specialist. These professionals provided direct services to the students approximately once a week, then consulted with the teacher and demonstrated how to continue implementing the skill development activities throughout the remainder of the week.

Karla was surprised and somewhat disconcerted by the number of adults she was introduced to within the first hour. She had more trouble remembering their names than those of the children. She was only twenty-two herself and didn't know how she would ever feel confident directing the activities of two paraprofessionals, both of whom were the age of her mother. To make it worse, one was even the parent of a child in the classroom. And, maybe it was too soon to judge, but it seemed that the paraprofessionals spent as much time talking with each other as they did working with students.

Karla sensed that many things in this room would need to be changed if she was going to demonstrate the skills she knew she had. She wondered if this was possible, or even her role? She was ready to try lots of ideas and wanted to make a real difference in the lives of these students. A fleeting question crossed her mind about why the university had chosen this placement for her. Before lunch, her head was swimming with a host of unanswered questions. What would her role be? How could she tighten up the schedule and keep everyone working productively with students? How was she going to plan for herself as well as Mrs. Spencer and Mrs. Gonzalez? It was clear that they were used to a lot of freedom; would they even be willing to do what she asked? What was the meaning behind that look she kept getting from these two women? How would she handle the fuzzy line between paraprofessional and parent? What was a parent doing in her room on a daily basis anyway? Reconsidering her original impression, maybe the ratio wasn't "dreamy"; it was "burdensome."

Consider This

1. Can student teachers learn as much from problematic placements as from more ideal ones?
2. In terms of the responsibilities of novice teachers, what do they need to know about working with paraprofessionals? Where can they seek help if they are unsure how to proceed?

3. Is it realistic for the student teacher to plan for instruction provided by all adults in the classroom?
4. How can a novice teacher establish credibility with older adults who have been in the classroom longer and know the students better?
5. Was Karla justified in worrying that one of the paraprofessionals was also a student's mother? Why?
6. Should Karla attempt to gain control over the schedule? If so, how might she do this?
7. How can related service providers and special educators work together effectively to benefit students? How important is it for the special education teacher to regularly implement the suggestions of related service providers?

Differences between University Ideals and Implementation in Schools

The discrepancy between theory and practice sometimes seems like a chasm to novice teachers. This is especially true for a student teacher who may feel like a guest in the school and classroom. While the classroom teacher's primary objective must be student outcomes, he or she must balance providing the student teacher with opportunities for growth with maintaining consistency and routines in an established school program. Teacher educators, on the other hand, hope that student teachers and university supervisors will positively impact the schools with new approaches and ideas. The following case illustrates gaps between what was learned in a teacher preparation program and the reality of daily classroom practices.

Theory or Reality?

Mario stared at his syllabus for student teaching. He didn't know how he would be able to fulfill these requirements in his placement with Mr. Cooper at Sharks Run Middle School. During the first meeting with the cooperating teacher and his university supervisor, Mario sensed that there were discrepancies between what the faculty at the university and the faculty at the school expected. The first requirement listed on the syllabus involved lesson plans. Dr. Cordoza required detailed plans for lessons to remediate specific academic and social skills, but how could Mario ever provide this, given Mr. Cooper's inclusion schedule? He didn't have responsibility for academic teaching and didn't write lesson plans. In the general education classrooms, these special education teachers functioned in support roles, mainly keeping a low profile so as not to stigmatize the special education students. Mr. Cooper assisted any students who appeared to need help during the period but seldom singled them out for special attention or instruction. Mario could still hear his Collaboration course professor warning them not to become a "glorified teacher's aide."

Resource room time was used to help students keep up in their academic classes. Daily work was dependent on individual student needs regarding homework, upcoming projects, or tests. Because Mario didn't know what help the students would need from day to day, it was impossible to write any kind of lesson plans.

As he glanced back at the syllabus, the second requirement—developing a behavior intervention plan—loomed before him. Mr. Cooper worked in a variety of general education classrooms with several teachers. Each teacher had his own established system for managing behavior, and Mr. Cooper adapted to these teachers' styles like a chameleon. In his resource room, however, he believed that students needed a break from the structured requirements and behavioral expectations of larger classes and so allowed students to relax in a casual atmosphere while they were with him. The students liked him, and their relationship was more like that of friends than the student-teacher relationships Mario observed in other classrooms. As long as students were not injuring themselves or others, Mr. Cooper tolerated their antics. During his supervisor's first observation in the resource room, Mario could almost feel Dr. Cordoza's blood pressure rising as he watched the students' behavior and off-task performance. Because of an unexpected parent conference, Mr. Cooper was not able to join them for the postobservation meeting, so Mario got an earful about both the lesson planning and the need for a well thought-out behavior management program. Dr. Cordoza cautioned, "Think about what you learned in Behavior Management 101. I'd like to see you implement some of those strategies."

Mario knew that Dr. Cordoza wanted him to fulfill the requirements on the syllabus. He had been told that these expectations were carefully constructed based on skills developed in courses, and student teaching was viewed as the opportunity to try out these important skills. Mario was required to identify one student with reading deficits and to develop and implement a remedial plan. Mario agreed, since he realized remediating these basic skill deficits might ultimately allow the special education students more independent access to the general curriculum. He was willing to attempt to establish resource room rules and implement a system for reinforcing appropriate behavior. He might even have risked trying one of the co-teaching roles he remembered seeing in a collaboration video. But as he thought about all this, he understood that the school culture contributed to the current model of inclusion and that Mr. Cooper had not necessarily chosen the support role in which he found himself. The teacher had confided that he felt tremendous pressure to help his students pass their academic classes as well as master the new state curriculum standards. With so many different subject area teachers to work with, it was a constant struggle to keep one step ahead. Students and their parents were depending on him because obtaining a regular high school diploma was at stake. Relieving this pressure was his rationale for providing a more supportive, relaxed resource environment. The students were like corks ready to pop out of the bottle when they entered during the last period of the day. Mr. Cooper told Mario to follow the routines already in place and learn how special educators in the real world had to work.

Mario truly felt caught in the middle. He needed to satisfy Dr. Cordoza to pass student teaching and get his special education teaching license. He also had six more weeks of working with Mr. Cooper in classrooms with routines established since the beginning of the school year. He didn't see how he was going to be able to satisfy everyone and still look out for himself. Should he be trying to implement theory or stick to reality?

Consider This

1. Describe co-teaching models that might be effectively used to maximize the different skills of two professional teachers in a single classroom.
2. What are some of the obstacles that must be dealt with before co-teaching will be successful?
3. How can a special education teacher assure that students with disabilities are getting what they need in a general education classroom?
4. What are the advantages and disadvantages of having different behavioral expectations in special education classrooms and in general education settings?
5. During his next communication with Dr. Cordoza, how might Mario approach the dilemma resulting from the difference between theory and actual practice?
6. How can novice teachers be change agents for practices they want to implement within a school?

Changing Faces of Instruction

Novice teachers have an image of themselves teaching students effectively in an ideal, or at least appropriate, instructional environment. Actual teaching conditions in today's schools, however, may be less than ideal, and control of some of the instructional variables may not be in the special educator's hands. In the following case, a student teacher faces a range of instructional difficulties in a high school setting.

Biology, Page 112

There seemed to be no end to the number of students in the school division who were found eligible for special education services, and by the time they reached high school it was tough to provide the services they needed, cover the curriculum, and prepare them for the state tests. Jefferson High was a large urban school, and despite a special education staff of fifteen teachers Dennis still couldn't quite see how they would get it all done. He was formally placed with Mrs. Lombardi, a very busy teacher with an eclectic schedule of classes.

Although she was officially a special education teacher, Mrs. Lombardi taught biology first period and a study skills class second period, did planning third period, and, after a late lunch, taught one period of basic skills remediation. Mrs. Lombardi attended weekly meetings as a member of the school's special education department as well as the science department.

During his visit before starting student teaching, Dennis had initially been pleased with the small number of courses he would be teaching, though he immediately started worrying about the science course. Mrs. Lombardi took great pride in her biology class and spent most of the hour-long meeting describing various aspects she wanted to make sure Dennis continued. Words and phrases like "differentiation of instruction," "textbook modification," "adapted lab activities," "cooperative learning," "performance-based assessment," "compensatory skills," "mnemonic strategies," and "graphic organizers" all became lost in a sea of jargon.

Biology! Dennis had taken the minimum number of science classes both in high school and college. His love was history; before entering the special education program, he had considered becoming a social studies teacher. Why couldn't he at least be in a history or government class, where he would have something to contribute? The worst was that these classes were interminable. The school was on a 4 "TIMES" 4 block schedule with 90-minute periods. How would he ever keep an active class of sixteen ninth-graders with disabilities focused on the science content for an hour and a half, especially when they had minute attention spans, severe memory deficits, and reading skills typically at the fourth-grade level? On top of all this, Dennis knew he didn't know enough about biology to teach it and certainly had no enthusiasm for the subject. He was at least happy that Mrs. Lombardi had agreed to let him get his feet wet with the other classes and take over biology last.

Dennis remembered the first time he had been expected to write a lesson plan. He had had no idea how much thought and consideration went into developing or "designing" (as his professor called it) lessons. There were so many factors to think about, and a lot of these were supposed to be written down. At first, Dennis had oversimplified the process and received a bad grade on the lesson plan assignment. He made an appointment with the instructor because he knew this was going to be an important skill, and he wanted to be successful when lesson plans really counted.

That had been two years earlier. Since then, Dennis had learned to write detailed plans for the practicum students he worked with and the student he tutored in the after-school program. He devoted a significant amount of time to these plans for several reasons. First, he was being graded on them. Second, the plans were a way to communicate what he was doing with the student to others who needed to know (the supervisor, the classroom teacher, his peer partner, and, at times, the parent). Third, these plans helped him think through the lesson and make the very best use of the instructional time. He learned that on days when he had not planned adequately, his lesson did not go as well. They were his security blanket, especially when someone was observing, because at these times he tended to become very nervous. He'd lose track of what he was supposed to be doing and skip parts of the lesson.

Dennis was faced with a dilemma. He knew not only why he was required to, but also why he should write lesson plans. However, he also knew that Mrs. Lombardi had a different idea about these plans. She told him that she expected him to have written plans and proceeded to show him an example from her plan book. She used one of those plastic-covered teacher plan books with 2-inch by 2-inch boxes for each instructional period; a week was visible at any one time. Dennis's eyes widened when he saw the neatly written biology textbook page numbers, names of lab activities, and lists of instructional materials that comprised the plans. Mrs. Lombardi was an excellent creative teacher; how could she possibly teach from these shorthand notes?

At first, Dennis held to his high standards and wrote detailed plans for each lesson he taught, but Mrs. Lombardi barely looked at them and gave him very little feedback. His university supervisor stated that he only wanted to review the plans on the days that he observed, and Dennis usually knew when the supervisor was coming. So Dennis quickly fell into the habit of writing less and less. With increasing lessons to plan for, assessment reports to write, weekly paperwork for student teaching, and his other added responsibilities, he justified that he didn't have time to write so much detail. Accordingly, he shortened his plans and subsequently his planning time. Dennis assumed that if Mrs. Lombardi could do it, then he must be ready, too; it really didn't matter anyway because she wasn't going to look at them. Suddenly, however, he did not have as much confidence in his teaching and would glance up hoping that Mr. Stone, the university supervisor, would not walk in unannounced.

As Mrs. Lombardi sat in the back of the room working on a draft of an IEP for an upcoming conference, she was wondering why Dennis's lessons seemed to lose their effectiveness and the students didn't seem as interested as before. She would have to discuss this with Dennis as soon as possible, especially since he was scheduled to take over the biology class next week.

Consider This

1. Why could Mrs. Lombardi teach effectively from sketchy lesson plans while Dennis could not?
2. What did Dennis include in his original plans that he still needed now? Why does Dennis refer to his lesson plans as his "security blanket"? Is this unusual for a novice teacher?
3. What should Dennis do to balance his need for more detailed lesson plans and the time constraints he faces?
4. Identify the decisions that a teacher makes in planning instruction. List as many as you can and then place them in a logical sequential order.
5. Why would a special educator be teaching a high school content area course?

6. How would you prepare to teach a subject you were unfamiliar with and/or unenthusiastic about? Where will Dennis find the general education curriculum objectives for biology?
7. How might planning for instruction be different in a block schedule? What should Dennis consider in order to meet the needs of his students with disabilities in this schedule?

Seamless Integration of Skills

Juggling lesson plans, instructional materials, assessment of student performance, and student attention is often difficult for the beginning professional. Courses, as evidenced by their titles, are developed to focus on somewhat isolated aspects of the overall teaching role, but effective teaching demands the fluid integration of skills. Student teaching challenges the novice to balance and seamlessly integrate a wide range of pedagogical behaviors.

You Didn't Tell Me

Tamara just knew she couldn't handle it if Ms. Hannah, her university supervisor, called in the big guns from the university. During her last visit Ms. Hannah subtly mentioned talking with Dr. Kiser about her progress. Tamara wondered what Ms. Hannah was saying and what the head of the special education program was thinking. What if Dr. Kiser actually came out and observed her? Feeling increasingly threatened, Tamara wondered, "Why is Ms. Hannah doing this to me?"

Everything seemed to be going all right during her initial week in the self-contained classroom for students with emotional and behavioral disorders. Placement in a classroom that was part of a specialized center attached to the elementary school was a dream come true for Tamara, who knew she would learn a great deal from her cooperating teacher, Mrs. Curtis, and the students. Including this placement on her résumé would be the ticket to a good-paying job only a short eight weeks away. Tamara had always worked hard in her university courses and received good grades as a reward for this effort, and so she felt prepared to tackle the demands of this setting. She knew that the students' primary needs involved behavioral support, but she would also be responsible for planning all academic instruction. Tamara thought she'd spend a lot of time observing how Mrs. Curtis handled the students and thus would be able to follow the model she set.

Problems started on the day of her first supervisor observation, however. When Ms. Hannah arrived for her first visit, Tamara was still taking a fairly passive role trying to absorb all she could about this classroom. Ms. Hannah and Mrs. Curtis left for a while, and when they returned they asked the paraprofessional to continue with the students so that Tamara could meet with them for a few minutes. Ms. Hannah made a few brief positive remarks about the setting and opportunities for professional growth and then asked Tamara what her goals were for this placement, her third and last before obtaining her special education licensure. Tamara quickly stated that she wanted to learn all she could from Mrs. Curtis. Ms. Hannah and the teacher exchanged a quick glance, and then Ms. Hannah said she was hoping to see Tamara more integrally involved in the classroom by now, especially since this was her final placement. Surprised, Tamara responded by saying, "You didn't tell me that I should be doing more." Ms. Hannah took out a long-range planning form and suggested that they map out more clearly when and how much responsibility Tamara should begin to assume.

Two weeks later, when Ms. Hannah returned to Riverside Center, she found Tamara teaching a reading lesson with a small group of students. Tamara knew Ms. Hannah was coming, so she had developed a fun activity related to the story. During the lesson, Tamara found she was having difficulty maintaining the students' attention, but she kept going until the activity was finally completed. In the postobservation conference, when Ms. Hannah asked to see Tamara's lesson plans, Tamara said, "Since Mrs. Curtis didn't always have written plans for every part of her day, I did not write down today's lesson." Ms. Hannah explored further, asking Tamara about her instructional objectives for the lesson, projected time frames, preventative behavioral considerations, and ways she would know if the students achieved the desired outcomes. Thrown for a loop, Tamara said, "No one told me that I had to have plans written in so much detail." When Ms. Hannah asked about Tamara's preparation in this area, Tamara responded, "In the course on special education program planning and also in my methods class, I learned to write detailed lesson plans based on a direct instruction format, but that takes too much time. I know experienced teachers don't plan this way, and pretty soon I'm going to be teaching. I can do it, but you should have told me that you expected written plans."

Somewhat amazed, Ms. Hannah thought to herself, "How explicit do I have to be, and why is Tamara having so much difficulty applying skills from her courses to the requirements for this experience?" Rather than voicing these questions, Ms. Hannah said in a calm manner, "It is very important to write complete plans for each lesson you teach. A critical part of the plan should be appropriate instructional objectives, and these should drive the instructional activities, not the other way around. As you know, in an ED class it is also imperative to plan how you will prevent problems and manage misbehavior if it occurs. I especially want you to identify how you will know when each student has mastered the objectives. Can you go back to your textbooks and notes from your classes to refresh your memory on these topics?"

Tamara thought to herself, "This sounds like one of those beginning courses Dr. Kiser taught. I should be beyond this by now." When Mrs. Curtis arrived, Ms. Hannah reemphasized that Tamara was expected to have written lesson plans and that she should be showing them to her cooperating teacher before the lessons. Mrs. Curtis shot Tamara a look that meant, "This is what I have been telling you. I am glad we are all on the same wavelength now."

During the third observation, Ms. Hannah walked in expecting Tamara to exhibit skills more representative of all those A's she had received in her courses. It was a good sign that she had not had another phone call from Mrs. Curtis. The students were returning from music and Tamara walked in with a coffee cup in hand. She looked surprised to see Ms. Hannah but immediately smiled and began to get ready for her science lesson on simple machines. The students wandered around for a while, and once she was prepared Tamara called across the room to them that it was time for science. She walked over and handed Ms. Hannah a piece of paper and then began. Ms. Hannah glanced at the lesson plan, trying to get her bearings on what she would be observing. It seemed as if this was the introductory lesson, but Tamara was jumping right in, showing and labeling three different types of simple machines. She drew some illustrations on the board and then distributed a textbook work sheet requiring the students to label various simple machines and their parts, even though not all of this matched what she had just tried to teach. Students began raising their hands and started calling out for Tamara to come over and answer their questions. Ms. Hannah sat there dumbfounded, wondering how she would approach this one. She was really beginning to question what Tamara had learned in her classes at the university.

When they met with Mrs. Curtis after class, Ms. Hannah began by asking Tamara how she thought the lesson went. "It's always like that when they come in from music," Tamara said. "They have a hard time settling down and science isn't their favorite subject anyway." Mrs. Curtis looked exasperated and gave Ms. Hannah a look that showed she was having a hard time controlling her anger. It was obvious that things were not going as well as Ms. Hannah had assumed. Ms. Hannah broached the subject of the instructional objectives and teaching methods that Tamara had chosen, asking how she might better have introduced the lesson to capture the students' attention and give them the big ideas before delving into the smaller details. Looking at Mrs. Curtis as she answered, Tamara said, "You told me to make sure I covered the necessary content standards related to simple machines in the state science curriculum." Ms. Hannah and Mrs. Curtis both began talking at once. Ms. Hannah realized she would have to seek the help of faculty at the university to sort this out. What skills did or didn't this student have? Maybe it wasn't Tamara's fault, and she had not been prepared for a teaching role that required her to juggle multiple responsibilities and apply a range of teaching skills? Maybe they were being too hard on Tamara to expect her to perform like an experienced teacher?

Consider This

1. What is the relationship between instructional objectives and the rest of the lesson plan?
2. What might the student teacher do to help students appropriately transition from another class and not lose valuable instructional time?

3. How might Tamara have effectively introduced the lesson on simple machines?
4. What could Tamara do to assess student mastery of the curriculum objectives? Why is this an important part of planning?
5. How can preservice teachers organize the handouts and materials from their classes for later reference when they are student teachers or beginning professionals?
6. How can student teachers consciously bridge the gap between what they learned in their classes and the skills they must demonstrate in the classroom?
7. How can gaps in communication among the university supervisor, cooperating teacher, and student teacher be resolved? What is the student teacher's responsibility in this situation?

Documenting Professional Knowledge and Skills

In an era of increasing accountability, portfolios are gaining popularity as evidence of professional knowledge and skills. From the beginning of their teacher preparation program to the final stages of their careers, teachers should be able to provide evidence of continued professional development. How can a teacher document pedagogical expertise?

Let Me Show You

Alex wished he had not waited until now to get serious about his portfolio. He needed to have it ready by the end of student teaching; more important, he wanted to have it completed for his interviews, which would start at the end of the month. Regrettably, he had not kept his coursework from his practicum classes or artifacts from student teaching in a very organized manner. His apartment was littered with stacks of papers, folders from courses, projects, instructional materials, and the like. Although he had been encouraged along the way to take photographs of materials he had made or bulletin boards he'd created, Alex had only done this sporadically and was not sure he could even find them at this point.

During the student teaching seminar meeting, several of his peers had shared their portfolios, and it was then that Alex realized exactly what was involved and why it was important. It really was impressive to see concrete examples of many things they had learned and skills they had mastered. Chris Wang's had been especially remarkable. Not only was it glitzy—with an attractive cover, well organized with dividers, illustrated with purposeful photographs, and displayed in plastic pages—but as Chris talked about the contents, Alex was amazed at the depth of reflectivity. Chris spoke articulately not only about his experiences, but also about the teaching profession and him-

self as a professional. His philosophy was well thought out and concisely artic-
ulated. The arrangement and focus of various contents actually captured some
aspects of Chris' personality. Alex thought to himself, "I would hire him in a
heartbeat if he brought this portfolio to an interview."

Alex made a commitment to return home that evening and make assembling his portfolio a priority. With several weeks of student teaching left, he
could already think of things he wanted to capture and include. Tomorrow Alex
wanted to talk with his cooperating teacher, Ms. James, about the materials she
was assembling for her own portfolio. After fifteen years of experience, she was
preparing to apply for National Professional Teaching Standards Board (NPTSB)
certification.

That evening, Alex sat on the living-room floor overwhelmed and wondering where to begin. What should he include? How could he provide tangible evidence of his teaching skills? How should he organize the materials to
reflect his growth over the past four years?

Consider This

1. What broad areas would you include in a well-designed portfolio? How
   would you organize the materials?
2. Identify specific examples of content you might place in each section of your
   portfolio.
3. What types of artifacts would you not include, and why?
4. What does it mean to be "reflective" in a portfolio?
5. How might you use a portfolio in an interview?
6. How might you use a portfolio for continued professional development
   throughout your career?
7. Consulting the National Board for Professional Teaching Standards' literature or website, describe what is required for the NBPTS portfolio.

Differentiating Instruction

There is no single correct way to meet the various needs of learners in a mixed-
ability classroom. Effective differentiation requires knowledge of the learner and
the learning goals as well as a flexible approach to teaching. Just as "one size
doesn't fit all," one instructional approach won't work for all students. Teachers
need to systematically evaluate the demands of the task in light of their knowledge
of student characteristics. Only then can they identify modifications or develop
alternatives.

The Many Faces of Instruction

Sue Ellen, a second-year teacher at Carterville Elementary, reviewed the files of
the students on her caseload. Most of them were identified as learning disabled
and had academic skill deficits ranging from one to four years below grade

level. She worked very hard to schedule her students to that she could provide direct instruction as well as co-teach when needed.

Sue Ellen began by working with Yvonne, one of the fourth-grade teachers who had five of her students. They became friends last year shortly after being hired, and both were looking forward to this opportunity to work together. Enough discussion had occurred to make them optimistic that two teachers in the classroom during science would improve instruction and alleviate some of their isolation as well as teaching load. They both loved kids and enjoyed their jobs.

"I hope we can meet our goal of differentiating instruction so that all students succeed," said Sue Ellen. "I'm really pleased that my schedule worked out so well. I ended up being able to schedule my kids for direct instruction in reading and writing at times when they wouldn't miss subjects like math, social studies, and science. This will work out great because when my students are working on language arts, the kids back in their classroom will be doing the same thing. As we hoped," she added, "I was able to fit in one co-teaching period with you because you have so many students with LD."

"It'll be great to work with you," Yvonne agreed. "I hope to learn more about teaching your students."

Picking up on the opportunity, Sue Ellen quickly replied, "I'm really looking forward to working with you, too. I learned a lot about modifying materials in a course I took. We adapted materials or developed alternatives that really helped the students who had organization, attention, memory, reading, and writing problems. I really think it's kind of fun, like solving a puzzle. We used a strategic process called 'IEP-DR.' If I remember right, the letters stand for: *I*dentify student's strengths and weaknesses, *E*valuate the demands of the task, *P*redict potential problems, *D*evelop modifications, and *R*eflect on results and revise as needed."

Yvonne thought for a second. "What exactly did you do when you developed the modifications? I'm not sure if I had to change the things I do in science that I'd know what to do. Predicting potential problems doesn't sound too hard because I've seen how some kids struggle, but developing modifications is another story."

"That's why we'll make a good team," Sue Ellen responded enthusiastically. "You are more of the science curriculum expert, while I can contribute ideas to help us reach all the kids." She made a mental note to go over the students' IEPs with Yvonne and create a chart with brief summaries of each child's reading level and IEP accommodations. They could keep this chart in the front of their plan books.

Meeting 1: First, the teachers briefly reviewed the IEPs for the five students, paying special attention to the accommodations. Yvonne gave Sue Ellen a copy of the pacing guide that she and the other fourth-grade teachers had developed and said, "This pacing guide accompanies the state curriculum standards showing the sequence of our fourth-grade science units and how much time we'll spend on each unit." Sue Ellen noted that according to the guide, the first unit was on "light and sound." At that point Yvonne took a box labeled

"Light & Sound" off the shelf and passed it to Sue Ellen, suggesting, "Rather than explaining the box of materials page by page, why don't you take a look and see what we'll be doing. This is one of my favorite units. There are lots of interesting science experiments and projects we can do." Anxious to get started, Sue Ellen took the materials back to her resource room and gradually went through the box. Forty minutes later she closed the lid. It was obvious from the instructional materials that Yvonne was very knowledgeable about science, "much more than me," Sue Ellen thought, "but I wonder how much she knows about students with special needs?"

Meeting 2: Yvonne and Sue Ellen discussed the first lesson. Yvonne thought it would be best for all the students to take a pretest and then read the first section of the science textbook chapter on sound. "I can just picture the frustration level rise rapidly as the students look at a pretest full of vocabulary and dense print they couldn't read. We're going to have trouble getting them interested in anything about light and sound after this," Sue Ellen thought. "Would it be possible to grab their attention with a novel demonstration or some stimulating questions related to everyday application of information related to light?" she said aloud. "My students are often unmotivated on the surface. Unless we grab their attention right away, they are bound to say something like, 'That's boring,' or 'When can we do something else?' It's definitely a challenge to stimulate their interest, but if they are curious and it looks like it will be fun and something not too hard for them, then we'll hook them."

"We could get at the information you have in the pretest using a KWL chart." Yvonne said excitedly, "Sounds great. Why don't I do the lesson intro and you can lead the chart activity? I've already got some intriguing things in mind." Each teacher left with a clear understanding of her role in the first science lesson.

Meeting 3: After a successful first day, Yvonne and Sue Ellen were inspired to continue planning. They looked at Yvonne's plans from the previous year in light of the new students that were in the class. The science textbook had chapters on both light and sound, over forty-five pages of reading altogether. Yvonne said, "I usually assign sections of the reading for homework first, then we read at least some of it aloud in class. I like to call on students to read so I know if they are paying attention."

"What will happen when you call on Jeremy or Sean?" Sue Ellen said gently. "They will either refuse, distracting everyone with some antic, or comply, thereby embarrassing themselves with stilted monotone reading, stopping every 5 seconds at words they don't know."

"I know the textbook is too hard for some of the children, but I don't have anything else on 'light and sound' for them to read. What can we do?" asked Yvonne. Sue Ellen reminded her about the IEP accommodations, which had included books on tape for at least two of the students. "I was relieved when the taped copies of the textbook arrived last week along with the variable speed tape recorders. Sean and Jeremy can use these to compensate for their reading problems while in science, but I'll still work on improving their reading skills in the resource room during language arts," Sue Ellen explained.

"The audiotapes will really help," Yvonne remarked, "but if they don't have to read the materials, then the others won't want to do it, either. Everyone will want one of those tape recorders, won't they? I can just picture one of my students telling me that it isn't fair." Although this was a tough question, Sue Ellen knew it was a realistic one, so she explained her definition of "fairness."

The next 20 minutes were spent discussing how to reinforce the science vocabulary and provide an alternative to writing the answers to countless text-book chapter questions. Both teachers agreed the questions were good ones but they brainstormed ways to accomplish this comprehension check without as much writing. The result involved a cooperative learning activity called "Send a Problem."

Future meetings: Plans were proceeding smoothly, and both teachers were pleased with how they were working together to improve instruction and split the load. Sue Ellen enjoyed gaining a more in-depth understanding of the science content, and Yvonne was becoming increasingly adept at predicting the potential problems the students might have and suggesting alternatives. They both were amazed how much better a lesson went when they developed modifications collaboratively. As they became increasingly attuned to the needs of other students in the room, Sue Ellen and Yvonne found themselves considering how to accommodate students with gifts and talents as well as those with language barriers. Before the unit ended, they still had to tackle an experiment using flashlights, remembering the essential information from the unit, active studying, and modifying the test.

Consider This

1. Construct a response to Yvonne's concern that accommodations for some students were not "fair" to the other students.
2. What are some other instructional accommodations that can be made for students who have difficulty reading the textbook material? How would you deal with the need to know difficult but essential content-area vocabulary words?
3. Activities like science experiments are multistep tasks. What are some of the potential problems that Sean or Jeremy might face as they complete and write up a science experiment? Extend your thinking to the potential problems of completing a six-week science project using the scientific process.
4. Predict the potential problems the boys might have remembering information in the "light and sound" unit. What mnemonic strategies could be used?
5. Passive learning is a characteristic of many students with disabilities. How might the teachers increase the active involvement of students in both class review activities and independent studying?
6. If the end-of-unit assessment was a paper-and-pencil test, describe how it could be designed to make it appropriate for Sean and Jeremy. What other types of assessment would be appropriate?

7. Do you think accommodations benefit only the students with identified disabilities? Who else might need additional instructional support in order to
   learn, and why?
8. What is the purpose of the IEP in this co-teaching scenario? Who should
   attend the IEP meeting, and why?

The Cycle of Assessment and Instruction

Teachers are increasingly accountable for assessing and documenting students'
knowledge and skills. Assessment in special education includes formal diagnosis
for the purposes of identification and determination of students' skill levels in a
variety of academic and nonacademic areas. On the basis of this assessment initial
IEPs are written, delineating instructional goals and objectives. From here, teachers need to assess specifically at what level a child is in a given skill and, once they
implement instruction, when to move forward or backward. This assessment
involves ongoing data collection and analysis. Finally, teachers are required to
monitor, provide feedback, and periodically report each student's progress in the
curriculum and on individual objectives. This case highlights a variety of assessment issues that novice teachers face as they diagnose, instruct, evaluate, and
report students' performance.

Keeping Track of Their Progress

It had been a difficult decision to return to college at my age, especially with so
many family responsibilities. Three busy kids, one with a learning disability,
and a husband who travels a lot for business made for a hectic life, but I was
determined to pursue my lifelong dream of becoming a special education
teacher. After having volunteered in my children's schools, I was even more
confident that I wanted to enter the teaching field and that I could make a difference. So once my youngest started kindergarten, I started graduate school.
The picture of the four of us leaving the house on the first day of school with our
backpacks still hangs on the refrigerator. That seems like a long time ago now.
Chipping away at the required courses, one or two per semester, delayed my
progress compared to that of the full-time students, many of whom were considerably younger than I, but I worked hard and achieved excellent grades to
show for it. I found it interesting to learn in school about things that I had experienced firsthand as a parent of a child with a disability. It made me appreciate
our school division and my son's teachers, most of whom had been excellent.
Now I am almost done. Once I've completed this final field experience, I will
have my own classroom. Bonita Lopez, a special education teacher. I can't wait.

Tonight, we are all sitting in a semicircle at the biweekly university seminar for student teaching. I rushed home from student teaching, fixed the kids
a quick dinner, started everyone on their homework, and then raced to find

parking at the university so I wouldn't be late. The topic for the evening was assessment because of the difficulties some of us were having in this area, and Dr. Carter, the seminar leader, thought it might help if we shared not only the problems we were experiencing but some of the questions we continued to have or solutions we had come up with. We all found out that it wasn't as easy as we thought to generalize from what we learned in a book or from tutoring a student last year to the skills needed to manage a busy classroom. There were so many things to attend to and decisions to make. I could tell from how we were seated that I would be the last person to share, so I sat back and listened to other students describe their experiences related to assessment, thinking about what I would do in these situations.

Janice began with a description of what had happened when her supervisor came to observe earlier that day. "I was working with the students on telling time to the half hour. They had finished making their paper-plate clocks and I called out times, like 2:30 or 8:30. They each formed the hands on their clock to show the time. The lesson went even better than I expected and the students were really involved and paying attention. After the lesson, my supervisor asked, 'How do you think the students did on today's lesson?' I told her that I was very pleased and they did great. She asked, 'What exactly do you mean by great? Did they meet your lesson objective of 85% mastery?' I told her I thought so because they did so well, but she asked, 'How do you really know, and where is your data to show how each student did?' I was at a loss because I didn't even think to write anything down during the lesson. Then she asked, 'How long will you be working on this skill?' I told her that tomorrow I'd move to telling time to the 15-minute interval. She asked, 'Do you really know if each of the children mastered today's objective and is ready to move on? Is there anyone that has to go back and review time to the hour? Is there anyone that needs more work on the half hour? Is there anyone that already knows how to tell time to the quarter hour?' I have to admit, I was at a total loss for what to say. Of course, she was right, and I knew she could tell from the look on my face that I couldn't answer her questions. Can you all help me figure out how to know where each child is on specific skills?"

The next person to share was Raymond. "Remember in our instruction course when we learned about precision teaching and then used it with the student we were tutoring? I kept data on my third-grader's progress and then charted his performance. He was so excited to see the positive steps he made, and it made me feel good to see that I had actually taught him something. But we all know this was with one kid in a perfect scenario. Now I have twelve kids to keep track of. How can I possibly do this?"

The next situation involved how best to assess students' learning at the end of a unit and Rasheed described what happened to him. "This group of kids is terrible at paper-and-pencil tests. In fact, typical tests just don't seem appropriate. The students know how to do the skills, but they can't show me on a regular test. I was really stumped for a while, but my supervisor pushed me to solve the problem. Although I wasn't sure this would work, I developed a series of activities related to our instruction and made them into learning stations. The students rotated through the series of stations, calling for me to look at their work in each station when they were done. I marked down how they did on a checklist I had developed and let them move to the next station. In the end, I captured a lot of data about the students' skills and they were able to truly demonstrate their performance. The best part is how excited they were about doing it this way. 'Mr. Ammhad, is this really a test? This is so cool.' I wonder why I didn't think of this sooner?"

Leif was the fourth person to share. "In my ED class I have to keep track of not just their academic progress but also their behaviors, and each student has different behavioral goals! My teacher is awesome, and she showed me a neat way of doing this. For each student, she and the student jointly identify one to three behavioral goals to work on. These goals are written on a form with space to record a number from 1 to 5, indicating how well the student demonstrated the behavioral goal. After each period, both in our room and in their other classes, the student puts a number showing how he thinks he did and the teacher also writes a number. If there is a discrepancy, they briefly discuss the behavior and agree on a rating. At the end of the day the teacher records progress on a behavior chart tacked to the bulletin board. Students who make 5s for one week can take that behavior off their card. What is really great is that students are responsible for their cards, and there is a set routine for assessing the behavior. We have objective data to go on rather than just the subjective 'teacher observation' I have seen on so many IEPs."

When Marcie spoke up, it was clear that she had given her problem some thought. She reported, "My supervisor wrote on my plans that my instructional activities and materials were excellent, but they were not clearly associated with specific goals and objectives. How do I develop lesson objectives that correlate with the student's IEP objectives as well as the state curriculum objectives? There are just too many different objectives to worry about! I asked my cooperating teacher how she kept track of all the different types of objectives and she said that she is so familiar with the state curriculum and the students' IEPs that she can make these links in her head. She told me, 'You can't be expected to do this yet, so let's figure out a way to help you see the relationship among the different objectives.' We decided that I would write lesson-plan objectives at the top of the lesson plan as I had been doing but then I would also note the numbers of the state curriculum objectives and student's IEP objectives. Even though this is a pain, it really helps because it makes me look at both other documents each time I plan a lesson. I, too, am becoming more familiar with curriculum objectives. What I now don't understand is how to fill out their progress reports based on all this information. They may have mastered the lesson objective and I know which other objectives it relates to, but does that mean all the kids get A's?"

At this point Jamie jumped in. "I know what you mean. I hate to grade these students. I don't even like marking their papers because I don't know if I should mark the answers that are wrong or indicate the ones that are correct. It's even worse to decide what grade I should put on their report cards. Should I give a grade based on their effort? Johnny tries so hard, but he often can't do the problems the next day. Or should I give grades based on individual progress, even though it is still below grade level? Or is it important for students and their parents to realistically understand where they are functioning in comparison to typical seventh-graders? I really don't know what kind of feedback is required or which is most useful."

We all listened while J.T. read the questions his supervisor wrote on his observation sheet. "Why did you write '70% mastery' on all your lesson objectives? Did you just copy this number from the IEP? Is this the passing rate for the school? How should you decide what the level of mastery should be?" J.T. said to the group, "I'm not sure how this number jumped into my head and I don't really know how to select the desired mastery level. I know it shouldn't be 100%, or should it? Are there times when 100% mastery is necessary? What do you all think?"

Next was Johanna, who described what happened when she tried to grade a writing assignment. "I asked the students to write a short essay describing what they would do if they won a million dollars. I thought this would be a fun topic that would stimulate their interest and motivate them to write more than a couple of sentences. I specifically said that it had to be at least three paragraphs long and contain creative ideas. All the students turned in their papers on time, and I started to grade them that evening. After reading the first one, I put it down and picked up another. I read it and then read a third. I couldn't figure out how to grade these. What was I looking for—creative ideas? grammar? punctuation? vocabulary? spelling? correct length?"

As the discussion gradually wound around to me, I admitted to myself that these were some of the same problems I was facing. When it was my turn, I shared my assessment dilemma. "We had a new student come into our class today. My teacher asked me to review the file as soon as possible. She wanted me to summarize the basic information and determine what we should start working on with this child. After getting the file from the guidance secretary, I sat for two hours trying to make sense of all the papers and reports, especially the IEP. It was so vague that I could basically only tell what subjects we were supposed to cover. There were only one or two short-term objectives or benchmarks for each broad goal . . . really no help at all. Do you remember our professors talking about IEPs as working documents? Well, about all you could do with this one was put it in a file drawer. I'm sure glad my son's teachers were better prepared and more professional. For this child, I had to go back through the referral information, assessment reports, and eligibility information to get anything specific. Even then I didn't have much to go on. I hate to admit to Mr. Elias that this is all I could find, but I don't know what else to do. How will we know what to do with this new student?"

After we finished discussing the issues, the room was silent. I think we were all awed by how much we did know about assessment when we had time to reflect and brainstorm, but we also realized how much more we had to learn.

Consider This

1. How would you respond to Janice's supervisor's questions about data showing how the students were performing on the math skills for telling time?

2. Raymond had difficulty generalizing from a data collection skill that worked with one student to a larger group. How would you keep data on a group of students? Could you document that they mastered lesson objectives, IEP objectives, and possibly state curriculum objectives?

3. What were the strengths and weaknesses of Rasheed's "learning station" approach to assessment?

4. Leif was pleased with his students' involvement in maintaining their own behavioral points. Can you also envision a way to involve students in tracking their academic progress?

5. Why is it important for Marcie to be able to link instructional objectives from her lesson plans to both the IEP and state curriculum objectives? In what other ways might this linking be accomplished?

6. Jamie identifies several different ways to think about grading. Which do you think is the most appropriate, and why? How might you reflect this emphasis on a report card?

7. How might J.T. best determine the appropriate criteria for mastery of objectives?

8. How might Johanna use a scoring rubric to evaluate the written essays? Develop a sample rubric.

9. Bonita is frustrated with the lack of relevant instructional information available in the student's file and IEP. What will she and the teacher have to do to determine what and how to teach this new student?

6 Special Education Procedures and Legal Issues

Special education law affirms the rights of exceptional children and their families and guides the development of procedures that ensure these rights are honored and this population receives appropriate services. As schools attempted to educate exceptional children, parents and professionals questioned the adequacy of schools' efforts through litigation. Over the years, courts have interpreted laws and legislators have worked with advocacy groups to clarify and expand the support to individuals with disabilities and their families. As a result, the special education process has become extraordinarily complex and the need for documentation frequently overwhelms even veteran educators. In addition, each state legislature passes its own version of federal laws, and local school districts attempt to make sense of laws and mandates in their community context. Therefore, it is no wonder that preservice and novice teachers have much to learn about special education law generally and its applications within individual districts and schools specifically. Cases in this chapter explore several critical special education legal issues as preservice and novice teachers become aware of and question practices they observe or are asked to participate in.

Confidentiality

Information gathered during the special education assessment is sensitive and must be kept confidential. However, learning about unique conditions of students and complex family dynamics can be intriguing to novice educators. Special education student teachers must learn the importance of maintaining confidentiality. In the following case, a student teacher learns about the information available about exceptional students and related sensitive issues.

Know Your Students

One of the themes that permeated Brenda's teacher education program was that the heart of special education is individualized service and instruction. Her characteristics course had addressed the ways students vary, and her methods courses presented how to tailor education to individual needs. In her assessment class, Brenda learned the sources of information about students, the interpretation of data, and planning appropriate instruction. Brenda couldn't wait to student teach; she planned to learn everything she could about her students and to develop lessons that fit their individual needs. Brenda tried to imagine what she would find in each student's confidential file containing special education documents.

In January, Brenda began student teaching at Prairie View Elementary School. Her cooperating teacher, Mrs. Weaver, had a neat and orderly room. "These bulletin boards would get an A from my methods teacher," Brenda judged. The efficiency of the schedule and the way students knew what to do when they entered the room were impressive. Mrs. Weaver assigned Brenda to three students for a half hour of individualized reading instruction in the morning.

As Brenda began to work with the students, she noticed that the third-grader, Janees, did not remember new words from day to day; the second-grader, Jared, guessed at words using only the first sound; and the fourth-grader, Tori, read all the words correctly but did not comprehend a single sentence. Brenda pondered, "What could I learn about these students to really help them? Mrs. Weaver would be so impressed with me if I could develop lessons that truly responded to the individual needs of these three students. We haven't spoken about their folders, but won't she be impressed with my initiative if I read their files and come up with something insightful?"

After school, Brenda scurried to the main office and excitedly told the secretary, "I need to see the files for my three students, Janees, Jared, and Tori." Her exuberance was so persuasive that the secretary responded, "Well, I guess if you're Mrs. Weaver's student teacher, it's all right." The secretary retrieved the files, showed Brenda where she could sit to read the files, and explained where to return the files when she was finished. Brenda enthusiastically opened the first file and began taking copious notes. She didn't even notice when the secretary said, "I'm leaving. The door is locked. Just pull it closed behind you."

Brenda looked at her watch and couldn't believe it was 6:00, and she had only begun reading from the second file. Tori's file described many learning problems among family members. Brenda wondered about calling Tori's parents to learn more about what worked with older siblings. The second file, Janees's huge folder, really fascinated her, however. There was so much family and medical information from questions about the mother's substance abuse, a difficult birth, and later slow language development. "Could this explain memory problems? I'm going to ask about this in seminar tonight!" Brenda realized it was getting late, and there was still so much to read. She wanted to show these interesting reports to her seminar leader to get some insights into teaching a student with this background. Brenda decided to return two of the folders but take Janees's file with her to class.

Several students had arrived early for class. Brenda pulled the file from her bag and showed her peers the interesting reports she had been reading. Her enthusiasm was contagious. When the seminar leader, Mrs. Toklas, arrived, six students were gathered around the folder poring over the reports. "Look at this about the mother's drug use," commented Bridget. "This medical information is hard to read," Matt observed. "Wow, the IEP must be forty pages," Sheila exclaimed. Mrs. Toklas saw the obvious excitement and asked, "What has everyone so engaged?" Brenda explained proudly, "I began working with new students and wanted to learn as much as I could about them. I figured that their files might offer me some insights into how to individualize their instruction. This is Janees's file, and it's full of really interesting background information. I brought it tonight because I thought if I read some of the details, you might have great ideas about teaching a student like this." Brenda was pleased with the way she encapsulated the events leading up to seminar and how she set up the conversation in such a positive way. "What a great opportunity for everyone in the seminar to apply what we have learned to a real student!" she proudly thought.

Mrs. Toklas's eyes grew large, and Brenda realized something was wrong. The seminar leader tried to control her outrage, understanding the student meant no harm. She asked pointedly, "Is that one of your student's confidential files?" "Yes," Brenda responded with a sinking feeling. The leader continued, "You took the file from your school?" "Yes," the student responded and began to panic. Mrs. Toklas could not control herself any longer, "You shared confidential information with the class as if it were was a case study from a book?" This time Brenda realized the question was rhetorical, and she prepared for the worst.

Consider This

1. What might the seminar leader say to the group?
2. What types of sensitive material might be found in a confidential file?
3. When is it appropriate for special educators to share confidential information?
4. Why is confidentiality a critical legal issue in special education?
5. What procedures typically govern the location and use of student files?
6. How could this situation be resolved with the least harm?
7. Write a dialogue that might transpire between Brenda and her cooperating teacher the next day or between Brenda and the principal.

Sharing Power with Parents

The nature of the relationships between parents and educators has undergone substantial change in recent years. Parents have joined the system as partners and policymakers and have challenged the system as advocates and adversaries. There is a growing awareness that involved parents can powerfully affect the outcome of their children's education. Many school districts are directing efforts toward building and maintaining relationships within their school and communities that foster openness, honesty, and cooperation between parents and schools. On the other hand, it is difficult for educators to relinquish power when they believe they are better prepared to make decisions about children than the children's parents are. In the following case, a student teacher sees the conflict firsthand.

Getting That Signature

"Would you like to be part of a special education referral from the beginning?" asked the special education teacher, Mrs. Cho. The new student teacher, Connie, responded without hesitation, "Absolutely!" Mrs. Cho continued, "There is a child study team meeting (school-based team that determines appropriateness of assessing a child for special education eligibility) this afternoon about a second-grade student. His teacher has been to see me several times asking for suggestions and materials. I feel sure the team will refer him for special education testing."

"What luck," thought Connie. Some student teachers had talked of their teachers discussing students who were having problems, but their teachers were trying some strategies before referring the students for testing. Other student teachers had commented on observing testing or an eligibility committee meeting. "Maybe I'll finally understand the whole process if I see it from the beginning," Connie reflected.

The Child Study Team met that afternoon in a small conference room in the main office. There were six participants: the referring teacher, the child's mother, the special education teacher, the school psychologist, and two classroom teachers. The principal was unable to attend and asked Phildra Johnson, the school psychologist, to be his administrative designee. Mrs. Cho introduced her student teacher to the group and asked if she could join them. There were no objections.

It became immediately clear who was leading the meeting. One of the classroom teachers, Mrs. Rigsby, began authoritatively, "Last year, Michael Kemper's teacher asked for help in teaching him to read. We have a report here from Michael's teacher. 'When Michael entered first grade, he knew only ten letters and three letter sounds. In the fall, we tried volunteer tutors to give him additional one-on-one attention. By January, he knew his letters but could not read any words, while his peers had begun reading books. I expressed my concern about Michael throughout the year to his mother. Mrs. Kemper worked with him at home but did not want to refer him for special education until he had a chance to catch up. We tried two different reading programs, but progress remained slow. Michael is clearly behind all his peers.' "

Mrs. Rigsby continued, "This student's file also contains a document from the Teacher Assistance Team proposing that an older peer work with Michael one on one to develop sight-word vocabulary using flash cards. There's a note attached that explains a sixth-grade student came twice weekly and kept track of words learned—forty-two by June. There's his report card, too. Mostly C's and D's with a few F's. Mrs. Kemper, If I'm not mistaken, the first-grade teacher talked to you about holding Michael back, but you refused, saying that Michael would catch up."

The referring teacher, Kevin Malcolm, set the tone by chiming in, "I am not willing to let Michael go on struggling. I think he needs special help. But his mother is still opposed to special education." The lead teacher turned to the parent and gently explained, "At this point, we are talking about whether or not to assess Michael, not whether he receives special education services. Right now we are deciding if we should gather information about him, and then in a few weeks we would discuss if he qualifies for special education." Mrs. Kemper appeared upset. "You are making such a big deal out of this. He'll be fine. His brothers were slow, too. But they're all nice boys. They are good in sports, they have lots of friends, and they do what they are asked at home."

Connie felt the tension in the room and wondered who would respond. Michael's teacher had obviously had this conversation before, because he responded somewhat impatiently, "If he doesn't get help in reading, school will always be a frustrating place for him. Is that what you want?" The mother looked down and shook her head saying, "No." "I say we get on with this and get Michael some help," Mr. Malcolm continued.

Connie realized how intimidating this whole process must be for this parent. The school psychologist decided that conflict resolution was in order now, "Kevin, I hear how concerned you are for Michael." Mr. Malcolm agreed. The psychologist continued, "Mrs. Kemper, I know you want what is best for your son. You have worked with him on reading. What's it like for Michael when you read together?" The mother responded, "He doesn't want to work with me any more. He's always outside playing or watching TV. My husband says I should leave him alone."

The teacher shot a glance at the psychologist that communicated, "You see what I'm dealing with here." Then he turned and said to the parent, "We're trying to help Michael. The testing will tell us what he needs. All we're asking for is your permission to allow us to learn more about your son." The psychologist cautiously intervened, "Mr. Malcolm, this is a group decision. We all need to decide that a referral for testing is the best alternative here." Mr. Malcolm responded, "The mother just admitted she's not helping him anymore, he struggled all through first grade, and now I'm the one who sees this student failing day after day. What's to discuss?"

Connie could not believe the drama unfolding. The lead teacher attempted to get control back of the meeting, "This would be a good time to review the purpose of this meeting. . . ."

Consider This

1. What is the purpose of a Child Study Team meeting?
2. What role should the referring teacher play? parent? lead teacher?
3. What documentation or evidence should be available at Child Study Team meetings?
4. How could a special education teacher prepare for a challenging Child Study Team meeting?

5. What is the responsibility of the general education teacher at Child Study Team meetings?
6. What power issues between educators come into play when deciding whether a student should be assessed for special education?
7. Tell the case from the point of view of the mother . . . referring teacher . . . school psychologist.
8. Report the results of this meeting to the principal.

Most Appropriate and Least Restrictive

There is an ongoing debate over what services constitute the most appropriate education and which placement is the least restrictive environment for individual students with disabilities. Some parents and educators advocate almost total integration of students with disabilities into general education classrooms, while other parents and professionals demand a full range of services to meet every educational need. Special education law requires that each student is considered individually to ensure access to learning and to receive services that are provided by trained professionals along a full continuum of services from least to most restrictive. However, interpretation of what is appropriate for each child varies so widely that even high-court decisions seem to contradict each other. Parents and professionals are left to selecting the interpretation that supports their own needs and belief systems, each adult believing they are doing what is best for the child or their classmates. In the following scenario, a student teacher experiences the intensity of feelings surrounding a debate over what is most appropriate for a student with emotional/behavioral challenges.

Get Him Out of Here

Everyone in Woodward Elementary School knew Alex Teliak. The teachers knew him from either bus or lunch-room duty because Alex was in the center of a ruckus one place or another almost daily. On the playground he could be the best ballplayer but the worst teammate. The principal knew him very well because they spent time once or twice weekly reviewing how Alex could have handled situations with more self-control. By November of second grade, his teacher, Mrs. Lecus, felt at her wit's end and referred Alex for special education testing. Mrs. Lecus had plenty of convincing anecdotes to portray a student in need of assistance. She recounted, "Last week, Alex stormed in from the bus cursing and knocking things off students' desks. Later he explained that someone on the bus had called him a name, and he was going to get that kid. Then there was the time Alex poked a pencil through students' sandwiches because he 'hated his stupid mother' who didn't know how to make a good lunch." The eligibility committee found Alex eligible for special education services based on evidence of emotional/behavioral disabilities and asked the special education teacher, Mr. Garfalo, to develop an individualized education program with Mrs. Lecus and the parent.

Mr. Garfalo sketched out a plan for Alex and invited Alex's mother and Mrs. Lecus to the IEP meeting. Alex's mother hoped the services would include someone to help control his temper and teach him to comply with instructions. Mrs. Lecus expected to tell the special education teacher what Alex needed to learn in the special education classroom. However, Mr. Garfalo knew that the prevailing philosophy in his school district was to maintain students with disabilities in general education classrooms to the greatest extent possible. The special education teacher anticipated that there would be a conflict among the participants' expectations.

Patti Annunciado was Mr. Garfalo's student teacher. The teacher and student teacher talked about preparing for the IEP meeting. Mr. Garfalo strategized, "I think we can maintain Alex in his second-grade class with the right support system, but we will have quite a battle with Lecus. She expects us to take him full time." Patti responded, "Actually, I'm surprised, too. I expected Alex to be with us most of the time. I've been thinking about how to motivate him here with our point system." Mr. Garfalo explained, "Once you remove a student from the general education classroom, getting them back is almost impossible. They have to remain connected and work on their social skills in a real context. That way, students and teachers continue to think of them as part of the community. When you move a student out completely, that student becomes 'your student' forever." Patti could see the logic but was not looking forward to the meeting with Alex's second-grade teacher. Patti wondered what the parent expected. Would Alex's mother want her son to get full-time, intensive special education, or was she anticipating that Alex would continue in his second-grade class?

As a precaution, the special education teacher asked to speak with the principal before the IEP meeting. Mr. Garfalo explained, "We want the most appropriate education for Alex. I believe we can maintain him in his second-grade class if I can work with the teacher and Alex in that setting and of course use our special education room whenever he needs to be removed." The principal responded, "I trust your judgment, but you realize that Mary Ann is worn out and looking forward to a break from Alex. This could be very sensitive. You know I am a student advocate; on the other hand, I have to support my teachers. I'll attend the meeting and try to balance everyone's needs."

Mr. Garfalo returned to his room and gave Patti a summary of his meeting with the principal. Patti responded, "I had no idea this would be so political. I thought all you have to do is read the reports, figure out the goals and objectives, and talk about what is best for the student."

The IEP meeting was held immediately after school on Thursday. Alex's mother, Mrs. Lecus, Patti, Mr. Garfalo, and the principal met in a conference room. Mr. Garfalo had all the paperwork and notes on a pad of paper. Mrs. Lecus had Alex's books and complete notes to share with Mr. Garfalo about where he should begin with Alex.

Mr. Garfalo introduced everyone to Patti. Then he suggested the group work together to list the goals and objectives for Alex. Alex's mother wanted him to work on anger control and following directions. Mrs. Lecus agreed and added a long list of academic goals, including reading comprehension and regrouping in math. Mr. Garfalo reminded everyone of diagnostic testing results showing Alex's weaknesses in written language. When a list had been developed, Mr. Garfalo introduced his strategy to move the conversation in the direction he desired. He suggested, "Let's go back over these goals and mark whether each goal needs the intervention of a specialist, has to be taught in a specially designed environment, or could be accomplished in the current second-grade classroom."

"Why would we do this?" Mrs. Lecus asked. "I assume Alex will begin with you as soon as this IEP is signed." Patti realized she had stopped breathing. Since the principal was silent, Patti wondered how Mr. Garfalo would handle this. He responded calmly, "I'm really pleased with this comprehensive list of goals for Alex. Now it seems to me that some of them sound like goals you might have for many of your second-graders. If that's true, then Alex should work on those goals with his second-grade peers." "Wait," interrupted Mrs. Lecus, "I have already talked with you folks about how to teach Alex better, and it didn't work. I am here to tell you where to start in his books. I even brought the books along to pass off to you." Mary Ann looked at the principal for support. When the principal didn't speak, she prompted him, "It's not fair to the others. We all need Alex out of the room. Have you two conspired to keep him in my room? What was all that testing and meeting we went through?" The second-grade teacher realized Alex's mother was embarrassed and hanging her head. The principal began to intervene, "We are trying to design the most appropriate program for Alex."

Consider This

1. Why are IEP meetings political?
2. What factors must be considered in making a placement decision?
3. What is the role of the general education teacher in IEP development?
4. How might participants be encouraged to think about contributions before IEP meetings?
5. When is it appropriate to involve students in IEP meetings?
6. How could the student be involved?
7. Recount the events as Mrs. Lecus might have told them to another teacher.
8. How could the parent become involved in this scenario?

Increasing Responsibility for Medical Care

Educators declare that their roles are increasingly complex. In addition to instructing students in subjects with high standards set by state officials, teachers find they must attend to a wide range of issues and individual student needs. One area of increasing concern is the medical care that educators find they must perform to enable some students to have access to an education. Teachers are finding that they must be aware of multiple symptoms and keep track of devices and medications to enhance learning and avoid life-threatening situations. In the following case, a special education teacher wonders if anyone can attend to the diverse and serious needs of her students.

Teacher or Nurse?

"Julie, I think Albert is having an allergic reaction," the cafeteria aide exclaimed at the door to the teachers' lounge. Julie jumped from her seat and reached for the medical kit she had learned to keep ready at lunch time. Albert was allergic to peanuts and sesame products. Julie had asked the parents of her special education students to avoid sending peanuts and seed items in their children's lunches. She also asked Albert to stay with this class at lunch, but Albert had made friends in his fourth-grade class and he liked to sit with them. "Do we need a peanut-free school?" wondered Julie as she moved quickly through the cafeteria.

When Julie reached Albert, he was having difficulty breathing. The teacher opened her medical kit and removed the Ziploc bag with Albert's EpiPen hyperdermic needle. Julie offered it to Albert, who knew what to do. He grabbed the needle and jabbed his leg. Soon Albert's breathing began to return to normal. The children around him stared in awe. But as Julie watched the scene, she had mixed feelings. She liked Albert and felt good that she supported his health and learning needs. If only he were her sole medical challenge. In addition to Albert, she had five other students with medical concerns.

Julie recalled this morning when LaShanda arrived. The teacher asked, "Did you remember your inhaler? Your class is going out today in physical education and the teacher won't let you leave the building without it." LaShanda said sadly, "I forgot." Julie knew this meant phone calls home, arrangements to drop off the inhaler, and waiting for it to arrive. By the time someone could get the inhaler to school, the PE class was frequently already outside and LaShanda had to stay in.

Then Jorge came blasting through the door. Without asking, Julie knew his mother had forgotten or run out of his Ritalin. "Jorge, may I see you?" the teacher requested. "Did you take your pill this morning?" Julie inquired. "My mama don't have any money. She says she can buy them Friday," Jorge offered without concern. Julie knew she had to prod the social worker to explore other options. Without the medication, Jorge would be on task about half the time for the rest of the week. Julie could see a dramatic difference in his learning when he arrived "medicated."

At the same time that she was informally observing Jorge, Julie was supposed to formally observe Wanda for trial dosages of a new stimulant medication. It was less obvious with Wanda because the student was more "spacy than hyperactive." Julie was asked to record what percent of the time Wanda was on task over a six-week period. The pediatrician was trying different dosages and wanted Wanda's teacher to keep records to determine the optimal level of medication. "Unfortunately," Julie thought, "I'm distracted by my other duties, like teaching."

Julie looked around the room as the rest of the class arrived. Cari had a serious seizure disorder which did not affect her performance most of the time; she had had only one seizure so far this fall. However, Julie knew the symptoms that led up to a seizure. If Cari began to complain of blurry vision and a funny "glowing" feeling, Julie had to get her to the clinic quickly.

Finally, there was Margie, who was diabetic. Up until this year, Margie controlled her diabetes with a careful diet and pills. Now a new diabetic monitor enabled Margie to "read" her blood sugar level to determine if she needed a pill or a snack. Connie felt much better when she did not have to take the pills; on the other hand, it meant she had to visit the clinic regularly to use the monitor.

Julie pondered, "If I were a nurse, this is what I'd be focusing on every day. However, this is all secondary to the reason students were assigned to me. Aren't I supposed to be paying attention to teaching reading and math? With all this new talk about my students passing tests of standards at each grade level, the pressure is worse than ever. I don't feel I can meet all their needs. Can anyone?"

Consider This

1. What is a teacher's role in administering and monitoring medication? A call to local school districts about their policies and procedures may be enlightening.
2. Who is responsible for keeping children away from possible dangerous allergens?
3. Who might provide assistance and support to teachers on medical information and procedures?
4. Why do you think recent litigation continues to hold schools responsible for ever-increasing medically involved procedures?
5. How might the parent of one of these children describe the teacher's role?
6. How could teacher preparation programs prepare teachers for these new responsibilities?

The Challenge of Advocating for the Rights of Exceptional Students

Special educators find they must design the best instructional arrangement for their students and then keep a constant vigil over the delivery of those services. Through the IEP process, special education teachers work with parents, general education teachers, and administrators to establish the most appropriate instructional settings and delivery models. After signing the IEP, special educators often find that the challenge has just begun. Integrating exceptional students into the general education environment requires negotiating, facilitating, and asserting students' rights. In this last case, the special education teacher feels alone at every turn, learning how many different ways there are to lose ground every time she thinks she is gaining.

Alone

"Latisha, I'm so impressed that you have your homework done every day!" Lucy Thorpe, the special education teacher, praised. Latisha glanced up and then shyly back down, replying, "I do it during PE." The special education teacher looked quizzical and asked, "Mr. Reed [the physical education teacher] gives you time to do homework every day?" Latisha nodded her head. "When do you work on your special exercises?" Lucy probed. Latisha explained, "The PE teacher said if I can't play with the others, then I should sit on the bleachers and do my homework."

Mrs. Thorpe was furious. Latisha had IEP goals for her physical education class to improve visual-motor skills and to learn to be a team member. Instead, the PE teacher banished to the bleachers her student with limited sports ability and fledgling social skills. "I spent hours with that PE teacher observing the class, reviewing IEP goals with him, and actually writing sample lesson plans to implement," the special education teacher fumed. "We need to have a little chat."

That afternoon, the special education teacher dropped by the physical education office. Mr. Reed was just leaving. As he rushed by, he waved and said, "Gotta coach soccer." Mrs. Thorpe called after him, "I need to talk with you about Latisha." Mr. Reed paused and blurted somewhat defensively, "Look, she couldn't catch a ball if you handed it to her, and the other kids tease her mercilessly. Maybe she should stay with you during PE?" "No," the special education teacher said, "I want her to learn to play games and get along with others." "Wish I could talk about this more, but I gotta run. . . ." the PE teacher's voice trailed off as he headed for the field. "We're not finished," the special education teacher said aloud but to herself.

As she walked back to her room, Frank Johnson, the eighth-grade English teacher, called to her from down the hall, "Lucy, you have got to do something about Angela!" As the English teacher approached, the special education teacher braced herself for the usual barrage of negative rhetoric. Mrs. Thorpe wondered, "What will it be today—Angela can't read the novel, Angela can't write a paragraph, or Angela didn't turn in her homework?" "Lucy, this charade has gone on long enough," puffed Mr. Johnson. The English teacher's introductory statement was so pompous that it seemed humorous to Mrs. Thorpe and took the edge off of her increasing frustration. The special education teacher gained her composure and asked, "How can I help you?" "Look, you know and I know Angela can't do the work. What's the point of taking up a seat in my room when she doesn't have a clue about what's going on? Angela will never pass eighth-grade English. I implore you, for her sake, place Angela where she belongs!" Mr. Johnson demanded.

It was only two months into the school year, and Lucy Thorpe was growing weary of the battle. The special education teacher summoned her confidence and countered, "Frank, there are so many reasons why your class is the place Angela belongs. She achieves more by hearing the other students and seeing what they can do. Plus, you're a better English teacher than I am." Mr. Johnson closed his eyes, then he interrupted, "I thought you were trained to teach kids like Angela. You place her in my class and then spend all your time keeping her there. Just take her and spare us all the misery." Lucy was speechless. Mr. Johnson stared and prompted, "Well?" The special education teacher responded, "Angela, her parents, and I believe that with the proper support she can succeed in a general English class, and we need your support." Mrs. Thorpe was proud that these words came to her despite how hard her heart was pounding. "Obviously, you are not listening to me. I want her out of my class," Frank Johnson commanded. She shook her head. "No." Frank Johnson's face turned red, and he blurted, "If you won't do it, then it's time Lora [the principal] finds out how poorly your students are equipped to succeed and how unresponsive you are to teachers' requests." Mr. Johnson turned and marched to the office. Lucy Thorpe was so hurt and angry, she couldn't move. She thought, "Why would I want someone like that teaching one of my students? Angela never complains about him, but I have to wonder how he treats her."

There was barely time to recover as the assistant principal rounded the corner and began speaking, "There you are. I have been looking all over for you." Suzanne Martin was more cheerful than usual. Lucy Thorpe was relieved to see the assistant principal's friendly face but worried about this overly enthusiastic greeting. "I have a big favor," Ms. Martin pleaded, "I have parents in my office right now, and I wonder if you would speak with them." Mrs. Thorpe responded dutifully, "Sure," but began creating worrisome scenarios in her mind. The assistant principal physically ushered her in the direction of the office and said, "I'll explain on the way."

Walking briskly, Suzanne Martin talked rapidly. "Mr. and Mrs. Shellen showed up today at 3 without an appointment and asked to see 'someone in charge.' They claim their daughter, Megan, received special education services in Jefferson County Schools. They are moving to our area this weekend, and they don't want any lapse in support services." Mrs. Thorpe anticipated where this was going and questioned, "Did they bring an IEP or file with them?" The principal blushed and said, "The parents have not shown us anything. Mrs. Shellen reports that she requested the files from Jefferson County three weeks ago, but no one knows where the files are. The father is calling everyone incompetent. Lucy, a promise from you to work with their daughter as soon as she arrives could defuse this whole mess."

Mrs. Thorpe was trying to be helpful but cautious at the same time, "Suzanne, I'll talk with them if you'd like, but I can't promise them anything without seeing an IEP or some paperwork." The assistant principal replied anxiously, "Lucy, they say it was sent, but no one at central office can find it or has any record of it." Mrs. Thorpe surprised herself by retorting, "Then maybe it wasn't sent, or maybe there isn't any." Suzanne Martin stopped in her tracks, "What are you saying?" The special education teacher did not want to appear confrontational with her administrator, so she offered support, "I'll just ask some questions and see what I can do."

As they approached the main office, Mrs. Thorpe noticed three teachers leaning against the wall beside the door. They were obviously upset, speaking in exasperated tones, two with arms crossed and one with arms on her hips. As Mrs. Thorpe approached, they turned and glared at her. The special education teacher barely knew these seventh-grade teachers, and yet she felt she had offended them. "Is something wrong?" she forced an inquiry.

"Yes, something is very wrong," began the woman with hands on her hips, "Your student, Arturo, started a fight with two seventh-graders, and now guess who is still in school while our students are home for a week?" Lucy felt the sting of sarcasm. She knew there was no point in explaining the legality when the teachers were so upset, and since she was frustrated with Arturo's behavior as well, this was not a good time to talk. In the meantime, the assistant principal avoided the teachers' glances, quietly mumbled, "Excuse me," and slid through the office door into the conference room. Lucy did not know what to do, so she offered, "Could we talk about this later? We have parents waiting for us." Lucy Thorpe forced a smile and jumped from the frying pan into the fire.

In the conference room, the assistant principal introduced her to the parents as "the special education teacher I told you about." Mrs. Shellen muttered, "Finally we're getting somewhere." The assistant principal continued, "I'm sure Lucy can help." Mrs. Shellen began, "I hope you know what you're doing. So far I'm not impressed. Our daughter, Meg, will be here on Monday, and we expect her to receive services as soon as she arrives." When Lucy appeared to hesitate, the assistant principal took control, "I can assure you, Mrs. Shellen, that our capable special educators will be ready for your daughter on Monday." Once again, Lucy Thorpe felt overwhelmed by the difficulty of knowing what was the right thing to do and feeling quite alone.

Consider This

1. What role should special educators play in assuring the legal rights of their students?
2. Why does it seem that asserting the rights of exceptional children is a continuous battle?
3. How would you suggest responding to the PE teacher? the English teacher? the teachers angry over disparities in discipline? the parents of the new student?
4. What effect does this interaction between special and general education teachers have on the job satisfaction of special educators?

5. Assume the role of a principal and explain these legal responsibilities to a new special education teacher.

6. Role-play a principal interviewing a special educator for a new position and assume the applicant has to educate the principal about the legal responsibilities of special educators.

CHAPTER

7 Induction

Teachers receive preparation primarily through university coursework and field experiences. At the end of their university program, they become licensed to assume the demands of independent teaching. At this point, these novice educators seek employment in which they are given the same responsibilities as experienced teachers. Before research was done on the induction of new teachers and their gradual skill development, it was assumed that new teachers had gained the knowledge and skills necessary to perform their roles. According to this belief, new teachers only had to remember what they were taught and determine when to apply it. If this were the case, why did beginning teachers feel so challenged, why did supervisors spend so much time supporting novice teachers, and why did so many new teachers leave the profession after only two or three years?

Researchers have investigated these issues of teachers' experiences during their induction into the profession. They have concluded that career teachers move through developmental phases as they continually reflect and renew. Teachers' professional development follows a series of stages in which *beginners* survive and discover, *advanced beginners* experiment and consolidate, *experienced teachers* master and stabilize, *proficient teachers* analyze and deliberate, and *experts* become fluid and flexible.

Novice teachers require unique types of support during their first years. New educators express idealism, energy, courage, and passion while feeling overwhelmed, disillusioned, insecure, and exhausted. Novices need reasonable assignments, clear expectations, and systematic support from well-trained mentors. Mentors provide a wealth of information, guide the development of skills, encourage in the face of failures, celebrate successes, and promote collaborative problem solving so that novices learn to think like an expert teacher.

In this chapter, a new teacher experiences the complexity of teaching demands and requests help with a series of frustrating situations over the first few months of teaching. As the reader, you are asked to provide mentoring for the teacher in the form of collaborative problem solving while the new teacher responds to a barrage of information and learns to perform multilayered roles effectively. You will help the new teacher by providing multiple interpretations of the events from a broader range of perspectives, asking questions to clarify observations, and empowering the new teacher to experiment with solutions.

September

The Schedule

Good morning. Thank you so much for agreeing to be my mentor. I thought this day would never come. After all those years of undergraduate school and student teaching, I am so excited to finally have my own resource room and my own kids. I only have fourth-, fifth-, and sixth-graders but they're a handful. I don't know where to begin. There's so much I need help with.

I guess I better start with setting up the students' schedules. I should be able to catch their teachers this afternoon during the workday. So far I only know my students on paper. What a group, mostly boys, of course! A few of them seem like such a challenge. I have all their IEPs. I'll just list the subjects they need, group students by subject, and then let their homeroom teachers know when I've scheduled them. I wonder if any of the teachers would be interested in co-teaching. I have so many great ideas. I'll let you know how it goes later. . . ."

That afternoon: Okay, I had my first two surprises. First, you don't get to work on anything without interruptions around here. Lots of teachers stopped by to introduce themselves. They seem really nice. But then I had phone calls from parents, the principal asked me some questions about one of my students like I was supposed to know something, and there was an emergency meeting called about a new student that may be moving to this school soon.

Second, I just wasted two hours designing a schedule. I tried to put all students with similar needs together. I must say I had a cool spreadsheet developed so that I could show the other teachers clearly when I'd be working with each of their students. I went to Alice Washington [the fourth-grade teacher] first. When I showed her my chart, she tried not to burst my bubble too badly. Alice said, "I look forward to working with you and your students, but you have this schedule thing backwards. First, you get all the classroom teachers' schedules to see when your students have subjects and specials with them, and then *you* work around their schedules. you can copy my schedule from the board while you're here."

Is that the way it's supposed to be? Does everything revolve around their schedules and 'specials'? Am I powerless here?

Consider This

1. The new teacher was unprepared for the number of interruptions and expectations that faced her on the first day. Help the new teacher to develop some

strategies for balancing the role of teacher with the surprise of multiple demands placed on a member of a school team.

2. What factors must be considered in scheduling?
3. What political issues are involved here?
4. Who ultimately sets the schedule?
5. From the general educator's point of view, comment on scheduling students for resource room assistance.
6. As the new teacher's mentor, help analyze this scheduling frustration and determine a course of action.

Chaos

After the first day with students: I don't know whether to celebrate surviving a whole day or to weep over all the mistakes and disasters. Do you have a few minutes? Good, I promise not to stay long. First thing in the morning I had four wild boys from the fourth grade who acted like they'd never been in school before. They ran in the room, threw their stuff everywhere, wouldn't listen to me, and began pummeling and shouting at each other. We didn't even get started with my math activity. At the same time, there were sixth-graders who came to have their math homework checked before they went to class. How will I pay attention to them? I'm too busy trying to get Mark, Antonio, Elliot, and Tran to sit down. Mark has a huge file of behavior reports, including several suspensions last year. Antonio pretends he doesn't understand; he has that quizzical look perfected. Elliot and Tran are supposed to take Ritalin for their attention deficits, but it sure didn't look like they did today.

The sixth-graders just sat and watched and then checked for my response. I'm afraid it looks like a lot of fun and then Emily, Peter, and LaTanya will join right in.

Consider This
1. What questions do you have about the organization of the classroom?
2. Ask questions about how classroom expectations are communicated.
3. Suggest routines or practices to manage the two different groups and to provide the students what they need.
4. How might peers be encouraged to support each other positively?

End of day 2: Thanks for those great ideas. I tried a couple, and it went a little better today! I'm exhausted, though. Mark and Elliott are going to wear me out. I have them both for half the day. Mark can't seem to do anything on his own. I got him started on the problem set, walked away to help someone else, and when I checked back, he had done nothing. On the other hand, Elliott had a thousand excuses for not starting: "Can't find my pencil," "Gotta sharpen this stupid pencil," "Make him stop looking at me," "Wanta know what my father said about you?" But once Elliot got started, he kept going and finished. Of course, I have sixteen other students to teach during the day as well. How will I know if they are getting anything done when I'm focusing on two attention seekers?

Consider This

1. Ask questions about the new teacher's motivation systems for students.
2. Help the new teacher to clarify expectations for the students' behavior.
3. Make suggestions for keeping track of what students are working on and what they complete.
4. Make suggestions for working with students who have difficulty staying on task.
5. Help the new teacher develop strategies for dealing with students who have a high need for attention.

Who Decides?

Afternoon of day 3: If I talk about someone, I mean a teacher, will it, you know, stay just between us? Good. I need some advice about how to work with Larry. At 10:15 today, I was expecting his four fifth-graders. At the same time, I have Mark and Elliot, who cannot go unsupervised. The fifth-graders didn't show up. Finally, at 10:30, I asked my two students to go with me to check on Larry's students. When we got to the classroom, I opened the door and Larry looked at me as if to say, "May I help you?" I smiled and pointed to my students. I was so happy to see them included in a small group activity. When they saw me, they started to get up, but Larry stopped them cold in their tracks with, "Have your groups answered all the questions?" My kids froze. They were torn between us. He continued, "No one is going anywhere until their groups have answered the questions. If you are having trouble, ask your team captains." Then he turned to me and stated matter-of-factly, "They'll be down later," as if I had no schedule. I swallowed and suggested, "Maybe 11:30?" Larry just glared at me and countered, "We'll see how they're doing."

Well, they showed up at 11:15, when I have my largest language arts groups. That's not the end of the story. On my way down to see you, I stopped by Larry's classroom. With all the confidence I could muster, I offered, "If 11:15 is a better time for you, shall I switch the schedule?" He shrugged his shoulders and responded, "It depends what we're doing. You want them included in our activities, don't you?" I nodded in agreement, "Yes." Larry closed the conversation with, "Fine, then we both want what is best for them," and he got up.

What do I do?

Consider This

1. Does the special education teacher need to be more flexible than general education teachers?
2. Should a special education teacher assert the importance of students keeping a schedule?

3. Describe the situation from Larry's point of view.
4. Students' IEPs designate how much time they are to receive special education services. What are the legal ramifications of general education teachers holding special education students from that guaranteed amount of special services time?
5. Which do you think should take precedence, inclusion or special services?
6. How would you recommend the new teacher respond?

The Discouraging Grade

I thought it would be easier to agree with teachers about basic things, like tests and grades. I had no idea it was so personal! Hanifah, my star fourth-grader, was crying today. When I asked what was going on, she showed me her last science test with a big red D on top. I was just as upset as she was. I helped her to study. She knew the material, but she didn't know how to answer the questions. I told Hanifah I'd talk to her teacher, Candace. As soon as the kids left today, I took the test with me to her fourth-grade classroom. Candace saw what I had in my hand. Somewhat defensively she asked, "Did Hanifah study for that test?" I bristled and countered a little too quickly, "I helped her to study, and I believe she knew the material. I'm not sure if the test was a good measure of what she knew." Poor wording on my part. Candace dug in her heals and said, "I hope you don't expect me to change her grade because you think she knows the material. Every parent of every child in my room wants to tell me that their child knew the material the night before. And, if she continues to make grades like that, she'll get a D on her report card. Last year, your predecessor tried to get me to give higher grades to the LD students because they were trying so hard. I said, 'No' then, and I hope you won't even try now."

Everyone raves about Candace and her high expectations and how all the parents want their kids in her room. But frankly, I was shocked by her lack of sensitivity. I offered to create an alternative format test that was better matched to Hanifah's learning style and that Candace could approve. Candace lectured me, "It would not be fair to the others who did poorly, or for that matter to the students who did well because they studied hard and knew how to answer challenging questions. I just can't let you lower my standards because you feel bad about your students' failures."

I was speechless. I let Hanifah down. What do I do now?

Consider This

1. Why do teachers respond personally about tests and grading?
2. Should different students get different tests? Should there be different grades for students with learning challenges?
3. Describe Candace in a positive light.
4. What would you recommend to the new teacher?

On Their Own

This is not a criticism of last year's teacher, but has anyone ever expected these kids to work on their own? I bought notebooks for everyone to begin journaling. I thought that would really interest them in writing. But every day it's the same whine: "I don't know what to write," or "Why do we have to do this?" I spend 15 minutes walking from one student to the next, asking each one questions and helping them get started. I get Amy started and then walk to Eileen's desk, and Amy stops, puts her pen down, or whispers to another student, and they both collapse in laughter. Carl writes a word and then tears out the page; he's the only one almost at the end of his notebook, but not because he's accomplished much. And, that's just writing the first 15 minutes.

Math is the same, whether it's work sheets, textbook, or learning center. Yesterday Elliot could subtract with zeroes, but today he says, "Nobody ever taught me how to do this." Carla cries and Mark gets mad, but neither begins on his own. Sometimes I've tried doing the first math problem aloud for them. That usually results in one or two completed problems after I leave.

Reading is complicated but the same. We have silent reading (well, sort of silent) for 10 minutes every morning. The entire time I answer Amy, Steve, and Antonio's relentless question, "What is this word?" by encouraging them to start with the sound of the first letter, and so on. I've tried easier books, but they accuse me of giving them "baby books." When I read with them in small groups, they spend more time "I-don't-knowing" than decoding.

Following written directions is a joke. If the instruction says, "Circle the words with 3 syllables," Mark will circle *all* the words. If I write on the board, "Math book, page 67, multiplication problems 1–10," Tina asks, "What are we supposed to do?"

I guess I'm a glutton for punishment because I assign homework, too. Before students go home, I check their homework assignment pad and have them tell me what they have to do. Can you believe that I get phone calls from parents saying their children don't know what to do? Shandra's mother asked, "Why did you give my daughter homework she says you never taught her?" Mark's father ordered, "Don't send homework we have to teach him to do. That's your job, not ours."

What's going on here? Shouldn't they be able to do some work on their own?

Consider This

1. Are the new teacher's expectations reasonable?
2. What is the new teacher doing well?
3. What systems might help students be more independent?
4. What might help parents assist their children with homework?
5. Help the new teacher focus on ways to improve her situation.
6. Who else in the school might offer helpful insights, information, or assistance?

October

I Lost It!

I feel terrible. I really lost it today with my afternoon math group. I was everything I promised I would never be: I was impatient; I was sarcastic (I hate when teachers use sarcasm); I threatened them and then I just gave up. I walked away from my students and just sat down at my desk. I didn't care what happened. Maybe I'm just not cut out to do this. There's too much to pay attention to, so many demands. Teachers are frustrating. Parents are frustrating. Students are frustrating. It seems so hectic. I have meetings before school and after school. I make phone calls at lunch or eat with students who've been kicked out of the cafeteria. There's no room to breathe.

All right, I'm just worked up. I thought we were making progress. Today Elliot had been doing work without my standing by his side, and Jamel finally stopped hitting and taunting everyone in the math group. I had all seven students working for a few minutes when Elliott started madly scribbling over his math paper in that crazy way he does with his eyes wild. Jamel started laughing at him, and Elliot shouted at him, "Shut up, n. . . ." They were at each other's throats in seconds. While I was in between those two, holding them at arm's length, Shandra and Mai Li both whined, "I can't do this," as if nothing else were going on. They wanted attention precisely when I could not give it to them. And the other three students started acting silly, falling out of their chairs, laughing, and hitting each other. It was just like the first few days all over again. We've made *no* progress. They haven't improved; I haven't learned anything. Will they never learn self-control? Don't you think the honest and noble thing for me to do would be to admit my failure and move on? Tell the principal to find someone who can really teach?

Consider This

1. Help the new teacher to sort out the elements of her frustration.
2. What perspectives do you think she needs?
3. What questions would you ask to decide what to do next?
4. Recommend a course of action that helps the new teacher work on weak areas but keeps in mind the progress that has been made.

I Had a Great Lesson Plan!

I had a great lesson plan for my language arts group today. It was in one of those teacher idea books. I spent hours last night making colorful posters with envelopes that held cards. It was a mystery activity where all the children would get different pieces of information. They had to write about what they knew and then find out from other students more information and keep writing. I even designed different reading level cards so all students could be part of the activity. I was so excited coming to school today with these posters and something that would be a definite success. I couldn't wait for this afternoon.

But after lunch I got a call from the office. "Two of your students have been in a fight in the cafeteria." The principal wasn't going to treat it like a big deal and wasn't going to suspend them. They had just gotten into a heated argument, shouted at each other, and knocked over lunch trays. I went to pick them up from the office. When I arrived, they would not look at or even speak to me. They walked down the hall quietly looking at the floor the whole way. When we entered the room, the boys went right to their seats and dramatically turned their chairs so that they couldn't see anyone. The other kids had seen the fight start but hadn't known what had happened. They kept asking, "What happened, and who started it?" The boys wouldn't talk, so the students asked me. I said, "I don't know. Can we start our lesson now?"

I tried to show excitement about my great lesson. When I took out the colorful posters, I thought they would get excited or at least act interested. Instead, the two boys were in their own world and the others just kept asking them questions like media vultures after some tragedy, "What did you say? Who won? What did the other kids in the cafeteria do? Did you get in trouble? What did the principal do?"

I took a deep breath and announced, "All right, let's move on. I have something here I know you will really enjoy!" Tina whispered, "Yeah, right" and a couple of kids laughed. I was about to give up when I thought, these kids have got to be able to pay attention to teachers and do their work. So I said, "It's important to know how to have a problem but still do your work anyway. That's the only way you will be successful in your other classes." Tina rolled her eyes, the boys didn't even look up, and the others looked my way without interest. I started the activity telling them about the mystery and how they were going to be detectives. Carla said, "That sounds stupid." I was about to tell them to give it a try when I realized 20 minutes had gone by and there was no way to get far enough into the lesson to get a good start and finish tomorrow. I put the posters aside and said a little sarcastically, "Fine, why don't we just write about fighting at school." The students all looked at each other, perked up and said, "Okay." Although I had mixed feelings about making a big deal out of this fight, I realized I had their interest. I went to the board and asked what words they might want help spelling. They actually wrote something today.

So what's the point of planning? It rarely ever works out. They have got to learn to roll with the punches. They will never succeed in general education classes until they can pay attention no matter what happens. Should I have made them do the lesson I planned? Are they going to learn anything if I just keep making up activities based on events I have no way of predicting?"

Consider This

1. Why should special educators spend time developing elaborate lesson plans that have to be abandoned when students are focused on other needs?

2. What advantage may result from special educators' incorporating "events they can't predict" into lessons?
3. Should special educators make their students stick to the planned activity?
4. Do special education students have to learn to keep going in spite of what is happening to them?
5. What social skills instruction can help students to complete work despite preoccupying thoughts and feelings?
6. How might the teacher have met the emotional needs of the students after the fight?
7. Describe the situation from the students' point of view.
8. Talk to the new teacher about how this lesson was handled.

Parent Partnerships

Something that happened before the kids arrived affected me all day. I cannot shake the feeling of being accused by Tina's mother of being insensitive. But then I'm not sure what I feel about her as a parent.

When I was in school, my professors talked about parent partnerships. We had assignments about getting parents involved and being culturally sensitive. On paper, I am an A student of parent partnerships, but where it counts, I get an F.

I have been trying to get hold of Mrs. Porter for two weeks to schedule an IEP meeting. Finally, after no response, I sent a note home with Tina asking her mother to call me. Mrs. Porter works nights and sleeps during the day. She unplugs the phone until she wakes up and is ready to face the world. I thought my note to her was sensitive and positive. I wrote that I cared about Tina's success and wanted the best for her. I said, we needed to have this IEP meeting to consider her daughter's schedule and time in special ed. I'd been trying to call her for two weeks but then thought maybe a note would work better.

This morning before students arrived, I was called to the office for a phone call. It was Mrs. Porter, obviously mad. She screamed at me, "Are you saying I don't care about my daughter? Are you saying I don't want the best for Tina? Don't you know I have to work at night? Maybe you can get a job in the day, but I can't get a break. You don't have any idea what it's like to raise three kids on your own, do you?"

It just got worse and worse. She misinterpreted everything I said. She concluded, "If you want me at a meeting at that school, I come with my other children tomorrow at five." I agreed, but I know I really need help. How do I prepare for this meeting?

Consider This

1. What might this parent be communicating?
2. What suggestions do you have for talking with angry parents?
3. How should the new teacher prepare for the meeting?
4. Who else might the new teacher talk to before this meeting?

5. Should she involve anyone else in the meeting?
6. What suggestions do you have for child care during the conference? Are there other ways to communicate with families with complex child care needs?

Reading

What I don't know about reading would fill a book. It's become painfully clear to me that most of my students are poor readers and six are terrible readers. All right, I shouldn't be surprised. But, if I can't help them improve their reading, they will never make it in general education classes. And the parents are always so concerned about reading as well.

Elliot and Mark are fourth-graders who barely read at a second-grade level. Elliott struggles to blend three sounds together. Once he reads the sentence, he understands and can answer questions. Mark, on the other hand, can call words. He usually refuses to read aloud, but when he does, there's no inflection because he has *no* comprehension of what he's reading. They're with me half the day, so you would think I could do something about their reading. But, so far I don't see any approach that works for either. Elliott practices sound-symbol association daily, but if I'm not listening to each one, he says the wrong sound half the time and then practices his errors. For Mark, I've written sentences to match picture cards, but he gets so frustrated I can barely get him to try.

Antonio is another story entirely. He learned to speak English in kindergarten. Although everyone says his English is good, I know better. He doesn't seem to be able to predict what word might be next in a sentence because he doesn't have a grasp of English structure. I copy pages from his reading book and white out a word from each sentence for him to guess. But he hates it because he is always wrong. Even Hanifah, who is bilingual in Farsi and English, reads better (although her writing is worse).

Tina and Jamel are fifth-graders who cannot read for information. Their classroom teacher has given up and sends them to me whenever the class has to answer questions from science or social studies reading. I can even read the passage aloud to them, and they still can't answer the questions. I've started highlighting the answers in their book for them to match to the questions. They worry me. How are they ever going to pass their standards-based assessment?

Steve is my almost nonreading sixth-grader. He is a really sweet kid, and his classroom teacher likes him to be there most of the day, but it's questionable what he is learning. It's unbelievable what he will guess when he tries to read a word he doesn't know. Yesterday he read "circus" for the word "science" and "bend" for the word "dead." He barely uses phonetic or context clues. I don't even know where to start with him.

Can I use first-grade books with a sixth-grader? Can I use different basal series than the school district uses? Should I have supplemental reading resources in my class? Where do I get materials? Should I be trying different remedial programs? Do I make my own? Who do I ask? Can I spend my own money at teacher stores and get reimbursed? Where do I start?

Consider This

1. What is the new teacher doing well?
2. How can the new teacher learn more about reading instruction?
3. What specific suggestions do you have for helping each of the six challenging students to read better?
4. How would you answer the teacher's questions about reading materials?
5. What are sources of materials?

They Hate Me

You know that fifth-grader, Carla, I've talked so much about? The one I've spent so much time helping after school, and the one I've fought for to get so many classroom accommodations? The one I would have taken home if she needed anything? Today she snarled at me, "I hate you!" And, her buddy, Tina, chimes in, "You got that right," and high-fives her, slapping hands and both giggling. I felt so betrayed. They acted as if I have no feelings or haven't done everything I could for them.

I don't know what I thought before I got my own class. I guess I imagined a big, happy family, or maybe I dreamed that when they talked about me, they'd say, "My teacher is so cool." I let them bring their own music. We talked about popular groups and their favorite TV shows and their computer chat rooms. Sometimes I'm sure they know I care about them, and they talk to me. Other times it's not like that at all. When I try to ignore their cursing or little transgressions, other students say, "Last year the teacher never let us get away with that. She was a good teacher!" But when I remind them of the rules, they say meanly, "We know. You don't have to always be telling us," like I'm a nag! I can't win.

My mother said, "Don't smile until Christmas or they'll walk all over you." But I didn't become a teacher to be a dictator. I wanted to show them someone cared. I wanted to comfort them when they were frustrated and build them up when they were scared.

I advocate for them with their classroom teachers. I get their parents' support. I have even argued for them with the PE teacher, who scares me. I beg for one more chance from the bus driver. And in return Carla says, "I hate you." And, the other kids think it's funny. Is it unreasonable to want my students to like me? Do I have to be a tough-skinned ogre?

Consider This

1. What are this new teacher's fears?
2. What is the reality of working with children and things they say?

3. Is it unreasonable or appropriate for special education teachers to expect to be liked by their students?
4. Is it possible this teacher is doing something to elicit this negative student response?
5. Help the teacher make sense of her dedication in light of the recent student feedback.

November

Over Their Heads

The principal came for my first observation today. Earlier in the week he came to my room and asked if he could see how things were going. He asked about observing at the worst time of my day, when I have Mark, Antonio, Elliot, Tran, and Hanifah for math. I didn't want to appear like I was making excuses or having trouble so I agreed without hesitation. But as he left, my knees got weak.

Because they are such an active group (wild, actually), I planned an interactive lesson with things to hold, paper-and-pencil tasks, and several parts to keep them involved. We've been working on measurement, and they have been struggling with greater than/less than, so I thought a lesson with rulers would keep their interest.

I designed a page of lines to measure with a place to write their answers after each line. We would compare the number measurements to figure out which was greater or less than, and then we'd look at the lines to make it more concrete.

The principal arrived early, as I was finishing up with another group. I started to explain that I would begin a lesson about greater than/less than in a few minutes, and he said, "It's fine. I like to see the transition times as well." When the fourth-graders arrived, late of course, I was nervous and not thinking and anxious to get started. I told students we were doing a lesson about greater than/less than. I gave each one a ruler and the work sheet and told them to go to their seats. Bad move right off the bat. I should have had them sit down first. Mark and Elliot were instant musketeers, dueling all the way across the room to their seats. I got them settled and separated.

When everyone was seated and ready, I thought we'd better do the first example together. So I instructed, "measure the first line, and write your answer on the line next to it." Then I saw my next mistake. Antonio did not know which line to measure and which to write on. I should have made boxes instead of lines for answers. Mark blurted out, "eight." I was just about to remind him to raise his hand when I thought to myself, "How could you get eight for a 3- inch line?' Then I saw he was using the metric side. I held up my ruler and clarified that we would be using inches and to look at the edge that only goes up to twelve. Elliot raised his hand and answered, "five." I asked him to show me how he measured five. He just plunked his ruler down without lining up the zero with the end of the line. I looked up and saw that none of them were lining up the zero on the ruler with the end of the line. It quickly became apparent to me that we would be doing a ruler lesson, not greater than/less than. So I regrouped and said, "let's look at our ruler. . . ."

Consider This

1. What part of this lesson could have been done more effectively?
2. Does even an expert special educator have to rethink the goal of a lesson?
3. What might the principal say about this lesson?
4. What positive things would you say to the new teacher?
5. If you had the chance to speak to the principal on behalf of the teacher, what would you say about the lesson?

Are They Learning?

It's been two months now! I feel like I can start paying attention to important instructional questions like: Are my students learning? To tell you the truth, I think they're learning, but I'm not sure. I figure I need to give them tests, but every time I tell students, "Tomorrow is your test," they beg me not to be like their other teachers. "We don't need tests in here. You know what we can do." I'm supposed to give tests, right? How else can I tell if they're learning?

Well, I decided to give spelling tests to all the students. Everyone gives spelling tests. No big deal, right? Wrong! It was a disaster. Carla cried, "I can't remember." Elliot didn't care and wrote letters whether they made sense or not, like "mrt" for "people." They all begged me for hints, "Is that an 'i' or an 'e'? Just tell us how to spell this one, and we can do the rest." They stalled, "Slow down. What was that word again?" Mark tore up his paper after five words. Jamel laughed at him, and they were at it again. All the while they were saying, "I hate tests. You're so mean."

Are the students right that I know what they can do? When I see a student multiplying three digits times two digits correctly, does that mean he has mastered the skill? I worry that if I don't give tests, then when they take tests in their other classes, they won't be prepared.

We talked about authentic assessment in my college classes. It seems there are other ways of measuring progress. But, if they can't take tests, they will never make it in their other classes, and they'll never pass the state assessments of learning. What do you think?

Consider This

1. Do special education students need to take tests?
2. What skills do special education students need to be successful on tests?
3. What alternatives could be used to monitor progress?
4. What elements may be confounding the present situation?
5. Recommend a course of action for the new teacher.

Computers for Games

I guess I've been in survival mode. I'm sure there's a lot I haven't noticed, but it's hard to admit there are two computers in my room that I haven't thought about seriously. I mean, I noticed them the first day and felt pleased to be so well equipped. And from the start, the students have been asking, "When can we use them?" But with so much else to pay attention to, I haven't been able to give technology much thought.

I have learned a few things, though. If Tran finishes his work early, he will keep himself busy at the computer. He's good with it, so I don't have to spend any time helping him find programs or figure out how to follow directions. Elliot loves the computer, but he's not independent at all. If he has extra time, he'll turn on the computer and start asking me questions: "Where are the games? How do I get started? I can't remember how to go to the next level." So that doesn't keep him occupied independently.

Amy and Eileen are happy with the "Paint" program, making colored pictures. Mai-Li taught some of the girls how to go to Internet chat rooms. Once they figured out how to go to the Internet, I really lost control. At the end of the day, sometimes I'll make sure the computers are turned off and find them logged on to very interesting sites, like shopping networks, sports rooms, and sex information. I should have known something was up when all the boys crowded around the computer screen yesterday but were quiet instead of loud like when they're watching someone play a game.

For a while I have been using the computers for rewards. Completed work equals five minutes of computer time. I negotiated for extra time based on difficulty of work and how quickly the work was completed. So, the computer has helped with behavior management. I let the students bring in games to show me. It helped my "cool" index when I would watch them play and cheer them on.

Yet I know there are ways I could enhance instruction by using the computers. I just don't know where to start.

Consider This

1. Help the new teacher to evaluate the current uses of the computer.
2. Is it appropriate to use time on a computer as a reward?
3. What are the pros and cons of students having access to the Internet?
4. What school policies relate to use of the Internet?
5. What should the new teacher do first to make better use of the computers in her room?

Grades

It's hard to believe eight weeks have passed. I didn't think about it until the principal reminded us that the nine-week report cards should be ready to send home next Wednesday. I have to admit something. It's probably simple, but I feel kind of stupid. I don't know how to figure out what grades to give my students.

When I started, I didn't give any tests and I put only verbal comments on their papers. How do I turn a "good" into a grade, or what grade do I assign to "This is not a sentence. Use capital letters at the beginning of your sentences"? I wanted to encourage the students, so I was overly generous with my positive comments. When Mark and Elliot did three or four of twenty math problems, I wrote, "Good start." Their classroom teachers would have given them an F. After a month of positive comments, should I tell them they were actually doing failing work? Even a grade of C doesn't match all the students' papers I posted on the "Good Work" board because the students finally did something. But then how do I give a grade to students who need assistance to finish anything?

After a month I started giving tests, but that was a disaster. It was emotionally wrenching for them and me. I didn't know how to make good tests or at what level the students were actually performing. So I decided not to grade those first tests. That leaves me with about three weeks of grades. Should I use those to calculate grades for the whole quarter?

You know how they tell you to form good relationships with parents? Remember how the principal encouraged me to make positive phone calls home and not to call just to report bad news? Well, I called every one of the parents every week and said mostly positive things. I didn't want to admit how badly they were doing academically because I felt guilty it was my fault. Those parents are probably expecting straight A's.

Oh, and there's another piece. I guess IDEA (Individuals with Disabilities Education Act) mandates regular progress reports to special education parents. I thought the report card was going to be enough and plenty of a challenge for me. But our special ed supervisor has directed us to report on every student's progress toward the IEP objectives. How am I supposed to do that? Should I be testing every student on all those objectives? There are a lot of objectives that are all important, but I can't assess everyone. I won't have time to teach them anything. It seems like too much time devoted to assessing and too little time spent on instruction.

Sorry, I guess I'm overwhelmed once again. Where do I start?

Consider This

1. The new teacher asks many questions about assessing, grading, and reporting. Respond to her questions as the mentor.
2. Discuss the pros and cons of special educators giving students grades based on effort. Should these grades be converted to report card grades?
3. Why does IDEA mandate regular reporting to special ed parents about IEP progress?
4. Will the new teacher have to test every child's progress for every IEP objective?
5. How could the new teacher integrate assessment into her routine?

An Invitation

I have to admit I'm amazed. I'm such a novice; I do so much wrong. Yet Mrs. Toklas approached me today and began talking about co-teaching in her fourth-grade classroom. I know I talked about co-teaching at the faculty meeting in August; but the teachers acted like I was crazy. They wondered what I would do in their room. They said,"Your students would be better off getting undivided attention in the special ed room." So I gave up hope, and anyway I realized pretty quickly how much I had to learn about teaching and my students. But Mrs. Toklas told me she liked my energy and appreciated how much I seemed to know about our kids. That's the first time any general ed teacher said, "our kids."

There is so much Alice and I will have to figure out. I'm so excited, but so nervous. The other teachers will be watching, too. Alice proposed co-teaching for social studies. She said our students like the subject, but they get frustrated because they need help with reading the textbook and writing essays and papers. That makes sense to me, but I don't know what I would do with them in her class. Would I sit with my group apart from the rest of the class whenever they have reading or writing to do? Is it OK to include some of the other kids if they are having difficulty? What if my students don't want to sit with me? Maybe they're hoping the other kids don't know that they come to my class. Should I find a different text for them, one that has a lower reading level? Should I design different assignments than the rest of the class gets, assignments that are easier? Do I have to get Mrs. Toklas's okay on everything I do in her room? For that matter, when I'm in that room, is it Mrs. Toklas's room?

Maybe I'm not so excited anymore. Why is everything so complicated?

Consider This

1. The new teacher is surprised by an invitation to co-teach from a veteran teacher. Why might a veteran teacher reach out to a new teacher?
2. What benefits might the teacher and her students receive from co-teaching?
3. What challenges are inherent in two teachers working together?
4. Answer the new teacher's questions about methods that might work best in Mrs. Toklas's class concerning different materials and assignments.
5. When the special education teacher goes to the general education teacher's classroom, whose class is it?
6. What concerns might the general education teacher have?
7. Encourage both teachers to experiment! Describe how they might effectively work as two professionals in one classroom.

CHAPTER

8

Write Your Own Cases

Writing cases can be a valuable experience in professional reflection. This process facilitates movement from an orientation focused solely on your own perceptions and feelings to one in which you have increased ability to take into account the insights of others and the broader perspectives of the teaching profession. In addition, cases contribute to the special education literature on teaching and learning. As you have observed from the examples in this book, cases are rich contextual descriptions of problematic situations that present the reader with a dilemma to be resolved. These cases are multilayered and open-ended, calling for analysis as well as problem resolution. Writing cases based on personal experiences with real-life classroom dilemmas is a powerful reflective tool. In addition to writing up the case, using this case as the basis for reflection and discussion enables teachers to move to a higher level of analysis. Cases promote analysis of complex issues, development of a richer understanding of the situation, and generation of practical solutions that ultimately empower teachers to take appropriate action.

Asked to write a case, preservice or novice teachers may wonder what they have to offer. They may have read a variety of cases as well as the ones in this book but doubt that they "know enough" to write a case. This concern is real, as indicated in the following case.

I Don't Have Enough Experience

All semester I had weekly seminar meetings with my university supervisor and other student teachers. After a long day of teaching, often without time to grab dinner, it was difficult to motivate myself to drive to the university, find a parking space, and prepare to think when I was so tired. However, once I arrived, had a chance to hear what my friends were doing, and became involved in discussing what was happening in our classrooms, I had to admit I appreciated this support offered each week.

We were placed in a variety of classrooms within a 50-mile radius of the university. One obvious difference in our placements involved the diversity of students in abilities, disabilities, and backgrounds. Other differences included the varied teaching styles of our cooperating teachers, the culture of individual schools, and the range of placement models, including full inclusion.

When the syllabus for student teaching was distributed at the first meeting, it was evident that all of the requirements related directly to this culminating field experience. We were expected to have written lesson plans for all our teaching, to write weekly journal entries, to continue working on our portfolios, to videotape and analyze a lesson we taught, and to write a case. Although we had used cases periodically throughout our courses and case analysis was incorporated into this seminar, at first I couldn't imagine writing one myself. I was sure I didn't have enough teaching experience or insight to complete this assignment.

Consider This

1. Why might a case written by a novice or student teacher be as useful as one written by an experienced professional?
2. What criteria would you use to identify a problematic situation that might provide the basis for a case?

Getting Started

Students may either over- or underestimate the effort involved in writing a case. Without support and structure, they may find it a daunting task, may not know where to start, or may merely write a simplistic list of events that occurred in the classroom. It is important to provide a step-by-step approach to this new experience of writing cases.

Writing My Case

Now, weeks later, I thought back to the initial stages of writing the case. The first task involved identifying a problem I was experiencing in my student teaching. We were even encouraged to discuss this with our cooperating teacher and, if possible, choose a situation the teacher found problematic also. In my case, this was easy. In our classroom, Mrs. Harmon and I seemed to be constantly referring to the many difficulties surrounding our students taking the spring tests measuring mastery of the state curriculum standards. All the teachers and administrators in the school were anxious about the students' performance on these tests, but the special education teachers in the building really appeared to have a problem on their hands. Since the first day, I felt the sometimes subtle but everpresent pressure on students to demonstrate mastery of curriculum standards. Mr. Gillam and other general education teachers were worried about the performance of their whole class, while Mrs. Harmon and her special education colleagues feared what would ultimately happen to those students who did not pass the tests. I expressed frustration about this situation in my journal, secretly hoping the whole standards situation would blow over before I was settled in my first teaching job. So when I thought about a possible focus for a case to write, this pressure cooker scenario immediately came to mind. As the weeks progressed, I became an acute observer of all that was taking place related to the high-stakes testing. There was a lot of written communication, including memos from the principal and central office supervisors to teachers as well as notes from parents. I kept written summaries of issues as they occurred to me; things we tried, reactions of the students, input from others in the school, and interactions with parents. At times, I was overwhelmed with the complexity of the situation and could see from Mrs. Harmon's anxiety that I was not the only one who felt this way. Although there were students with disabilities who should and could take the tests, it was readily apparent that other students did not yet have adequate basic skills to succeed. As a matter of fact, I knew students like Lauren and Carter were going to find it a very negative, stressful experience.

At first I wasn't sure where to start, but just as we teach the kids, it was helpful to begin with a prewriting activity to brainstorm clusters of ideas. Several methods were suggested, and I chose one that intrigued me called "cubing" that involved quickly generating issues on the six sides of a cube. Once the scope of ideas was recorded, I began to think about how I could best tell this story. I had read cases presented in the form of a letter, written like a narrative, or developed into a play with dialogue. It seemed that a series of notes and memos to and from the various participants would be a realistic way to illustrate the many sides of this situation.

I then began to write the case, including rich contextual detail of problems surrounding this situation. I wrote about the many people involved and even inserted actual quotes by students and parents. Part of the value and beauty of the case was leaving it open-ended, just as it continued to feel to me. As the series of drafts unfolded, the case became increasingly realistic.

One thing I worried about was my writing skills. Since I had majored in psychology, not English, I was concerned that I would not be able to describe the true dilemma adequately or help the reader fully understand the ramifications of this frustrating situation. All of us were feeling this way, and it was a relief to learn that this first writing attempt was a draft that we would be able to revise. One evening we spent time during the seminar doing what the supervisor called "case conferencing." This involved trading our case drafts and using a simple form to offer informal written feedback. When I read Amy's and Minh's responses to my case, I realized I needed to add more detail for readers to fully comprehend the magnitude and complexity of the situation. They didn't seem to understand how many people were affected and the serious nature of the consequences for certain special education students. I had to make this reality come alive.

I took time to revise my case and was pleased with the depth of the end product. The memos and letters turned out to be an effective presentation format. During various stages of writing the case, I found it therapeutic to reflect on the situation. Having to complete this assignment forced me to think about this problematic issue, but ultimately it became clear that another step was needed if we all were not to be simply left hanging. The case begged for solutions. The whole situation felt like a jet plane out of control, and I still couldn't imagine what I could possibly do to help. I desperately wanted to feel more in control of implementing practical solutions. The more I heard Mrs. Harmon and others talking in the teachers' lounge or at special education department meetings, the greater number of issues I wrested with and the more confused I became. It did not seem like there could possibly be real solutions for some of the students that most needed our help and advocacy.

Consider This

1. What problematic situation in your present classroom experience would you select for writing a case?
2. How might you gather data to help readers gain an understanding of the multiple perspectives of the participants in your case?
3. Can you envision how much contextual detail would be necessary to portray the situation realistically?
4. Will your colleagues be able to relate to this problematic situation?

Planning to Teach a Case

Even though preservice teachers might have been involved in case-based learning, they may not be able to envision how to present their own case during the seminar. There are a variety of ways to do this, but a key ingredient is being open to feedback and new ideas.

Presenting My Case

Although I felt somewhat surprised, I now knew I was able to write a case. It seemed to me, though, that the real question was whether realistic solutions would arise out of using the case as a problem-solving tool. Several of my friends had already presented or "taught" their cases during seminar meetings, and participating in their case analyses was really very interesting. I began to realize that I could contribute in valuable ways to helping others objectively identify the issues surrounding their problematic situation and actually suggest viable solutions. Jared's case, which he called "Math Baggage," was about a group of middle school students who came to math class not ready to learn because of all the "baggage" they brought from their chaotic home situations and personal lives. Rachel described another really challenging situation in her case, "Bart," about a little boy with a behavior disorder who was not responding to any of the management strategies used in the classroom, even those of an experienced master teacher. "The Unfolding of Madelyn" examined the issues involved in providing instruction to a medically fragile child in Minh's class, while "Brian and the Dream Team" focused on the teaming difficulties experienced by a group of middle school teachers and how this situation impacted the learning of one student with a disability.

Each of us was expected to plan our presentation of the case, make accompanying materials, and facilitate the group discussion or activities. The authors thought of creative ways to effectively help seminar participants identify both surface and underlying issues in the cases and then transition to the problem-solving stage. Some of these presentation strategies were hard acts to follow. For example, with "The Unfolding of Madelyn," Minh dramatically unfolded a collection of paper dolls, each representing a character in the case, and then gave a paper doll to each of us. We began the case analysis by jotting down the feelings and concerns of our character on the paper doll. For the "Bart" case, Rachel included some realistic props related to some of his episodes (for example, a milk carton from the "big spill" episode in the cafeteria). She distributed laminated parts of a picture on which we wrote issues related to the case, and these parts were assembled to form a large picture of the child. The completed "Bart" puzzle served as a visual display of the main problems in the case.

Once we understood the main issues in each case and were able to see the case from the multiple viewpoints of the characters, we began to explore potential solutions. Minh had us work in small groups to devise solutions to issues previously identified on the paper dolls. We wrote these solutions for the medically fragile child on paper "prescriptions." Afterwards Minh said, "I learned so much from writing and presenting my case. It's really important when you're solving problems not to just move chaotically from one thing to the next in the classroom. Often you don't get a chance to sit back, think about the problem, and generate new ideas. This case allowed me to step back and look at the issue in more depth."

The discussion of "Bart" helped Rachel move beyond seeing only the problems to identifying the strengths of the case. "There were so many problems to focus on but the discussion helped me to see that potential solutions could arise from the positive aspects of the situation." The value of using a case as a problem-solving tool became clearly evident to me and I hoped it would work for my case as well as it had for the others.

I wondered how I could best present the issues in the case. Would I be able to help the seminar participants understand not only the facts but the complex nature of the problems surrounding state standards and assessment of the students in my class? It was important to understand the situation intellectually as well as emotionally. For me, this wasn't merely an exercise in problem solving; it was a serious situation demanding some very real answers. I decided to go back to the idea of the cube I used for brainstorming. As part of my case presentation, I planned to assign a viewpoint to each of six groups. They would write the various perceptions and/or emotions on pieces of paper that would then be pasted onto the sides of a cube symbolizing the multidimensional complexity of the case. Individual perspectives would then be shared with the larger group. I planned an activity to facilitate each group's generating solutions and recording their ideas on simulated test forms.

Even though I was proud of the case I'd written and was prepared to present my case, I worried about being able to step back far enough to be objective.

Rachel had done a particularly good job with this aspect. I didn't want to sound defensive about suggestions that might be made or as if I already had the answers. I knew I'd be frustrated if the seminar participants just "didn't get it" or misperceived the seriousness of the situation. Had I written the case combining enough detail with broader contextual information, so the reader would see what I saw? If the solutions they suggested were truly helpful, then they had to be based on the real facts. It seemed as if I now had more questions than when I began this reflective journey. I knew that merely setting aside time did not guarantee that reflection would occur, but that this structured activity promoted reflection and analysis. I was looking forward to reflecting rigorously with others about a problem that was important to me, hoping not only that it would result in some potential solutions but that others would benefit from exposure to a situation possibly similar to ones they might encounter in the future. I wanted to be free of my own assumptions and open the door to additional options. Maybe I would be able to see the issues as well as possible solutions more clearly .

Consider This

1. Can you think of effective ways to assist readers of your case in understanding the perspectives of the various participants?
2. Would you be able to present the facts in your case objectively and be open to, not defensive about, solutions proposed by your colleagues?
3. Do you believe that it is possible for your colleagues to develop salient solutions involving suggestions you have not yet tried?
4. Could case writing and problem solving be as useful for practicing teachers as for student teachers? As a teacher, how might you realistically use this strategy?

The End Result

It is possible for others not directly involved in the case to help a teacher clearly understand the issues and identify potential realistic solutions. Are there other benefits to case-based learning? As seen in the following cases, students seek to understand what they have ultimately learned from this experience.

What I Learned

I couldn't wait to return to school the next day and share what I had learned with Mrs. Harmon. Although these ideas were not quick fixes, they were a series of steps, both large and small, that we could take to chip away at the problem. I now felt empowered rather than immobilized because I had things I could actually try. These actions might not resolve all the problems, but they would help us move forward in the right direction. I was somewhat surprised at how much my guilt and confusion lessened. For one thing, it became increasingly clear during the case discussion that some of the issues I was worrying about were truly not in my control. This helped me to realize that it would be most productive to focus my efforts on tackling the problems that were within my reach. This was an important lesson to learn.

Guidelines for Writing a Case

1. Identify a topic.
   a. Identify three to five problematic situations involving you, the teacher. Let them arise out of actual dilemmas you are presently experiencing. Does one present itself as needing attention, possibly a priority or something immediately pressing?
   b. Keep in mind that not all problems are worthy of incorporating into a case or require the level of problem solving facilitated by case analysis.
   c. Select a problem that especially evokes your emotions. Do you find yourself overwhelmed, confused, or anxious?
   d. Choose a situation in which the teacher has some control. Be open to a variety of situations, including those focusing on students, colleagues, school environment, interactions with parents, instruction, behavior, or school policy.
2. Brainstorm contextual details.
   a. Use a prewriting activity (for example, concept mapping, outlining, cubing, looping) to develop specific written ideas to include in the case.
   b. Take time to reflect on what is happening in relation to the problem. Who is involved? Can you portray the situation from more than one perspective? What are people thinking or feeling? What emotions are you experiencing? What is the context, including positive aspects of the situation? What background information is necessary to understand the scope and basis of the problem?
3. Develop a draft case.
   a. Consider a variety of writing styles such as a play, journal entries, a series of letters, and the like as ways to help readers effectively understand your case.
   b. Encourage readers to really feel what the characters are going through. Show not just the "big picture" but the interconnections among the smaller related pieces.
   c. Make the case three dimensional by including real details, but leave the case open-ended.
   d. Insert dialogue and descriptive comments to add to the richness of the case.
   e. Protect the identities of people and situations by maintaining confidentiality. It may be necessary to alter the situation slightly or use pseudonyms in order to protect people.
4. Obtain feedback and revise as needed.
   a. Use a case-conferencing format to obtain feedback on the draft case. Readers can comment on areas of possible confusion, need for additional supporting details, need for further character development, and overall clarity.
   b. Carefully read the reviewers' comments and make revisions as appropriate.

Guidelines for Teaching a Case

1. Prepare to present the case.
    a. Plan ahead to use time effectively as you move from identification of issues to brainstorming of solutions.
    b. Plan ways to actively involve participants throughout the case discussion.
2. Remain objective.
    a. Even though you are involved in the case, take as objective a stance as possible. Use this as a healthy opportunity to remove yourself emotionally from the situation.
    b. Open yourself to viewing the problem from new or different vantage points and gaining new ideas.
    c. Avoid leading the discussion too much, bringing up information that was not included in the written case, biasing the participants with your opinions, or reacting personally to comments made during the discussion.
    d. Analyze the dilemma from alternative points of view.
3. Foster active involvement of the participants.
    a. Devote adequate time to case presentation and analysis (possibly up to two hours).
    b. Use techniques to actively involve participants. Include as many people as possible, but avoid letting any one person monopolize the conversation. Help participants step into the shoes of the characters and view the situation from various perspectives.
    c. Generate lists of issues, but do not forget to focus on "analyzing" in addition to listing.
    d. Encourage participants to support their suggestions or arguments in a logical, concise manner.
    e. Consider how time is allocated so that there is a balance between small-group brainstorming and larger-group discussion.
4. Brainstorm potential solutions.
    a. Avoid promoting the idea that solutions come in the form of prescribed "right answers."
    b. Model openness to the "messy" side of cases. Case analysis may not solve the problem, but it is a tool for solving problems.
    c. Focus on actions within control of the teacher. Think about what you would do if you were the teacher.
    d. Avoid limiting discussion to one solution but develop alternatives and possibly prioritize them.

W9-AXK-293

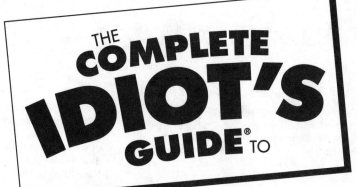

Creating
CDs and DVDs

Third Edition

by Todd Brakke

ALPHA

A Pearson Education Company

For my wife Angela. Our road hasn't always been a smooth one, but I wouldn't trade one single second of it. Your love and support means everything to me.
"Dream by night, wish by day ..."

For marketing and publicity, please call: 317-581-3722

The publisher offers discounts on this book when ordered in quantity for bulk purchases and special sales.

For sales within the United States, please contact: Corporate and Government Sales, 1-800-382-3419 or corpsales@pearsontechgroup.com

Outside the United States, please contact: International Sales, 317-581-3793 or international@pearsontechgroup.com

Publisher: *Marie Butler-Knight*
Product Manager: *Phil Kitchel*
Managing Editor: *Jennifer Chisholm*
Acquisitions Editor: *Eric Heagy*
Development Editor: *Ginny Bess Munroe*
Copy Editor: *Ross Patty*
Illustrator: *Chris Eliopoulos*
Cover/Book Designer: *Trina Wurst*
Indexer: *Angie Bess*

Contents at a Glance

Contents

Appendixes

Introduction

It's a Brave New World

Welcome to the third edition of *The Complete Idiot's Guide to Creating Your Own CDs and DVDs*. In a way, I suppose that technically this book is a first edition. This is, after all, the first time we've included coverage of recording to DVD. But being that recording to DVD isn't a whole lot different from recording to CD, this book is still an extension of the roads we already traveled in the first and second editions.

While still a medium in its infancy, recordable DVD is poised to take over the disc recording industry in the next few years. The drives can still read and write to CDs, so the only roadblocks remaining (as I discuss in Chapter 2) are price and standards. Both of these obstacles should start passing into our collective rearview mirror by the end of 2003.

Lest you think that DVD is the only thing we've updated in this edition, keep reading. For the third edition, I've almost completely reorganized the content, so that it's easier than ever before to quickly find the material you're looking for (see the later "How to Use This Book" section).

In this edition I've also swapped out one of the core programs we covered in the second edition. As I discuss in the next section, NTI CD-Maker 2000 was a fine program, but this year I've replaced it with Nero Burning ROM. For users who want all the power in their hands, this is *the* tool to use.

Fans of Easy CD Creator shouldn't feel gypped, though. I've updated, reorganized, and refined every page related to using this application, including the addition of using it to burn DVDs.

Combine all that with coverage of MusicMatch Jukebox updated for users of version 7.x and all new coverage of the video-disc authoring tool Ulead VideoStudio, and I firmly believe that you'll find this to be the best edition yet. There's something in this book for anyone interested in recording CD or DVDs using a home computer.

The Programs Used in This Book

There are a lot of tools out there that you can use to record audio, video, or data to a CD or DVD. Many are all-encompassing software suites that let you perform almost any operation you might need. Others are more specialized, focusing only on one aspect of disc recording (providing you with many more features and much more power to do it).

This book focuses primarily on Easy CD Creator 5 Platinum from Roxio and Nero Burning ROM 5.5 from Ahead Software. Each of these applications has its strengths and weaknesses, but I chose them for good reasons:

- ◆ Both are commonly included in software bundles that come with recordable disc drive upgrades and pre-built PCs that come with these drives.

- ◆ Both provide you with tools that you can use to create data, audio, and video discs.

- ◆ Both support recording to CD and DVD (make sure you have at least ECDC version 5.1 and Nero 5.5.8).

If you purchased the second edition of this book you'll no doubt notice that instead of Nero, we elected to cover NTI CD-Maker 2000. With apologies to those of you who swear by NTI's product, I felt that this was no longer the way to go. ECDC and Nero are clearly the two front-runners when it comes to full-featured disc authoring software. But not only that, covering these two products allows me to address two different families of recording enthusiasts.

Don't Get Burned _____

> The chapters in this book are based on using the full versions of each program I cover. Nero, Easy CD Creator, and the others can also be found in "basic" or "demo" versions. Often, these are the versions that are packaged with recordable drives.
>
> If you have a demo version of this software, the basics I cover in this book should still be the same for you, but you will find that certain features and options are off limits. If you want access to them, you need to pay for the full version of the application.

If there's one trend I noticed as I began researching how to update this book, it was that everywhere I looked I found two camps of people: those who hate Nero and love Easy CD Creator, and those who hate Easy CD Creator and love Nero.

Which is right for you?

Generally, it seems like ECDC is more popular amongst users who are either new to disc recording or are generally not comfortable with personal computers. Nero, on the other hand, is extremely popular with many of those who feel as though they've graduated from the world of ECDC and want something that provides more options and more control.

Personally, after putting Nero through its paces I have to say that I'd never go back to ECDC for personal use. I like having the control over the recording process that Nero provides. I also like that it boasts more features, like being able to create inserts for more than just jewel cases, and recording Super Video CDs (the video DVD recording option could still use some fleshing out).

The only place where I feel both of these programs fall short is in the realm of managing a large PC-based audio collection and recording DVD video. That's why I've also included chapters on MusicMatch Jukebox and Ulead VideoStudio in this book.

MusicMatch Jukebox is simply the best tool I've ever used for ripping, managing, and recording my music collection. Ulead VideoStudio on the other hand, while not perfect, is the only reasonably-priced tool I've seen that allows you to capture, edit, and record video to both CD and DVD.

Each person's tastes are different and surely some of you have other programs that you prefer. That doesn't mean this book can't be of use to you, though. The basics and general concepts that I cover throughout the chapters in this book are applicable to any disc authoring application you might have. What will differ is the options you have and how you're able to use them.

How to Use This Book

For your ease of use, this book is organized into seven different parts, plus three appendixes:

Part 1, "The Digital Revolution," deals mainly with recordable disc and drive technology. It also contains a chapter that provides you with a basic understanding of copyright law, Fair Use, and what the content producing industry (note I do mean "producing" and not "authoring") is doing to inhibit your ability to engage in Fair Use practices.

The chapters in this part aren't required reading, but if you're new to disc recording or are unfamiliar with what you do and do not have the right to do with copyrighted content, I strongly recommend that you give them a look.

Part 2, "Quick and Painless: Duplicating CDs and DVDs," helps you get your feet wet by showing you how to perform a simple disc copy.

Part 3, "PC Life Insurance: The Zen of Making Data Discs," starts with an introduction to the world of data discs and formats, this part provides you with all the information you need to make a data CD for backup or other purposes.

Part 4, "Digital Jukeboxes: The Tao of Making Audio Discs," is the part for you if you've got a hankering for making custom audio CDs. The first of this part's three chapters gives you the straight dope and audio recording basics and file formats. The next two show you how to actually produce a disc.

By now, I've covered data and audio disc recording so **Part 5, "Eat Your Heart Out, Mr. Spielberg: Creating Video CDs,"** moves on to the world of video. If you've been waiting for the opportunity to dump your VCR, the chapters in this part show you how to make it happen.

Once you've created your discs you need someplace to put them. The jewel cases you get with your recordable discs (or that you purchased separately) are all fine and dandy, but they sure are drab. The chapters in **Part 6, "Picasso Was Overrated: Creating Great-Looking CD Labels and Jewel Case Inserts,"** provide you with all the tools and knowledge you need to make custom jewel case inserts and disc labels.

So I've shown you all the crucial tools and features of Easy CD Creator and Nero Burning ROM, but you still want more. Well then buckle up, because **Part 7, "Putting the Cherry on Top with More Great Tools and Software,"** takes you through the basics of three great specialized tools: MusicMatch Jukebox (for audio), Ulead VisualStudio (for video), and Roxio PhotoRelay (for making digital photo albums). I've also thrown in a troubleshooting chapter that gives you basic tips and advice for what to do when your recording efforts have only brought you to coaster city.

If you're an experienced user or someone who has no interest in learning the basics, then not every chapter in this book is for you. You can pretty much write off Part 1 and the first chapters of Parts 3 through 6. Each of these chapters is designed to give you the background knowledge you need to understand the content provided in the succeeding Easy CD Creator and Nero Burning ROM chapters that actually show you how to get things done. However, if you do skip any of these chapters and then find yourself getting confused when terms like MPEG, WMA, packet-writing, and others get thrown around, make sure to flip back a chapter or two where these basics were probably covered.

Disc Burning Lingo

As with any new technology, a new language has grown up around the practice of writing information to a disc. Terms you should make sure you know before cracking Chapter 1 are:

- **Ripping.** While the term might sound like it means you're going to be running at mach 5 from a music store with stolen CDs, the term "ripping" actually applies to the process of copying music files from tracks on a CD to files on your hard drive. At this point, I'm convinced it's a record company term used to make you think you're doing something wrong. Remember, there is nothing illegal about ripping tracks from CDs you've purchased to your PC; though in the world of the DMCA (see Chapter 3), if you circumvent any copy-protection schemes to do so, then you're on your own.

- **Burning.** This term, which describes the process of recording information to a disc, is actually very accurate. When you record to CD-R, DVD-R, or DVD+R discs your drive is actually burning a series of tiny holes in the surface of a disc. That's why these record-once media cannot be erased.

- **Coaster.** When using record-once media like a CD-R, you only get one chance. If you experience an error or other problem that prevents the burn from completing, then the disc is ruined and only suitable for use as something on which you can put tasty, cold beverages.

- **Recordable (R) versus rewritable (RW).** Be they CD or DVD, you can only record once to discs that carry the recordable "R" designation. However you can erase, rewrite, and modify a disc bearing the letters "RW," which stands for rewritable.

- **Disc or disc drive.** Any time I write the words disc or disc drive, without specifying a type, I mean that the information it pertains to could apply to either CD or DVD media and drives.

- **Recordable disc or recordable drive.** While there is a distinct difference between "recordable" and "rewritable" media, it's a pain in the butt to read or write "recordable and rewritable" every time I'm talking about both formats. So when you read these words, remember that I'm referring to both formats.

There is, of course, other lingo scattered throughout the book that may not be familiar to you. Most of the time you should find that I explain uncommon terms as I use them. The ones listed here consist of those that I use repeatedly throughout the book.

Other Goodies You'll Find Herein

Similar to a child, we like to write in the margins and all over the page. In this book, you'll find some examples of this in the following forms:

Between Tracks

These small bits of text are inserted here and there to provide tips, notes, and extra information that isn't in the main body of the text. You might find a shortcut or possibly a topic you may want to explore further in another chapter of the book.

Don't Get Burned

Caution! Caution! Caution! Can I make it any plainer? These notes point you away from potential pitfalls and help you keep from spending hours working on your pet project only to have something go wrong in the process.

Arcane CD Speak

Sometimes words just say too much—so much that they don't make sense. In these little text bites, we explain some of this terminology. You don't need to know these words to get the job done, but they'll make you sound smarter when you're spouting off to friends about how clever you are.

Cross Reference

Need more information? These cross references will point to other locations in the book where further discussion takes place.

Closing Thoughts

I used to think that one of the best investments I ever made was upgrading my PC with a CD-RW drive. I don't think that anymore. Now it's the money spent on my DVD+R/RW drive. Burning CDs is great. I don't think I could've survived some of my long road trips if it weren't for the compilation CDs that have accompanied my journeys. Being able to record to DVD, though, just makes it better.

With recordable DVDs it's no longer necessary to have seven or more discs on hand just to back up all your crucial data, graphics files, or MP3 collection. In my case, I can record it all to just two or three DVDs (bearing in mind my MP3 collection is rather large). I particularly like that I can now truly bid adieu to my VCR (as can you). Once you get the basics down, capturing video and recording it to a video DVD is a snap. At long last I need no longer groan any time I watch one of my old *Cheers* or *Murphy Brown* recordings, as I realize the degree to which my rotting VHS tapes have eroded away the video and audio quality.

Life in the disc-recording world would just about be perfect if not for the copyright cops in the content producing industry. These guys seem to think owning a PC, especially one with a recordable disc drive, and having an Internet connection automatically makes you a copyright pirate (read all about it in Chapter 3). As the saying goes, though, "into all things a little rain must fall."

When all is said and done, all I can say is, read this book fast! The sooner you do, the sooner you can make backups of your precious CDs. Put your family photographs on CD for long-term digital storage. Save your VHS collection. After you get started with your CD or DVD recorder, you'll wonder how you ever got along without it. CD and DVD recording for the home user really is a *digital revolution!*

Acknowledgments

As always, a great author must give credit where credit is due. As a thoroughly mediocre talent, I endeavor to do the same in the hopes I might one day be great.

First off, I'd like to thank my acquisitions editor, Eric Heagy. Eric has been a tremendous source of support in helping (and allowing) me to produce this book and it's been a pleasure to work with him. Hopefully, this edition will continue to do well and we can hook up again for another one.

I'd also like to thank Ginny Bess Munroe, who developed this edition. As a developer myself, I know how tough a job it can be. A development editor who knows when to be firm and when to be fair is an invaluable asset. Ginny's comments, criticisms, and suggestions helped make this a much better book. You did a first-rate job, Ginny. Thanks!

Big props as well to senior production editor Christy Wagner (and the pinch hit from Billy Fields) who made sure I didn't sluff off during the review process and genuinely helped make the ship run more smoothly.

Likewise, copy editor Ross Patty not only helped make me sound like one o' them fancy educated folk, but also provided a lot of extremely helpful thoughts and insight that helped make this a better book on all fronts.

Finally, be sure to look through the entire list of credits for this book. All of these talented professionals who handled laying out the book, designing the cover, and more deserve credit for work which goes largely unnoticed. All in all, Alpha has put together a top-notch team who all deserve a well-earned thanks for their efforts.

On a personal note, I'd like to thank my wife, Angela, and my many parents (Gayle, Jim, John, and Nancy). Angie is, without any doubt, the most special person I've ever known. The fact that someone like her was willing to marry me is a testament to her compassion and patience (particularly while writing this book). Thank you again, my love, for sharing your life with me.

As for my parents ... they're okay. I mean yeah, they loved me, raised me, convinced me I wasn't really descended from carnival folk and all. But really, I ask you: Where are they when I tell them we need a plasma TV for Christmas? Kidding aside, these four very special people mean the world to me and the confidence they instill in me is as big a reason as any that I could actually take on a project like this one. I love you all very much.

Finally, I owe countless thanks to Terry W. Ogletree. While Terry will tell you that I (as his editor) wrote as much of the first edition as he, I assure you, he's lying. Terry produced a great book the first time around with little help from me. The fact that he recruited (i.e., coerced) me into co-authoring the second edition with him only demonstrates what a generous person he is.

Terry, my wife and I now live in our first house because of the generosity you showed in letting me tag along for the second edition (just ask the mortgage company). The fact that you've one-upped yourself by letting me take sole authorship over this fine title in the third edition is astounding to me. I know you claim you've got too many other projects going on, but truly, your generosity is one of a kind. If you ever need a kidney give me call ... I'm sure I can talk somebody into giving one up.

About the Author

Todd Brakke has been an editor and writer for various online and print publications for about five years. As a development editor for a computer book publisher he, among many other projects, helped develop the first edition of Terry Ogletree's *The Complete Idiot's Guide to Creating Your Own CDs*, later bribing his way to co-authorship of the second edition. As a writer, Todd has produced content for various online PC gaming websites as well as some print articles for *Computer Games Magazine*. He also helped lay the groundwork for the dot-bomb implosion as the editor-in-chief of the PC gaming website, Computer Games Review (a dot-com casualty).

Special Thanks to the Technical Reviewer

The Complete Idiot's Guide to Creating CDs and DVDs, Third Edition, was reviewed by an expert who double-checked the accuracy of what you'll learn here, to help us ensure that this book gives you everything you need to know about creating your own CDs. Special thanks are extended to Dallas G. Releford.

Trademarks

All terms mentioned in this book that are known to be or are suspected of being trademarks or service marks have been appropriately capitalized. Alpha Books and Pearson Education, Inc., cannot attest to the accuracy of this information. Use of a term in this book should not be regarded as affecting the validity of any trademark or service mark.

Part 1

The Digital Revolution

There's a lot to know about recording to a CD or DVD before you actually throw a blank disc in your recorder and start burning. In Part 1, I discuss the various aspects of both recordable CD and DVD technology, including both the discs and the drives. I also give you the basics on copyright law and Fair Use, so that you have a basic understanding of what you can and can't do with your drive.

Chapter 1

Recordable CDs: Not Just for Geeks Anymore

In This Chapter

- Why analog sucks
- What to look for in a CD-RW drive, including buffer-underrun protection and support for CD-MRW
- The difference between CD-R (Recordable) and CD-RW (Rewritable) discs
- Information on the various recordable CDs and their capacities, including discs that hold 90 to 99 minutes of audio

Compact discs, as I'm sure we're all aware, started out as a much-needed medium for storing music. If you're one of those whippersnappers born in the 1980s or sometime after that, you will never know the time that some people devoted to protecting their music collection before CDs came along. Analog phonograph records were fragile platforms to hold music and—other than various forms of magnetic tape, such as cassettes or reel-to-reel—there was no alternative. Music was either recorded as an audio signal that was laid down on tape or it was etched into the surface of a master platter that would eventually lead to stamped phonograph records.

Such fragile things are subject to quick deterioration. Despite audio quality that some people still prefer to CDs, all you have to do to damage a record is walk across the floor not-too-softly, making the needle skip across the record. There's the first scratch and more would surely follow.

And audio tape? Heck, audio tape quality can degrade just sitting on the shelf for a few years. Considering its quality was nothing to write home about in the first place, the medium made for a pretty lame format.

When the compact disc was finally released, its capability to store audio digitally was heralded as a great leap forward in the music industry. And, indeed, it has come to prove itself to be just that … not just for music, but for storing data as well. Over the years, recording audio and data to a compact disc went from an expensive manufacturing process requiring tens of thousands of dollars of equipment to something Joe the couch designer could do at home on his new Pentium 4 after putting the kids to bed.

In this chapter, I show you the basics of the CD recording medium, including what to look for in a CD-RW drive and the types of media you can use in one.

Buying a CD-RW Drive

Not long ago, the province of recording music or data to a CD belonged to computer "geeks" (like me) who had little else to spend money on than PCs and bootleg special editions of *Terminator 2* on VHS or laserdisc. Nowadays, though, almost every new computer purchased has a recordable drive in it that can make backups of your precious PC data and record audio to CD. Even if your PC doesn't have one, you can get a brand new 40× drive (among the faster drives currently available) for as little as $60.

Between Tracks

At the dawn of home CD recording you had to choose between recordable drives that could only record to a blank disc and rewritable drives that, with RW media, could rewrite a CD. These days, CD-R only drives are harder to find than a participant's pride or self respect on a typical "reality" TV show.

If you got your CD burner with a new computer, it should be installed and set up already. If you have just purchased—or are about to purchase—a new drive, you need to follow the drive's instructions to install it properly. This is not an impossible task, even for the inexperienced. However, it's still not for those afraid to remove even one screw from their PC case. If that's you, call that computer nerd friend on your speed dial or see if the place from which you bought your drive can install it for you (for a price).

CD-RW Drive Terms and Technologies

If there's one thing that's been a consistent trait for the disc burning hobbyist, it's been the invention of a new language that can be more difficult to understand than Swahili. If terms like buffer underruns, packet-writing, or x-ratings, sound like something you once heard about while watching Star Trek, then this is your section.

Buffer-Underruns

The term "buffer-underrun" was once synonymous with the process of burning a disc. Usually when a technology's defining characteristic describes an error, that technology is in big trouble. The technology behind burning a disc, however, has progressed significantly, and this disc-killing error is fast-becoming little more than a speed-bump on the way to a disc authoring superhighway.

When writing information to a disc, your drive depends on a constant stream of data from your PC. It uses a special buffer to store this data. If that buffer should be empty when your CD-RW drive is eagerly looking for more data, then you're about to experience a buffer-underrun. In the case of a record-once, CD-R disc, this means the disc is a coaster. That is, it's given its life to the disc recording gods and is now more functional as something for putting a cold drink on than for storing audio or data.

Originally, to combat the buffer-underrun menace, drive manufacturers tried increasing the size of the memory cache. This is an allotment of memory built into your drive that's meant to give the PC a cushion in providing data or audio for it to record. This solution is only marginally effective since any truly meaningful increases in the amount of physical cache memory also increase the cost of the drive.

> ### Cross Reference
>
> Several key terms to the disc-burning world are covered in the introduction to this book.

> ### Don't Get Burned
>
> While this should not be a concern for any up-to-date software, keep in mind that buffer-underrun protection only works if it's built into both the drive and the software you use to record your discs.

Fortunately, the need for a larger cache has gone away with the invention of various buffer-underrun protection technologies. Yes, technologies. As in plural. Because each drive manufacturer to come up with a technique for putting an end to buffer-underruns decided to patent their technology as quickly as possible, they didn't all use the same name. Additionally, rather than develop their own solutions, many manufacturers simply licensed someone else's buffer-underrun protection technology for their own products.

Sanyo, for example, was among the first to produce a buffer-underrun protection technology. Theirs is called BurnProof, and has been licensed to several drive manufacturers. The important thing in choosing a drive is not to focus on the name, but rather the existence of some kind of buffer-underrun protection.

CD-MRW (Mount Rainier)

CD Mount Rainier Rewrite (CD-MRW) may seem like a variation on the CD-RW disc, but it's actually a combination hardware and software technology that's used in conjunction with normal CD-RW discs. Mount Rainier, at its heart, is a packet-writing technology. Packet-writing is a term applied to how files are written to the disc. Normally, it's the province of CD authoring software, as discussed in Chapter 6. However, Mount Rainier is different. The technology for CD-MRW is built into the drive hardware and into the latest PC operating systems, like Windows XP.

While I discuss Mount Rainier a bit more in Chapter 6, it is important that I bring it up now because it's an important feature to look for when purchasing a new CD-RW drive. It makes the process of writing packets of data to a CD simple and error-free, just as you would write to any other drive on your computer.

If you've used packet-writing software like Easy CD Creator's DirectCD or Nero's InCD, you're familiar with the benefits and detractions of current packet-writing formats. Normally, you have to pre-format the disc, just to make it work with these programs. This formatting process can take upward of 20 minutes to an hour to complete! With Mount Rainier, your drive can format the disc in the background as it writes the data. No more waiting! Not only that, but if for some reason you need to eject the disc before the format is complete, you can do so. When you put the disc back in later, your drive will complete the formatting process on its own. No errors!

Also, because of more efficient writing algorithms built into the hardware and Windows XP, it makes better use of space. A disc formatted for CD-MRW can hold more data than one formatted using a typical packet-writing program like DirectCD or InCD.

Finally, protecting recorded data from errors (defect-management) is handled in the drive's hardware, rather than packet-writing software. This not only frees up your PC's resources while writing, it further improves the reliability of the data you write to the disc. All in all, CD-MRW is probably the most significant new disc recording technology since buffer-underrun protection. (And it's also available in the latest DVD recorders!)

X-Ratings

Before you get too offended (or excited, as the case may be), we're not talking about videos featuring scantily clad resumé builders for plastic surgeons.

No doubt you've noticed drives on store shelves boldly proclaiming they support 32×, 40×, or faster. This designation refers to the speed with which the drive can spin the disc and still read from or write to it. The speed at which a drive can operate depends on the task it is performing (read/write) and, in the case of writing, what medium to which it's writing (R/RW). Usually you'll see a designation like 32×10×40. Whenever you see this, 32× is the CD-R write maximum write speed, 10× is the CD-RW write speed and 40× is the speed when reading from a CD-ROM.

Don't Get Burned

If you're an audiophile, keep in mind that a drive's read speed doesn't always translate into its abilities to "rip" (copy) audio tracks to your PC. Some drives can read and rip at the same speed, but most rip audio at speeds much lower than they can read ordinary data.

Also, understand that the ratings used to promote a drive are maximum performance ratings. A drive that writes CD-Rs at 40× doesn't maintain that 40× *all* the time. That's just where it peaks.

So let's translate these numbers into real-world performance. At 1× speed, recording a CD takes about 74 minutes. 1× is the same speed at which you listen to an audio CD, which I suppose is why the measurements start there. At 2×, the time to complete a recording drops to 37 minutes, more or less. Today's 32× drives can burn a disc in less than 3 minutes. As you can imagine, there comes a point (and I think we've hit it), where a drive's speed is no longer the primary factor to consider when choosing a new drive.

What to Look For

So if speed isn't a big issue, what features should you be looking for? Well, that can vary based on your budget and needs. If can afford to drop a few hundred dollars, you might even want to consider buying a DVD+R/RW or -R/RW drive. Not only can these drives burn to DVD discs, they can still record to CD-R/RW discs, too! However, this chapter is about recordable CDs so that's what I focus on here. Any drive you buy today should:

- Support CD-RW discs and CD-R discs (I'd be shocked if you found a new drive that didn't).

- Support some form of buffer-underrun protection, like BurnProof. Most new drives today do protect you from this coaster-producing error, but some might not.

- Support the new Mount Rainier packet-writing standard. This might be a *little* more difficult to come by, but it's well worth any added cost to have this ability. Sometimes support for this technology is referred to as CD-MRW.

- Be able to record a CD-R at a speed of at least 12×. In 2001, 12× was pretty much the standard speed for recording a CD-R. What a difference a year makes. Now drives can write a CD-R at 48× or more! Pretty soon I guess you'll just hit a button on your keyboard and be done.

This list narrows the playing field slightly when choosing a new CD-RW drive, but it certainly doesn't make it a small list. There are as many CD-RW drive manufacturers these days as there are American corporations with lousy accounting practices.

Choosing a drive manufacturer is purely a personal choice. I will tell you, though, that most drives from companies like Plextor, HP, TDK, Yamaha, and Philips do have predominantly good reputations. Typically, you get what you pay for with these things, so if you find a deal that's just too good to be true, don't be surprised when it starts spitting out charcoal briquettes instead of newly recorded CDs!

Recordable CDs: A Revolution in Data Storage

Digitally recording music on a CD improves on the analog record in two major areas. First, the actual sound quality is much better on the CD than on the record. The digital recording method used to sample music at thousands and thousands of times per second almost guarantees that you won't miss a beat.

The second area in which CDs can be said to excel is in their durability. Now, I'm not saying you can take your CDs and use them to play Frisbee with your dog. However, in normal everyday use CDs are much more durable than most other storage mediums (especially analog tapes, vinyl records, and floppy disks).

The laser used to read a CD does no damage to speak of to the CD itself. It simply reflects off the disc back to a receptor in the drive. Nothing touches the surface of the CD other than a clamping device, which holds the CD in the drive by clamping onto the very center of the disc, where there is no recording surface. The wear and tear factor for CDs, when compared to vinyl, tape, and floppy is almost nonexistent.

Between Tracks

You might wonder why CDs were developed first to store 74 minutes of audio information. The "urban folklore" answer is that it was selected because it could hold the entire performance of Beethoven's Ninth Symphony. This is, however, not true, at least as far as this author has been able to determine. The amount of audio data was more likely determined by the technological capabilities available at the time the compact disc was first introduced. As technologies are further developed, we are able to fit more and more information on a much smaller amount of disc (or disk) real estate. Thus, we now have 80-, 90-, and even 99-minute CDs. Of course, there are also DVDs, which can hold more than seven times the information of a typical CD, despite being the same physical size.

Digital vs. Analog: Analog Gets Its Butt Kicked

After you get past the physical advantages of the CD itself, the digital method used for recording audio needs to be considered. Vinyl records and older audio tape machines used analog methods to encode sound. When a copy was made, the sound quality was degraded a little each time. Lost sound quality comes about partly because of the wear and tear on the original and the condition of the recording equipment. And let's not even get into making copies of copies with analog music. Have you ever made a photocopy and then tried to copy that copy, and copy the copy after that, and so on? The same gradual demise of the image you see in a photocopy also happens to your music when making copies of copies using a cassette tape. Major bummer! Of course, it makes one wonder if, when it comes to cloning human beings (something that is fast becoming a reality), we can expect the same results? I mean if we think Anna Nicole Smith is the "before" poster-child for Hooked-on-Phonics now, I guess her clone would have trouble finding a multi-syllabic word with two hands and a flashlight!

Digital recording writes audio on the CD in a digital format that is similar to the way your computer stores its data. As a matter of fact, you can, using the right program, extract songs from your favorite CDs and store them as files on your hard drive. Because the music is stored in a digital format (rather than analog), it is even possible to do a little error correction to help ensure that the sound quality is up to par.

When using CDs to store computer data, the error correction scheme used is even more powerful than that used on audio CDs. This is because there is less tolerance for a mistake in a computer program or the data it uses than there is in an audio file. You probably wouldn't even notice if one zillionth of a second of music got screwed up while burning your favorite CD. Having your CD-RW drive flub those few bits when burning a computer program or word processor file, however, could cause a complete disaster!

For Computer Nerds, as Well as Aspiring Musicians!

As you can see, buying a CD burner gives you the chance to get a lot more out of your computer. If you follow this book's lead and use Roxio's Easy CD Creator 5.0 Platinum, or Nero Burning ROM 5.5 for your CD-burning pleasure, the sky is very nearly the limit. If, for example, you happen to be someone who has a large collection of LPs just sitting around the house, you're going to find it impossible not to use SoundStream (part of Easy CD Creator) to clean up the sound and make CDs from those LPs. After waiting all these years, you could even put the songs in the order in which *you* think they should be. To heck with those dopey record producers!

When you're finished copying all your LPs, making backup copies of your CDs, and backing up all the crucial data on your PC, you can get started scanning and storing all your family photographs on CD. Want to annoy relatives and friends? Capture all your home videos to your PC, burn them to a Video CD and send everyone you know movies of Junior dropping an ice-cream cone in Grandma's hair.

The number of practical and fun applications for burning information to these small shiny discs seems to grow by the day.

Recordable CD Media

When home disc recording first got started there was only one medium from which to choose: CD-R. Since that time, your options have grown significantly. In this section, I take a look at the various types of discs you might see hanging around on store shelves.

Between Tracks _____

You'll find that there are many kinds of CD-R and CD-RW discs available on the market today. The most common are the same size as a commercial CD. Yet you'll also find "business card" CD-R discs as well as mini-discs that are much smaller and meant for playing in portable players. However for all practical purposes, the main two differences between discs, other than size and capacity, are whether the CD blank disc can be recorded once or if it can be erased and used again.

CD-R

Compact Disc Recordable, or CD-R, is the old stalwart of the disc recording family. CD-R is a write-once, read-many format. That is, you can write to a CD-R once, but after that you can only read it. This is fine in most cases, since very often the discs you write you won't have any need to alter. However, it also has a rather big drawback. If the burn should fail at any point after the first bit of data is written to the disc, then the whole disc is toast. Throw it out, or use it as a drink coaster, and get ready to start over. For those of you with unreliable drives, this can be an expensive proposition.

Fortunately, the cost of CD-R media is its other key feature. At this very moment you should be able to walk into your local Best Buy or Circuit City and pick up a spindle with 50 to 100 CD-R blanks for as little as $20 to $30, respectively. If there's a rebate going on, your bottom line could be even lower. In the summer of 2002, I picked up a spindle of 100 Memorex CD-R blanks for a base price of 25 cents a disc (including rebate). I expect that I'll still be using discs off this spindle when it comes time to start the fourth edition of this book!

Finally, CD-Rs are, by far, the most compatible disc format out there. Nearly all set-top, car, and compact CD players can play audio CD-Rs. Most all CD-ROM drives can read CD-R data. In fact, most set-top DVD players can play audio CD-Rs and video CDs. No other disc format can be used in such a wide variety of devices.

Between Tracks

You can also, of course, buy your CD-Rs in jewel cases, but most of the time it's not worth the added cost. If you must, buy your jewel cases separately, in bulk. In a time where 401(k)s are falling, you should pinch every penny, right?

CD-RW

When they first appeared CD-R discs were great. But there was no one who wouldn't have preferred the ability to erase and rewrite a disc, rather than have to start a new disc for each new project. Fortunately, Compact Disc Rewritable (CD-RW) discs soon emerged on the market. While a bit more expensive than their record-once cousins, these discs can justify their extra cost each time you're able to erase one with outdated data and use it for a new recording.

While these discs are not nearly as compatible across a large spread of devices, as CD-Rs are, they are ideal for users who perform regular data backups. While not fun or exciting, using your CD-RW drive to back up your data is as important a function as you're likely to perform using your drive. If you make weekly backups, the number of CD-Rs you could go through can pile up quickly. CD-RW discs can reduce your disc needs to a small backup set. Once you've filled up your set of discs, erase the oldest one and start anew!

How CD-R and CD-RW Discs Are Different

I can pretty much guarantee you that rewritable discs didn't come about because some schmoe decided, "Hey, let me use my Revers-O laser to undo my recording!"

When burning a CD-R, a recordable drive emits a laser that literally pokes miniscule holes in a very thin layer of dye that makes up part of the CD-R disc. This physically creates the "pits" and "lands" in a manner similar (but not the same) to a commercially manufactured CD. This is why CD-Rs are so compatible with older CD players. The CD-RW burning process, which produces discs that are not nearly as compatible, is actually quite different.

When your recordable drive burns a CD-RW, it doesn't actually burn any "holes" in the dye layer of the disc. Instead it physically changes the reflectivity of the disc in a way that simulates the same effect as having the pits and lands a conventional CD player looks for when reading a CD. The disc is rewritable because the same process can be used to reset the reflectivity of each "spot" on the disc. Because the drive only simulates the pits and lands of a manufactured disc or CD-R, many older CD players and CD-ROM drives are unable to read these discs.

CD Media Capacities

When buying CDs for your CD-RW drive, not only must you decide whether you want recordable or rewritable discs, you must also decide what capacity of disc you want.

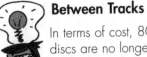

Between Tracks

In terms of cost, 80-minute discs are no longer significantly more expensive than their smaller cousins. In fact, many stores these days seem to stock more 700MB discs than they do those of the 650MB variety.

It used to be that all CDs held 650MB (megabytes) of data, which equates to about 74 minutes of audio on a disc. As CD-manufacturing processes have evolved, it has become possible to produce 700MB, 80-minute CDs that are just as compatible as the 650MB versions (though you may occasionally encounter players and recorders that balk at 80-minute discs).

While these two formats are by far the most common recordable CD formats you're likely to encounter, there are some others that bear a mention here.

Low-Capacity Discs: 50MB and 180MB Data Discs

While the norm for the tech industry has been to find a way to squeeze more and more information onto the same amount of space, there's also a niche market for squeezing a small amount of information onto a much smaller disc. 50MB "business card" CDs and 180MB 3-inch Mini-CDs have emerged to fill that need. These discs can hold up to 5 or 21 minutes of audio information, respectively. However, because of their limited capacity and nonstandard physical size, they're much more suited to holding data than audio. For folks who want to create video discs, this format is all but useless.

High-Capacity CDs: 90-, 99-, and 100-Minute CDs

Predictably, a mere 80 minutes of recording time hasn't been enough for some people. In the continuing effort to pack more data onto a CD-sized disc, 90-, 99-, and 100-minute CDs have come available on the market.

Despite the benefits of having an extra 10 to 20 minutes of recording time, these discs come with some hefty detractions. First of all, your recording software has to be able to recognize that your disc has a higher capacity. If it doesn't, it may not let you create a layout that holds more information than a conventional 74- or 80-minute CD. Second, your drive has to be able to write that much data to a disc. These discs achieve their higher capacity by tightening up the tracks on the disc, making them closer together. If the recorder can't handle burning data that way, then it can't burn the disc. Finally, these discs often have considerable problems playing in drives and players outside of the one that created them. In the case of an audio disc, what usually happens is that your CD player will play it normally until it reaches the 80- to 90-minute mark and then it will lock up.

DDCD

Whereas high-capacity CDs like those I discussed in the previous section are somewhat a "home-cooked" solution for getting more data on a disc, Sony and Philips (the creator of the CD standard) have developed a disc format called Double-Density Compact Disc (DDCD). Going by the "rainbow" standards discussed in Appendix C, this standard is known, unofficially, as part of the "Purple Book."

These discs hold up to 1.3GB (gigabytes) of information. Unfortunately, they're not compatible with non-DDCD-enabled disc drives and CD-players, so there's no point in recording audio or video to them. Nero Burning ROM, which is covered in this book, does support the format, but I don't recommend you run out and buy a drive that supports it. Because of the limited compatibility and because DVD recording technology is becomingly increasingly affordable, I don't expect this format to live for very long.

> **Between Tracks**
>
> Some CD burner software applications allow you to *overburn* a CD. That is, they let you record a few minutes of additional audio or a few extra megabytes of data beyond the reported capacity of the disc.
>
> Overburning can be a risky process, however. Recently there have been reports in Internet newsgroups that some CD-RW drives can actually be damaged if you try to use them for overburning. So while your software application may allow this feature, use it at your own risk! If you want to record 80 minutes, buy 80-minute CD-R discs! Don't try to put a few extra minutes on a 74-minute CD-R disc!

What Should I Use?

There is an easy answer to that question: use the discs that work best in your recorder! Because several combinations of dyes and metallic reflecting materials are used to construct a disc, what works well in one recorder or player might not work well in another. Furthermore, because several brands exist on the market—even though there is only a handful of manufacturers—you can not even be sure that when you continue to buy the same brand, you're getting the same disc. The brand-name distributor might be buying batches of discs from other manufacturers based on whoever has the lowest price at the moment!

> **Between Tracks**
>
> You may have noticed that the bottom of your recordable discs sometimes have different colors. Usually this is because manufacturers use various dyes and metals to construct their recordable discs. This results in different colors for the media. Originally, the color of the data side of the disc was just a reflection of whose discs you purchased. Lately, though, it's become something of a marketing gimmick; especially where the so-called, "black," discs are concerned.
>
> When you look at the bottom of the CD-R blank, if it's a greenish color then most likely there's a gold metallic layer underneath. If it is more of a bluish color, silver is probably being used instead for the metallic reflective layer. This isn't a guarantee, but I just mention it to let you know different kinds of recordable CD blanks exist.

Now that makes for a confusing situation! So buy first in small quantities, find a brand that works, and stick with it until it doesn't! Also, be sure you use a recording speed for which the media is rated. You'll usually see them rated for various speeds, such as 4×, 8×, 32×, etc. If higher speeds don't produce good results, and you have a higher-speed drive, try lowering your recording speed to around 8×. If that fails then try a different brand of discs. If it works, try bumping up the speed a notch until you find your drive's sweet spot.

The Least You Need to Know

- When you buy a CD-RW drive, look more at features like buffer-underrun protection and Mount Rainier support than for recording speed.

- Mount Rainier (CD-MRW) is the newest recordable CD standard. It uses hardware technology and support built into Windows XP to allow you to write to any CD-RW disc like it were an ordinary floppy disk or hard disk drive.

- You can buy CD-R (record once, read forever) or CD-RW (rewritable) discs. CD-Rs are cheaper and more compatible with a wider variety of ROM drives and CD players than are CD-RW discs. But you can erase an RW disc and re-use it.

- Recordable CDs come in a variety of storage capacities. The two you should look for, though, hold 650MB of data (74 minutes of audio) or 700MB of data (80 minutes of audio).

Rewritable DVD: The Next Generation of Recording Comes Home

In This Chapter

◆ What makes a recordable DVD different from a recordable CD

◆ An explanation of the different recordable DVD standards, including DVD-R/RW and DVD+R/RW

◆ What to look for in a recordable DVD drive and how compatible the media it produces is with existing DVD set-top players and DVD-ROM drives

◆ What to expect in the future for recordable DVD

You don't need a magic 8-ball to see the future of optical storage in home PCs. DVD is following a road to the home PC not unlike that of the compact disc. At this point, it's all but killed off VHS tape in the home movie market and while it may take time, it will eventually eat into the dominance of the CD.

The Evolution of DVD

When CDs first jumped into the public spotlight, it was as a medium for storing high-quality music in a format that is durable, portable, and relatively inexpensive. It was also a read-only medium at the beginning. Until the mid- to late 1990s, the idea of using a home PC to record not only audio, but also data and video, to a compact disc was about as likely as the Patriots winning the Super Bowl … ahem. But it happened, and now CD-RW drives are found in almost every new desktop and portable PC sold.

Now let's look at a DVD. In the late 1990s, DVD emerged as a medium for storing high-quality video in a format that is, let's see, durable, portable, and relatively inexpensive. It was a read-only medium designed to make VHS tape obsolete. Sound familiar? And it is. Many brick-and-mortar retail chains have dramatically cut back on (and even eliminated) their stock of movies on VHS. Even as early as 2001, though, the idea of adding a PC-based DVD drive capable of recording to DVD discs for less than the cost of a big-screen television sounded as likely as, well, the Detroit Lions winning the Super Bowl (could happen … someday). But guess what? It is happening; and it's happening quickly.

By the end of 2002, a drive capable of recording to DVD media could be purchased for as little as $250! Depending on your budget that may not be chump change, but it's a heck of a lot less expensive than a big-screen TV.

Recordable DVD Technology

DVD discs don't look much different from a typical compact disc. They're the same size. They've got one really shiny side, and they store lots and lots of information. It just so happens that a DVD stores a lot more. A recordable DVD disc can hold approximately 4.7GB (gigabytes) of data. That's more than seven times the standard CD capacity of 650MB (megabytes). To put it in perspective, if a music CD can hold about 70 minutes of CD-audio data, a DVD could hold about 490 minutes (using the same CD-audio encoding standards).

So what does DVD stand for? Truthfully, it doesn't stand for anything anymore. It's just DVD. There are camps that will tell you that it stands for Digital Video Disc and others that insist it stands for Digital Virtual Disc. But at this point, DVD is just DVD.

One thing, however, that is certain is that the terminology used to rate DVD recording speeds is sure to confuse the average Joe. Like CD-RW drives, DVD read and recording speeds are measured in factors of "x." So in the next few sections when I talk about DVD drives burning at 1× and 2.4× you might think this is rather pathetic. After all, CD-RW drives can burn at about 40× these days. Fortunately, that's not the case.

The "×" rating for a DVD drive has no relationship whatsoever with that of a CD drive. DVD drives and players, as designed, access their discs much more quickly than do their CD-spinning cousins. For example, writing to a normal CD at 16× takes roughly six minutes. So were you to insert a CD capable of holding 4.7GB of data instead of 650MB, we can guess that it would probably take about 42 minutes. Well, a 2.4× DVD+RW drive can burn a DVD+R or DVD+RW disc in roughly 15 minutes.

Unfortunately, these numbers don't work in reverse when you attempt to burn a CD-R or CD-RW disc in a 2.4× DVD+RW drive. Recordable DVD drives are also rated for burning CDs, but as mentioned earlier, they're quite a bit slower at it than today's top of the line CD-RW drives, usually topping out at about 12× (CD-speed).

> **Between Tracks**
>
> Commercially released video DVDs can use a technique called dual-layering which doubles the capacity of a single-sided DVD to about 8.4GB. Many of these DVDs have data written to both sides of the disc for a whopping 16GB+ of information on a single disc!

Format Wars

The recordable DVD industry has a problem. There are too many (incompatible) standards for its discs. Originally, there was DVD-RAM. DVD-RAM discs had to be put in cartridges that you inserted into the recordable drive. A bit clumsy, but for storing data they were effective. They weren't much of a solution, though, for folks who wanted to record their decaying VHS collection to a disc they could put in their set-top DVD movie players.

Unfortunately, while new solutions would soon come along, they've also ignited one of the biggest format wars since VHS versus Betamax.

DVD-R and DVD-RW

Not long after the introduction of DVD-RAM, along came the DVD Forum, which you can pay a visit to at www.dvdforum.com. The DVD forum was founded by 10 companies who wanted to set a new standard for recordable DVD. These companies included such heavyweights as Pioneer, Philips, Time Warner, and Sony. They agreed on a format for recordable and rewritable discs called DVD-R and DVD-RW.

Between Tracks

The DVD Forum also recently announced a specification called DVD-Multi. Billed as a universal DVD format, the only recordable format that it adds compatibility for is DVD-RAM. If you're wondering why the +R/RW format isn't part of this universal compatibility, you have to read the fine print, which states, "all currently developed formats which have been approved by DVD Forum." DVD+R/RW doesn't make their approved list.

Maybe it should've ended there. But it didn't.

DVD+R and DVD+RW

Unhappy with various issues surrounding the standards set for DVD-R/RW, several developers (including some founders of the DVD Forum) jumped ship and formed the DVD+RW Alliance. Guess what standard they produced?

The founders of the DVD+RW Alliance, which included DVD Forum co-founders Philips and Sony in addition to companies like HP, Dell, and Ricoh, also developed a standard for both recordable and rewritable DVD discs: DVD+R and DVD+RW.

Was this necessary? Many people, including myself, think that it was. The +R/RW standard has a lot of advantages of -R/RW. For one, it could initially record discs faster. DVD+R/RW was the first to reach speeds of 2.4×, while DVD-R/RW was still topping out at 1×, and later, 2×. By the end of 2002, both formats were heading towards 4×, but DVD+R/RW looked to be getting there first. In the fall of 2002, Mitsubishi announced a technique for recordable DVD drives that would allow all formats to write to disc at 8×!

DVD authoring software can also format +R/RW media much more quickly (just a few seconds) for the purposes of storing data. Additionally, a technology called loss-less-linking allows you to add, change, and remove files from a +RW disc without having to erase the disc or rerecord the existing data in a separate session.

Between Tracks

As I discussed earlier in the chapter, the x-ratings for recordable DVD drives is not an equal match for the x-ratings listed for CD-RW drives.

Finally, according to the DVD+RW Alliance, this format is also much more compatible with existing set-top DVD players and DVD-ROM drives. This claim is one that is pretty difficult to back up, and the DVD+RW Alliance, itself, has yet to really do so. However, a study by Intellikey Labs produced some interesting results that would seem to confirm the Alliance's claim. On the tested DVD players:

- ◆ DVD+R was compatible with 90 percent

- ◆ DVD-R was compatible with 77 percent

- ◆ DVD+RW was compatible with 72 percent

- ◆ DVD-RW was compatible with 66 percent

Pioneer, who originally commissioned the study (and is a supporter of DVD-R/RW) called the results into question, but the general consensus is that DVD+R/RW is a more universal format.

Unfortunately, DVD+R/RW does have an Achilles' heel. It's expensive. Not obnoxiously expensive, mind you. Just more expensive than -R/RW solutions. And that doesn't just apply to the drives. That's true of the media as well. Typical +R/RW discs typically cost in the range of $4 to $6 per disc. On my most recent check, I found Internet offers that had -R/RW media selling (in bulk I'm sure) for as little as $1 per disc. Considering that the drives, on average, are anywhere from $100 to $200 cheaper, DVD-R/RW does have some significant advantages.

Which format should you choose? That, dear reader, is up to you. While I still firmly believe that the +R/RW camp has the superior technology, that doesn't mean it will emerge victorious. Just ask Amiga if, in the mid- to late 1980s they thought they had a better gaming computer than Apple or IBM!

Buying a Recordable DVD Drive

Buying a recordable DVD drive really comes down to whether or not you want a -R/RW or +R/RW, though there are a few other factors to consider.

Between Tracks _____

All recordable DVD drives are also able to record to CD-R and CD-RW discs. Though they tend to peak out at around 12x when recording to a CD-R, which is roughly one-third the speed of the higher-end CD-RW drives available. Still, recording a CD-R at 12x only takes about 7 to 10 minutes, so there's really no need to have separate CD-RW and DVD-R/RW or +R/RW drives.

Right now the number of manufacturers putting out recordable DVD drives is significantly lower than those making CD-RW drives. Also, at least one of the old standbys in the CD-RW market, Plextor, had yet to release a recordable DVD drive by the end of 2002. The limited number of choices (especially once you side with a format), has at least one worthwhile side effect: there's not much difference between the drives. So whether you, for example, buy a +R/RW drive from HP or Philips, isn't going to make a huge difference. This will likely change, however, as time goes on.

First Generation Drives

By the end of 2002 there were at least three distinct generations of recordable DVD drives on the market. The first generation of drives was comprised of DVD-R/RW drives that recorded both -R and -RW media at 1× and DVD+RW drives, capable of recording at 2.4×.

Notice I wrote DVD+RW and not DVD+R/RW. That's not a typo. While the boxes on these first generation drives often boasted differently, they did not support the yet-to-be-released DVD+R disc format. It was thought at the time that the *firmware* in these drives could be upgraded to add the support once the discs were available. They were wrong.

Arcane CD Speak

A lot of PC hardware components these days are embedded with a small amount of static memory. That is, unlike the system RAM in your PC, the contents of it aren't lost when you turn your computer off. **Firmware** is the term applied to the data held in this static memory. In the case of recordable DVDs, this data helps tell the drive how to burn a disc and interpret commands from Windows. Drive manufacturers often provide firmware updates that you can download and install to fix bugs and occasionally improve reliability and features.

The DVD+R/RW format was dealt a serious blow when it was discovered that these first-generation drives couldn't be upgraded to support DVD+R. Given that +RW is still a spotty format where compatibility with set-top DVD players and DVD-ROM drives are concerned, this left a lot of people with very expensive data backup devices.

Fortunately, it didn't take long for a second generation of drives to hit the market.

Second Generation Drives

In the summer of 2002, the first of the second generation of recordable DVD drives started to emerge. For DVD-R/RW, this generation's primary asset is the bump to 2× recording. For DVD+R/RW, the main improvement was a bit more noticeable.

That's right, upon reloading, members of the DVD+RW Alliance finally produced recordable DVD drives with support for DVD+R and DVD+RW discs. So far, DVD+R has shown itself to be extremely reliable in both other DVD-ROM drives and in set-top DVD players.

Third Generation Drives

The third generation of recordable DVD drives (set to release soon after the time of this writing) should see the emergence of 4× drives. However, many third generation drives should have one more bonus in store: support for the new Mount Rainier packet-writing standard that first started to become popular in the CD-RW world.

For more information on Mount Rainier, see Chapter 1, and for more information on packet-writing, see Chapter 6.

The Future

The future of DVD recordable drives and media is uncertain. Undoubtedly, recordable DVD drives will eventually replace CD-RW drives as the prime method of recording audio, video, and data to a disc. However, I don't expect that prices on recordable DVD drives and wide-spread consumer acceptance will truly begin until either the -R/RW or +R/RW format becomes dominant. Expect that to happen by the time the sun sets on 2003.

In the foreseeable future, though, expect to see:

◆ DVD+R/RW drives that can write a DVD at speeds above 4× to 8×.

◆ A generation of DVD-R/RW drives that conform to the DVD-Multi format which guarantees compatibility across the -R, -RW, and -RAM recordable formats.

◆ At least a few drives emerge that actually support both -R/RW and +R/RW. Oak Technology has already announced a chipset that can be used to produce recordable DVD drives that support both of these competing formats.

The big issues that all these technology folk must deal with is compatibility. Neither format achieves 100 percent compatibility with any device capable of playing a DVD disc. If you're interested in what your set-top DVD players and DVD-ROM drives can support, check out www.vcdhelp.com/dvdplayers.php. This site lists just about every piece of DVD-playing hardware known to man (and a few of those only known to beasts, or so I hear).

Between Tracks

For those looking for a clear, "buy this, don't buy that," I'm afraid you'll be disappointed. At this point, there's just no way to predict whether +R/RW or -R/RW will become the de facto standard.

As I think it's a better technology, I favor +R/RW. Many favor -R/RW (cost is a prime factor there, I suspect). I don't think you'll be too disappointed either way as I think the -R/RW and +R/RW media will be available for at least a few more years (regardless of which one becomes dominant). Realistically, a drive you buy today only needs to be usable for a couple years, anyway.

Within a year or two we'll likely see recordable DVD drives become standard on new computers (as with CD-RW drives today). Typically, a PC is only good for two to four years before it is in need of an upgrade. So if you buy a drive today, odds are you'll be ready to upgrade to a newer model before +R/RW or -R/RW can become truly obsolete.

If that's just too much of a gamble for you, my advice is to wait for a drive that can read and burn all the formats, or wait the year or two it will take for one of them to win out.

However, before you get too excited because this list shows your Panasonic A-110 is compatible with every recordable DVD disc format under the sun, step back and take a breath. There is more to disc compatibility than just plusses and minuses. Note that all of the following have an effect on whether or not your recorded discs will work in any particular device:

- The brand of media you use

- The specific drive you use to record the disc (in terms of manufacturer)

- The condition of your set-top DVD player or DVD-ROM drive

The Least You Need to Know

- There are two camps for recordable DVD: -R/RW and +R/RW.

- -R/RW discs and drives, at this time, are considerably less expensive than the +R/RW format.

- +R/RW drives are able to record data to disc faster and more reliably, which many feel justifies paying more for both drives and the media.

- Compatibility with existing DVD-ROM drives and set-top DVD players is still spotty for both -R/RW and +R/RW formats. However, both formats usually work in newer model drives and players.

Chapter 3

What You Need to Know About Copyright Law and Fair Use

In This Chapter

- ◆ What you need to know about Copyright Law

- ◆ What Fair Use says you can and can't do with copyrighted content

- ◆ What the music and movie industry is doing to combat piracy and how it effects you (and your jones for disc recording)

This chapter is the one chapter in this book that doesn't deal exclusively with information related to recording data, audio, or video to a CD or DVD. It does, however, deal with what you can and cannot do, legally, with your disc recorder and how your ability to use it may become more limited in the future.

Copyright, Fair Use, and how the entertainment industry is seeking more control over what you can do with content you put on your PC is becoming an increasingly hot topic. Although I believe this chapter to be a must-read for anyone interested in what rights they have in terms of copying copyrighted content for personal use, it is not strictly necessary that you read it if you're only interested in burning data to a disc as quickly as possible. So feel free to skip it or come back to it later if what you want to jump right into using your disc recorder.

The Dicey Copyright Landscape

While, as you'll soon read, I am a strong advocate of Fair Use and the rights of consumers to use legally purchased content as they see fit, it is equally important to understand that I do not condone that you break the law. Trading copyrighted material online with others who have not paid for that content is illegal. Artists, writers, musicians, etc. work very hard at what they do. If you like the fruits of their labors, the best way to pay tribute to it is buy it, not steal it.

However, that doesn't mean you should buy into the notion that the file-sharing on the Internet and burning custom CDs is at the heart of declining recording industry revenues. In fact, in the summer of 2002, Forrester Research revealed a study that indicated that profits from music sales actually went up during the year in which Napster was at its peak.

Firstly, the most damaging piracy doesn't come from our living rooms, but from organized groups of people who duplicate copyrighted content on mass and sell it for their own gain. Secondly, the recording industry has taken to clamoring quite loudly about how much money they lose to piracy. It's true. They do lose a lot. But they also lose a lot because the quality of much of the content they produce is questionable at best. The prices they charge for their product are on the rise (and many argue that music CDs were overpriced to begin with). Plus, the economy isn't exactly booming these days. Few industries are increasing their profits, so why would the recording industry be any different? To top it all off, let's remember that when a music company speaks of declining revenues, that doesn't mean they're actually losing money. It just means that they're not making as much. How often do you hear about a cash strapped record label laying off hundreds of employees because their profits are in the red?

Between Tracks

Any opinions I express in this chapter are most certainly my own and not necessarily those of Alpha Books or Pearson Education, Inc.

Still, the law is the law and I do encourage you to abide by it. Though what the law says is certainly not a black and white issue. As I'll explain in this chapter, there are legitimate questions regarding some existing and proposed copyright laws that seem to contradict both Fair Use and even free speech.

Know the Law and Know Your Rights

Knowledge is power, as they say. When it comes to the topic of burning any kind of information to a digital medium, it has become increasingly important to understand just what you do have the right to do, and what you don't have the right to do.

It's very likely that in the future this decade will be thought of as the one to redefine copyright and privacy in a time of unheard of technological advancement. The entertainment and software industries are *very* interested in seeing how far they can push their "rights" as holders of intellectual property copyrights. How far they're able to do so will have a direct effect on what you can do with your recordable disc drive.

In the next few sections, I offer you a crash-course on copyright law, Fair Use, and the Digital Millennium Copyright Act.

Copyright

To say that copyright law is tricky is to say that the Joker was just a nuisance to the Batman. I've read up on copyright law. I've attempted to interpret it. I've listened to others try to interpret it. I've even tried playing recorded readings on the subject while I sleep, on the off chance that some glint of understanding will seep in through osmosis. No such luck yet.

Regardless, it is clear what copyright is supposed to do. It's intended to protect the rights of those who produce original works; a very noble and worthwhile goal. Areas considered to be, "original works," include (but are not exclusive to):

- Drama
- Literature (both fiction and nonfiction)
- Music
- Art
- Other works of an intellectual nature

If you write a song, for example, you own that song. No paperwork needs be filed, no forms submitted. It's yours, and as such you have the right to:

- Display or perform your work publicly
- Make copies and distribute for public consumption the work you've created
- Create derivative works based on your original content

Seems like a pretty good piece of legislation doesn't it? I mean if I'm J.R.R. Tolkien (may he rest in peace) and I found out some wonk has made huge sums of money selling a book about a midget who finds an invisibility ring while stumbling around a mountain looking for a dragon, then I'm going to be a little hot under the collar. Copyright law, plain and simple, is intended to protect someone's creative work and that's a good thing.

> **CAUTION**
>
> **Don't Get Burned** _____
>
> There's a world of difference between knowing you produced an original work and being able to prove you produced original work. Just because you saw your joke on *The Simpsons* last week and you know you thought of it first (or even wrote it down first) doesn't mean you get to sue the show's creators.
>
> Also, to have copyright over an original work, that work must be conveyed in a "tangible" format. That would include written or recorded works. It doesn't apply, for example, to a joke you thought of on the fly while improvising at the local comedy club's open mic night.

Unfortunately, in the world of commercially published media, the authors of copyrighted works very rarely hold the copyright to the material they produce. For example, I wrote nearly all the content in this book. But I don't own the copyright to it. I voluntarily forfeited that right in order to convince the good folks at Alpha Books to put it on a store shelf and charge money for it (and give some of that money back to me). In most cases, though, if a published work becomes unavailable for a set length of time, then the copyright for that work reverts back to the author, artist, etc.

Fair Use

Copyright law specifically states that the rights of a copyright holder are *not* unlimited in scope. That's where the term, "Fair Use," comes in.

Fair Use, introduced as part of the 1976 Copyright Act, dictates that you can legally duplicate copyrighted work for:

- ◆ **Creative Uses.** This includes Fair Use by authors who copy from other works to create their own work, so long as that work is not derivative of the original.

- ◆ **Personal Uses.** This includes Fair Use by individuals who copy from works for their own learning or entertainment.

- ◆ **Educational Uses.** This includes Fair Use by teachers, scholars, and students who copy for educational purposes.

In the case of using copyrighted work in a public arena, you can only use, "limited portions," of a copyrighted work. What constitutes limited portions mostly depends on the judge assigned to your case when the copyright holder sues you. In general however, the key points that determine whether "infringement" of copyrighted work fall under the category of Fair Use are:

♦ **The purpose and character of the use.** That is to say, you can use portions of copyrighted work for nonprofit or educational purposes.

♦ **The nature of the copyrighted work.** This requires a determination of whether the work is a creative work, a compilation, or a derivative work.

♦ **How much of the copyrighted work was used as compared to the whole.** In other words, the higher the percentage of a copyrighted work you use determines whether or not you've infringed upon the copyright.

♦ **The effect of your use of copyright material on the market and value of the original work.** That is, if someone has duplicated copyrighted material, are their actions hurting the copyright holder financially (say, from lost sales)?

So far, this may not seem like Fair Use specifically protects your right to make a backup copy of your new game, or copy your new Sammy Hagar CD to MP3 files on your PC. However, and perhaps most important to the nature of this book, Fair Use dictates that copyright law should only apply to the *marketing* of a work. It does not extend to individual copies of the work that the copyright owner has sold. In other words, duplicating a VHS movie you purchased onto a DVD so you can watch it in your DVD player instead is not a violation of copyright.

Naturally, the entertainment industry has an answer for this too. Fair Use does not specifically state that you have the *right* to personal use for any copyrighted material you purchased. Consequently, the music and video industries believe they are free to introduce schemes and technology that prevent you from making full use of the media you purchase. You don't have to be John Nash (think *A Beautiful Mind*) to see that argument for what it is: a loop-hole.

The Digital Millennium Copyright Act

In the fall of 1998, the U.S. government enacted into law the Digital Millennium Copyright Act (DMCA). The DMCA was supposed to be a law that further protected the rights of content creators in a time when digital storage and digital information makes infringing on copyright increasingly easy; certainly, a legitimate goal. Instead, what we (in the USA) got was a law that is so loosely worded and potentially far reaching that it severely represses Fair Use and generally leaves educators, journalists, and consumers at the mercy of any copyright holder with the resources (money) to haul you into court. It doesn't matter whether or not the accusation is based in established fact. Most people and organizations can't afford to be dragged into court regardless of guilt or innocence.

The DMCA also puts part of the burden for protecting copyright on the Internet Service Providers. In other words, your ISP can be held responsible if you trade in copyrighted content online. In practice, usually what happens is that if a copyright holder determines (or thinks they've determined) that you're one of the more flagrant violators of copyrighted content, they'll contact your ISP (with lawyers) and demand that they discontinue your service. They may even demand your name, address, or other personal information so they can get you in court. Big Brother, you have a call on line one.

The other egregious aspect of the DMCA is the provision that makes any product designed to circumvent a copy-protection scheme illegal. For example, it's currently illegal to make available a product (even for free) that disables the CSS copy-protection found on nearly all commercial video DVDs. In fact, the law's wording is loose enough that it's been used to dissuade publication of the methodology used to break a copy-protection scheme. In other words, not only can you not distribute or provide access to the tools, you can't even publish, in any form, how it's done. The fact that technologies like CSS prevents you from using legally purchased DVDs within the limits of Fair Use doesn't seem to matter.

Between Tracks

Here's just one example of the DMCA being put to nefarious use. In 2000, the Secure Digital Music Initiative (SDMI) and RIAA issued a *public challenge* to see if anyone could break their latest copy protection technology. When a team led by university professors from Princeton and Rice was able to circumvent the copy protection and sought to publish their findings the RIAA and SDMI immediately used the threat of the DMCA to suppress that information.

To date the paper produced on the subject has yet to see the light of day. All it took was the threat of the DMCA and some high-priced lawyers. Check out www.eff.org/sc/felten/ for more information.

Not all is gloom and doom. At this time Fair Use is still very much alive. It's not illegal to download songs you paid for to your MP3 player or make backup copies of your software. However, if your media is copy-protected, it's no longer legal to circumvent that copy-protection, even if the end goal is make copies of copyrighted material that conform to Fair Use standards. How's that for a contradiction in terms!

Cross Reference

When you read about using Nero to make a data disc in Chapter 8, you'll notice that Nero does indeed contain options that can aid you in copying a disc that has some forms of copy-protection on it.

Given the DMCA, how is this legal? Honestly, I've been unable to find a definitive answer to that question. I suspect this is legal because the program is capable of merely ignoring certain methods of preventing a PC from properly reading data from the disc. So technically, it's not circumventing anything.

Copyright Violation

Under current copyright law, if someone or some entity knows that you have infringed on their copyright, they do have grounds to sue you in a civil (not criminal) court. (As they should.) Criminal proceedings could also follow in some cases depending on whether or not you significantly devalued said material. This is right and just. Under no standard should anyone support the idea that you should be able to buy a CD and then share copies of it with 10,000 of your best friends.

The notion, however, that a copyright holder must work through the legal system to stop someone from infringing on their copyright is an important one to understand. At this time, a copyright holder cannot go outside the legal system to protect their content. They can't knock on your door and demand a check for reparations. They can't hack into your PC to see what you might or might not be doing. Put simply, a copyright holder cannot enforce the law.

Now, that may seem like common sense, but stay tuned. You might be surprised to learn that this situation could change, and not for the better.

The RIAA and MPAA Want You! (and Your Computer)

Make no mistake about it. If you own a disc recorder, the entertainment industry (comprised of the major music, video, and software publishers) does not like you. In fact, it's their firmly held belief that you either are a copyright criminal or are likely to become one. Your crime? You own a computer or other device capable of storing digital content and you *might* want to use it to store copyrighted material you didn't purchase.

I've already covered the framework for copyright, Fair Use, and the dreaded DMCA. But as someone with a recordable disc drive, I think it's worth your time to find out just how organizations like the Recording Industry Association of America (RIAA) and the Motion Picture Association of America (MPAA) are working to further insert themselves between you and everything you do on your PC. That includes burning audio to a CD or video to a DVD.

Don't believe me? Consider the words of Sony Pictures Entertainment U.S. senior VP Steve Heckler at a public conference in 2000 (the middle of Napster's hay-day):

> "The [music] industry will take whatever steps it needs to protect itself and protect its revenue streams. It will not lose that revenue stream, no matter what ...
>
> Sony is going to take aggressive steps to stop this. We will develop technology that transcends the individual user. We will firewall Napster at the source—we will block it at your cable company, we will block it at your phone company, we will block it at your [ISP]. We will firewall it at your PC."

It's statements like that, that make it hard to sleep without the lights on.

I don't think many people support the idea that you should be able to freely distribute and download copyrighted material at will. And certainly groups like the RIAA have a responsibility to protect their interests. But the power they wield in this regard is well beyond any reasonable standard. There is a line between legitimate infringement concerns and instituting a virtual copyright police state.

These organizations believe they have a right to know what you store on your computer, how you use it, and who else you give access to it. After all, how do *they* know that the Tom Petty song, "Joe," was burned onto that CD-R in your car radio from a legitimate source? Shouldn't *you* have to prove it to *them*?

What They've Done

Using the DMCA as its shield, the RIAA, MPAA, and various other organizations have already inflicted a considerable amount of damage to your ability to exercise Fair Use.

As I type this, the media industry in the United States (with the DMCA as their weapon) is actually suing several major *Internet Service Providers* for *not* blocking your ability to access a website called Listen4ever. True, the site does store and allow anyone to download copyrighted music tracks, but is that the ISP's responsibility? If these groups can sue ISPs for not blocking your access to one website, what's to stop them from banning your access to any other site they don't like?

It doesn't end there. One of the things that finally brought DVD from the drawing board to actual movies on disc is the inclusion of a copy-protection technology called CSS (Content Scrambling System). It's also the reason you can't copy any portion of a DVD movie off the disc onto another medium (like a hard disk drive or DVD+RW disc). The movie industry devoted enormous resources to the development of this technology. From the day CSS source code was anonymously posted to the Internet it took just 48 hours for someone to break it, using a program called DeCSS.

Between Tracks

DeCSS actually appeared on the Internet before DVDs containing CSS technology made it to market.

How did the media industry react to the revelation of DeCSS and other tools that appeared for circumventing DVD copy-protection? Predictably, in late 1999, they gathered their lawyers and sued for violation of the DMCA. The hit list included more than 500 individuals in over 11 countries whose biggest crime was making various DeCSS programs *available* for download or even *claiming* they had links to other sites where the files were available. Remember, DeCSS's sole function was not to allow people to violate copyright law. It was to allow you to circumvent a DVD copy-protection scheme that inhibits your ability to copy a DVD within the guidelines set forth by Fair Use.

What They're Trying to Do (Proposed Legislation)

It's said that the wheels of justice turn slowly. Too slowly for a media industry bent on stopping file trading at all costs, no matter how they have to go about doing it. So if you can't beat them in the courts, get that congressman out of your pocket and have him write a new law.

Arcane CD Speak

Peer-to-peer networks are those that allow various users to connect with each other over the network for the purposes of swapping data.

It's similar to Napster, except that with Napster, files went across Napster-owned servers (that's how the media industry got them). In most peer-to-peer networks, developers only produce the software. People actually connect directly to one another.

It's important to understand that peer-to-peer is a technology. There is nothing about it that is designed for "trafficking" in copyrighted content. That's just the aspect that gets all the media attention.

In the summer of 2002, the media industry sent a letter to Attorney General John Ashcroft (not an aide, not his department, the attorney general of the United States of America) demanding that the government devote more resources to finding and prosecuting people who traded copyrighted material online and to shut down peer-to-peer networks (remember that not all traffic on these networks consists of trading copyrighted content). Is this really how we want someone of this importance to be spending their time, resources, and your tax dollars?

On another front, the RIAA has been trying for a long time now to push through legislation that would tax all blank CDs to compensate its member companies for all the money they lose to "piracy." Perhaps we all missed a step, but when did having a disc burner and recording data to a disc (be it music, video, or Quicken files) make us responsible for any amount of lost revenue for the music industry?

The RIAA is even attempting to get legislation passed that would give them legal authority to hack peer-to-peer networks in search of illegally distributed copyrighted content. If found, they would have the power to conduct denial-of-service attacks and any other hack against the network, and against *you*, that is successful in preventing you from having or distributing files on your PC that *appear* to be copyrighted.

Earlier in the chapter I mentioned that the entertainment industry can't enforce copyright law. If this legislation passes, that will change. Not only would it give them legal authority to nose around the data on your PC through the Internet (without your knowledge or consent), it would put the burden of proof on you if, while they're there, they happen to do damage to your data. So what if the "Enter Sandman" file they deleted from your hard drive wasn't the Metallica song, but rather your Master's thesis on narcolepsy.

Between Tracks

To be fair, the entertainment industry insists that they would never use such a law in this manner. But the fact is that according to many quoted legal experts, the wording of the law makes just such an event perfectly legal. This law would give copyright holders the power to *enforce* the law. Thanks, but we already have folks who do that. They're called the police and they're a nonprofit organization.

Finally, we come to what many consider to be the most invasive measure yet. Senator Fritz Hollings (South Carolina), someone to whom Hollywood gives generous campaign contributions, has introduced a bill called the "Consumer Broadband and Digital Television Promotion Act."

It's a swell name, I'll give it that. But the legislation is designed to require hard-coded copy-protection measures to be included in *any and every* electronic device capable of storing or using digital content. This potentially covers everything from hard disk drives, to recordable disc drives to televisions to calculators. What this does to promote broadband and television on the behalf of consumers I have no idea.

It is very possible that in the next few years the only data we can copy from one electronic device to another is data that the content provider says we can copy. If this should come to pass, the only thing your recordable disc drive is going to be good for is making data backups (as long as it's data that you own and have not installed from a copyrighted source).

What's Next?

The amazing thing about the entire mess that the entertainment industry has made of copyright law is that their efforts are fruitless. At best they are attempting to criminalize millions of their own customers. At worst they've wasted millions of dollars researching and developing ways of "protecting" content that a 14-year-old kid on the other side of the world spends a day and a half figuring out how to break.

No one is saying that we should condone people downloading thousands of songs, movies, written work, etc. Certainly we should endeavor to protect the rights of copyright holders. But that doesn't mean it's right to adopt legislation that makes the accused guilty until proven innocent.

In a digital age there may be no way to adequately protect both consumer Fair Use rights and those of copyright holders. Odds are someone will get the short end of the stick. But do you believe you should have to prove to anyone that you use your CD-RW drive legally? Shouldn't it be the other way around?

The Least You Need to Know

◆ Copyright law is important and necessary to protect the rights of those who create original content.

◆ Fair Use does dictate that it is legal for you to make copies of copyrighted content for your personal use. It does not, however, give you the legal right to do so.

◆ The RIAA, MPAA, and other content publishers are lobbying heavily in the courts and in Washington for complete control of digital content and its distribution. This could severely affect what you can and cannot do with storage devices like your recordable disc drive.

Part 2

Quick and Painless: Duplicating CDs and DVDs

The fun begins in Part 2. What follows are chapters that tell you how to easily duplicate both audio and data discs so you'll never have to worry about losing or damaging an original disc again. Keep a spare copy of your favorite audio CD in your car and leave the original at home! Or make copies of your newest software so that you don't risk damaging the original from everyday use. The chapters in this part guide you through the disc copying process using both Easy CD Creator and Nero Burning ROM.

Easy Copying with Easy CD Creator

In This Chapter

- ◆ What you can and cannot copy with Easy CD Creator's CD Copier

- ◆ Copying disc to disc!

- ◆ Using a single recordable drive for copying CDs

- ◆ Advanced options that can help fine-tune the copying process

One of the simplest Easy CD Creator Platinum programs to use is also the one most record executives would rather you didn't have: CD Copier.

If all you want to do is make a straight copy of a disc, why go through the hassle of creating an audio or data disc? When making copies you don't have to create a disc layout, and you don't have to worry about editing audio tracks or using special effects such as fade in, fade out, or cross-fade. Indeed, making a copy is much simpler. To sum it up in just a few words: launch Easy CD Copier, insert the CD you want to copy and the blank recordable disc into the correct drives, and click OK—then you're on your way.

So why devote a chapter to such a simple process? Well, there are a few twists to this process, and there are some tips I will show you that can make the job easier. However, it really is a simple matter to make a copy of almost any disc that isn't shielded by some form of copy-protection, or unless your particular recordable drive has some problems with the blank media you have purchased.

Copying a Disc

Using CD Copier is an exercise in simplicity. To start up the CD Copier, click Start, All Programs, Roxio Easy CD Creator 5, Project Selector (or double-click the Easy CD Creator icon on your desktop). This brings up the menu shown in Figure 4.1.

Figure 4.1

The Project Selector gives you access to all of Easy CD Creator's programs.

From this menu, briefly hover your mouse pointer over the CD Copier button and then click the second CD Copier button that appears in the middle of the window. If this is your first use of CD Copier, a warning dialog box pops up on the screen, essentially reminding you to use the program responsibly. To keep it from popping up every time you use CD Copier, put a check in the Don't Show This Again check box and click OK. From there CD Copier launches and it's time to start copying CDs!

Cross Reference

For more information on the technologies used to prevent disc copying, see Chapter 3. To learn about the various disc formats and mediums you may have to use to copy a disc, see Chapters 1 and 2.

Prepping for the CD-Copying Process

When used in conjunction with a second disc drive, the easy task of copying a CD gets even easier. After all, with two drives, you can just put the disc you want to copy (your source) into your regular CD-ROM or DVD-ROM drive and insert the blank recordable media (the target) into your recordable drive (CD-RW, DVD-RW, or DVD+RW). The only thing you have to be extremely careful about is matching the blank disc media you're using to the format of the source. Making this match requires you to take into consideration two factors:

♦ The type of media: CD or DVD

♦ The capacity of that media. Remember from Chapter 2 that commercial DVD media often holds much more data than a -R/RW or +R/RW disc can. Additionally, as I noted in Chapter 1, compact disc media often features variable recording capacity, the most common being 74 minutes and 80 minutes. If you try to copy an 80-minute disc (that's full) to a 74-minute blank, you'll have problems.

Once you're sure you have the media you need, you need to configure CD Copier for copying with two drives, or just one. You do this through the main interface window that appears when you launch the program (see Figure 4.2).

Source disc drive

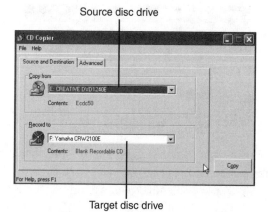

Figure 4.2

Insert two discs and click Copy. The CD Copier program is much simpler than other programs in this suite.

Target disc drive

Notice in this figure that there are sections for two discs: Copy From and Record To. If, as in this example, you have a ROM (use as Copy From) and an RW (use as Record To) drive, you need to make sure that you use both scroll boxes to select the appropriate drive.

If you only have a single RW drive, the copy process will involve a couple extra steps, the first of which is to make sure both the Copy From and Record To scroll boxes are set to use your single recordable drive. The other difference we'll mention in the next section.

Between Tracks

CD Copier will not let you select a nonrecordable drive as the Record To device.

Now, insert each disc, as appropriate, into your disc drives (if you only have one drive, insert the source disc). When you do this, give CD Copier a few seconds for your drives to spin up and for it to detect the newly inserted disc(s). When it does, you should see a screen similar to the one shown in Figure 4.2.

When choosing disc formats for each drive, keep in mind that you can mix and match between formats. You can copy a CD-ROM to a DVD+R/RW or -R/RW disc. Likewise, you can copy a DVD (so long as it contains less data than the target disc) to a CD-R/RW. Remember, though, you must also have the necessary drives to perform this operation. If your source drive is a CD-ROM you can't use it to copy a DVD to a disc in your DVD+R/RW or -R/RW drive. You can however use your DVD recorder as both the source and target drive.

When you have the discs inserted in the correct drives, and have ensured that the Copy From and Copy To drives have been selected correctly, the program tests the drive that holds the disc to be copied (see Figure 4.3).

Figure 4.3

Because no two drives are equal, CD Copier likes to test yours to see what it can and can't do.

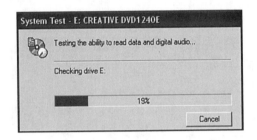

CD Copier only performs this test once, so it can be sure that the drive can support audio extraction and data copying at the rate necessary to write the disc. This happens whenever you use one of the Easy CD Creator 5 Platinum programs for the first time, or after you add and use a new disc drive. After the initial test, the program stores the results so it won't happen again.

> **Between Tracks**
>
> If the Copy button is grayed out, it's because the program has determined that there is either no source or target disc in the designated drive, or that the target disc is not recordable. The reasons for the latter could be that it's a bad disc, a nonrecordable disc (R/RW), or that it's a recordable disc to which information has already been recorded.

Start Copying

As you've probably noted from Figure 4.2, the disc we're copying in this example is the Easy CD Creator program disc. Making backup copies of your important software discs protects you if the original becomes corrupted or otherwise unusable (you will still have a copy from which to work). Actually, once you've made a backup copy, it's best to use the copy for primary use and keep the original protected from repeated use.

Once you and the media are ready to go, give the Copy button a click. After you do, another program window appears, called the Record CD Progress (see Figure 4.4).

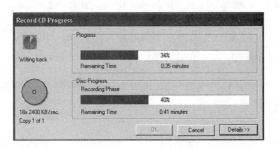

Figure 4.4

You can follow the progress as the CD is written.

Over the course of burning a data disc, it goes through several steps. These steps include the following:

1. **Prepare Data.** During this phase, the program examines the disc that will be copied.

2. **Writing Table of Contents.** Because the information on a disc starts at the center and is written from there toward the outer portion of the disc, the table of contents is the first thing that must be written after CD Copier prepares the data.

3. **Writing Track.** In this phase, CD Copier begins copying the actual data off the source disc and writing it to the target. Because the example shown here is a data CD, only one large track is written. That track, however, contains dozens of files and folders.

4. **Closing CD.** Once the data copy process is complete, CD Copier must close the disc. Basically, this means it is setting the data so that it can be read in other disc drives and players.

As the disc is written, you can use the Record CD Progress window to glean other information on its progress. On the left are two icons. The upper one lists the current stage in the burn process. The other is a visual depiction of the copy's progress (with only one track to copy, the disc pictured remains shaded until the copy is complete). On the left of the dialog box are two progress indicators. The upper one indicates the time to completion for the current stage in the burn, while the other indicates the time remaining until the burn is complete.

You can also get more detailed information on the recording process by clicking the Details button. Clicking the Details button opens up some extra information about the disc-writing process. This information includes a monitor that keeps track of your disc drive's buffer, how much data remains to be written, and the methodology being used to write to the disc. The method used to write a disc is typically disc-at-once, session-at-once, or track-at-once. I describe all three of these methods in Appendix C. The buffer indicator is very important for drives that lack BurnProof technology (refer to Chapter 1). It lets you know if you're likely to experience a buffer underrun (if it hits a very low number or bottoms out at 0 percent, expect an error message to appear).

You can get a good look at the information the Details button reveals in the next section.

Between Tracks

When copying a disc using just one recordable drive, this process works a little differently. Instead of copying directly from disc to disc, CD Copier copies the source disc to a temporary file on your hard disk drive. When it's done, it then prompts you to replace the source CD with a blank recordable one. Once CD Copier determines that your blank is good, it records that temporary file to the disc.

Before you attempt to make a single-drive disc copy, keep in mind the following:

◆ Make sure enough space is available on the hard disk! A full CD-ROM can hold up to 650MB of data, 700MB if it was written on an 80-minute blank. A recordable DVD holds up to 4.7GB (4,700 MB, or more than seven CDs).

◆ Keep your hard disk in good shape. Windows has a variety of system tools you can use to keep things running smoothly. If you're unfamiliar with them, you should seek out a Windows-specific book tailored to your version (9x/Me, 2000/XP). The main program to look for is Disk Defragmenter. Getting to this utility varies based on the operating system, but generally look in your Start menu under All Programs, Accessories, System Tools.

Crossing the Finish Line

As you can see, this is hardly a time-consuming process (unless you're recording at 4× or slower, of course). Figure 4.5 shows the dialog box that appears when CD Copier has successfully finished copying a CD. It's not particularly exciting, but it does let you know that the process was completed successfully.

Cross Reference

If you are having problems, such as a buffer underrun, that prevent this process from successfully completing, consult Chapter 21 for some troubleshooting tips.

From here you can select the CD Label Creator button at the bottom if you want to make a label for the CD and create inserts for the jewel case. Chapter 16 can give you more information on that creative endeavor. Or if you want to do that at a later time, just click the Close button to dismiss the Record CD Progress dialog box and return to the main CD Copier screen.

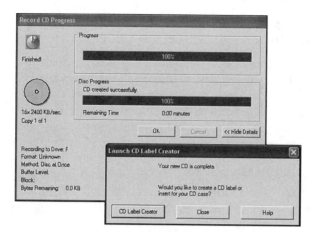

Figure 4.5

CD Copier tells you when the CD has been successfully copied. Notice the dialog box in the background indicating that one out of one tracks were successfully copied.

Using Advanced Copying Features

Now that we've made a simple copy, let's look at the advanced features you can use to control the copying process a little more precisely. For the most part, you can use the procedures we've just discussed to make all your copies. However, if you plan to make several copies and want to speed up the process, you might want to use the advanced features of CD Copier to change the speed at which the copying is performed.

Figure 4.6 shows the CD Copier program with the Advanced tab selected. Since this tab doesn't have a ton of features to choose from, you might want to consider trying each one, just to see what works best for you.

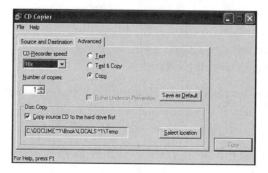

Figure 4.6

The Advanced tab of CD Copier enables you to more precisely control the copying process.

The advanced features include the following:

♦ **CD-Recorder Speed.** If your disc drive can write at a faster rate, you can select it here. CD Copier will display only speeds at which your drive is capable of performing. Thus, you might see higher speeds on one computer versus another one.

CAUTION

Don't Get Burned _____

If you find that CD Copier is not finishing successfully, and you're recording to a CD-R/RW and attempting to record at your disc drive's maximum speed, it might be that the disc media you are using doesn't work well at that speed. I've had trouble recording at 12x with media that specifically said it was rated for 12x speed. It just goes to show you that you can't always trust the manufacturer to give you all the facts. If this happens, try dropping the recording speed down from the maximum available (depending on the speed of your drive, you may have to resort to 1x, but any recent drive should have no troubles recording at 8x). If it doesn't work at a significantly lower speed, then you have some other problems. If it does work at that speed, try increasing the speed a notch at a time with future copies until you find out how well that particular brand of media works with your drive.

- ◆ **Number of Copies.** If you want to make more than one copy of the disc, select the number of copies here.

- ◆ **Copy Source CD to the Hard Drive First.** Rather than copying directly from one disc to another, this method first copies the source disc to a file on your hard drive. This file is then used to record to the target disc. This option is a good one to use if you are making more than one copy of the CD or are having problems with buffer-underruns. Click the Select Location button if you want to select a new temporary location on your hard disk to store this file.

- ◆ **Test.** Use this option if you want to test whether or not the disc can be successfully written. When you select this option, CD Copier performs the copy process, but no data is actually copied to the blank disc. Use this option if you are having problems copying a disc or if you have just installed a new drive and want to ensure it is in working order.

- ◆ **Test & Copy.** Similar to the preceding option, this one enables you to perform the test first, and then, if the test is successful, automatically begin burning the disc.

- ◆ **Copy.** This is the default. Just go ahead and make the copy without any of that sissy testing stuff!

- ◆ **Buffer Underrun Prevention.** If your disc recorder supports buffer underrun protection, make sure to put a check in this box. (It is disabled if your drive does not support this disc-saving feature.)

♦ **Save as Default.** If you make changes to these options and want to make your changes the new default settings for when the program is started up again, click this button.

As you can see, there aren't many options to worry about, and for the most part they are self-explanatory.

The Least You Need to Know

♦ Use CD Copier, not Easy CD Creator, when you want to make a copy of a single disc.

♦ You don't have to have two drives in your computer to use CD Copier. You can use your recordable disc drive as both the source and destination discs.

♦ Use the advanced options to copy the disc to your hard disk when making multiple copies or having troubles with buffer underruns. This speeds up the copying process and makes it more reliable.

♦ Some discs simply cannot be copied. These are usually PC software applications and games, but some newer audio CDs also employ various protection schemes.

The Magical Nero Disc Copy Wizard

In This Chapter

◆ How to copy a CD with Nero

◆ Configuring Nero's basic recording options

◆ Getting around copy-protection schemes when making backup discs

◆ How to copy a DDCD or DVD with Nero

Copying a disc using Nero Burning ROM 5.x is about as easy as it gets. There's a few more extra steps than copying a disc with Easy CD Creator, but then Easy CD Creator can't help you out if you try to make a backup of a disc made to thwart most conventional disc-copy methods.

Starting Nero Burning ROM

To get things kicked off, open Nero Burning ROM. If the Nero Wizard opens up, close it. Choose File, New from the Nero window. This brings up the New Compilation window. Get comfy, this is where you'll spend a lot of your disc recording time when using Nero.

There are three types of discs you can copy using Nero:

♦ **CDs.** These include CD-Rs and CD-RWs.

♦ **DDCDs.** These are Double Density Compact Discs, which hold twice the data of a typical compact disc.

♦ **DVDs.** These include both -R/RW and +R/RW discs.

When you open a new compilation, you'll see a window like the one shown in Figure 5.1. Use the scroll box on the top left corner of the window to choose your disc type.

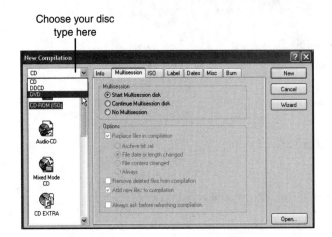

Figure 5.1

Nero Burning Rom allows you to copy three types of discs.

The remaining sections in this chapter cover making disc copies with each type of disc.

Copying a CD

To copy a compact disc, choose CD from the scroll box shown in Figure 5.1. When you select this option, the list of icons on the left of the window changes. These icons allow you to choose what type of recording you want to make. Choose CD-Copy. When you do, the display to the right of these icons changes to one geared toward copying a compact disc (see Figure 5.2).

There are four tabs available that allow you to configure the disc copy process:

♦ **Image.** This tab gives you control over where to put a disc image (if you choose to have Nero create one using the Copy Options tab) on your hard drive. It's best to choose an empty folder on your fastest hard disk. If you're not sure, click the Test All Drive Speeds button.

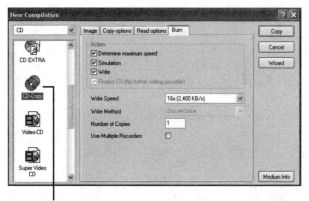

Figure 5.2

Use the CD-Copy icon when copying a compact disc in Nero.

Click to select Nero's copy options

♦ **Copy Options.** This tab allows you to choose the disc drive for your source disc and its top read speed (best to leave the latter at the default setting). Use the On The Fly check box to tell Nero whether or not to use a disc image to record to the target.

♦ **Read Options.** This is by far the most complex of the four tabs (see Figure 5.3). If you're dealing with a disc designed interfere with typical disc-copy routines, this tab gives you the best chance of getting around it.

Between Tracks

For more information on disc images, see Chapter 6.

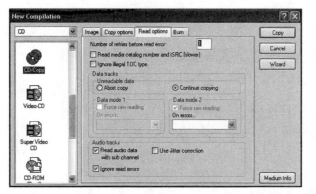

Figure 5.3

If Nero has a chance to bust through a copy-protected disc when you want to make a backup, the Read options tab is the place to try.

First, enable the check boxes Ignore Illegal TOC Type and Read Media Catalog Number. In the Unreadable Data section, choose the Continue Copying radio button. If necessary, Nero chooses from one of the Data Mode types (1 or 2). Use the On Errors scroll box to select Write Uncorrected. Finally, keep all three of the check boxes selected in the Audio Tracks section.

◆ **Burn.** Nero defaults to this tab when you click the CD-Copy icon. Nero correctly sets most of the options in this tab by default. However, if you want to change the selected disc recorder or recording speed you can. If you don't want Nero to perform a test recording before actually writing the disc, disable the Simulation check box. If you only want to perform a test, disable the Write check box.

Between Tracks

Most early disc protection schemes centered around manipulating how data can be read from a disc, as opposed to implementing true copy protection technology. The main reason, I suspect, that the features included in Nero aren't a violation of the Digital Millennium Copyright Act is because they don't appear to break actual copy-protection schemes. Though I'm sure the Recording Industry Association of America would beg to differ. For more information on the DMCA, Copyright, and Fair Use, see Chapter 3.

Once you've got your options set (most of the time, all the defaults will suffice), click the Copy button. This opens the Read CD dialog box, initiating the copy process. Nero first processes the source disc (writing it to the hard drive if you chose to disable the On The Fly check box). If the Determine Maximum Speed or Simulation check boxes are selected, Nero then performs both of these tests. Sooner or later though, it begins copying your disc (see Figure 5.4).

Nero's log of the recording process.
You can save or print this later if you want.

Figure 5.4

Nero's log of the recording process. You can save or print this later, if you want.

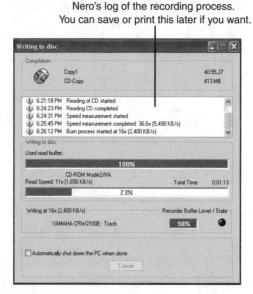

If you want to leave the burn unattended, you can use the Automatically Shut Down PC When Done check box to, big surprise, shut down your PC automatically when the copy is complete.

Assuming you have not enabled this check box, when the burn is complete a dialog box, like the one shown in Figure 5.5, appears.

Figure 5.5

If all goes well, this is the dialog box you'll see when your burn is complete.

Click OK to close this dialog box. This returns you to the CD Recording window. You'll probably notice that Nero has kept a log of all the steps in the copy process. If the burn failed, you can Save or Print this log to help you troubleshoot the problem. Assuming the burn went as planned, click Discard to delete the log.

Copying DVDs and DDCDs

In terms of process, copying a DVD or DDCD is no different than making a compact disc copy. The exception is that your options are a bit more restricted. There is no Read options tab for breaking through copy-protection schemes when making your backup. There's a good reason for this, for both disc types.

If you're copying a DDCD, it's not likely to be copy-protected. Virtually all copy-protected discs are commercial in nature. This isn't exactly a big consumer market at this point so you shouldn't expect to see any commercially produced DDCD software applications released in the near future.

The same holds true for a DVD. While there is the occasional application released as a DVD, most DVDs that you're likely to make a copy of are other recordable and rewritable DVD discs. True, you might *want* to copy a DVD movie, but virtually all DVDs use a copy-protection scheme called Content Scrambling System (CSS), so don't expect to accomplish this feat very easily. Because of the Digital Millennium Copyright Act (DMCA), not only is it illegal to sell tools that break this scheme, it's illegal to break it period.

> **Cross Reference**
>
> For more information on copy protection schemes, and copyright legislation like the DMCA, see Chapter 3.

Find that hard to believe? Just ask the unfortunate university professors about the nightmares they went through when they tried to release the DeCSS utility as a proof of concept (i.e., they weren't selling it). This "Copyright Protection" Act makes the circumvention of this technology illegal, regardless of the use for which it is intended. Land of the free, indeed.

The Least You Need to Know

◆ If you have problems copying discs with Nero, use a slower write speed or create a disc image instead of copying directly from one disc to another.

◆ The Read options tab in Nero allows you to get past basic copy-protection schemes for the purposes of making backup copies of your CDs.

◆ When copying DDCDs or DVDs, you cannot use Nero's copy-protection circumvention tools.

Part  PC Life Insurance: The Zen of Making Data Discs

Are you prepared to lose all your e-mail, Internet favorites, Quicken, or MS Money records to a hard drive failure or other PC catastrophe? Keeping your data safe by burning it to a CD or DVD is one of the most important uses you can come up with for your disc recorder. Chapter 6 provides you with a basic understanding of terms and techniques involved in burning a data disc. Chapters 7 and 8 show you how to use Easy CD Creator and Nero Burning ROM respectively to record a data disc.

Chapter 6

Protecting Your Precious 1s and 0s

In This Chapter

♦ Find out why backing up your data is the most important thing you can do with your disc recorder

♦ Learn about the various file system formats used to write data on a CD, and determine which are important to you

♦ Check out how packet writing works, and see how the Mount Rainier format promises to change how you write data to a disc

♦ Find out when you should create a disc image before you write data to a disc

When it comes to recording information to an optical disc like a CD or DVD, most of the attention is paid to the concept of making music or video discs. Certainly, the results of a successfully created music or video disc can provide much more entertainment value than archiving data.

On the other side of the spectrum, however, is the fact that for home usage one of the most important aspects of owning a disc recorder is the ability to back up data.

Why Make a Data CD?

If you're like me, you probably don't spend much time worrying about backing up the data on your PC. If so, that's unfortunate, because you probably have a lot to lose.

Think about it. Perhaps you take work home at night, or maybe you work from home full-time, using your PC. What happens in the event of a hard disk failure, power surge, or some other freak of nature? What happens if a hacker makes his or her way into your computer's sensitive files and erases, corrupts, or steals them?

It's not just business either. What if one of these events occurred while you were just hours away from finishing a computer role playing game that took you 50 hours to complete. Good-bye save game files!

Do you students want to know what it's like to lose a 20-page term paper the day before it's due? Do you want to risk losing many years of financial records you had so carefully recorded in Quicken or Microsoft Money?

If you don't have backups of your data, you're constantly at risk of losing data that took you hours, months, and even years to compile!

Between Tracks

Even if you have no interest in backing up your personal data, you should consider using recordable discs to store information that takes up a lot of space on your hard drive, but that you don't use very often. Do you have a lot of video, picture, or audio files that you don't need on a regular basis? Recordable discs, DVDs in particular, are a wonderful medium for keeping data close at hand but off your hard drive's limited real estate.

Fortunately, the minute you buy a CD or DVD recorder, you instantly have access to the best form of backup tool around. These drives are easy to use to store data files and the process of writing that data to disc is generally much less error prone than for CD audio or video CDs and DVDs.

Actually, recording data to a CD is covered in Chapters 7 and 8. However, many of the basic concepts for recording data to a CD are true regardless of what program you use. That information is what we cover in this chapter.

Data Disc File Systems

No matter what type of disc you want to create, be it a music, video disc, or a data backup, the disc media must be encoded with what is called a file system. A file system is basically a standard by which all those 1s and 0s that comprise your precious data are written to a disk (or disc). Windows XP, for example, supports a couple of file systems, called NTFS and FAT32. When you launch a program like Microsoft Word, the type of file system determines how Windows finds Word's application files. Optical discs like CDs and DVDs don't use a conventional file system like NTFS or FAT32. Instead, they have their own format standards. These include the following:

♦ **ISO 9660.** This is a standard developed by the International Organization for Standardization (how that equates to ISO, I have no idea). This format is the quintessential data CD used with Windows PCs. When you make a data disc using Easy CD Creator or Nero Burning ROM, this is the format you'll most likely use. The format has a couple of flavors: 8.3 and Joliet. 8.3 refers to the filename conventions used in DOS and Windows 3.x PCs (file names were limited to eight characters). Joliet, the format you'll most likely use, supports long file names and can be read on any PC running Windows 95 or later.

⚠ CAUTION   Don't Get Burned _____

Remember, that although any Windows PC can recognize the ISO 9660 file format, that doesn't mean the drive can read the disc. A DVD+RW disc, for example, cannot be read in a CD-ROM drive no matter what format you use. Also, many older CD-ROM drives won't recognize a CD-RW disc. Be sure to keep in mind the PCs you might need to use the disc in before you settle on a type of media and recording format!

♦ **Bootable CDs.** In terms of file format, these discs are no different than an ISO 9660 CD. However, these discs have special operating system files included on them that allow you to boot your computer from the disc. Windows XP, for example, ships on a bootable CD. Unless you're making an emergency disc in case your PC fails to boot, you probably won't need to make a bootable CD.

♦ **HFS.** Short for Hierarchical File System, this is the format used to store files on Macintosh computers. There is also a revised format called Sequoia or HFS+. More than likely, this is not a format with which you need concern yourself.

💡 Between Tracks _____

Unless you plan to port your data between PC and Apple computers you should never need to create hybrid discs. Usually the only time this format comes into play is for software developers that put out multiplatform products.

◆ **Hybrid.** In a hybrid CD, the same data is written to the disc twice. One instance is recorded using the ISO 9660 format, while the other in HFS. This makes the disc usable in both PCs and Apple computers, though having to write the same information twice limits how much you can store on the disc.

◆ **UDF.** Also called the Universal Data Format, UDF is the primary file system used to write all DVDs. It was intended to be a replacement for ISO 9660, but has only achieved popularity in the CD-R and CD-RW mediums as a packet writing format (see the following "Packet Writing" section).

Between Tracks _____

There are also CDs that hold both audio and data. We don't address the process of making these discs in this book. However, information about the two types of discs recorded in this format can be found in Appendix C.

In the case of making generic data discs for use in Windows PCs, the only formats you should have to worry about are ISO 9660 and UDF. If you're using the main Easy CD Creator or Nero Burning ROM programs, you'll use ISO 9660. If you're using the packet writing programs InCD (included with Nero) or DirectCD (included with Easy CD Creator), those programs will format your discs for you using a derivative of UDF. So with that said, let's dig into packet writing!

Packet Writing

When you write a data disc using the main Easy CD Creator or Nero Burning ROM programs, you have to create a kind of "to-do" list before you start recording. In other words you have to create a list in your recording software that lets it know exactly what files and folders you want recorded, before you can actually begin the recording process. You can't just type away on a Word document, click the Save As button and choose your disc recorder as the target.

Ever since the first CD-R drives appeared on the market, users have wanted the ability to treat their recordable discs like a hard disk. Just save from whatever application you're using and forget it.

Fortunately, as the years have gone by, methods for accomplishing this have emerged. The process of writing an optical disc like you would any storage device on your PC is called packet writing. It gets its name from the fact that data is read and written from a drive in bunches, called packets. This is much different from writing data to a CD in a conventional way, which involves recording all the data as a single, long stream, rather than in bits and pieces.

As in all things related to computers there are various different packet writing formats, and they don't all play nice together. In this section we focus on three of them (there are others):

- **DirectCD.** This is the packet writing format used in Easy CD Creator. It's based on the UDF file system discussed in the previous section, which means that for a PC to read the disc it must have DirectCD or a compatible UDF reader installed. Discs using DirectCD must be formatted as such before you can write to them. This can be a time-consuming process.

Arcane CD Speak

A UDF Reader is a software utility that allows your PC to read discs formatted using the UDF file system.

- **InCD.** This is Nero's answer to DirectCD. Compared to DirectCD, InCD is generally a little bit more stable and reliable. It cannot, however, write to recordable (R) discs, meaning you must use RW discs if writing with InCD. Like DirectCD, you must pre-format the disc before you can write to it using InCD.

Between Tracks

While DirectCD does support writing to recordable (R) discs, that's not necessarily a great thing. Packet writing is supposed to be like using your disc as a hard drive. Well, if you're using a hard drive, you want to be able to write to it, change the contents around, rename contents, and remove contents. You can't do that with an R disc, be it CD or DVD.

When you "change" an R disc's contents with DirectCD, the program is actually writing a new copy of that data. The old data is still stored on the disc and cannot be removed.

In essence, this means the fact that InCD only supports RW discs is not really a shortcoming after all (excepting that RW discs are a smidge more expensive than their R counterparts).

- **Mount Rainier.** Like InCD and DirectCD, Mount Rainier does use the UDF file system. However it's supported in both the recording drive and the PC operating system (Windows, for our purposes), rather than in separate software like Nero. Mount Rainier drives don't require RW discs to be formatted before writing, and defect management is built into the drive. If there is a problem writing to a specific part of the disc, Mount Rainier drives can automatically seek out the next best spot to write, rather than produce an error. Best of all, with Mount Rainier drives data can be written as a background process. This means you can go on with whatever PC chores you were doing while the disc is written, instead of having to sit there like a rock until the process is complete.

Clearly, Mount Rainier is the top dog. While still not widely supported at the time of this writing, Mount Rainier is destined to be the packet writing format that ends the competition. It is already widely available in many CD-RW drives and has begun to emerge in rewritable DVD drives as of late 2002.

General Recording Strategies

No matter what type of disc you intend to record, there are usually two strategies you can employ when writing data with whatever authoring software you have. These are:

♦ Create an image of the recording on your hard disk

♦ Record the data directly to the disc

Both have their advantages and disadvantages. If you have a reliable recording drive (with buffer-underrun protection), a good hard drive, and a fast computer, you should have no troubles recording data directly to a disc. However, if any of the above are not true, you might be better off opting to create a disc image.

Between Tracks

Remember that the strategies I discuss in this section apply only to standard methods of writing to a disc, like ISO 9660. These strategies do not apply to packet writing, which handles the process very differently.

Cross Reference

If you're looking for information on sessions or disc writing methods like Track-at-Once (TAO) and Disc-at-Once (DAO), refer to Appendix C.

When a program prepares to write data to a disc, it must first convert that data from the file system format used on the source (most likely, your hard disk), to the format used for the CD (ISO 9660, for example). This process happens quickly, but not always quickly enough for your disc recorder. Because disc data must be written in a flowing "stream" of information, an interruption in that flow can cause the burn to fail.

If you instruct your recording program (Easy CD Creator, for example) to first create a disc image, it will take all the data meant to go on the CD, convert it to the format it will use when stored on a disc, and store it all in a single *image* file. Once that image file is complete, it can be recorded to a disc without your PC having to convert that data on the fly. Especially for slower PCs or recording drives without buffer underrun protection, this can make the whole process much more reliable.

Additionally, if you intend to make multiple copies of a disc layout, it's much faster to record it all to an image file and create multiple discs from that than it is to keep reformatting the same data for each copy you intend to make.

The Least You Need to Know

- ◆ Using your disc recorder as a data backup device may be the most important task you perform.

- ◆ Like your hard drive, data recorded to optical discs must conform to a standard file system that dictates how that information is stored or retrieved.

- ◆ Mount Rainier is destined to become the industry standard packet writing format for optical discs.

- ◆ Create an image file before recording data to a disc if you want a more reliable burn or if you intend to make multiple copies of the same disc.

Easy CD Creator: Says What It Does and Does What It Says

In This Chapter

- ◆ Creating and editing a data CD layout
- ◆ Burning a data CD with Easy CD Creator
- ◆ Making a CD image file and using it to burn multiple CDs
- ◆ Using DirectCD to make your disc an optical hard drive
- ◆ Formatting a DirectCD disc

There is, as they say, more than one way to skin a cat—or so I'm told. Obviously, this is not something I've confirmed. I'd never do such a thing, especially because I have nosy neighbors and no desire to explain myself to the ASPCA. There is, however, also more than one way to create a data disc using Roxio Easy CD Creator software. That's what this chapter discusses.

Starting Roxio Project Selector

To get started you need to open the Roxio Project Selector through the Easy CD Creator folder found in the Start menu. Open the Roxio Project Selector and hover your mouse pointer over the Make A Data CD button (see Figure 7.1).

Figure 7.1

When making a data disc you need to select from three of Easy CD Creator's applications.

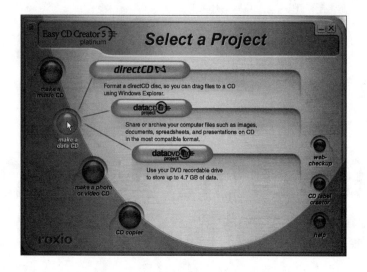

Assuming you've upgraded to at least Easy CD Creator 5.1 (which adds support for DVD), you'll see three options at your disposal:

- DataCD Project
- DataDVD Project
- DirectCD

While this chapter does examine all three of the methods listed here, keep in mind that outside of the media used, the processes used to record a Data DVD and a Data CD are the same.

Creating a DataCD or DataDVD Project

If you've already skipped ahead and learned about creating an audio CD using Easy CD Creator, then I have some good news for you. It's not a whole lot different creating a data disc. You audiophiles may be wondering why you'd want to take time out of your day to make a data CD when you've found the inspiration to create a "Top 10 Songs Based on Superheroes" audio disc. Well, remember that your

Between Tracks

Version 5.0 of ECDC doesn't have the option for burning a Data DVD. It does, however, have one for the Take Two backup software. If this is the case for you, you should immediately download the most recent point release of ECDC. For more information on bringing Easy CD Creator up to date, see Appendix A.

Cross Reference

If all you want to do is make a copy of an entire CD, use Roxio's Easy CD Copier, see Chapter 4.

computer isn't infallible and accidents do happen. If you value what's on your computer, backing up your key folders and files to a data disc is the surest protection you can have. After all, no power surge or hacker is going to affect a small disc sitting on a CD rack next to your PC.

The first step is to choose the type of project you want to create from the Project Selector window, shown earlier in Figure 7.1. Because the interface is the same whether you choose to create a CD or DVD, the examples used in images for this chapter are based on creating a data CD (see Figure 7.2).

Use the scroll box and buttons to locate sources, files, and folders

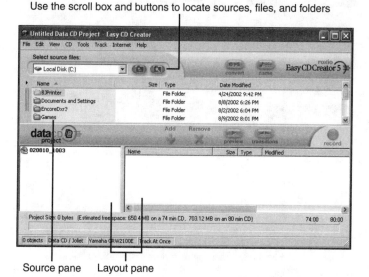

Source pane   Layout pane

Figure 7.2

Whether you choose DataCD or DataDVD from the Project Selector, Easy CD Creator brings you to this screen.

When you launch a new data disc session from the Project Selector, this window immediately appears with a new project already open. However, should you find yourself wanting to start from scratch, you can click File, New CD Project, Data CD. Actually, you can use this method to start a new project of any type, be it one containing audio, data, or both.

The Data CD Project window is broken down into two main pieces. The pane that runs across the top of the window is called the Source pane. The pane on the lower half of the window is called the Layout pane and is divided into two sections. The left-hand section shows a "tree" of the data folders that you plan to burn. The right side shows the contents (files and subfolders) of whichever folder is selected on the tree.

Cross Reference

For more information on creating discs with both audio and video content, see Appendix C.

Creating a Data CD Layout

Creating a data disc layout is a simple matter of finding the information you want recorded in the Source pane, and copying it to the Layout pane. You can select individual files, groups of files, or even entire folders. To copy this data to the Layout pane you need just select it in the Source pane and then drag it to the Layout pane (see Figure 7.3). (You can also select the data and click the Add button located between the two panes.)

Figure 7.3

Getting data to your disc layout is a simple matter of drag and drop or clicking the Add button.

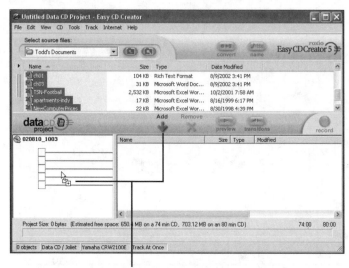

Drag and drop or click the Add button to add selected data to the source pane

When you add data to the disc layout you should notice that at the very bottom of the application window you can see indicators of how much space you've used up, based on the type of media you're recording to (see Figure 7.4). Whereas with audio CDs you needed to worry about how many minutes of recording time your tracks use up, when recording data discs you have to view capacity in terms of megabytes (MB) and, in the case of DVDs, gigabytes (GB). If you don't really understand what these terms imply, it's not a big deal. Just be wary of having more MB or GB of data than your recording media can handle (Easy CD Creator does let you know if that's the case).

Between Tracks _____

If you're accustomed to using My Computer or File Explorer, then finding data to record shouldn't be much of a challenge. However, on the off chance the Window in Figure 7.3 looks like Greek (or geek) to you, don't worry; it's not as bad as it looks. For example, let's say you want to back up all the documents in your My Documents folder.

The first thing you need to do is navigate to that folder using the options in the Select Source Files section above the Source pane. You can use the scroll box to move up to a higher folder level than the one currently selected (My Computer is the top-most level). You can also use the first button next to it to move up just one level at a time. If you're not sure of the location of the file or folder you're looking for, click the next button over. This one opens up the Windows Search engine.

To find the My Documents folder, use the scroll box to bump up to the My Computer level. The Source pane should then show your PC's storage devices and, depending on your Windows version, some extra "key" folders. If you use Windows XP you can go straight to your My Documents folder from here, by double-clicking it. Otherwise, you may need to get there from your hard disk drive. Double-click the icon for your hard drive (probably Local Disk [C:]), and then double-click on the My Documents folder.

From here it's just a matter of selecting the file or folders you want to drag to the Layout pane as shown previously, in Figure 7.3.

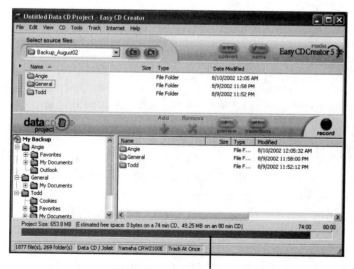

Figure 7.4

The layout for this data CD is too big for a 650MB CD, but it has room to spare on the CDs with the larger 700MB capacity.

This indicator measures available recording space based on how much data is in the Layout

You probably noticed in Figure 7.3 that Easy CD Creator gives your data CD a default name comprised of a series of numbers akin to a serial number. This is probably fine if you're John Nash (if you don't know this reference, do yourself a favor and watch *A Beautiful Mind*), but it leaves something to be desired for the rest of us. If you want to change this to something more descriptive, click the label to highlight it, pause for a second and click it again. The name should now be selected with a blue highlight with a cursor at the end. Just type in the disc's new name and press Enter when complete.

> **Between Tracks**
>
> Unlike creating an audio CD (which typically requires a CD-R disc for compatibility with home CD audio players), it doesn't matter much whether you want to use a recordable or rewritable disc (CD or DVD). However, if you do make a data DVD, keep in mind all the computers on which you may want to use it. DVD drives are still not standard on all PCs so if you want your data to be portable, CD may be a better choice for you.

When creating the layout, if you find that you need to remove files or folders, just select them and either press Delete on your keyboard, click the Remove button between the Source and Layout panes, or right-click your selection and click Remove From CD Project.

After you have your layout set, there's just one more step you should take before actually burning the disc. It's always a good idea to save your project to your hard disk, just in case something goes wrong or if you want to use the same layout again later. That way you can just load it back up as needed, using the Open CD Project option on the File menu. To save your project, click File, Save Project List. Saving and loading a project is no different than saving and loading any other type of document.

Starting the Recording Process

After your data CD layout is set and saved, it's time to start burning the CD. Put a blank recordable disc in your recordable drive, and then click the big red Record button located between the Source and Layout panes (you can also click File, Record CD). This opens up the Record CD Setup dialog box. To see all the options you have at your disposal, click the Options button. Figure 7.5 show the Record CD Setup window with all options shown. Notice that the Options button now reads Hide Options.

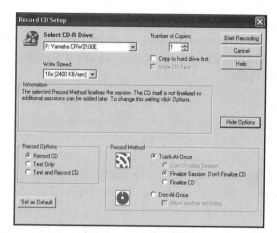

Figure 7.5

The Record CD Setup window gives you control over various aspects of burning a disc.

The options on this screen allow you to select:

♦ The target disc drive.

♦ The write speed of the drive. If you're having problems recording to disc successfully, try a slower speed.

♦ The number of copies to make.

♦ Whether to copy the disc to an image file on your hard disk first. Choosing this option can be more reliable when recording to drives that lack buffer underrun protection. It also makes the process faster if you are making more than one copy.

Between Tracks _____

Keep the following in mind before you record:

♦ If you're recording to a RW disc that needs to be erased, click the CD menu and choose Erase Disc. You can choose between a Quick and Full Erase. If you want to ensure the disc is "clean," take the 20 minutes or so it'll need to do a Full Erase.

♦ The Record button is grayed out unless you have inserted a recordable disc (with space available) into your recordable disc drive.

♦ If this is the first data CD you've created, Easy CD creator may run a data transfer rate test on your CD or hard disk drives to determine their capabilities. This should be a quick, error-free process that won't cause you any problems.

◆ Recording options. If you've recorded data CDs successfully before, choose Record CD. If you're unsure, choose Test and Record CD. If you're troubleshooting an existing problem and want to see if you've managed to beat it, just choose Test Only.

◆ The recording method. Choose between Track-At-Once or Disc-At-Once. If you choose Track-At-Once, you must also choose whether you want to finalize the session (you can still record more data to the disc later) or the disc (you can never record to the disc again, unless it's of the erasable RW variety). If you want to ensure compatibility across a variety of disc drives, choose to Finalize the CD (this option is implied if you choose Disc-At-Once recording).

Once you're ready, click Start Recording. The Record CD Progress display pops on the screen and the theatrics begin (see Figure 7.6). (To see the information in this box, click the Details button. Click the Hide Details button to hide the options.)

Figure 7.6

The Record CD Progress dialog box allows you to monitor Easy CD Creator's progress as it records your data disc.

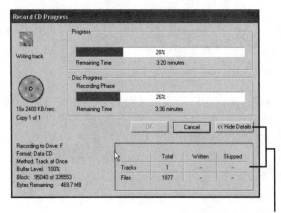

Click the Details button to show or hide the extended display information

The steps that are performed to create a data CD are as follows:

◆ File system generation

◆ Copying files

◆ Writing track

◆ Closing session (or closing CD)

After the program finishes creating the necessary data structures on the CD, it then starts copying files from your hard disk to a temporary location. Next, it writes a single track out to the CD-RW drive. If you chose to finalize the session, but leave the CD open, you'll see Closing Session as a step in the CD creation process. If you selected to close the CD, you'll see Closing CD in the CD Creation Process dialog box.

If you leave the disc open, you can keep adding sessions to it until you run out of space on the disc. Even if you leave the disc open, you can use the disc in your disc recorder or in most CD and DVD-ROM drives—just as long as the *session* itself is closed.

Once complete, a screen like the one shown in Figure 7.7 confirms your earth-shattering success!

Figure 7.7

If all goes as it should, you should see this dialog box once your disc recording is complete.

From this screen you can either click Close to return to Easy CD Creator or click CD Label Creator to create a label based on your new disc's contents. (If you feel the need to click Help on this window then you do need help, just not the type ECDC can provide.) For more information on creating labels and inserts with Easy CD Creator, see Chapter 16.

Now that we've created a data disc from an Easy CD Creator layout, let's take a look at how ECDC lets you use your recorder like a hard drive.

Dial Direct with DirectCD

While creating a data disc by first creating a specific layout and then burning a batch of files and folders to disc is not a great challenge, that doesn't necessarily mean it's convenient. Wouldn't it be nice if you could just record to a disc like it were any other storage drive on your

Cross Reference

If problems occur during the creation process, then something has gone terribly wrong and the CD will most likely not be playable. Check out Chapter 21 for help and insight as to what may have gone wrong.

Don't Get Burned

Always check any disc you burn to make sure that it did record successfully. Just because Easy CD creator or Nero tells you that all went to plan doesn't always mean it did. Try reading and accessing the data on your disc before you assume that it's perfect!

PC? Easy CD Creator's packet-writing software, called DirectCD, allows you to do just that!

Packet writing, as I discussed in Chapter 6, enables small amounts of data to be written to a disc, instead of having to write a whole track of data. This takes up a little more space on the disc, but the convenience it provides to the user can make up for that.

Between Tracks

Another advantage of using the RW discs is that if a problem occurs during recording to the disc, you can always erase it and start over. With a CD-R disc, if the write fails for any reason, the disc is toast.

You can use both R and RW discs with DirectCD. But while it may appear that DirectCD enables you to update or modify data on both disc formats, that doesn't mean you can change or remove what was already written to an R disc. Where recordable drives can erase RW data that's no longer needed, remember that it cannot do the same with R discs. Instead, it simply marks any changed or deleted blocks of data as something to ignore and then writes new blocks of data instead. Of course, because the "deleted" material is technically still on the disc, you'll eventually run out of space.

Starting Up DirectCD

By default, when you install Easy CD Creator 5 Platinum, Easy CD Creator sets Windows to load DirectCD automatically whenever you turn on your computer. Just double-click the small disc icon in the Windows System Tray. However, should you need to bring up DirectCD manually, open the Project Selector, select Make A Data CD, and choose Direct CD. Either way, you'll be brought to the main DirectCD interface, as shown in Figure 7.8.

Figure 7.8

The DirectCD system tray icon gives you quick access to DirectCD options.

Before you can use DirectCD to write data to a disc, the disc has to be formatted to meet certain requirements. If the disc in your drive has not been set up when you launch DirectCD, you must tell DirectCD to format it for you. If you have already formatted the disc in your hard drive, you can simply start using it just as if it were a floppy or hard disk installed in your computer.

Formatting a Disc Before Its First Use

To format a disc to meet DirectCD standards, click the Format button in the middle of the Direct CD window. Figure 7.9 shows the Format dialog box that appears. There are a few options you must select here in order to proceed.

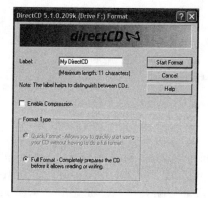

Figure 7.9

The Roxio Format CD dialog box allows you to set up a blank disc for use with DirectCD.

On the Format dialog box you configure the following options:

◆ **Label.** This option allows you to assign a name to the disc that your PC can use to identify it. You don't have to assign one, but it's not a bad idea to come up with something for this field.

◆ **Enable Compression.** If you format the disc to use compression, DirectCD will attempt to make the files you write to it more compact so that they take up less space on the disc. If space is a big issue, then you may want to consider using this option. However, having to compress the file for writing and then decompress it any time you need access will slow you down.

◆ **Format Type.** If your disc recorder supports the Quick Format feature, you can choose between a Quick Format and a Full Format. This feature is not found in all drives, but it's a nice one to have, since a full format can take upwards of 40 minutes depending on the speed of your drive.

When you're ready to format a disc, click the Start Format button. DirectCD pops up with a dialog box informing you of how long it will take to format the disc. For a full format, expect it to take between 25 and 45 minutes (so be sure you're ready to begin this process). When you do click the OK button to continue, you'll see the screen shown in Figure 7.10.

Figure 7.10

Measuring the progress of a DirectCD format operation.

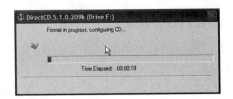

During the progress of the format, this dialog box enables you to see the elapsed time, allowing you to come up with a reasonable guess as to when the disc format will be complete. When the formatting process has completed successfully, this dialog box disappears, returning you to the main DirectCD interface.

Once formatted, if you look at the CD Info pane in the DirectCD window, you'll see that you lost a little real estate during the process. The DirectCD program has to use up some of the space on your disc to properly format it. In my case, a 650MB CD (a normal 74-minute disc) was left with 533MB of space after the format. While that is a fairly large chunk of space, it's the price you pay for the convenience of not needing Easy CD Creator and all that data layout stuff to write to your discs!

So long as you keep DirectCD turned on, you can now use your disc just like it were any other storage drive on your computer.

DirectCD Options and Utilities

If you take a look at the main DirectCD window (refer to Figure 7.8), you'll notice a few buttons we have yet to discuss. These buttons include:

- **CD Utilities.** This button provides access to the DirectCD ScanDisc and UnDelete utilities.

- **Erase CD.** If you formatted an RW disc for DirectCD use and have decided you no longer want to use it as a DirectCD disc, use the Erase CD button to restore it to its original unformatted state.

- **Make Writable.** If you have recorded files to a R disc and closed the session (you must still have left the disc open), using this handy button reopens the existing session so you can add more data to it. (For more information on sessions, see Chapter 8 and Appendix C.)

◆ **Web Checkup.** Like the Web Checkup button on the Project Selector (which I discuss in Appendix A), this takes you to Roxio's Web support page in search of an update to DirectCD.

◆ **Options.** Provides a series of options that allow you to customize how DirectCD functions.

In the next couple of sections I take a look at two of the more involved buttons listed here: CD Utilities and Options.

DirectCD Utilities

To access the DirectCD utilities, click the CD Utilities button on the DirectCD window. This window provides you with access to a pair of tools: ScanDisc and UnDelete.

If you're having problems writing data to your DirectCD disc, then there could be something wrong with the disc. While it's always preferable to copy any critical data off the disc when you suspect trouble, that's not always an option (in other words, the disc may not be readable). If all else fails, you can try using the DirectCD ScanDisc tool to find and fix common problems. Click the ScanDisc button on the CD Utilities dialog box and then click the Scan button on the dialog box that appears. This initiates the disc scan (see Figure 7.11).

Figure 7.11

Depending on the amount of information on the disc and any problems with it, Scan-Disk should complete in just a few seconds.

Once you click the Scan button, ScanDisk immediately checks various parts of the disc for common problems. If it finds any, it will attempt to correct them, but don't expect miracles. If you've turned your DirectCD disc into a charcoal briquette, then the data it housed is probably toast.

The UnDelete option in the CD Utilities dialog box is actually only good for recovering deleted files from a Recordable disc. When you erase from an RW disc, the files are literally erased. You can't get them back. However, because an R disc only marks deleted files as hidden, you can actually still gain access to them. Click the UnDelete button to recover files from a recordable disc. UnDelete asks for a quick confirmation that this is what you want to do. Click Yes and UnDelete will begin searching the disc for recoverable information.

Options

The options available in version 5.x of DirectCD are much simpler than what you had to choose from when using it with Easy CD Creator 4. Rather than having to sort through several tabs of information, very little of which you need, in this version you only have to click the Option button, which brings up the Direct CD Options dialog box (see Figure 7.12).

Figure 7.12

The DirectCD Options dialog box contains all the controls you need to determine how the DirectCD program works.

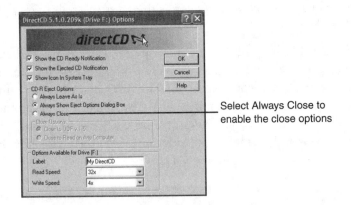

Select Always Close to enable the close options

Leading off this Options dialog box are a series of three check boxes:

♦ **Show the CD Ready Notification.** Selecting this check box causes a prompt to inform you when a DirectCD disc has been inserted in the drive.

♦ **Show the Ejected CD Notification.** Selecting this causes a message to be displayed when you eject a DirectCD disc.

♦ **Show Icon in System Tray.** This option controls whether or not the Direct-CD icon appears in your system tray. Disabling this icon does not disable DirectCD, so I'd advise against doing so. However, if you've got a system tray full of icons that you don't want to see, this is one way to get rid of one of them.

Of these three options, the only one I would recommend leaving enabled is the Show Icon In System Tray check box. If you insert or eject a DirectCD Ready disc from your CD-RW drive, do you really need an annoying message telling you so?

The middle section of the DirectCD Options dialog box has two parts. The CD-R Eject Options section allows you to control what happens when you eject a recordable DirectCD disc. The options included here are:

♦ **Always Leave As Is.** This means that the disc remains "open" after you eject it. Leaving a disc open makes it less compatible with other disc drives.

♦ **Always Show Eject Options Dialog Box.** Each time you eject a DirectCD disc, this option gives you a choice between leaving the disc open and closing it.

♦ **Always Close.** This option means that Direct CD will always close the disc when you eject it.

If you enable the Always Close dialog box, you also enable the Close Options section of this window. This provides you with two choices for how to close a disc: Close to UDF v 1.5 or Close To Read On Any Computer. As I covered in Chapter 6, Direct-CD writes data to a disc using the UDF format. Any computer with a UDF reader installed can read a DirectCD disc. However, if you think you may need to use this disc in a PC without such a reader, choose the other option.

Finally, at the bottom of this dialog box is a section that lets you select the read and write speeds for your recorder. The values available in these drop-down menus depend on the capabilities of your disc drive, so you cannot actually choose an incorrect setting. However, you will probably do best to take whatever the default values are for these and adjust them later, based on your experience. If you have problems reading from or writing to a DirectCD disc, try lowering the associated speed a notch or two.

Using the DirectCD Disc

Once formatted, you can treat the DirectCD disc just like it is a hard drive on your system. You can save files to it, copy files to it, or use other commands from application programs. In Figure 7.13, you can see that a disc I formatted and named "My DirectCD" is in my DVD+RW drive. (Keep in mind when looking at this figure that I use Windows XP, which shows file icons a bit differently than previous Windows versions.)

Between Tracks

The dialog box that usually appears when you eject a DirectCD disc won't pop up if you used the Options section described earlier to disable eject notification.

Figure 7.13

I've been using this DirectCD disc to save my MS Word documents for this book to a CD.

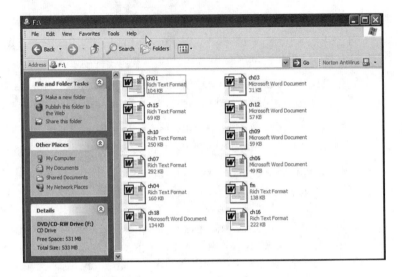

When you want to eject a DirectCD CD, you can use the eject button on the CD drive, the button on the main DirectCD window, or you can right-click the Direct-CD System Tray icon and choose Eject. In any case, a dialog box pops up after the disc has been physically ejected. The information displayed tells you on what types of systems you can use the disc. Click the OK button to dismiss this dialog box.

The Least You Need to Know

◆ Easy CD Creator can write data to both R and RW CDs and DVDs.

◆ Avoid finalizing (closing) a data CD until you can no longer fit any more data onto them or you know you'll never need to add more.

◆ You can use DirectCD with CD-R/RW, DVD-R/RW, or DVD+R/RW discs.

◆ DirectCD has to format a disc before it can use it.

◆ Once formatted, a DirectCD disc acts just like a hard disk or floppy.

Chapter 8

Drag and Drop in Style with Nero

In This Chapter

♦ Using Nero Burning ROM and InCD to make a data disc

♦ How to configure Nero data CD compilation settings for maximum disc compatibility in other PCs

♦ Creating a compilation of data files and folders that you can burn to a data disc

♦ Formatting a disc for use with Nero's InCD packet-writing software

Hopefully, when you bought your disc recorder, making data backups and transferring large chunks of seldom used files and folders off your PC's hard drive was one of the uses you had in mind. Nero Burning ROM includes two primary tools that allow you to get your data on one of those shiny discs, whether it's a CD, DDCD (double-density compact disc), or DVD.

♦ **Nero Burning ROM.** This, obviously, is the package you purchased. Using the compilation system discussed in this book's introduction, you create a variety of data discs.

♦ **InCD.** If you've already read Chapter 7, which covered Easy CD Creator's DirectCD program, think of InCD as the Nero equivalent. This packet-writing software allows you to treat your discs like they were any other storage drive on your computer. You can just save files right to them, without first having to create a compilation of files and folders!

In this chapter, I cover making data CDs using both programs. First, we take a look at using the main Nero Burning ROM application.

Types of Data CDs Burnable in Nero

To get Nero Burning ROM started, click Start, All Programs, ahead Nero, Nero—Burning Rom. As you can see from Figure 8.1, Nero automatically opens the New Compilation window and defaults to the options for creating a conventional data CD. If the Nero Wizard opens first, click the Close button. If for some reason the New Compilation window doesn't appear, just activate the File menu and choose New.

Click to choose   Click to enable the
a media type   Options section

Figure 8.1

The New Compilation screen allows you to create various data discs, video discs, audio discs, and more.

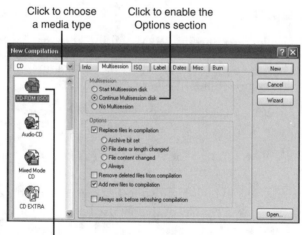

Click to create a data disc

Cross Reference

For more detailed information on the various types of discs and for an explanation of ISO, visit Chapter 6.

The default disc type for a new compilation is a conventional CD. If you want to burn a DVD or a DDCD, use the scroll box in the upper-left corner of the window to select your format preference.

Regardless of which type you choose, you'll no doubt notice the series of icons in a vertical scroll box on the left of the window. There's an icon for every type of disc type you can make for the selected format. In this chapter, we're going to stick to the ROM (ISO) types, which can be DVD, DDCD, or CD. This icon is always the first one on the list, regardless of the disc media type. Click the icon once to select it (if it's not selected already).

The New Compilation Window Tabs

When you select to create an ISO disc you'll see a series of tabs appear across the top of the New Compilation dialog box (refer to Figure 8.1). Regardless of whether you are making a CD or DDCD, there are seven tabs:

- ◆ Info
- ◆ Multisession
- ◆ ISO
- ◆ Label
- ◆ Dates
- ◆ Misc
- ◆ Burn

If you intend to create a data DVD you'll see every tab listed here, except for the Multisession tab. DVD discs don't require the use of sessions to store data. Their contents can be added to as you see fit (as long as adequate space is left on the disc). Yet another nice convenience feature for DVD!

In the following sections we take a look at each of these tabs.

The Multisession Tab: Only CDs Need Apply

Since the Multisession tab, which was shown earlier (refer to Figure 8.1), can only be used with CDs and DDCDs, I'll stick to the term CD when referring to recordable discs in this section.

Because of how data is organized on a compact disc, they must be written to in sessions. The number of sessions can vary based on the nature of the disc. An audio disc, for example, would have just one session (conventional CD players can only read one session on a CD, so adding

> **Cross Reference**
>
> For more information on the concepts of multisession CDs, see Appendix C.

more to an audio CD would be fruitless). However, if you're making a data CD that you don't fill up after just one burn, the use of multiple sessions can be invaluable.

The Multisession tab, which is divided into two sections, controls how sessions are used on the data CD you intend to record.

The first section is also called Multisession. In the Multisession section you can choose to create the following:

♦ **Start Multisession disc.** Choose this option if you're recording to a new disc but either know, or think it possible, that you'll want to write multiple sessions to it before it's filled.

♦ **Continue Multisession disc.** Choose this option if you want to add a session to an open CD that already contains at least one session.

♦ **No Multisession.** If you know that once you write to this CD for the first time you're never going to want to write to it again (except to erase it, if it's a re-writable disc), then choose this option.

If you choose to create a new multisession disc or to not create a multisession disc at all, the second section of this tab is grayed out. However, if you choose to add to an existing multisession CD, then you'll find that Nero has made the fields in the Options section available for your use.

If you're into making frequent backups of data folders on your hard disk (and you should be), the Replace files in compilation check box should be of significant importance to you. This is because if you're continually backing up the same set of data, you may no longer need older backup sessions on the disc. By enabling this check box, Nero provides you with a series of options that allow you to "replace" data from the existing session (remember, even if marked as deleted, no program can actually replace data on an R disc):

Don't Get Burned

If you choose to enable the Archive Bit Set button, be sure you also have backup software installed that uses this bit to track changed files and folders. If you're not sure, don't choose this option!

♦ **Archive bit set.** All Windows files have a component called an Archive Bit. Backup utilities use this bit to keep track of whether a file has been changed or not since a prior backup. As long as you use backup software that sets this bit, Nero can also benefit from it. Choose this option to perform backups that only copy selected files and folders where the archive bit indicates the file has changed in some way since the previous backup.

◆ **File Date or Length Changed.** Whenever you use an application to modify a document, Windows marks the date that file was modified. Enabling this radio button enables Nero to backup files or folders whose modification dates or file size have changed since the previous backup. (Nero compares the documents you've selected to the last time you recorded the compilation to disc.)

◆ **File Content Changed.** Unfortunately, file modification dates aren't always reliable. If you're concerned about the possibility that a backup file will be overlooked even though it's changed, choose this option. This causes Nero to perform a bit-by-bit comparison of all files and folders on the existing disc's session with those you want backed up. This can take much longer than backing up using the other methods, but it is more reliable.

◆ **Always.** If you're really concerned about not missing a single change, you can choose this option to have Nero forgo checking for file comparisons or archive bits and instead just replace every file in the backup compilation. Usually this option requires the most time to perform, but it's also the most reliable.

Between Tracks

As you'll soon find out when you actually get to making a data disc compilation, Nero saves information about that compilation to your hard disk. Nero can use this saved compilation data as comparison to any updates you attempt to make to it.

Odds are that every document or data file you create is not so important that you'll want to keep it forever. During backups, Nero can look for files in the previous backup that may no longer exist in the new one. If Nero doesn't find a file, then most likely it's because you've deleted it. If you also want the file removed from your existing backup sessions, make sure the Remove deleted files from compilation check box is enabled.

The Add new files to compilation check box operates in exactly the opposite manner as the Remove deleted files from compilation check box. Enabling this check box causes Nero to look for new files in the backup folders that you designate. If it finds any, it adds them to the compilation.

Finally, the Always ask before refreshing compilation check box allows you to forgo making decisions here. By enabling this option, Nero instead asks you to choose between these options if and when you decide to "refresh" the compilation. That is, if you burn an existing compilation to a disc multiple times, Nero will only then ask you how to handle managing file updates, changes, deletions, etc.

If you do intend to add to the session on an existing disc for the purposes of making routine data backups, I recommend you choose to always replace files in the compilation, leave deleted files intact on the disc, and add new files to the compilation as they're detected. In my opinion, this is the configuration that leaves you the most margin for error.

The Info Tab

The Info tab does not have any controls with which you need interact. Instead, this option tells you about the active compilation. If you're creating a new compilation, don't expect this to tell you much. If you're updating an existing compilation, this tab provides you with the big picture in terms of how much data is set to be written to disc and how much space Nero needs to create the file system that allows Windows to find all the data on the disc (see Figure 8.2).

Figure 8.2

The Info tab can help you gauge how much disc space you have to work with before writing the disc.

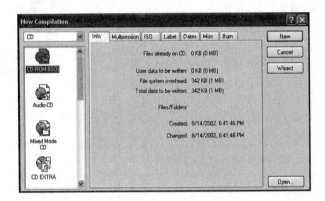

The ISO Tab

The ISO tab dictates how Nero writes data to a disc. Primarily, you should use these options to help ensure disc compatibility in the drives in which you intend to use it (see Figure 8.3). Some of the terms used in this tab are fairly obscure, but I covered most of them in Chapter 6. Others I consider beyond the range of your need to know (this is an *Idiot's Guide* after all). In any case, I'll only go into this deep enough for you to decide which options you need to set.

The tab is divided into the following sections:

♦ **File-/Directorynames Length.** If you want your disc to be compatible with DOS disc drives and Windows 3.x (not likely), choose ISO Level 1.

♦ **Format.** If you think you might need to use your disc in an older CD-ROM drive (and I do mean old), you might want to choose the Mode 2/XA option.

However, I recommend you stick with Mode 1. (If you chose to continue a multisession disc on the Multisession tab, this section is disabled. Multisession discs are Mode 1 only.)

- **Character Set.** Unless you know differently, stick with ISO 9660. Unless you intend to use the disc with an operating system older than Windows 95, enable the Joliet check box. This option allows you to write file and folder names to the disc that are more than eight characters in length.

- **Relax ISO Restrictions.** These options deal primarily with the character length and depth of folder paths that you intend to include in your compilation. If you intend to burn data that is more than eight subfolders (folders within folders) deep on your hard disk, you should enable the Allow Pathdepth of More Than 8 Directories option. If you have extremely long folder and filenames that, when combined as one line, are longer than 255 characters, then you should enable the Allow More Than 255 Characters in Path check box as well. (Enabling either of these options reduces the number of drives with which your disc is compatible.)

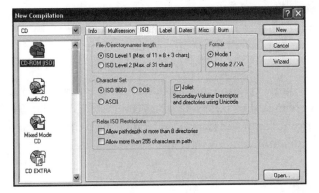

Figure 8.3

This tab contains as many obscure options as you're likely to encounter in using any part of the Nero Burning ROM software.

Generally speaking, if you're not sure what to change on this screen, then don't change anything. Nero's default options should not steer you wrong for any generic data disc you want to create.

The Label Tab

You can completely ignore the Label tab if you like. It contains a series of fields that allow you to include custom information about the disc during its creation. This information includes things like the name of the disc (Volume Label), Publishers, Copyright file, etc.

To fill out any field on the tab, just click it and enter the appropriate information.

The Dates Tab

The Dates tab allows you to configure the dates used in creating the disc and the dates of the files recorded to it. Both the Volume Dates and File Dates sections are disabled by default and I recommend you leave it that way (see Figure 8.4).

Figure 8.4

Unless you know better, it's best to let Nero assign current date and times to your disc volume and to keep the existing date and time applied to the files you record.

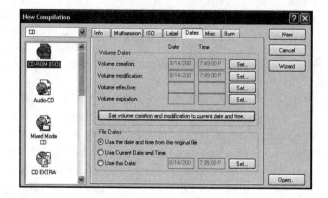

If you want more control over the dates used, you can click the Set buttons in the Volume Dates section to chance the information contained there. In the File Dates section, you can choose to label all files with the current date and time or to use a date of your choosing.

Finally, click the Set volume creation and modification to current date and time button if you've spent a great deal of time setting up the New Compilation and want to use more updated current times and dates (by default Nero fills out these fields the second the New Compilation window opens).

The Misc Tab

The Misc tab is practically a waste of a good tab. It contains just one small section with just two check boxes to choose from:

- **Cache Files From Disk And Network.** If some of the data you intend to write to disc is coming from a floppy disk or across a computer network you should make sure this option is enabled.

- **Cache Files Smaller Than.** This option, which is enabled by default to cache files smaller than 64KB, helps increase the speed of the recording process. I recommend you leave this option alone.

The Burn Tab

The Burn tab is the last tab you have to deal with before finally deciding what data you want burned to disc. In the Action section of this tab are four check boxes:

◆ **Determine Maximum Speed.** Enabling this option determines the speed of each source from which you have selected data to record. This can increase burn reliability because it lets Nero get a good idea of how quickly it can expect to draw data from each source.

◆ **Simulation.** If you want Nero to test write the disc before writing it for real, enable this check box. Unless you're burning with Nero for the first time with your recordable drive or are having problems burning a disc, you are probably safe disabling this check box.

◆ **Write.** This check box is enabled by default. If you only want to test your recording and don't want to record a disc regardless of test results, disable the Write check box.

◆ **Finalize CD.** If you know that you don't ever want to add more data to this disc, enable this check box. Finalizing a CD helps ensure that it's compatible with the widest range of disc drives.

Underneath the Action section is a series of options that allow you to configure your maximum write speed (on the recordable drive), write method (consult Appendix C for information on these methods), number of copies to make, use multiple recorders (if you have them), or to do a virus check on the data you want to record. This does require that you have antivirus software installed. However, hopefully you perform routine antivirus checks as a matter of routine anyway, making this option unnecessary.

When you're satisfied that all is as you want it, click the New button to choose the data you want included in your compilation.

Choosing Data to Record

When you click the New button on the New Compilation window as described at the end of the previous section, you are sent to the main Nero Burning ROM window.

This window has two other windows contained within it: ISO2 and File Browser (see Figure 8.5). The name of the ISO2 window can vary depending on the exact specifications you chose in the New Compilation window.

Between Tracks

By default, Nero names any new data disc, "New," in the ISO2 window. If you want to change that name, right-click it, choose Rename, and enter the name you want.

Figure 8.5

Use the two windows (ISO2 and File Browser) to create your data disc compilation.

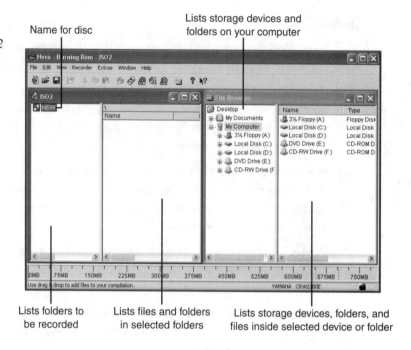

Name for disc

Lists storage devices and folders on your computer

Lists folders to be recorded

Lists files and folders in selected folders

Lists storage devices, folders, and files inside selected device or folder

If you're familiar with the Windows File Explorer or My Computer functions then the File Browser window should be old hat to you (if you don't know how to use these applets, you should get yourself a book that discusses Windows).

Use the File Browser window to locate the data you want included on your data disc. When you find it, select it and drag and drop it on the ISO2 window (see Figure 8.6). You don't have to select individual files. If you drag and drop a folder onto the ISO2 window, all of its contents are also included.

As you add data to the compilation, you'll notice a blue bar creep along the bottom of the window. If it reaches the dotted red dash bar on the left side then you've exceeded your disc media's capacity and must remove something from your compilation. To remove files or folders from the ISO2 window, select and right-click the files or folders you want removed. In the menu that appears, choose Delete. Don't panic over using this option. It only removes these files from the compilation, not your hard disk.

> **Cross Reference**
>
> For visual learners, I've found *Easy Windows XP* and *How to Use Windows XP* to be excellent full-color tutorials. For a more text heavy introduction to Windows, check out *The Complete Idiot's Guide to Windows XP* or *The Absolute Beginner's Guide to Windows XP*. Finally, *Special Edition Using Windows XP* is an excellent reference book to have on hand for all things Windows.

Click to save
the compilation ── ┌─ Click to record current compilation

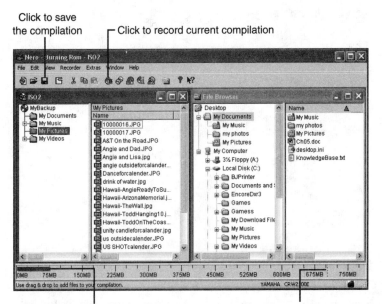

Figure 8.6

The ISO2 folder now contains the contents of the "My" folders (Documents, Music, Pictures, etc.) on my hard disk drive.

This bar measures the amount of   Dotted line marks the storage limit
disc space the compilation requires   of selected recordable media

Saving Your Compilation

Before recording your compilation to disc, it's a good idea to save it to your hard disk. You never know when you might need to duplicate it (especially if you're making routine backups) or use it as the basis for a future compilation.

To save your compilation, click the floppy disk icon on the toolbar or click File, Save. This opens up a Save dialog box which you've likely seen a million times. Enter a name for your compilation and click Save. If you've already saved your compilation once and want to save it again under a new file name, choose File, Save As instead.

Recording the Disc

When you're ready to start recording, click the burning disc icon on the toolbar or select File, Write CD. When you do, the Write CD window appears. Surprise! Aside from the fact that you can no longer change the type of disc you're recording to, this window is no different from the New Compilation window we spent half this chapter discussing.

If you want to change any options here you can. If you need help, refer to the "New Compilation Window Tabs" section earlier in this chapter. When you're ready, click the Write button to initiate the recording process (see Figure 8.7).

Figure 8.7

Burn, baby, burn! From here your disc recording is in the hands of Nero and your disc recorder.

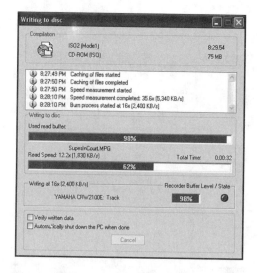

The recording process could take just a minute or two or an hour or more depending on the speed of your drive, whether your disc media is recordable or rewritable, and whether you're using CD, DDCD, DVD-R/RW, or DVD+R/RW to write the disc. When the disc is complete, you'll see a dialog box confirming the successful burn. Click OK to close this dialog box.

This returns you to the recording window where you have three options. Nero keeps a log of the entire recording process, which can be seen in the scrollable box near the top of the window. If you're having problems with successfully recording to disc, you can Save or Print this log for future reference and troubleshooting. Most likely you'll just want to press the Discard button to close the window.

Congratulations! You've got yourself a data disc! Now let's take a look at writing data to a disc via InCD's packet-writing tools.

InCD

Nero's InCD is a packet-writing utility that allows you to write data to a rewritable disc as though it were any other storage device on your computer. No need to create those time consuming compilations. The upshot of this process is that it's quick, easy, and painless. The downside is that you have to spend a good chunk of time formatting the disc to conform to InCD's packet-writing standards, the formatting process eats up a big chunk of your disc's available space, and the disc is only readable in other PCs that either have InCD or another UDF Reader installed.

> **Cross Reference**
>
> For more information on packet-writing and on the UDF file system, see Chapter 6.

When you install InCD, as covered in Appendix B, Nero configures it to launch automatically whenever you boot your PC. You've probably noticed a large, and rather ugly, InCD logo appear briefly when you boot or log on to Windows. Once that disappears, the only indication of InCD's presence on your system is an icon in the Windows System Tray. Everything you need to do to configure InCD and format a disc for packet writing can be accessed by right-clicking this icon (see Figure 8.8).

Figure 8.8

Right-clicking the InCD icon gives you three options for accessing InCD.

From the menu shown here, you have three options:

◆ **Properties.** This opens the InCD Property Page. This page has two tabs: InCD Page Information and InCD Page Settings. The first only provides information about the capacity of any inserted InCD disc and how much space is still free. The second tab displays information about your disc recorder, allows you to disable the InCD logo screen at startup, and sets InCD to a Safe Mode, in which it compares all files written to the disc with those on the original source. Use this option if you're having problems reading back files written to an InCD disc.

◆ **Format.** Selecting this option allows you to format a disc for use with InCD.

◆ **Version Information.** Opens a logo window similar to the one that appears when InCD launches at Windows startup. However, there is also an About button that you can click to see what version of InCD you have installed (useful to determine if a newer version is available for download from the Ahead Software website). Click OK on this window and on the InCD logo window to close.

Formatting a disc for use with InCD is the most complicated part of using InCD and even it isn't that complicated. If Nero Burning ROM gets knocked for anything in comparison to Easy CD Creator it's that many people find it difficult to use. This is one area where that's absolutely not true. Using InCD is much more simple than using the Easy CD Creator equivalent: DirectCD.

To get the format process started, click the Format option from the menu shown in Figure 8.8. This opens the InCD wizard shown in Figure 8.9.

Figure 8.9

It's not pretty, but the InCD Wizard makes formatting a disc for packet writing a snap!

Notice the message that indicates Nero is compatible with CD-RWs and DVDs of the +RW and -RW variety (standard recordable discs are not compatible). Click Next to continue.

The next step in the wizard allows you to select a recordable drive. As most of us only have one, that will be the only one available (as long as your recorder is compatible with InCD). If you do have more than one, click the one you want to use in this instance. Click Next to continue.

The next screen checks your recordable drive for a rewritable disc. Assuming one is there and that it is blank, you can click Next to continue. If you have not inserted an RW disc, or if the disc contains data, you must click the Back button and insert media that conforms to these standards. There is also a Properties button here, but it leads to the same window as described earlier in this section.

Finally, we've reached the last step in the process. Nero allows you to enter a name for the disc in the Label field. Unless you change it, the default name is InCD. Click the Finish button to begin formatting the disc, which takes about 10 to 20 minutes (see Figure 8.10).

When complete, you'll see a dialog box letting you know that it did complete the formatting process successfully (or you'll see an error dialog if it did not). Click OK to close this dialog box and start using your new InCD-formatted disc!

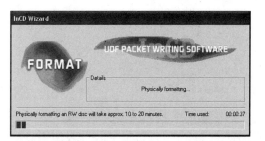

Figure 8.10

It's best to go grab a snack or tasty beverage once you start formatting a disc with InCD. The process usually takes a while.

Cross Reference

As stated, using an InCD-formatted disc is no different than storing files on your hard disk drive or floppy disk. Just copy/paste information directly to the drive from Windows File Explorer or My Computer or select your recordable drive in the Save dialog for your applications and choose Save. For an example, refer to the "Using the DirectCD Disc" section in Chapter 7. Yes, this section is specific to DirectCD, but if you've saved a file to CD in one packet-writing program then you've saved it in all of them!

The Least You Need to Know

♦ Nero includes two applications for recording data to a disc: the main Nero Burning ROM application and the packet-writing tool, InCD.

♦ Before you can create a compilation of data files for recording to disc, you must configure options for how Nero Burning ROM is to create the disc. These options affect what drives the disc can be read in.

♦ Adding data files and folders to a compilation is as simple as drag and drop using a pair of windows that operate no differently than Windows File Explorer or My Computer.

♦ The only thing you need to do to make use of InCD is format a disc for its file system. From there you can use the disc just like any other hard disk or floppy.

Part 4

Digital Jukeboxes: The Tao of Making Audio Discs

Despite what the RIAA (Recording Industry Association of America) wants to tell you, no audio CD is perfect (except, perhaps, for Van Halen's double-live *Right Here, Right Now*). Using your disc recorder you can make CDs that contain only what you want to hear. Record audio to MP3 files on your hard drive or burn it directly to a blank CD. Create custom greatest hits compilations or mix and match from various artists. It's all up to you! Chapter 9 explains all the basics you need to know about working with audio on your PC, while Chapters 10 and 11 tackle producing great audio CDs using Easy CD Creator and Nero Burning ROM.

Creating Your Own Music Studio

In This Chapter

♦ Learn about the various sources you can use to get music for recording on your PC

♦ Learn about the pitfalls involved in signing up for web-based music subscription services

♦ Find out what audio file formats are the most useful for ripping, listening to, and recording music

♦ Understand how recording quality is a balance between bigger files and better music

Putting audio on a disc is probably the reason you bought your disc recorder. That, or your drive was included with a new PC and you're just looking for an excuse to put it to good use. This chapter gives you the 411 on what's involved when recording audio to disc.

PC Audio 101

Cross Reference

This chapter focuses solely on understanding audio file formats and how to get them on your PC. For information on recording audio from your PC to a CD or DVD, see Chapters 10, 11, and 18.

Recording audio to a CD or DVD means you have to actually have audio on your PC in the first place (unless you plan to record directly from another audio disc). That means you need at least a basic understanding of the sources for music, the encoding formats used to store them on your PC, and how your choice affects what you can do with your music and how it sounds when recorded to disc. Consider this chapter a *Cliff's Notes* version of everything you need to know about audio on your PC.

Music Sources

Unless you're using it to create your own masterful works, getting music on your PC requires a source. You're not limited to getting music from other CDs. Indeed, there are a lot of options at your disposal, including the following:

◆ Commercial music CDs

◆ The various analog audio formats, like tape, vinyl records, and even 8-track tapes

◆ Recordable CDs and DVDs with either digital audio tracks or music saved in one of the formats outlined in the "Audio File Formats" section later in this chapter

◆ The Internet

The next few sections take a look at each method.

Music CDs

Recording audio from a music CD is generally a pretty simple process. You just put the disc in your PC and use your encoding program to record to your hard drive. This program could be one of those discussed in this book, like Easy CD Creator, Nero, or MusicMatch. It could also be one of hundreds of other audio players available on retail store shelves and downloadable from the Internet. One of the most popular of these, for example, is a program called WinAmp, which you can download for free from www.winamp.com.

If you have Windows 98 or newer, you have at least one program capable of *ripping* music from a CD to your PC: Windows Media Player. The latest version of Media Player, currently version 8 in Windows XP, is a decent all-around tool for ripping music from CD and organizing your music collection on your hard drive. It's not my first choice, but for those on a budget it'll do the job.

Arcane CD Speak

Ripping is the process by which you record audio from a disc into a file on your PC. While the name may make it sound like you're stealing, there's absolutely nothing wrong with ripping your CDs to your PC.

Audio Type, Vinyl Records, and Other Analog Mediums

If you're old enough, you no doubt have a collection of cassette tapes, vinyl records, or even 8-track tapes gathering dust in some dark corner of your home. No doubt many of these titles aren't available for purchase on CD. If not, that doesn't mean you can't get them there. All you need are the following:

♦ An analog player (cassette deck, record player, etc.) with audio output connectors (if the speaker is built into the player you may not have any audio out connectors).

♦ A sound card with an audio in connectors (you can try using the microphone connector, but don't expect to be happy with the results).

♦ A cable that can bridge the gap between your analog player's audio outs and your PC card's audio inputs. Cables of almost every kind can be found at consumer electronics stores like Radio Shack.

♦ A program, like MusicMatch or Easy CD Creator's SoundStream that can record audio signals from your sound card's inputs.

If you've got these tools then there's no reason you can't take a stab at getting your old record or tape collection onto your PC and, from there, onto a CD. Expect a lot of trial and error when using your recording software and at least some degradation in overall sound quality. Still, it's a lot better than watching all your old favorites turn to dust from age (tape) or repeated use (vinyl records).

Cross Reference

For more information on converting analog music recordings to a digital PC format, see Chapter 10, in particular the "A Word About Phonographs" section. You should also check out www. crazyformp3s.com for even more great tips!

Internet Downloads

While all the buzz in the news centers around free file-sharing services like the defunct Napster, there are plenty of noncontroversial ways of downloading music from the Internet. Of course, by noncontroversial, I mean services that the RIAA (Recording Industry Association of America) and music industry at large aren't attempting to shut down. Personally, I find paying for music downloads at a rate per song that is no better than buying the CD off a store shelf insulting. If I've got to pay $15 or more for a full CD's worth of music then I want the darn packaging, too!

> **Don't Get Burned** _____
>
> Remember that just because you paid to download an audio file, that doesn't mean you can do whatever you please with it. If the file format is not MP3 or WAV, you can bet that there are security features built into it that may deny you the right to copy it to an audio CD compilation or portable MP3 player. Heck, you might not even be able to transfer it off your hard drive if you buy a new computer. And to think that the music industry claims not to understand why few people sign up for their "legitimate" download services. Really, who's actually pirating who here?

Free and Pay Per File Downloads

One method of downloading music is to visit select music retailers on the web. While many charge you by the download, believe it or not, there is also free downloadable music available too that you can legally download. Amazon.com, for example, has an entire section dedicated to free music downloads, that at the time of this writing included select tracks from artists like Allison Krauss and Oasis.

Subscription Services

The music industry's idea of fair play when downloading music from the Internet is to sign up for a subscription-based service. The services include the following:

- **Press Play.** www.pressplay.com. Press Play is backed by Universal and Sony and allows you to pay from $10 to $18 a month to $180 a year for limited rights to streaming, downloadable, and portable music. (Portable music can be transferred off your hard drive to a different storage medium.) You can also purchase "packs" of portable music for $5, $10, and $18 a pack (in quantities of 5, 10, and 20 portable downloads). Gee … what a deal.

- **Rhapsody.** www.listen.com. Home of the Rhapsody music service, this one is backed by BMG, EMI, Sony, Warner Brothers, and Universal. Essentially a glorified Internet Radio service, for $5 to $10 a month you can listen to their, "CD Quality" radio broadcasts, and have on-demand access to all or a portion of their music library. Under the most comprehensive plan, you're allowed to download 10 tracks recordable to CD a month.

◆ **Emusic.** www.emusic.com. Perhaps the best subscription service online, you pay $15 a month (or $120 a year) for unlimited MP3 downloads (you can copy to CD or MP3 player as you like). This is what a subscription based service should look like. Given that it's, more or less, a fair trade for consumers, it's no wonder that Emusic does not receive backing from most of the major record labels (resulting in some large gaps in their music database). Still, if you want to use a subscription service, you're best off backing the one that offers the best deal. If Emusic receives the most support from consumers there is a better chance some of the major labels will come around.

Between Tracks

All prices and subscription service data is accurate at the time of this writing. However, as volatile as this environment is, don't be surprised if the details have changed from what I describe here.

There are certainly other subscription-based services out there (like StreamWaves and RealOne), but aside from Emusic, most are not worth your time, attention, or cash. In a January 2002 PCWorld.com article, Tom Spring wrote:

> One could even argue that their current digital online music subscription schemes do more to promote online piracy than prevent it. The inconvenience of the legit services may send music seekers back to the black and gray markets.

This is, unfortunately, no understatement. Until the major record labels and RIAA get serious about providing good content for a good value, their subscription-based music services will likely go nowhere (unless of course their lobby pushes enough legislation through to make theirs the only option).

Regardless, if you choose to go this route you should make sure you know the nomenclature many of these sites use to define what you can do with the music they make available. The terms may vary from service to service, but most are variations on the theme that Press Play uses:

◆ **Stream.** Songs you can listen to live, but cannot download to your hard disk drive.

◆ **Download.** Songs you can download to your hard drive but, due to digital rights management, can be played only on your hard drive.

◆ **Portable.** Songs that, once downloaded, you actually get to own and use as you want, even after you cancel your membership.

Truthfully, I think your best value is to stick to the world of compact discs available on sale or used.

Peer-to-Peer

If you've lived through the late 1990s and have never heard of Napster then you've no doubt been living under a rock (a heavy one) or have recently sustained a memory-altering head injury. Napster practically gave birth to the free music sharing phenomenon that made MP3 the most popular audio file format in existence.

Arcane CD Speak

Peer-to-Peer is a type of file sharing in which you provide access to specific folders on your computer that contain media files like MP3s in exchange to similar access to the folders of every other user of the service that is online.

Don't Get Burned

Right now no one can really stop you if you choose to trade and download copyrighted work that you do not own; that doesn't make it right. I have no love of music publishers or the Recording Industry Association of America (RIAA). However, the law is the law and you can be prosecuted for downloading or distributing work to which you do not hold the copyright. For more information on copyright and Fair Use, see Chapter 3.

Unfortunately for Napster, their computers played the middleman for users sharing files and that gave the RIAA and the rest of the music industry a clear legal target. Not surprisingly, they had it shut down. At one point the service was scheduled to relaunch as a subscription service, but it now looks like Napster is finished.

In Napster's wake, however, a variety of other services have come into the limelight. Services like Kazaa, Gnutella, and Audio Galaxy have provided users with free access to the music collections of thousands of other users. The difference is, they only provide the software. Not one byte of copyrighted content is traded across their own computers. Needless to say, the music industry is not ignoring these services just because of a legal loophole. As I type they are lobbying to shut down many of these services and have been successful in doing so (or at least forcing them to change how they work to filter out copyrighted content).

I'll not cover any of these services in detail in this book. However, if you want to learn more about them, all you have to do is run some of the names dropped here through an Internet search engine. You'll no doubt generate a few hits.

Understanding the Various Audio File Formats

Putting music on your computer requires that the digital audio data be encoded in a specific method that your PC, or more accurately, your player software, can read. There are about as many audio file formats as there are stars in the sky. Fortunately, there are only a few that you really need concern yourself. These are:

◆ **MP3.** MP3 files are, undeniably, the most popular format for audio files. An entire industry has sprouted up to support the format through software players on your PC, portable hardware players, and tools to convert your CD audio to the format and back again.

◆ **MP3Pro.** Think of MP3 Pro as the sequel to MP3. It offers the same quality of compression for your music files, but takes up only half the space.

◆ **Windows Media files (WMA).** WMA files are Microsoft's response to MP3. They provide similar sound quality, in file sizes that are generally a bit smaller than MP3, but much bigger than MP3Pro.

◆ **Compact Disc Digital Audio.** CD-DA, as specified in the Red Book standard (discussed in Appendix C), is the format in which audio CDs are recorded.

◆ **Wave.** WAV files are the equivalent of CD-DA audio when ripped from a CD to your PC without going through any kind of compression (like to encode as an MP3 file). These files provide the best sound quality, but take up an enormous amount of disk space compared to the others mentioned in this list. Using special (but generally inexpensive) software you can edit WAV files to trim or modify their contents. Both Easy CD Creator and Nero Burning ROM come with WAV file editors, called Sound Editor and Nero WAV Editor, respectively.

As mentioned, there are other file formats used to encode audio, like Real Audio and M3U. But the ones outlined here are the ones that you should give most of your attention. Once you know the players, though, it's time to learn some of the fine details about using these files.

Track Tags

The most popular consumer audio file formats like MP3 and WMA provide space in the file's data to store information about a track that a player can read and relay back to the listener. This collection of data is referred to as a track tag. In this section, we'll stick to MP3s as an example, but this does apply to WMA files as well.

Primarily, track tags are used to store information about the title of the track, the name of the artist, and the album in which the track was originally recorded. This information makes it easy for your MP3 software to log all your MP3s in a Media Library, like the Music Library in MusicMatch Jukebox (see Chapter 18).

When you rip a music CD to your PC, you can manually enter track tag information. However, this can be pretty time consuming if you're talking about every track on a CD for an entire music collection. Fortunately, the Internet has come to the rescue.

Services like Gracenote's CDDB (www.cddb.com) provide an online database of virtually every published CD in existence. Makers of digital music software, like MusicMatch's Jukebox (MMJ), pay Gracenote so that their programs have access to this database. What this means for you is that when you put a CD in your drive, your software gathers information about the CD and matches it to listings in the database. Once it finds a match (it's *very* rare that it won't), it downloads all information about that disc to your PC. When you rip the CD to your hard drive, this information is automatically used to fill out the key fields in the track's tag. Virtually all software players provide access to the CDDB database or one just like it.

> **CAUTION**
>
> **Don't Get Burned**
>
> This process of getting track tag information from an online database only works for commercially recorded CDs. Don't expect these online databases to recognize the *Steve-O's Collective Soul Greatest Hits* CD you burned last week.

Some software players, like MusicMatch Jukebox, allow you to go well beyond the generic title, artist, and album information usually stored in a track tag. These programs go so far as to let you store information about the music genre, lyrics, album art (which appears in the software when the track plays), preference, mood, and more. This kind of information is generally used to implement features like MMJ's AutoDJ, which automatically generates random music playlists according to your preferences.

Recording Quality

When you use a tool like Easy CD Creator, Nero, or MusicMatch Jukebox to rip music from CD to your PC, you have to choose not only a file format, but also the quality in which you want it recorded.

While it may seem like a no-brainer to say, "I want the highest quality," that's not really true. After all, the highest-quality way would be to use the WAV file format. Technically, you could do just that. But when you start wondering where all your disk space went, be sure to take note of all those 20+ megabyte music files on your hard drive.

Formats like MP3 and WMA have become popular because they compress audio files down to a much more manageable size (usually around 3 to 5MB for a 5-minute track). Compressing that audio unavoidably lowers the quality of audio in the file. Fortunately, only the best ears can really tell the difference.

The measurement use to let you determine whether you want better quality music or smaller audio files is kbps, or the number of kilobits of data recorded for each second of music in the file; the higher the number, the higher the quality, the bigger the file. The choices you have vary based on the file format, as noted in the following:

- ◆ **WAV.** Can only record to CD quality at 1411 kbps.

- ◆ **MP3.** Can record to CD quality at 128 kbps, near CD quality at 96 kbps, and FM radio quality at 64 kbps.

- ◆ **MP3Pro.** Can record to CD quality at 64 kbps, near CD quality at 32 kbps, and FM radio quality at 24 kbps.

- ◆ **WMA.** Can record to CD quality at 96 kbps, near CD quality at 64 kbps, and FM radio quality at 32 kbps.

Between Tracks

The options listed here are just the generic ones commonly used for music and generally found in ripping software. Some software does let you specifically set the kbps rate.

Which format you eventually choose and what quality you use is entirely up to you, so long as your ripping software supports it.

The Least You Need to Know

- ◆ As long as you have the tools you can record music from virtually any source to your PC. Even old cassette tapes and vinyl records!

- ◆ Downloading music from the Internet (legally) is generally not a cost-effective choice. Quality is spotty and the services that provide the most music generally provide the worst value for the buck.

- ◆ Music files can be recorded to your PC in a variety of formats. The most common, however, are MP3 and WMA.

- ◆ When recording music to your PC it's best to choose a setting that provides CD quality. For MP3 that is 128kbps. For WMA it's 96kbps.

Drag and Drop with Easy CD Creator

In This Chapter

◆ How to create and edit an audio or MP3 CD layout

◆ Creating an audio or MP3 CD with Easy CD Creator

◆ Use SoundStream to record music to your hard disk from CD or any analog source (like LPs or audio cassettes) by connecting through your sound card

◆ Build a Media Library in SoundStream from MP3 and WMA audio files

◆ Record audio from virtually any source to your PC using SoundStream

◆ Use SoundStream's sound cleaning tools to clean up pops and scratches and those other annoying sound problems found on older recording mediums

While making data backups of all your crucial documents is practically a necessity when it comes to how you put your disc recorder to work, it's a heck of a lot more fun to create audio CDs. Certainly you'll look a bit less

Between Tracks

Most of this chapter focuses on creating discs with the CD-DA (Compact Disc Digital Audio) format used to create commercial music CDs. Because CD-DA is a compact disc native format, most of the content here cannot be applied to creating DVDs. However, you can create a disc full of MP3s using a recordable DVD.

of a geek at work or school showing off your Collective Soul greatest hits collection than bragging about how you'll never lose your Quicken financial data to a hard drive crash.

If you open the Roxio Project Selector (by either double-clicking its desktop icon or clicking Start, Programs, Easy CD Creator 5, Project Selector) and move your mouse pointer over the Make A Music CD button, you'll find three different tools you can work with to create an audio CD (see Figure 10.1).

♦ MusicCD Project

♦ MP3CD Project

♦ SoundStream

Figure 10.1

Pick your audio poison with the Project Selector: Music CD, MP3 CD, or SoundStream.

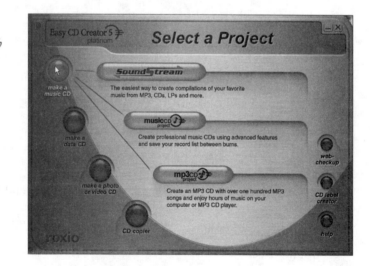

Over the course of this chapter we take a look at creating an audio CD using the tools provided with each of these options.

Creating a MusicCD Project CD

For your music listening pleasure, you can use Easy CD Creator to create audio CD-Rs that can be played in your CD or DVD drive or virtually any home audio CD player and most set-top DVD players (although your mileage on these may vary). You can also create audio CDs using CD-RW discs, but expect these to be much less compatible with home audio CD players and those found in car stereos.

I think the most fun to be had with this program is in selecting your favorite songs from various CDs for a mini-megahits collection that can get you through the commute to and from work or school. However, creating compilations that mix and match from your Tom Petty and Motley Crue discs are hardly the only use for your MusicCD Project. If it strikes your fancy, you can also recreate an existing audio CD by making a copy of it that just switches around the order of the songs (or leaves out the dogs). You can also create compilation CDs from music files, like MP3s, located on your hard disk drive!

> **Cross Reference**
>
> While several audio file formats can be used to store and play music on a PC, Easy CD Creator supports the three most important ones: MP3, WMA, and WAV. For more information on these file formats, see Chapter 9.

To get things cracking, use the Project Selector window described in the previous section to select MusicCD Project, which opens the Music CD Project window (see Figure 10.2). While just opening this window creates a new project, should you find yourself looking to start a new project from scratch, just click File, New CD Project, Music CD.

Source pane

Use scroll box and buttons to locate audio data

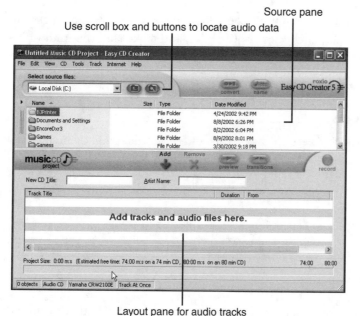

Figure 10.2

The MusicCD Project window provides a simple means for creating Audio CDs.

Layout pane for audio tracks

If you've already read Chapter 7, this window will probably look familiar to you. It is, however, a little different.

The upper pane is the Source pane. Use this section to find and select music for your audio CD layout. If you haven't already guessed, that makes the lower section the Layout pane. This pane tells you what audio tracks you've selected for recording to a CD.

> **Cross Reference**
>
> For more information on using the Select Source File controls, see the "Creating a Data CD Layout" section in Chapter 7.

Just above the Source pane is a series of three controls, labeled Select Source Files. Use these controls, in conjunction with the Source pane, to locate your files.

Creating the Audio CD Layout

The most important part of creating an audio CD is building a layout (truthfully, this applies to any kind of CD you create using Easy CD Creator). To do this, you must tell the program exactly which files or tracks you want to record, and in what order. The program then uses this information to burn the CD, rather like creating a building from a set of blueprints. You can also save the layout so that you can recall it for use at a later time.

Before you proceed, if you're creating an audio CD from files on your hard drive, then you don't need the distraction of seeing a bunch of Windows data files and documents. On the menu bar, click View, Show Files, and make sure the Audio Files Only options has a check mark next to it (if it doesn't, click it). This restricts the Source pane's listings to just audio files.

Between Tracks

If you are going to be doing a lot of audio CD recording and are using WAV or MP3 files, you can locate these files more easily if you keep them all in one folder or set of folders. Windows has a My Documents folder built in for this purpose. If you own Windows Me or XP, you will find My Documents also contains a My Music folder!

If you collect a lot of audio files, it's an even better idea to create subfolders in My Music for each artist. Otherwise, things can get pretty cluttered when you're trying to seek out one music track out of a few hundred.

Since the process for creating an audio CD can vary based on whether or not your source material is located on a single CD, multiple CDs, files on your PC, or a combination of each, we'll take a look at creating a layout from each perspective, in turn.

Adding Audio CD Tracks to the Layout

Identifying an MP3 or WAV file is generally not too difficult. They're almost always named after the song or artist they represent. Audio CDs can be a bit trickier. By default, Easy CD Creator just lists songs by their track number (see Figure 10.3).

Let's face it, it would be pretty mind-numbing if you had to go with titles like Track 1, Track 2, etc., and have to look on the CD cover to find out which track is which so you can decide what you want added to your layout. That kind of thing is more frustrating than a traffic jam while racing to the airport to catch a flight. After all, "Track 13" is not very descriptive, especially if you're dealing with tracks from multiple CDs.

Between Tracks

Generally, when you insert an audio CD with Easy CD Creator open, it immediately switches the Source view to the CD drive the disc is in. If it doesn't, click the Source scroll box to manually select the drive.

Click to identify tracks for a commercial audio CD

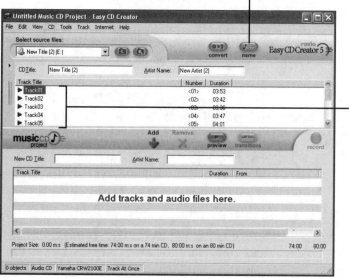

Figure 10.3

What's with this "Track 1," "Track 2" stuff?

Unidentified track data off a music CD

The good news is that, so long as you have an active Internet connection, you probably don't have to worry. Easy CD Creator can access web database and download information about almost any music CD.

To initiate this download, click the Name button in the Source pane (or click the Track menu and select Name CD Tracks). This initiates the download process. Sit tight for a few seconds while Easy CD Creator connects and locates the CD information concurrent with your disc. (If Easy CD Creator finds more than one likely candidate, you may be asked to choose from a few potential disc titles.)

Once Easy CD Creator has located the information for your CD, it replaces the generic information in the Source pane with that data (see Figure 10.4).

Figure 10.4

After the download finishes, the display makes a lot more sense!

Music CD with tracks filled in automatically using an Internet database

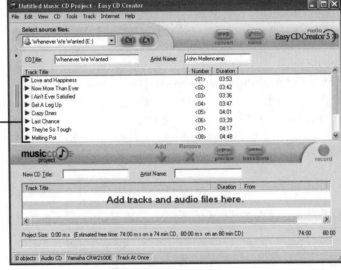

Between Tracks

Rare is the CD that Easy CD Creator can't find information about on the Internet (unless it's a custom compilation). If this happens, you can enter track information manually. Just select the track, click a second time (not a double-click) and type the track information in manually.

As you can see, the mystery CD from Figure 10.4 is actually the John Mellencamp disc, *Whenever We Wanted*. Each track is identified by the name of the song, which makes creating the layout for the new CD much easier. The good news is that you only have to do this once per CD. Easy CD Creator remembers discs that it's already identified.

If you'd rather not have to go through this series of clicks every time you insert a new CD, you can configure this service so that it works automatically. Click Tools at the top of the Easy CD Creator and then Options to open the Easy CD Creator options dialog box shown in Figure 10.5.

Three check boxes are available here. The first, Enable audio CD information download, is all you need to have Easy CD Creator get your CD's information from the web. However, if you are connecting to the Internet through a modem, it's a good idea to also check the second check box, Prompt me before attempting Internet download. This gives you a chance to establish your Internet connection (if you haven't already). Unless you're using a PC on a corporate network, you shouldn't need to worry about the third option: Access the Internet using a proxy server.

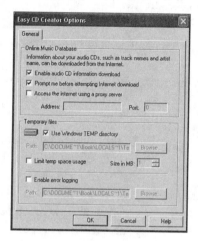

Figure 10.5

Use the Options properties page from the Tools menu to enable automatic download-ing of CD information from the Internet.

With CD information in hand, simply drag the tracks you want to record from the Source pane to the Layout pane. You can also just select the tracks and click the Add button located between the Source and Layout panes (see Figure 10.6).

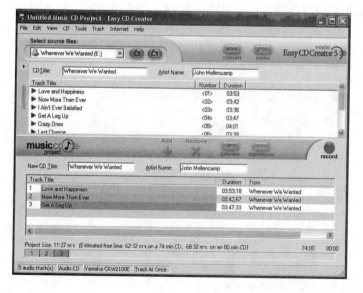

Figure 10.6

After you drag a track to the bottom pane, it becomes part of the new CD layout.

As you can see, tracks added to the Layout pane display the track number (in order), title, length, and source. Because we've only added tracks from a single artist's CD,

Easy CD Creator has also filled in the New CD Title and Artist Name fields (you can change these manually if you want).

Notice that near the bottom of this figure there is a timeline that shows how much of the CD's available time you've used up and how much free time you still have available (depending on whether you're recording to a 74-minute or 80-minute CD). Anyone who has ever tried to make audiocassettes from several sources will appreciate knowing exactly how much time they have to deal with, rather than having to guess as to whether or not they've got room to squeeze in just one more "short" track.

> **Between Tracks**
>
> Although rare, sometimes the information Easy CD Creator dredges up from the Internet is not as accurate as it should be. You should review the track names it generates to ensure there's nothing misnamed or misspelled. If there is, just rename the track, artist, or CD manually.

Here there's no running out of tape with just 30 seconds left on the last song. With Easy CD Creator (or virtually any other CD-burning software), if you use up more space than exists on the CD, the program tells you how much *overtime* you've run before the first track is ever recorded. This way, you can determine how many and which tracks you will have to remove from the layout to make it fit on a single CD.

Adding PC-Based Tracks to the Layout

Adding audio tracks, like MP3, WMA, or WAV files located on your PC is no more complicated than adding them from a CD. Use the Select Source Files scroll box and Source Pane to determine the location of your audio files. Once located, you need just select them and drag them into the Layout pane (see Figure 10.7).

Figure 10.7

This layout contains tracks from both a CD and MP3 files on a hard disk drive.

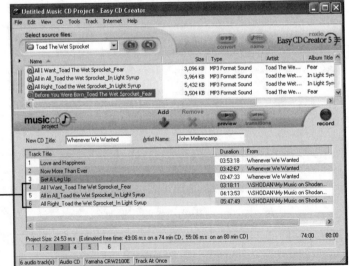

MP3s added to Layout pane from files on a hard disk drive using the Add button

As you can see, Easy CD Creator hasn't quite got the knack for using the Track Tag information I discussed in Chapter 9. If it did, this CD wouldn't still be named *Whenever We Wanted* by John Mellencamp. Nor would the track names for the MP3 files be based on file names, which on my system include the track title, artist, and album. Unfortunately, this is where making manual changes to the layout becomes necessary.

Using Multiple CDs

Unless you're making a backup of a newly purchased CD, there's not much point in recreating a duplicate music CD. Odds are you've drifted to this chapter because you want to create your own compilations. Unless you keep all your music on your hard drive (which for some of us would use a lot of hard disk space), you'll probably want to create a CD layout that contains tracks from multiple CDs.

To do this, just insert one CD at a time, selecting and adding the songs you want to the layout for each disc until you run out of space (see Figure 10.8).

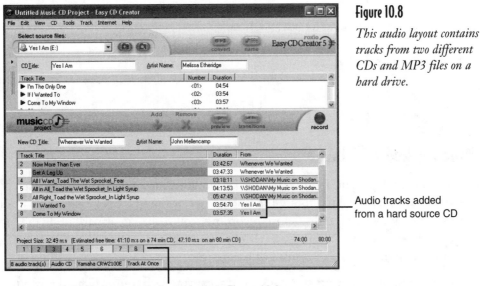

Figure 10.8

This audio layout contains tracks from two different CDs and MP3 files on a hard drive.

Audio tracks added from a hard source CD

Notice increase in Project size since Figure 10.6

Notice in this figure that as we keep adding tracks, the Project Size field continues to grow. If this project were to exceed the size of the CD to which we intend to record, we'd have to start cutting back.

This, by the way, is where it becomes important to download CD information from the Internet. Without that download, you'll have tracks from multiple CDs identified only as Track 1, Track 2, etc. To compound matters though, when you go to record, you'll be asked for Disk 1, Disk 2, and so on—instead of the actual CD and artist name. This can get really hard to keep track of if you're using a lot of CDs. Remember, if the CD information is not available online, never fear, you can put the information in yourself.

Between Tracks

While working with multiple CDs in one layout is possible, it can be a pain when it comes time to record. Even if it's only temporary, consider copying CD audio tracks to a folder on your hard drive as MP3, WMA, or WAV files.

Just select the track(s) you wish to store and click the Convert button near the top of the Source pane (or select the Track menu and click Convert to Audio File).

A Convert x Audio Tracks dialog box appears, where x is the number of tracks you selected. If using one track, you can customize the filename, but converting multiple tracks at once causes Easy CD Creator to generate the filenames automatically. Using the Save As Type scroll box, you can save the track as an MP3, WAV, or WMA file. If you're well acquainted with audio file formats, use the Format dialog box to set this option as well. If these file types and formats are Greek to you, stick with MP3 file types and the recording format (160Kbps).

Once you've set your file location, click Save and Easy CD Creator will convert the files as you've chosen. Do so for each CD you're using tracks from. Once that's complete add the files on your hard drive to your audio CD layout, rather than using the CDs themselves.

Editing the Audio CD Layout

Rare is the CD layout that doesn't need a modification of one sort or another. There's always a need to modify the track order or dump a track that won't fit on the disc. After all, what if, right before recording, you realize in a spark of divine inspiration that Van Halen's "Right Here, Right Now" should come right after Eric Clapton's "Running on Faith," instead of before it?

No worries! Simply select the track (or tracks) you wish to move, hold down the mouse button and drag it to a different location in the layout. When you move a track around like this, the program takes care of renumbering all the other tracks.

Just as adding a track to the layout is easy, removing one is also an exercise in simplicity. So when you decide that Prince's "Purple Rain" doesn't work on the same CD as John Lennon's "Imagine," you can use three methods to cut one of them:

◆ Right-click the track in the layout pane and, on the menu that appears, click Remove From CD Project.

◆ Click the song once in the layout pane and click the Remove button between the Source and Layout panes.

◆ Click the track (or tracks) and press the Delete key.

Changing the order of songs in a layout and removing songs from a layout are not only convenient when you are first creating the layout, but also when you decide to use a layout that was saved from a previous session.

Between Tracks

If hearing a track can help you decide where to put it in the layout (or whether or not it should be cut entirely), select it in either the Source or Layout panes and click the Preview button located between the two panes. This brings up a CD-player-like interface with which you can listen to the selected track.

Saving the Layout for Later Use

After creating the layout, you can then go right ahead and create the CD. However, if you think you might want to use this layout again or if you don't have time to create the CD right away, you can save it to your hard disk for later use.

To save the layout click File at the top of the Easy CD Creator program and select Save Project List. Assuming this is the first time you've saved this layout, a dialog box appears that you can use to select the location on your hard disk to which to save the layout. Just give it a name, using the File Name field and click Save.

Now, whenever you select File, Save, Easy CD Creator automatically overwrites the filename you just gave it. If you want to rename the layout, click Save Project List As in the File menu instead of Save Project List. Note that *saving the layout doesn't save any of the songs*—it just saves the information that Easy CD Creator uses to create a new CD. If you use a saved layout at a later time, you still must have the CDs or other files that were used to select songs to create the layout (and they must be in the same location as when you added them to it).

Don't Get Burned

There are two good reasons for saving the layout after it's created. First, you might want to change the order, or maybe add or delete some tracks in the future. Second, you never know when a disaster, like a Windows crash or power outage, might occur. Saving your layouts early and often can save you the extra work!

Creating an Audio CD

Having come this far, it's time to make a CD from the layout we've created. As you might guess, there are a couple ways to do this. You can use either of the following methods:

> **Between Tracks**
>
> You can also create an image of the CD you want to create. Just click CD Hard Disk Image. This puts all the data for the CD into a huge file on your hard disk (unlike a layout, this includes all your music tracks' data). You can't play this file, but you can use it at a later time to burn as many copies of the CD as you like using the File, Record CD From CD Image option. You can find more information on disc image files in Chapter 6.

- Click the Record button located between the Source and Layout panes.

- Select File from the menu bar and click Record CD.

Either of these two methods yields the same result, so it's completely up to your personal preference. However, in either case, the first thing you need to do is make sure a blank, recordable CD is in your recordable drive. Don't worry; if you forget this, you'll get prompted when it comes time to start recording. Once you click the Record button, the dialog box shown in Figure 10.9 appears (click the Options button to see the full dialog box depicted here; after you do so, the button's label changes to read Hide Options).

Figure 10.9

The Recorded CD Setup dialog box allows you to set the stage for the CD-burning process.

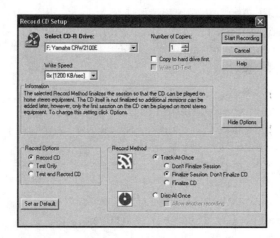

The Record CD Setup window you see here is no different from the one discussed in the section "Starting the Recording Process" of Chapter 7.

Because we're creating an audio CD, it is doubtful that there's going to be any need to create multiple sessions on the same disc. So make sure either Track-At-Once,

Finalize CD, or Disc-At-Once (leave the Allow Another Recording check box blank) are selected.

CAUTION

Don't Get Burned _____

Using the disc-at-once method has a few advantages over the track- or session-at-once methods. When recording from multiple source CDs with the other methods, you don't switch between source discs until each disc has written the track according to the order of the layout. This means you must baby-sit the entire burning process so you can switch discs when called upon to do so.

Disc-at-once prompts you to enter each CD right away so it can extract the audio tracks you have placed in the layout. So instead of writing each track out, and making you wait while it does so, it extracts each track and creates a temporary file on your hard disk. When all the tracks have been read, it then writes the entire CD, and you can go off and tend to other matters.

Finally, if you find that the preset options Easy CD Creator uses for this dialog box don't suit your needs, you can use the Set as Default button after making the necessary changes to make the program remember whatever changes you make.

When you are ready, click the Start Recording button. If this is the first time you've created a disc with Easy CD Creator, expect it to run a few tests on your drive to determine its capabilities before it actually gets to recording your disc.

It is important to understand that if you selected the disc-at-once method, after the laser starts to burn the CD, it can't stop or pause for even a second until the entire CD is written (unless your disc drive supports BurnProof technology). The burning of a track, session, or entire disc is a continuous process that cannot be interrupted from beginning to end. If the buffer becomes empty in the middle of writing a track, which can happen for various reasons, a buffer underrun occurs and your disc becomes a coaster.

After you click Start Recording (or after ECDC completes its initial test), the actual recording process begins. If you have one or more audio CDs for your source(s), Easy CD Creator prompts you for each CD in turn, collecting the necessary tracks from each disc before requesting the next CD it needs (see Figure 10.10).

After the program reads the last CD, the next step is to write the table of contents and then begin writing each track. In Figure 10.11, you can see the dialog box named Record CD Progress (be sure to click the Show Details button for the full view of this dialog box). This display shows you where the program is in the CD-burning process.

Figure 10.10

Easy CD Creator prompts you to insert each CD you have used for the layout.

Figure 10.11

The Record CD Progress dialog box shows the progress Easy CD Creator is making.

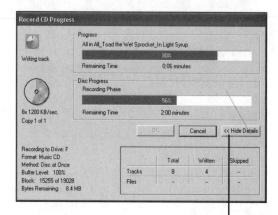

Click the Details button to show or hide
extra disc recording information

In the upper-left quadrant of this dialog box, you can see the stage of the burn process Easy CD Creator is currently at, along with an icon below that indicates the actual burn speed. The stages you should expect to see include preparation of the audio data, writing the CD-R table of contents, writing each individual track, and, depending on what record method you chose, closing the CD.

Don't Get Burned

When you are using your computer to record a CD, *don't use it for anything else* unless you have a very fast CPU, a disc recorder with BurnProof, and don't plan on making heavy use of other resources during the recording, such as your PC's memory and hard drive. As a rule of thumb, leave the computer alone while it's burning the CD!

To the right of the two icons is a pair of progress bars. The upper one indicates the progress Easy CD Creator has made on the current stage in the process. If it's recording an actual audio track, the name of the track appears above the progress bar. The second bar indicates how close to completion Easy CD Creator is in making the entire CD.

If percentages aren't enough for you, at the bottom-right you can see a small chart showing the number of tracks contained in the layout and the number that have been written so far. If you are having a bad day, you might also see something under the Skipped column, which means that the program could not write that particular track and moved on to the next one. If you're making more than one CD, text beneath the chart lets you know how many copies have been completed and how many are left to go.

If you get bored with the process, or decide you've made a big mistake, click the Cancel button at the bottom. This aborts the process, and regardless of what has been written to the CD, you'll have another coaster to put your drinks on.

After everything is finished, yet another dialog box pops up to let you know whether the process was successful or not. In most cases, you'll see the dialog box depicted in Figure 10.12.

Figure 10.12

Easy CD Creator tells you when it has finished successfully.

Notice that in addition to telling you the CD was created successfully, Easy CD Creator also asks if you'd like to create CD labels or jewel case inserts. If this is something you'd like to do now, click the CD Label Creator button and check out Chapter 16. Otherwise click Close.

Creating an MP3 CD Project CD

The key benefit behind the popularity of the MP3 file format is that it's a very compact way to store lots of near CD quality music. That music can then be offloaded to portable MP3 players, MP3-enabled car audio players, PDAs, and even some cell phones. Heck, there have already been demonstrations of MP3 watches! (Although I haven't seen one in the flesh, so to speak.)

As the capability to read and play MP3 files begins to invade every aspect of consumer electronic devices (normal CD and DVD players are starting to get in on the act), the capability to record *a lot* of MP3s to a single CD becomes more and more valuable. After all, a 64MB MP3 player might be able to store what? 12 to 15 songs or so? Compare that to the number of tracks a 650MB CD or 4.7GB DVD can store! Even if your car's CD player or your home theater's DVD player can't read MP3 files, you could still burn a single disc full of MP3s and play it in your office computer's CD-ROM. Who needs office Muzak when you can jam to Lenny Kravitz while trying to avoid any and all on-the-job responsibilities! Not to mention the fact that you've got a better chance of not hearing the same song twice when listening to a disc filled with MP3s than you do when listening to the radio, and without all those annoying commercials, too!

Although it's really little more than a glorified method of creating data CDs, Easy CD Creator comes with an MP3CD Project application that makes the process of producing an all-MP3 CD a simple one.

Creating an MP3 CD Layout

To get started, either use the Project Selector to select Make a Music CD, MP3CD Project, or use the Start menu to open Easy CD Creator, select the File menu and choose New CD Project, MP3 CD. Either way, you'll end up with the window shown in Figure 10.13.

Figure 10.13

Making an MP3 disc isn't much different from making an audio CD.

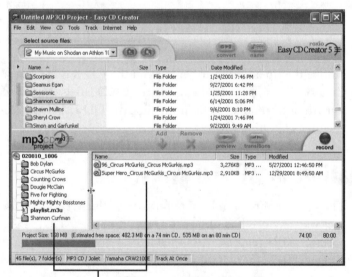

The Layout pane for an MP3 disc displays a "tree" of folders (left) and the contents of a selected folder (right)

In the default view, you may not see the tree listing on the left side of the Layout menu shown here. If you don't see it, move the mouse cursor to the left side of the pane until it becomes a horizontal double-arrow with two bars in the middle (refer to Figure 10.13) and drag it to the right. Notice in this new portion of the Layout pane there is a tree with both a disc name (the serial number) and an element called "playlist.m3u."

Just as with an audio CD, you can drag and drop (or use the Add button) every track you want to record into the Layout pane (you can add both individual files and folders full of files). Only with an MP3 disc, you can put a few dozen, a few hundred, or in the case of a DVD, a thousand MP3 music files from the Source pane to the Layout pane. The sky is very nearly the limit when making an MP3 disc.

Of course, if you have to sort through a thousand songs every time you play the disc, that sky may come tumbling down. That's where the Playlist.m3u field comes into play.

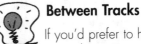

Between Tracks

If you'd prefer to have a more descriptive name for your disc or playlist—and who wouldn't—you can change it using the same click-pause-click method discussed previously. Unfortunately, the .m3u extension must remain, so you cannot get rid of it.

Working with Playlists

Since keeping track of hundreds of MP3s on a disc can be tricky, the main reason Roxio seems to have made creating an MP3 CD its own mini-application within Easy CD Creator is to let you organize MP3 files through the use of a playlist. The Playlist in the MP3CD Project window, which has the default name of playlist.m3u, allows you to customize the order in which MP3 tracks appear on an MP3 disc. However, unlike modifying track order in an audio CD, you cannot control play order in the Layout pane. Instead, you must double-click the playlist element of the Layout pane or select Edit in the menu bar and choose MP3 Playlist Editor (see Figure 10.14).

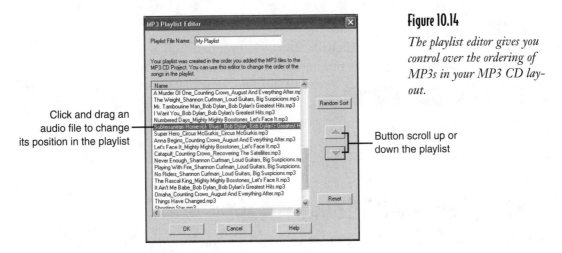

Click and drag an audio file to change its position in the playlist

Button scroll up or down the playlist

Figure 10.14

The playlist editor gives you control over the ordering of MP3s in your MP3 CD layout.

Notice in this window that in addition to being able to rename the playlist and shift tracks up and down in the list, there is also a button labeled Random Sort. After all, if you've got a CD jam-packed with MP3 files, do you really have the free time necessary to put them in a decent play order? By clicking the Random Sort button, Easy

CD Creator randomizes the play order of the MP3s in your layout. Once you're happy with the ordering of your playlist, click OK and get ready to burn.

Don't Get Burned

In testing different MP3 layouts in the MP3CD Project application, I've discovered what can only be a bug in the way the program interprets MP3 filenames. If you've got two song tracks from different artists that are similar only in that they have the same first word in the song title, Easy CD Creator interprets these files to be one and the same (overwriting the one originally added to the playlist with the one added most recently). For example, try putting "Little White Lies" from Sammy Hagar on the same MP3 layout as "Little Earthquakes" from Tori Amos. The only way to get around this is to manually alter the track name so that it's not an exact duplicate in the first word.

Copying Files for an MP3 CD

Once again, creating an MP3 CD is really no different than making an audio or data disc. However, if you want to have access to all songs at once, I do recommend that you burn only one session to a CD. This is because you have to manually switch between the sessions on a multisession disc. This is rather like having to get up to turn over a cassette tape or record. Who would want to go back to that dark age in home audio history?

To get the process moving, click the Record button to bring up the now familiar Record CD dialog box. After making sure that a blank recordable disc is in your recordable drive, click Start Recording and wait patiently for your work of digital audio art to be completed.

Cross Reference

Learn more about multisession discs in Appendix C.

Upon successful completion of the burn, give your new MP3 CD a whirl!

Getting Funky with SoundStream

If the audio features of Easy CD Creator don't get you everything you need, Roxio's CD-burning software suite has something else that probably will: SoundStream. SoundStream, which is essentially a new version of the CD Spin Doctor from previous versions of the Easy CD Creator suite, allows you to go beyond the capabilities of Easy CD Creator. In this chapter, we walk through the process of making a simple copy of a song using SoundStream. We also discuss some of the options you can use, such as recording music from a variety of sources to files on your hard drive. This, among other things, allows you to clean up audio by removing hisses, pops, and scratches.

SoundStream might sound like something that's caused by someone playing loud music on a jet, but in this case we're talking about a great program that comes with Easy CD Creator 5 Platinum. At this point we've already looked at using Easy CD Creator to duplicate CDs and to create audio and data CDs using the main Easy CD Creator application. The SoundStream application expands your recording abilities by letting you choose almost any source for which you can use a cable that attaches it to your sound card's input connector. For example, you can use SoundStream to create CDs from records (45s, 78s, and LPs), cassette tapes, radio signals, microphones, and even your TV or VCR.

After you've recorded the audio tracks you want, you can apply options that allow you to clean up some of the background noise inherent with older recordings such as records. Other options enable you to add special effects to the sounds you record. When you are ready to burn a CD, you can do it directly from the source, or you can create WAV, MP3, or WMA files on your hard disk that you can experiment with, using the clean up and sound effects tools, before sending them to a shiny new CD.

A Word About Phonographs

One thing that I particularly like about Sound-Stream is that it allows me to continue to listen to the many records I bought either as I was growing up or from yard sales and flea markets over the past few years. This way, I can make a CD copy of these fragile LPs so that they don't have to be subjected to an eventual, slow death when I play them over and over again.

To transfer the audio from old phonograph records you have lying around, you, obviously, must have a phonograph player. Although that might seem redundant, keep in mind that finding a good phonograph player in the new millennium might require the assistance of an

Between Tracks

Those of you who own Creative Labs Live 5.1 or Audigy Platinum (with the LiveDrive) will have extra appreciation for Sound-Stream's capabilities. It finally gives you an opportunity to put all those extra connectors and inputs to work!

Don't Get Burned

Playing vinyl records on a banged up phonograph, particularly one with a badly worn needle, can further degrade the only copy you own of a particular record. For this reason, backing up your LPs on CD becomes a valuable alternative.

archaeologist on par with Indiana Jones. You can look around in yard sales and such, but I caution you to beware of that source. You're likely to get a unit that either doesn't work, or that has a needle in such bad condition that the end results won't be worth the effort or cost.

Although you aren't likely to find phonograph players at the local discount retailers or even some of the supposedly totally audio/video concept stores, you will find them here and there. While the few totally new players that can be found might not be cheap, believe me when I say that it is worth the cost. Shelling out a little over a $100 is a worthy expense if you are going to use the device to transfer music from vinyl that might never be remastered on CD.

And, if you like the results you get using SoundStream, you might start frequenting yard sales a little more often to look for some long-out-of-print titles and discover music you once thought lost.

When purchasing a phonograph player, however, there is one important factor to consider. In the "olden" days of component stereo systems, you bought a receiver/amplifier, speakers, tape deck, and phonograph as separate items. The phonograph plugged into the receiver using a special port that directed its sound through a pre-amplifier. If you use this kind of phonograph with your sound card, there's no pre-amp, so you'll either have to buy one—check Radio Shack, they'll know what you're talking about—or buy a new phonograph that has audio/video outputs, which means that it has its own preamp built into its guts.

Between Tracks

If you're stuck trying to plug a preampless phonograph player into your sound-card, there's another way to get around the problem than buying a new "amp'd" phonograph player. If you can connect your current player to a component stereo system that has a headphone jack, you can connect your sound card to the receiver using a headphone cable that has the appropriate plugs at both ends. You might lose a touch of sound quality, but it's cheaper than buying a new phonograph player!

The SoundStream Interface

Because using SoundStream to create CDs from other music CDs or MP3 files is not much different from doing so in Easy CD Creator, this section focuses on getting tracks from multiple sources into your Music Library, cleaning up any imperfections in that music, and then burning it onto a CD.

Starting up the SoundStream application is simple. Just double-click the Easy CD Creator desktop icon, pass your mouse over Make a Music CD, and then click SoundStream from the options in the middle of the window. This starts Sound-Stream, bringing up an application window that looks very different from Easy CD Creator (see Figure 10.15).

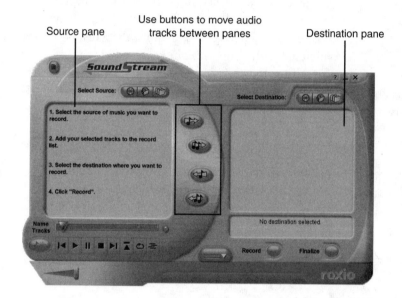

Figure 10.15

Using SoundStream to record a CD is a simple four-step process.

At the top of the SoundStream window is a Menu button, which gives you access to various micro-managing controls that, with the exception of Preferences, you'll likely never need to use.

This window is divided into two main sections: Source and Destination. The four buttons between the two panes are used to move tracks from one side to the other. The three buttons on top of each pane control the media type for that source or destination: CD, Media Library, or Hard Disk. (Recording tunes from an analog source requires the use of Spin Doctor, which I get to later in this chapter.)

Anyone associated with a home stereo or car radio built in the last 20 years recognizes the play control icons underneath the Source pane. Underneath those is a volume control.

Finally, the button between both panes is an Options Drawer that provides access to various controls and features that SoundStream can utilize. Keep this button in the back of your mind for now; we'll come back to it soon. Before we get to all that though, let's take a look at how to record music into the SoundStream Music Library.

Setting Your Recording Preferences

A new feature in SoundStream with Easy CD Creator 5 is the implementation of a Music Library for storing information about audio files on your computer. I'm beginning to believe that Music Libraries must be the big thing for the new millennium because virtually every audio related PC program, like MusicMatch Jukebox, Windows Media Player, etc., etc., uses one. Unfortunately, the Music Library included with SoundStream is not nearly as user friendly as those assembled in other applications (for reasons I'll explain as we go along).

Before you can get busy adding contents to the Media Library, you need to jump through a couple of preparatory hoops. In SoundStream, click the SoundStream Menu button and choose Properties from the list that appears. This brings up a properties dialog box, from which you should select the Music Library tab (see Figure 10.16).

> **Don't Get Burned**
>
> If you want a custom location in which to store audio files, make sure that location already exists on your computer. You cannot create new folders from within the Browse For Folder dialog box. If you don't know how to create a folder using My Computer or Windows Explorer, it's probably best that you stick with the default.

Figure 10.16

The Music Library tab allows you to customize the way in which SoundStream stores music on your hard disk.

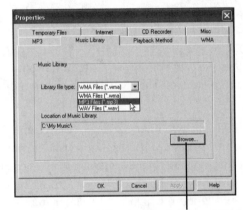

Click to change location of Music Library

This is where you select what kind of files you want the Media Library to record audio as and where you want those files stored. You can easily use the default location for storing your audio files, but you may already have a different location in mind. To change the location on your computer, click the Browse button. From the Library File Type scroll box select either MP3, WMA, or WAV files. The default is WMA, but as I've stated elsewhere, I think MP3 is a better format (certainly a more universally accepted one).

Assuming you didn't choose the WAV file format, there is still one more hoop for you to jump through. For both MP3 and WMA files you need to choose the encoding quality SoundStream will use to create these files. There are individual tabs for both MP3 and WMA files in the Properties dialog box. Click the one appropriate for your use and make the necessary adjustments to the Encoding scroll box.

Cross Reference

See Chapter 9 for more information on audio file format qualities.

The first step in making the Media Library useful is actually getting music stored in it. To do this you need to locate a folder on your hard disk with audio files or insert a music CD into your CD-ROM drive that contains music you want to store on your hard disk.

Putting CD Music in the Media Library

Getting music tracks into the Media Library is no big trial. To record from a CD, follow these steps:

1. Insert the music CD into your CD-ROM drive. SoundStream will immediately recognize it.

2. To get track names for an unknown CD click the Name Tracks button underneath the Source List. It will take a few moments for SoundStream to connect to the Internet and get the information it needs. Once it's done, you'll see the CD's contents displayed properly (as opposed to, Track 1, Track 2, etc.) in the Source List.

3. Once you have the CD information, you need to create a place on your hard disk to store it. On the Record List, choose the Music Library button. This opens the Save Album As dialog box.

4. Click the New button to bring up the Properties dialog box shown in Figure 10.17 and then enter the album's information (title, artist, and genre). The information you enter here causes folders to be created on your hard drive to store the music in (a folder for the artist with a sub-folder for the CD title).

 Between Tracks

If this is the first time you've used SoundStream to put music on your hard drive, it will need to test the audio extraction (or ripping) speed of your source CD drive.

5. This will add that CD's artist and album titles to the Music Library list on the left side of the Save Album As list. Select the folder you just created and click Choose. This sets your destination for the CD files.

Figure 10.17

The Music Library Properties dialog box uses the information you enter to create folders for the CD artist and title on your hard drive.

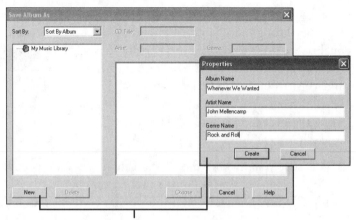

Click New to open the album Properties dialog box

6. If you only want certain files off the disc, either select them one at a time and click the Add Selected button or select multiple files by Ctrl-clicking each one before clicking the Add Selected button. To add all the files, click the Add All button.

7. Finally, you're ready to begin recording the CD to your hard disk. Clicking the Record button brings up a new recording screen where the Source List used to be. This screen has, big surprise, yet another record button (as if you didn't mean it the first time). Click this Record button to make all the magic happen (see Figure 10.18). Depending on how many audio tracks you're ripping, be prepared for a lengthy wait.

Once the recording is complete, a small dialog box pops up letting you know. Just click OK to send this message box packing.

Figure 10.18

The recording process is monitored where the Source List normally appears.

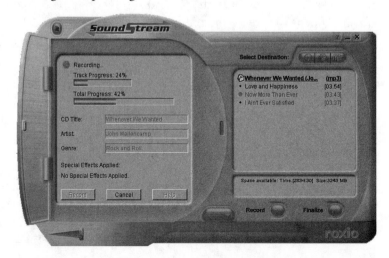

Putting Existing Audio Files in the Music Library

If getting files from music CD to the Music Library seems like a tedious process, you might want to just sit back and take a break. Logging existing files on your hard drive into the Music Library, which ought to be an easy task, requires a fair amount of hoop-jumping as well.

Because the Music Library is very specific (and inflexible) about where it wants to store audio files, a folder for the artist and a subfolder for the CD title, it can be a chore getting existing audio files in it without a lot of finagling.

If you've already got a ton of MP3 or WMA files on your hard disk in a filing system with which you're quite happy, but that's not like the one shown here, you may want to consider abandoning your use of the Music Library. However, if you're just starting out or don't mind the hassle, just use these steps:

1. In the Source List, click the Select Folder As Source button to bring up the dialog box shown in Figure 10.19.

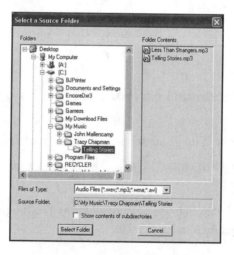

Figure 10.19

The Select a Source Folder dialog box allows you to browse for folders on your hard drive that contain audio files.

2. In the Select a Source Folder dialog box, browse to the location of your existing MP3, WMA, or WAV files. When you select a location with valid audio files in it, those files appear in the pane on the right of the dialog box. Once you've got the location you want selected, click Select Folder.

3. The tracks in this folder now appear in the Source List, so it's time to set your destination. Click the CD button in the Select Destination area (refer to Figure 10.15) and follow steps four and five from the previous section, "Putting CD Music in the Media Library," to add the destination folder.

4. Now select the tracks you want to add to the Record List and use the Add buttons to get them there.

5. Finally, click both the first Record button and the second one that pops up.

SoundStream begins copying the files to their new location, which is a much quicker process than for copying from CD. However, now you've got a new problem. The file or files you've just copied are taking up space in two different locations on your hard drive. If you only want to keep the new copy(s), make sure you use My Computer or Windows Explorer to delete the old one(s).

> **Don't Get Burned**
>
> Should you decide you no longer want to view a CD listing in your Music Library you can delete it from the Save Album As dialog box. Be warned however, that this not only removes the listing from the Media Library, but it also removes the tracks and folders from your hard drive.

Now, as this is all pretty simple you may think you're sitting pretty right about now. However, if you've already got hundreds of MP3 or WMA files on your hard drive that you want to convert, that smile is going to disappear. Remember that for every artist and every CD in your collection, you're going to have to repeat steps four and five from the previous section for every single one of them.

Recording from a CD to Folders on Your Hard Drive

Recording files from CD to your hard drive is a very similar process to putting files into the Media Library. The good news is that this is far simpler. Here are the steps:

1. With a music CD in your CD drive, select the Music CD button for the Source List.

2. In the Record List, click the Select Folder as Destination button. This brings up the dialog box shown in Figure 10.20.

3. Using this Save File As dialog box, choose a location to which you want to store the CD tracks you want recorded (if you plan to store them in folders named after the artist and CD title, just use the Media Library steps from the previous sections).

   If you want to put your music files in a folder that doesn't currently exist, get as close as you can in the folder tree to the location you want and click the New Folder button. This adds a sub-folder to the currently selected folder (type in a new name for it).

Figure 10.20

This dialog box allows you to select a folder on your hard drive in which to store audio files.

4. In the Save as Type scroll box, choose to record your music files as WAV, MP3, or WMA. Once you have the folder you want highlighted, click the Select Folder button.

5. Select the files you want recorded to this destination and use the appropriate Add button to add them to the Record List.

6. Once you're ready, click the Record button once and then click the second Record button that appears where the Source List used to be. This kicks off the recording process just as we described in the "Putting Music in the Media Library from CD" section.

Once the recording process is complete, click OK on the confirmation dialog box and you're good to go!

Recording to CD

For this example, we are going to keep it simple and add source tracks from both a CD and files on your hard drive that can be recorded to a CD-R disc. As with recording to your hard disk or Media Library, you must first select a source using the three buttons above the Source list that I've already described. Then select the Select Music CD As Destination button from the equivalent set of Record List buttons.

The list shown in Figure 10.21 has tracks selected from multiple CDs, a folder on my hard drive, and from my SoundStream Media Library bound for a final destination on the blank CD-R in my recordable drive.

Figure 10.21

The Destination List shown here includes three tracks from the Music Library, three from a folder on the hard disk, and three directly from another CD.

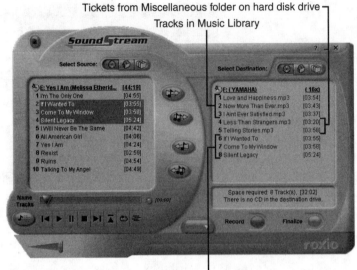

Tickets from Miscellaneous folder on hard disk drive

Tracks in Music Library

Tracks from the music CD

From here it's a simple matter of clicking Record (again, in two locations as described in the "Putting CD Music in the Media Library" section of this chapter).

The CD recording process begins. (The recording process for a CD is no different than what you saw earlier, in Figure 10.18.) Depending on the speed of your drive and how much music you're recording (up to 74 or 80 minutes, depending on the type of CD-R you're using), this could take anywhere from an hour to 5 or 10 minutes. When the process is complete, click OK in the success dialog box that appears. Assuming you don't intend to add anything more to the disc you've recorded to, click the Finalize button to close the CD.

Making SoundStream Sing with the Options Drawer

SoundStream contains a host of options you can choose from that can be used to obtain music from a wide variety of sources and modify the quality of sound you've recorded. These options can be found by clicking the Show Options button on the main SoundStream window. This opens up a tray of buttons that you can use to modify and record audio and open applications related to the music content creation and recording process (see Figure 10.22).

Click to
scroll right   Click to show or hide the Options drawer   Click to scroll left

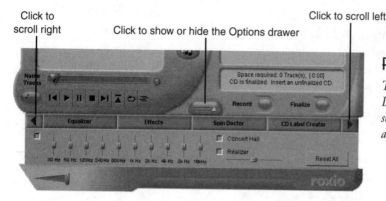

Figure 10.22

The SoundStream Options Drawer gives you access to several audio CD related applications and controls.

This Options Drawer contains a wealth of controls for you to make use of. These controls include the following:

◆ **Equalizer.** Brings up a graphic equalizer that allows those who aren't tone deaf (like myself) to change the amplitude of selected sound frequencies for an audio track. Unless you already know what all these frequencies are, I recommend you leave these alone.

◆ **Effect.** Gives you access to three audio quality-related controls: Sound Cleaning Level, Pop Removal Level, and the Normalizer. Use the check boxes associated with each option to enable or disable them.

◆ **Sound Cleaning Level.** A tool for removing the hiss if you're recording from an audio tape. Use the slider to control the degree of aggressiveness with which you want SoundStream to attempt to remove the hiss.

◆ **Pop Removal Lever.** If recording from an LP, the Pop Removal Level allows you to attempt to remove the pops that come from playing a scratched vinyl album.

◆ **Normalizer.** If you're looking to make a compilation CD from several sources, you'll no doubt find that many of those sources were originally recorded at different levels (so some songs play louder than others). Enabling the Normalizer tool causes SoundStream to analyze every track in your Record List for variances in recorded volume level. It then equalizes them.

Between Tracks

The Sound Cleaning and Pop Removal sliders are more aggressive when set further to the right and less intrusive (to sound quality) when set to the left.

◆ **Spin Doctor.** In Easy CD Creator 4 this was essentially what SoundStream is in Easy CD Creator 5. In Easy CD Creator 5, its focus has moved solely toward recording audio from outside analog sources, such as audio cassettes and LP records. We'll discuss the Spin Doctor in the "Using the SoundStream Disc Doctor" section.

◆ **CD Label Creator.** Opens the CD Label Creator application that we cover in Chapter 16.

◆ **Sound Editor.** This opens up the Sound Editor application. We don't cover this application in this book as it strays even further from the topic of actually creating CDs than I already have.

◆ **Internet Links.** Clicking this button displays a series of Internet links located on Roxio's website (if your connection is not active, SoundStream automatically dials it). None of these links are particularly useful unless there's information you need that only Roxio can provide (like information on product updates).

Using the SoundStream Spin Doctor

As we hinted at way back at the beginning of this discussion, you can use Sound-Stream to recover aging music collections from decaying analog sources like LPs and audio cassettes. This requires the use of the SoundStream Spin Doctor. To open the Spin Doctor, make sure the SoundStream Options Drawer is open and click the Disc Doctor's button from the list. The screen shown in Figure 10.23 appears.

Figure 10.23

The new face of the CD Spin Doctor is quite different from what users of Easy CD Creator 4 were used to.

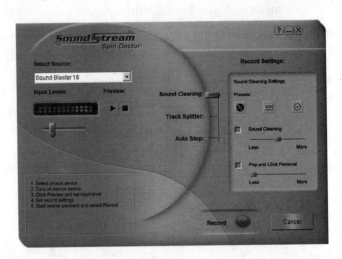

As you can see there are quite a few options listed in this window. However, as this screen indicates, it all boils down to five basic steps.

1. Select a source (like a cassette or record player)

2. Turn the source on

3. Set input levels

4. Set record settings (these are the pop and hiss removal sliders discussed in the options drawer section)

5. Start source playback and select record

Really, this is a bit of a simplification on Roxio's part, but we'll walk you through it, so don't worry.

Selecting a Source

Selecting a source involves making two decisions. One, what the real source of your music will be (like an LP or audio cassette). Two, what input connection on your sound card that will require. The available inputs are listed in the Select Source drop-down list. Generally, you'll want an option that indicates an input from your sound card.

Once your source is selected, make sure you've connected it to your PC's sound card and turned its power on. In Figure 10.24, you can see how I've connected my Sony Walkman to my PC using front-mounted ports that come with the Live Platinum 5.1.

Figure 10.24

Connecting an audio cassette player to a PC through the Creative Labs LiveDrive device.

Once connected, ensure that the cassette, LP, or whatever audio source you're using is set to the position containing the music you want to capture.

Setting Input Levels

With your audio equipment all set up and raring to go, you need to make sure you're recording at a level that's not going to blow out your speakers. First, make sure the Input Levels slider is set to a position somewhere in the left third of the slider.

Now it's time to preview your audio to ensure that you're hearing what you want to hear. Start playing the music from your source and then hit the Preview Play button. Once the audio begins playing, you should be able to hear it coming out of your computer speakers, and the Input Levels lights should spring to life.

Watch the Input Levels lights closely. What you want to see while audio is playing is the green lights consistently lit, with occasional spikes into the yellow range. If it gets as far as the red lights once in a while, that's okay, but if you find that you're consistently in the red, lower the Input Levels slider (if it's too quiet, slide it farther to the right).

Once you're satisfied with the input level, click the Preview Stop button and stop playing your source.

Adjusting Record Settings

Now that you're almost ready to go, it's time to deal with the issue of recording quality. Specifically …

♦ Cleaning up any fingernails-on-chalkboard type pops or hissing that might be present on your audio source.

♦ Splitting up multiple tracks (after all, vinyl records and audio cassettes don't have easily identifiable divisions between tracks like CDs do).

♦ Setting auto-stop options for controlling when the recording session should end. Making sure that the Record Settings slider is set to Sound Cleaning, notice that Spin Doctor contains three presets for recording audio sources and the level of cleaning these sources should get. You should feel free to experiment with these sliders manually, but generally speaking, you should just click the Presets buttons for Record, Tape, or CD and leave it at that.

> **CAUTION**
>
> **Don't Get Burned**
>
> Setting the Split whenever silence is detected slider too low will cause the Spin Doctor to split tracks too frequently (like between beats in a song). However, setting it too high will cause it to skip over silences entirely, causing separate tracks to not be split at all.

Taking the Record Settings slider down to the option for Track Splitting, you'll see options like the ones in Figure 10.25.

⚠ CAUTION

Don't Get Burned

Don't forget to clean up your source before you use the cleanup options of Spin Doctor. For LPs, use a good record-cleaning kit to make sure the LP is in tiptop condition before you record. If you haven't used the phonograph in a while, make sure the needle is clean and take appropriate action. For tape decks, you can usually use isopropyl alcohol and a cotton swab to clean the tape heads. Doing all this sort of work upfront can only help to improve the sound you get recorded to CD.

Although Spin Doctor can perform some cleanup of the sound outputted from your LP, this is done based strictly on the audio signal it gets. For some of its work, Spin Doctor looks for specific patterns in the signal based on the degree you tell Spin Doctor to look for (thus the sliding bars). When it sees these patterns it either eliminates them (as in pops and clicks from scratches) or tones them down (as when it performs a general sound cleanup). Sometimes a particular frequency is toned down or removed—whether it is background noise or part of the intended song; Spin Doctor cannot tell. You should record your audio to a file and experiment with Spin Doctor to find out which settings work best—for each LP from which you're recording!

Here you can control if you want Spin Doctor to determine when to split up tracks and, if so, how you want it to do it. To eliminate the option entirely, select No track splitting. If you want your audio stream to be broken up into tracks of equal lengths, use the spin-box control to select how many equal lengths you want. Finally, you can have Spin Doctor attempt to split the tracks whenever a certain amount of silence is detected. You'll need to experiment with the slider on this option to find an ideal setting.

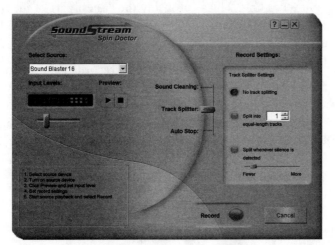

Figure 10.25

Use Track Splitter Settings options to control how Spin Doctor should split a single analog stream into multiple tracks.

If you ratchet the Record Settings slider down one more notch, you get the options shown in Figure 10.26 for Auto Stop settings.

Figure 10.26

Using Auto Stop settings, you can control when Spin Doctor stops recording from an analog device.

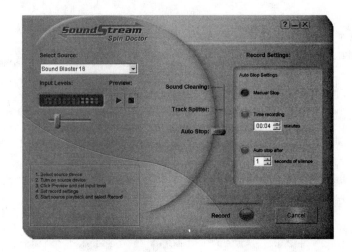

Auto Stop settings allow you to control when recording of analog audio should stop. The best option is probably to stick with the Manual Stop options and take care of it all yourself. However, if you want to turn over contro to the Spin Doctor, you can select either Time recording to record for a set amount of time before stopping, or to Auto stop after a specific period of silence. The former option is useful if you're recording a specific track and already know its length. The latter allows you to attempt to break after a break in songs, or by setting for a longer silence gap, at the end of a tape or record where there is nothing but silence.

Making It All Digital

Finally, it's time to begin recording. This is probably the easiest part of the whole process. Just get your source to its start point (don't start it yet!) and hit the Record button. This brings up the window shown in Figure 10.27.

From here you need to select a name for the track being recorded and the recording destination (File or CD). If you select File, you need to choose a folder on your hard drive in which to place the file (you can only record to WAV format). If you select CD (which I don't recommend, you can always record to CD later), make sure a blank disc is in your recorder before you start. When you're ready, click the Start Recording button and get your audio source playing. (When you click the Start Recording button, the interface changes to include Pause Recording and Stop buttons.)

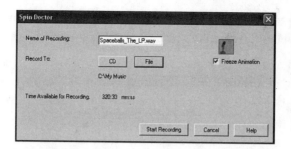

Figure 10.27

Choosing a location to store the analog audio stream and what to call it.

Between Tracks

Usually it's best to record to your hard drive first, without using any sound cleaning options. This way you're getting your audio, in its current state, into a digital format on your hard disk. Once it's there you can always experiment with different sound cleaning options or deal with converting it to the MP3 or WMA audio file formats. By recording directly to CD you're pretty much putting all your chips down on the idea that it will be perfect the first time, which probably won't be the case if you're not yet experienced using all these options.

The recording process now begins. While the recording is happening you can only choose to Pause Recording or Stop. Keep an eye on the Time Available for Recording field, as it will let you know if you're running out of storage space on your chosen location for the music. When you're ready to stop, click the Stop button and stop your source from playing. A small SoundStream dialog box pops up, letting you know that your recording was successful. Click OK and go enjoy your new digital music file!

The Least You Need to Know

- ◆ Easy CD Creator provides mini-applications that allow you to create CD-audio and MP3 discs.

- ◆ When creating an audio CD, make sure to finalize the disc before attempting to play it in a home audio CD player.

- ◆ A normal CD can store hundreds of near CD-quality MP3 files. A DVD can store upward of a thousand! That can get you through a long work day without having to hear the same song twice.

- ◆ Use SoundStream instead of Easy CD Creator when you want to build a Music Library or manipulate your audio using options the aforementioned program doesn't have.

◆ Use Spin Doctor to record from almost any analog source—phonograph, cassette player, and microphone—directly to the CD recorder or your hard drive.

◆ When recording from an analog source, use Spin Doctor's cleaning options to do some cleanup work on audio that doesn't play as clearly as it used to. Also, make sure you're starting with a clean source.

Chapter 11

Getting Jiggy with Nero

In This Chapter

- ◆ How to configure a new audio compilation

- ◆ How to add tracks to a new compilation

- ◆ How to identify and make basic edits to audio tracks

- ◆ How to burn an audio compilation to CD

While using your disc recorder to perform data backups is important, it's not nearly as much as creating an audio CD with a collection of your favorite music tracks. Nero Burning ROM makes this job a snap, using an interface not at all dissimilar to that used to create a data CD.

Discs created using Nero Burning ROM are built through the use of what Ahead Software refers to as *compilations*. When you create a disc you must first tell Nero how to configure a new compilation. Once set, you can begin "compiling" the source audio you want burned to disc (hence the name compilation). From there burning your audio CD is a snap.

Between Tracks

If you want to create a disc comprised of just MP3 or other audio file formats, you can just create a generic MP3 disc (CD, DDCD, or DVD). See Chapter 8.

Because this chapter focuses exclusively on creating an audio disc, I only cover CDs in this chapter. You cannot create an audio disc in the DDCD or DVD format (since there is no audio disc standard for these types of media).

Open Nero Burning ROM to get started (click Start, All Programs, ahead Nero, Nero-Burning Rom). (If the Nero Wizard opens, click the Close Wizard button.)

Between Tracks

There are two new high-fidelity disc audio standards that are in the early phases of warring for your consumer dollar: Super Audio CD (SACD) and DVD-Audio (DVD-A). No consumer application available, to the best of my knowledge, supports burning discs in these formats. Indeed, even finding set-top players with support for them is still a bit of a challenge. Finding affordable set-top players is just about impossible for those on any kind of budget.

New Compilation Options

When started, Nero should immediately open the New Compilation window. If it doesn't, open the File menu and select New (see Figure 11.1, in the "The Audio-CD Tab" section).

In the New Compilation window you must first select CD from the media type scroll box in the upper-left corner. From the list of icons underneath this scroll box, choose Audio-CD, just as in the figure.

As you can see if you skip ahead to Figure 11.1, there are four tabs on the New Compilation window that control how Nero configures your audio disc.

◆ Info

◆ Audio-CD (the default tab)

◆ CDA Options

◆ Burn

Each the following sections covers the controls and information found in these tabs.

The Info Tab

If you click the Info tab, Nero displays information about your current compilation. As this is a new compilation, you haven't yet selected any tracks to include on your audio CD. So the information here, disc Size (in time and duration) and Number Of Tracks, should both all be zeroed-out. When it comes time to burn the CD, Nero takes you to a window that contains the same tabs found here. At that time, if you return to the Info tab you should find that both fields contain information about your compilation.

The Audio-CD Tab

The Audio-CD tab is the tab that Nero selects by default when you choose to create a new audio CD compilation. It's broken up into two sets of information, neither of which do you have to fill in to create an Audio CD (see Figure 11.1).

Select to create an audio file

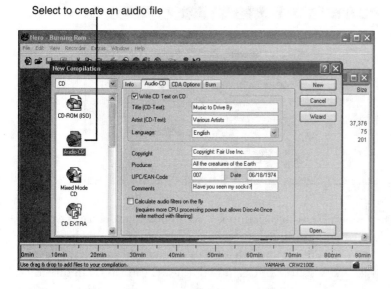

Figure 11.1

Fill in as much information as you want using this tab. You don't have to enter any if you don't want.

The first set of information contains fields for Title, Artist, and Language. As you can see from the figure, the Title and Artist fields have the words "CD-Text" in parentheses. If you enable the Write CD Text On CD check box, Nero burns this information in with the track data on your audio CD. Many newer CD players can read CD-Text information and display it for you while playing the disc. Though it's not listed here, CD text also includes each individual track title and artist (if there's more than one).

The only other non-self-explanatory option on this tab is the check box labeled Calculate audio filters on the fly. Nero includes various audio filters that you can apply to individual tracks. These filters take time to process, however if you have a fast enough processor in your PC Nero may be able to apply them as it writes the CD. This makes burning discs in which you've applied filters a faster process. However, if your PC can't keep up with the work load, the burn will surely fail. If you're unsure of whether or not to check this option, either leave it disabled or simulate the burn prior to actually making the recording.

The CDA Options Tab

The CDA Options tab allows you to configure various options that control which drive you use to rip audio (if your source audio is another CD) and how to handle audio tracks prior to burning them to disc. There are two sections on this tab: General settings and Track reference settings (see Figure 11.2).

Figure 11.2

Most of the controls on the CDA Options tab let you determine how to rip any source audio tracks from a music CD.

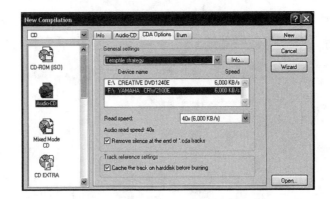

The first option in the General Settings section is a scroll box that determines the "strategy" Nero employs when writing the disc. To choose a strategy you have to understand that Nero can handle audio CD-based source tracks in two ways. It can rip them directly from the source to the disc you're recording, or it can store the tracks on your hard drive first. The former is faster, the latter is more reliable. Of course, you do have to have at least two disc drives to have much in the way of options here. There are four options from which you can choose that tell Nero how to handle CD tracks:

Don't Get Burned

If you choose a strategy that involves directly ripping source audio tracks from CD to your target disc then you cannot use your disc recorder to rip the source music (because that's the drive you're using to record).

- **Disk space strategy.** Using this strategy, Nero uses the amount of available disc space to determine whether or not to store CD tracks, temporarily, on your hard disk. By default, if there is enough space, it uses your hard disk.

- **Device Dependent strategy.** Using this strategy means that you can put your source disc in a ROM or recordable disc drive. If you use a ROM drive then Nero records directly from disc to disc. If you use your recorder, then Nero writes the source audio files, temporarily, to your hard disk.

- **Reference strategy.** Using this strategy Nero always copies CD audio from your source disc directly to the target. This means your source audio disc must be in your CD or DVD-ROM drive.

- **Temp file strategy.** Using this strategy, Nero always copies CD audio from your source disc to your hard drive first. With this method, you can rip the music from either your ROM drive or your disc recorder. This is the strategy I prefer as it is the most reliable and allows me to rip audio from my recorder drive, which it is faster than my DVD-ROM drive.

Once you've selected a strategy, you can choose the disc drive you want Nero to use if it needs to rip audio tracks from another music CD. Use the Read speed scroll box to select a maximum read speed for the selected drive. Nero automatically chooses your drive's top speed. But if you're having quality problems with your ripped audio, you should lower this setting. Beneath this scroll box Nero determines what it considers to be the fastest ripping speed the selected drive can support. Many disc drives cannot rip audio as quickly as they can other types of data, so often this indicator will be less than the maximum read speed for your drive.

If you've listened to CDs long enough then you know that there's usually a bit of "dead-air" at the end of each audio track. Sometimes this is a tolerable gap of silence, other times you'll find discs that put as much as 5 to 10 seconds of quiet at the end of a track. By enabling the Remove silence at the end of *.cda Tracks check box, you give Nero the right to chop this dead air off the track. Sometimes this is the difference between fitting one more audio track on your disc or running out of space.

Between Tracks

Though most of this section focuses on what to do when recording from one audio disc to another, remember that you can also record from audio files on your hard disk, such as MP3s.

There is only one option from which to choose in the Track reference settings section of this tab. If you enable this check box, then Nero automatically writes the CD audio to a special cache file on your hard disk before recording to CD. This is a little different from the temporary files Nero can create based on the recording strategy you select. Enabling this option also increases burn reliability, because it provides a more consistent flow of data from your PC to your disc recorder (lowering the chance of a buffer-underrun).

The Burn Tab

The Burn tab is where you get to configure the options for your disc recorder. This tab is no different from the one I showed you in Chapter 8 for recording a data disc (see Figure 11.3).

Figure 11.3

The options on the Burn tab let you configure how to burn your audio compilation to disc.

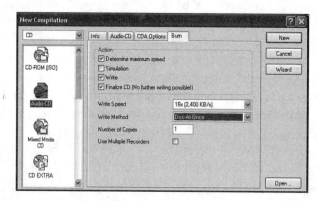

Use the Action section to enable or disable the following check boxes:

♦ **Determine maximum speed.** Enabling this option determines the speed of each source from which you have selected audio to record. This can increase burn reliability because it lets Nero get a good idea of how quickly it can expect to draw data from each source. (The fastest source of audio on your PC is usually your hard drive.)

♦ **Simulation.** If you want Nero to test write the disc before writing it for real enable this check box. Unless you're burning with Nero for the first time with your recordable drive or are having problems burning a disc, you are probably safe disabling this check box.

♦ **Write.** If you only want to test your recording and don't want to record a disc regardless of test results, disable the Write check box.

◆ **Finalize CD (No further writing possible).** If you know that you don't ever want to add more data to this disc, enable this check box. Finalizing a CD helps ensure it's compatible with the widest range of disc drives.

Underneath the Action section is a series of options that allow you to configure your maximum Write Speed (on the recordable drive), Write Method (consult Appendix C for information on these methods), Number of Copies to make, or whether or not you want to Use Multiple Recorders (if you have them).

When you're satisfied that all is as you want it, click the New button to choose the audio you want included on your CD.

Creating an Audio Compilation

When you click the New button from the New Compilation window you're taken to the main Nero interface. You should see two windows open inside Nero that look similar to the Windows File Explorer and My Computer (see Figure 11.4).

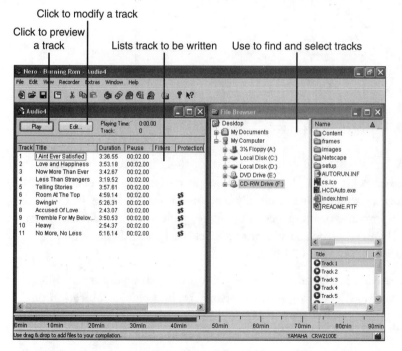

Click to modify a track

Click to preview a track

Lists track to be written

Use to find and select tracks

Figure 11.4

The tracks listed here contain audio from MP3 files and two separate music CDs.

By default, the window Nero opens on the left carries the name "Audio," while on the right, Nero opens a File Browser window. If the File Browser window does not open, or if you accidentally close it, click View, New File Browser to reopen it. To add audio to your compilation, just locate and select it in the File Browser window and drag it to the Audio window. You can select from any folder on your hard drive(s) or from any other attached storage device, like a RW or ROM CD/DVD drive.

You'll notice when you insert a music CD and select the source drive in the File Browser window it only identifies the tracks as Track01, Track02, etc. (It may also appear as Audio1, Audio2, etc.) When you drag tracks from the File Browser to the Audio window Nero attempts to identify the tracks (see Figure 11.5).

Figure 11.5

Use this window to automatically obtain information about any commercial music CD.

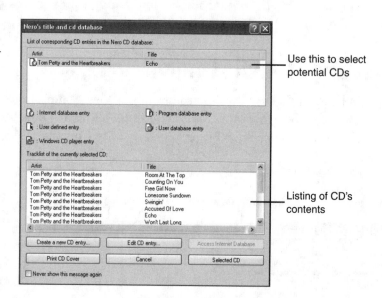

Use this to select potential CDs

Listing of CD's contents

If it does not already know what CD you have inserted, click the Access Internet Database button. This quickly identifies your CD. If more than one entry appears on the pane on top, select the one that most closely matches your CD. If any of the Artist or Title information is missing or incorrect in the lower pane, click the Create a new CD entry or Edit CD entry buttons to add or edit a selected track. When you're ready to proceed, click the Selected CD button.

If you have yet to create a User Database in Nero to store CD track information, a window appears asking you if you want to do so. Click Yes and choose a location on your hard disk to store this database (a My Music folder or the location to which you installed Nero should suffice). You should only have to create this database one time. After that Nero automatically uses it to store information about each CD you identify.

Once you have audio tracks in your compilation, you can arrange them in the order you want by clicking and dragging them up or down in the track list. If you want to preview a track, click the Play button. If you want to physically edit the audio in the track, click the Edit button. This opens the Nero Wave Editor program. You can use this program to cut audio from the track, add special effects, or perform other "enhancements." Discussion of this tool would require a chapter in and of itself and falls outside the focus of this book. For an explanation of Nero's more basic track editing tools, see the next section.

Once you've set your compilation, you have just a few more hoops to jump through before you can get the recording process started.

> **Don't Get Burned**
>
> Nero does not let you select audio from another networked computer. So if you have a home network and want to use audio files from a networked PC, you must copy them to the PC with which you're recording.

Tuning Your Tracks

Nero includes a few extra tools that allow you to tune your audio to your tastes. If you double-click any track in the Audio window, it opens an Audio Track Info window (see Figure 11.6).

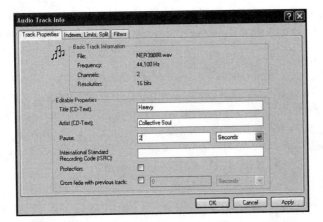

Figure 11.6

The tabs in this window allow you to tweak various components of the track to your liking.

This window has three tabs:

- ◆ **Track Properties.** This tab provides basic information about the track's audio quality. It also allows you to change the title, artist, and set the duration of pause between tracks after it has finished playing.

- ◆ **Indexes, Limits, Split.** This tab allows you to physically modify the track (see Figure 11.7).

Figure 11.7

You can split a track in two or mark edit points using the Indexes, Limits, Split tab.

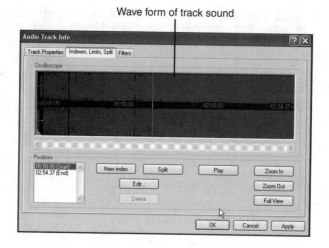

Wave form of track sound

Use the Split button on this tab to split a track into two separate parts. This can be useful if you have a track comprised of two separate songs (some CDs do this to "hide" an extra bonus track at the end of a CD). You can also create indexes in the track using the New index button to mark specific points in the track (click the wave form and use the Play button to find the location you want). To edit an existing Index, click the Edit button. Finally, use the Zoom and Full View buttons to control how much of the track's wave form you can see on the screen.

- ◆ **Filters.** We first mentioned Nero's filters when discussing the New Compilation window. This is the tab you use to apply filters to a selected track. There are several filters here, as you can see from Figure 11.8. To enable a filter, use the check boxes next to each filter. Depending on the filter you have currently selected, the main controls on the window change to reflect its needs. You can test the results using the Test Selected Filters button.

Once you're satisfied with any tweaking that you've made, click OK to return to the main Nero window.

Saving Your Compilation

Before recording your audio compilation to disc, it's a good idea to save it to your hard disk. You never know when you might need to duplicate it (especially if you decide to recreate it with just a couple of different tracks) or use it as the basis for a future compilation.

Select and enable special effects here

Which controls appear here depends on the selected filters

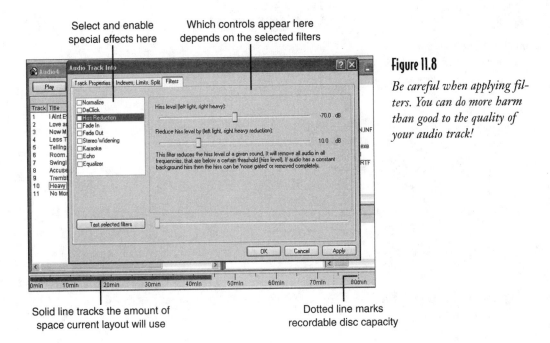

Figure 11.8

Be careful when applying filters. You can do more harm than good to the quality of your audio track!

Solid line tracks the amount of space current layout will use

Dotted line marks recordable disc capacity

To save your compilation, click the floppy disk icon on the toolbar or click File, Save. This opens up a Save dialog box which you've likely seen a million times. Enter a name for you compilation and click Save. If you've already saved you compilation once and want to save it again under a new file name, choose File, Save As instead.

Recording the Disc

When you're ready to start recording, click the burning disc icon on the toolbar or select File, Write CD. When you do, the Write CD window appears. This window is no different from the New Compilation window we spent half this chapter discussing (notice that the Info tab now has updated information).

If you want to change any options here you can. If you need help, refer to the "New Compilation Options," section earlier in this chapter. When you're ready, click the Write button to initiate the recording process (see Figure 11.9).

The length of the recording process will vary between a few minutes to a half hour or more, depending on your recording speed. When the recording is complete, a dialog box will appear that confirms your success. Click OK to close this dialog box.

This returns you to the recording window where you can view, save, or print a log of the entire recording process for future reference and troubleshooting. Most likely you'll just want to press the Discard button to close the window.

Figure 11.9

Burn, baby, burn! From here your disc recording is in the hands of Nero and your disc recorder.

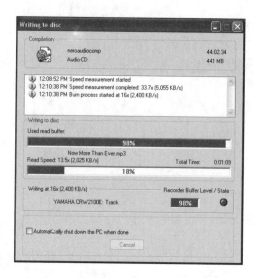

Congratulations! You've got yourself an audio disc. Now take it to the nearest CD player and give it a whirl!

The Least You Need to Know

◆ You can control how your source music tracks on CD are ripped to your recordable disc using the New Compilation window.

◆ Adding tracks to a new compilation requires only a simple drag and drop from the File Browser window to the Audio window.

◆ When you drag a track from an audio CD to the Audio window, Nero attempts to identify it. If it's a commercial music CD, use the Internet database option.

◆ Double-click any track in the Audio window to make basic edits to its information and structure.

Part 5

Eat Your Heart Out, Mr. Spielberg: Creating Video CDs

Video tapes aren't going to last forever. Even Circuit City dumped them from retail shelves. If you have a collection of tapes of popular movies that you bought, you can probably find them now or at a later date on DVD. However, what about all those tapes that you made of the family during holiday times or recordings of old *Cheers* episodes or *The West Wing?*

In Part 5, I show you how to take digitized video and create video CDs, Super Video CDs and even video DVDs that can immortalize your fragile VHS recordings. In Chapter 12, I give you the skinny on how to capture video: the devices, the video file formats, and where you can watch your recorded video discs. Chapters 13 and 14 cover using Easy CD Creator and Nero Burning ROM to actually create a video CD.

Pre-Production: What Any Home Video Producer Needs

In This Chapter

- ◆ What's the difference between a Video CD, Super Video CD, and a Video DVD, and why you should care

- ◆ Learn about the different video file formats

- ◆ What you need to get started recording video to a CD or DVD

In this chapter, we not only take a look at digital video mediums, but also at what you'll need to get started before using Roxio Video CD Creator or Nero Burning ROM to put audio and video onto a recordable disc that you can view on your computer or DVD player. Even though, in this book, we focus on just two applications you can use to create Video CDs, Super VCDs, and Video DVDs, it is important to remember that other software options are available: some better, some worse.

VHS Is Dead, Long Live DVD!

Ever notice how your older videotapes don't look quite as good as the day they were purchased (or first recorded)? Over time, colors fade, the video gets grainy, and the audio gets choppy. I've been using VHS tape for 20 years to watch movies and record television programs. When I compare a tape recorded a decade ago with one recorded five years ago with one recorded yesterday, the differences in video quality between all three can be astonishing. Analog tape is simply not a durable medium. It suffers from the wear and tear I just described and, of course, the ravages of time. The analog format in which the video and audio are recorded on a tape doesn't provide for the complex error correction that can be performed when recording digitally. Does that make digital better? Compared to tape, you betcha. (Most agree, however, that film usually still has an edge over digital in its ability to truly capture all facets of an image, rather than try to convert it to a stream of 1s and 0s and then back again.)

Video on a Disc?

Although your VHS tape might last a decade or two, the expected lifetime for recordable optical discs like CDs and DVDs is at least 100 years. Barring some major medical breakthroughs, that's long enough for most people! When you use a digital video creation program to make a video disc, there are a few tradeoffs, however. The first is in time, and the second is in quality. A commercial DVD disc can hold an entire movie, along with alternate camera angles and subtitles and so on, but a CD can't provide that kind of capacity. Actually, even a consumer rewritable DVD doesn't have that kind of capacity. Those discs are generally limited to an hour and a half to two hours worth of video. So if you are planning to put more than about a half hour to an hour of video on a CD or more than two hours of video on a DVD, plan on using more than one disc.

> **Between Tracks**
>
> A feature introduced in Easy CD Creator 5 Platinum is a tool called Video Impression. While it has nothing to do with actually recording video to CD, it can be used to edit your digital video content. Those of us who'd rather be tortured with 10 minutes, rather than 20 minutes, of someone's baby videos can appreciate the value of editing out the nonessential parts of a drawn out video. After all, who wouldn't want to see a much shorter cut of the pod race scene in *Star Wars: The Phantom Menace!*

The real key to how much you can store on a video disc is the format used to encode the video. There are three types of video discs you can create:

- **Video DVD.** Video on a DVD is encoded using a standard called MPEG-2.
- **Super Video CD (SVCD).** These discs are standard CDs that, like DVDs, contain video encoded using MPEG-2.

◆ **Video CDs (VCD).** These discs are standard recordable CDs that are recorded with video encoded in the MPEG-1 format.

While many differences exist between the MPEG-1 and MPEG-2 standards, the most important one is in video quality and the amount of storage space required per minute of video. MPEG-2 is higher quality, while MPEG-1 is more compact. For those with a jones for more information on these formats, stay tuned. I explain MPEG later in the chapter.

Between Tracks

Even though you can only use MPEG video clips to create a video disc, don't forget that you can still record video in any video format you want. There are as many (or more) video file formats as there are audio file formats. To record a VCD, SVCD, or video DVD that can play in a set-top player, you need to be able to convert that video to one of the required MPEG standards.

If you only wish to store video files on a disc and don't care about playing them in a set-top player, then you need not worry about the video format (as long as you have PC software that can read what you use). Just use Easy CD Creator or Nero to copy the actual video files to a disc (like you would when creating a data CD). This way you can still open the files using a suitable program if you want to view them. They won't be usable in a DVD player or any PC that lacks the software to read the format you use, but on your computer you should have no problems.

The type of disc to which you can record video depends entirely on the recordable drive in your system. Certainly DVD is preferable, because it can store so much more video than a CD. However, the drives are still expensive compared to compact disc recorders. Still, if for those with a decent tax return, DVD recorders are now available at fairly reasonable prices ($250 to $450). Unfortunately, there are still competing formats (DVD+R/RW and DVD-R/RW) to contend with; which will win out is anyone's guess (though this author is backing the +R/RW format). For more information on recordable and rewritable DVD, see Chapter 2.

The Discs

A VCD or SVCD should play in any CD or DVD drive in your PC, or in an ordinary set-top DVD player connected to your television. Ideally, a video DVD will play in any PC-based DVD drive or set-top DVD player, though compatibility is much better with +R and -R formats than with +RW and -RW. Because your mileage might vary as to whether or not the video discs you create are compatible with your playback devices, it's good practice to perform a test before you spend a lot of time and money creating video discs that might not work (some DVD players can't even handle video CDs). You can run into the same kind of problem when trying to play CD-RW audio discs on older CD players. Sometimes they just don't work.

Any VCD you create should also work in a CD-I player, if you have one. These are usually used for commercial purposes, and not commonly found at home.

What Is MPEG and Who Are These Motion Picture Experts, Anyway?

Video data, by its nature, takes up a lot of space on any storage medium. The amount of information needed to accurately store just a few minutes of video is enormous. Therefore, a way to encode and compress video data so that it can be more easily managed and stored became necessary.

Arcane CD Speak

When capturing video, your video capture software will need you to specify the capture format. Unfortunately, there are variations in MPEG-1 and MPEG-2 that can significantly impact on what devices you can play the video back. The key letters to look for when encoding to MPEG-1 or MPEG-2 are as follows:

- ◆ **VCD, SVCD, or DVD.** This, obviously, refers to the type of disc.
- ◆ **NTSC (National Television Standards Committee).** NTSC refers to the type of video signal used to display the image. Ever watched a TV in North America? That signal is NTSC. Many other countries use different signals (like PAL—Phase Alternating Line).
- ◆ **352×240, 480×480, 704×480.** These numbers refer to the resolution of the video (which affects the clarity and sharpness of the image). The first number indicates the number of "dots" used to create a single image line across the screen. The second number indicates the number of horizontal lines that fit on the screen. The higher the numbers, the more detailed the image. Your television doesn't necessarily need to be capable of displaying these higher resolutions to show the video (standard TVs have 525 lines of resolution). You just won't see all the detail the video has to offer.
- ◆ **29.97 fps.** This is the number of frames per second (fps) for the video clip. A video image is really just a series of still frames shown very quickly to create the illusion of motion. North American television shows 30 of these frames each second. So why does your software say 29.97 instead of 30? Well, if I ever meet the programmers, I'll have to ask.

The term *MPEG* comes from the standards body that created the MPEG standards: the Motion Picture Experts Group. This body has released several versions of MPEG standards, proving that even the "experts" can't get it right on the first try. The two most applicable to recording video discs are MPEG-1 and MPEG-2. These two standards outline how video is encoded into digital data and then decoded for viewing on a monitor or television. Whereas MPEG-1, which is the standard used for Video CDs, stresses compression over quality, MPEG-2 (Super Video CDs and video DVDs) provides a great deal of compression at extremely high video quality.

This is an important thing to remember if you decide to buy a video capture device so you can transfer videotapes or other recorded material to your computer for the purposes of creating a video disc. If you want to create a DVD or SVCD, for example, then you'll need to make sure it can encode video according to MPEG-2 standards. If you only want to create VCDs, the device must be able to capture MPEG-1. Really, if you're going to spend the money on such a device, it's best to buy one that can capture to both formats.

In the following table, I've provided a quick summation of the video disc types, necessary MPEG formats, and a few of the more specific details I discussed in the preceding sidebar.

Various Video Disc Types and Their Formats

Disc	Common MPEG	Format Type	Characteristics	Notes
CD	MPEG-1	NTSC	352×240, 29.97fps	Low quality, but compact
SVCD	MPEG-2	NTSC	480×480, 29.97fps	Higher quality, but limits amount of video you can put on a disc
DVD	MPEG-2	NTSC	352×480, 29.97fps*	Video quality slightly less than SVCD, but more compact
NTSC			704×480, 29.97fps*	Very high-quality video

For DVD encoding, you'll likely also see a number ranging from 3 to 5Mb/s. This number indicates the number of megabits per second of video to use on your hard disk for storing the video. The higher the number, the better the quality.

Regardless of their specifics, there are several video editors available on the market capable of working with MPEG video, and I don't want to make specific recommendations, as personal taste and certainly your budget are significant factors. However, keep in mind that most video capture cards, detailed in the following section, come with additional bonus software that does allow you to edit video.

Getting Video on Your PC

Before you can worry about recording video using your disc recorder, you need to worry about getting video on your PC so you have something to record. Unless you're downloading video from the Internet, this requires a video capture device or a digital video camera.

Video Capture Devices

If you want to transfer video to your PC from a conventional video camera, TV signal, VCR, etc., then you need a video capture device. Most video capture devices that I've seen lately can save a captured video in several formats, and MPEG-1/MPEG-2 are usually among them.

Between Tracks _____

In this chapter I refer to video capture "devices." These devices come in multiple forms. Some are cards that are installed inside your PC, with either input/output (I/O) connectors on the card or attached via a break-out box (a "box" housing several input and output connectors that won't fit on the add-in card). Others are external devices with video/audio I/O connectors that connect to your PC through a USB (Universal Serial Bus) or IEEE-1394 (FireWire) cable.

USB and FireWire are both technologies that allow you to transfer data to and from your computer at very high speeds. If you have at least a Pentium II computer you should have at least two USB ports on the back. While it's becoming more common, most PCs don't come with FireWire ports (which are more common on Apple computers). Instead they must be added using an internal add-in card.

If you have a capture device that doesn't support saving the video file in the MPEG format you need, you're not out of luck. If you have a video editing program, like Adobe Premiere or the Video Impression utility included with Easy CD Creator 5 Platinum, then you can probably read in a video file in one format (like AVI or QuickTime) and then save it as MPEG-1 or MPEG-2. Usually capture devices include an editing program of some kind, but they're not always the best. However, buying a quality capture device or editing program isn't always cheap. These devices can run anywhere from $100 to several thousand. These days you can usually find a worthy device for $200 to $300 that can also accept, record, time-shift, and pause live television feeds. The important thing is to balance your choice between what you really need and what you can afford!

As mentioned earlier in the section, you have several options when it comes to purchasing a video capture device. You can get an internal card to put inside your computer, or you can buy an external device that hooks up to the back of your computer via a cable. If you're comfortable working with the hardware in your computer, making a purchase and getting it all set up should be no problem. But for those who prefer to just let the magic happen, you should seek the help of that techno-geek friend of yours or the store where you buy the capture device.

Digital Video (DV) Cameras

If you have no interest in shilling out money for an expensive capture device, being that even the less expensive ones can set you back more than $100, then you might have another option. If you already own a digital video camera equipped with a FireWire connection for transferring video, then you might be in luck. Most digital video cameras, in addition to recording to digital videotapes in the MiniDV or Digital8 format, can receive video from a TV or VCR (though this usually requires special cables included with the camera).

In that case, all you need is a FireWire connection in your computer. Although most PCs don't include that connection by default, you can buy a FireWire card much more cheaply (less than $100) than the cost of a video capture device. The Adaptec FireConnect 4300 pictured in Figure 12.1, is one of the better cards you can find on the market.

Figure 12.1

The Adaptec FireConnect 4300 makes connecting a digital video camera to your PC for transferring video a simple task.

From here, the process is more time-consuming than difficult. If you have video shot with your digital video camera, then all you have to do is hook up your camera to your PC and transfer the video using the software provided with your camera or FireWire card. If you're looking to get your aging videotape collection onto a digital medium, be sure to set aside an afternoon.

First, you'll need to connect your camera to an output port on your VCR. How you do this depends on your camera and what cabling was included with it. On my JVC GR-DVL 9800, I received a cable with standard RCA jacks on one end and a headphone-style jack that connected to the camera on the other. The RCA jacks, pictured in Figure 12.2, have the familiar red, white, and yellow connectors and, in this case, are connected to the equivalent output connectors on your VCR.

Figure 12.2

This cable connects my digital video camera to a TV or VCR with RCA jacks.

Usually, at this point, you need to make sure your camera is configured to receive, rather than output video. Once set, you can start playing a tape or television signal through your VCR, then hit record on your camera. This is just like recording to a normal videocassette, except that now we're dealing with digital videotape.

Once you've recorded the video you want (most digital videotapes won't hold more than an hour's worth of footage), it's time to connect your camera to your computer via a FireWire cable, like the one shown in Figure 12.3.

Figure 12.3

The connector for this FireWire cable, which is already connected to a PC at the other end, plugs into a digital video camera.

Now you have but to use your computer's video capture software (again included with the FireWire card or digital video camera) to capture that video onto your PC. Once that's done you can you use that video however you want. That includes using your video software to convert it to a suitable MPEG format so that you can burn it to a disc using the Easy CD Creator or Nero software packages!

Don't Get Burned

Remember that moving video around in this fashion involves a lot of back and forth from analog to video (don't forget that the video is converted back to analog when played on a normal television). The transfer back and forth between formats (even from Digital Video to MPEG) causes some degradation of the video so don't expect broadcast quality results!

The Least You Need to Know

- Video discs come in three flavors: Video CDs, Super Video CDs, and video DVDs.

- If you want to create a video disc, you must have video files encoded in MPEG-1 (VCD) or MPEG-2 (SVCD and video DVD) formats.

- MPEG file formats are designed to compress large amounts of video data into smaller files. While both provide video of good quality, even MPEG-2 loses some detail during the encoding process.

- A video disc will play in your computer's DVD drive and on most set-top DVD players. DVD+R and -R media are more compatible with set-top players than DVD+RW or -RW.

- Getting video onto your computer from a videotape or other analog source requires the use of a video capture device or digital video camera.

Chapter 13

Toss Your VCR: Using Video CD Creator to Create Video CDs

In This Chapter

- ◆ Using the VCD Creator
- ◆ Creating simple sequence video CDs
- ◆ Creating video CDs with menus

Easy CD Creator comes with two video recording programs: Video CD Creator and Video Impression. In this chapter, I focus only on Video CD Creator. Video Impression, which is geared more toward video editing and capture than recording, is okay if you can't find anything better. But in truth, you could throw a rock at a Best Buy store shelf and come up with a better video editing tool.

While Video CD Creator is much better at actually creating a Video CD (VCD), it is quite limited, too. You cannot use it to create either a Super

Video CD (SVCD) or video DVD. Video CDs are okay, but you do have to make sacrifices in video quality if you intend to use them (of course, it's also much more compact). The good news is that most set-top and PC-based DVD players can play them.

Regardless, the overall process of creating a VCD in Video CD Creator requires just three parts:

> ### Cross Reference
>
> If you want to get more information on how to capture and edit video, especially DVD video, see Chapter 19. For more information on video disc formats like VCD, see Chapter 12.

- ◆ Getting the source material
- ◆ Prepping the video material (editing, creating a layout for the disc, etc.)
- ◆ Recording a VCD layout to disc

Over the rest of this chapter we take a look at how you can use Video CD Creator to make a Video CD layout based on video you've already captured and then burn it to a CD.

Starting Video CD Program

To gain access to the Video CD program, open the Roxio Project Selector. When you hover your mouse pointer over the Make A Photo Or Video CD, a button for each program related to this topic appears in the main window (see Figure 13.1). Click Video CD.

Figure 13.1

The only useful tool Roxio has for recording a Video CD is Video CD Creator.

The Video CD Creator Interface

As with the other Roxio programs that are part of the Easy CD Creator 5 Platinum version, you can start up Video CD Creator by double-clicking the Project Selector icon on your PC's desktop or by using the Start menu (click Start, Programs, Roxio Easy CD Creator 5, Applications, Video CD Creator).

Using the Project Selector, you simply select Make a Photo Or Video CD from the first set of buttons that pop up; then, from the second, click Video CD. When you open Video CD Creator, the VCD Creator window pops up. A welcome dialog box appears in front of it, asking you if you want to create a VCD using a wizard (see Figure 13.2).

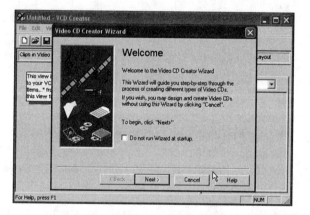

Figure 13.2

The Video CD Creator Wizard can help simplify the process of creating a VCD.

Two ways are available to create Video CDs. You can use the program itself, or you can use this wizard. Although easier, the wizard does limit what you can do with the program, so go ahead and dismiss this wizard dialog box using the Cancel button. This way we can get straight into the VCD Creator program itself, which really isn't that much more difficult to use than by going through the Wizard.

With the wizard out of the way, you're left to gaze adoringly at the main VCD Creator window (see Figure 13.3). Here you can see the recognizable File, Edit, and View menus. In addition, menus are available for Video CD and Playback. Help, as always, is there if you need it. As long as you have this book around, hopefully you won't ever need to use the Help option.

Between Tracks

To keep the wizard from popping up every time you use Video CD Creator, you can select the check box named Do Not Run Wizard at Startup from the wizard's first dialog box. You can re-enable the Wizard at startup by using the Preferences option in the File menu of the main program.

Figure 13.3

Use the VCD Creator program to create the VCD layout and burn the VCD.

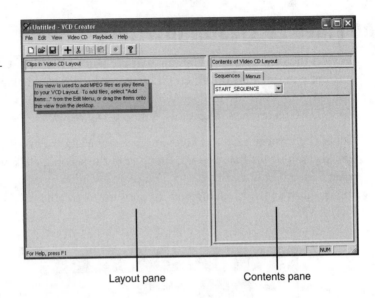

Layout pane   Contents pane

The pane on the left side of the program window is titled Clips In Video CD Layout. After you start adding segments of video (clips) to the layout, they show up in this pane. On the right side of the program window, you can see the Contents of Video CD Layout pane, which has two tabs. The first, Sequences, is where the order in which the video clips will play is determined. The second tab, called Menus, enables you to add menus to the CD so the viewer can choose to watch specific clips when viewing the disc.

As with many applications, you can set certain options for the program to customize it for your needs. The Preferences option on the File menu brings up the dialog box shown in Figure 13.4. This enables you to make decisions that affect some aspects of how the program works.

Figure 13.4

The VCD Creator Preferences dialog box gives you control over the program.

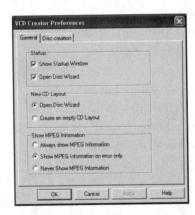

This dialog box has two tabs: General and Disc Creation. In Figure 13.4, you can see the General tab and the preferences it enables you to set. These preferences fall under the groupings Startup, New CD Layout, and Show MPEG Information.

Cross Reference

You can find more information on video file formats like MPEG in Chapter 12.

You can control the following program Startup options:

◆ **Show Startup Window.** If selected, this just means that the program's logo will be shown when the application is first started up. I know, big yeah! Feel free to disable this one.

◆ **Open Disc Wizard.** This is the check box you select or deselect, depending on whether you want the Wizard to be your main interface when you launch the program. I've disabled it as I don't think the Wizard is particularly helpful. However, if you're more comfortable using it, keep this box enabled.

Preferences you can set to control what happens when you select New CD Layout from the File menu are:

◆ **Open Disc Wizard.** If this option is selected, every time you want to create a new CD layout, the Wizard pops up to walk you through it. You won't have to restart the program to get the Wizard running as with the previous option.

◆ **Create an empty CD Layout.** If you select this, instead of the Wizard, the main VCD Creator program becomes the standard method you use to create the video CD.

Under the Show MPEG Information section, you can control when the MPEG information sheet is displayed.

◆ **Always show MPEG information.** If you select this, you'll see the MPEG information sheet for all files you choose to add. This includes files that meet the White Book VCD specifications as well as those that contain errors. (For more information on the White Book standard, visit Appendix C.)

◆ **Show MPEG Information on error only.** If you get tired of clicking a lot of MPEG information sheets that show good files, selecting this preference causes the program to show the MPEG information sheet only when a bad file crops up.

◆ **Never Show MPEG Information.** If, under no circumstances do you want to see MPEG file information, this is the option for you. At the very least, though, we'd recommend you choose to show information on error. It's always good to know when you're dealing with files that may not work!

Similar to Easy CD Creator, when VCD burns a disc, it places temporary files on your hard disk to make the process run smoothly. Under the Disc Creation tab on the VCD Creator Preferences dialog box you can control the temporary files created by the program. The default, as you can see in Figure 13.5, is to use the Windows TEMP directory, which already exists on Windows systems. However, you can deselect this check box and add other locations.

If you do elect to create other directories (click the Add button) instead of using the default, another dialog box pops up and enables you to enter the path and filename for the temporary file (there is a Browse button here you can click to select the new location). If you want, you can also set a limit as to the amount of space that can be used; just put a checkmark in the Limit disk space usage check box (see Figure 13.5). You can add more temporary locations as needed.

Figure 13.5

You can control the disk locations used for temporary storage.

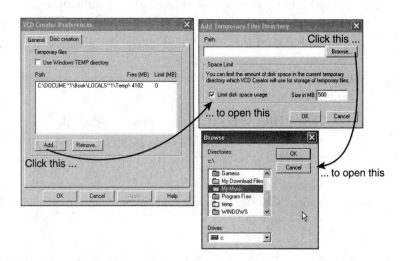

Generally, unless you really understand how to navigate your hard drive, create and move folders, and so on, you are better off leaving these options alone.

Creating the Video CD Layout and Adding Items

Starting with a clean layout—that is, you've just opened the program or you've selected New VCD Layout from the File menu—you need to add video clips to the layout you want to create.

To add a clip, click the Edit menu and then select Add Item (or click the Add An Item button on the toolbar). This brings up the Add Play Items dialog box, which really looks and operates no differently than opening up any other file in Windows. In this case, however, you can only open files that are of the MPEG-1 format.

To select a file for inclusion in the layout, double-click it in this dialog box or highlight it by clicking it once and then clicking the Open button. Continue using the Add Play Items dialog box until you have added all the video clips you want on the VCD.

Unless you chose to hide it using the Preference dialog box I covered in the previous section, each time you add a file using this method, an MPEG Information dialog box appears, telling you whether the clip to be added to the layout meets the MPEG-1 specifications. If VCD Creator has no complaints, this dialog box has a nice, friendly, green check mark at the top. If it gets finicky and doesn't like your files, however, a red X will appear. From there, click the Details button to show exactly which parts of it didn't measure up (see Figure 13.6).

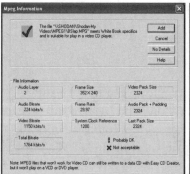 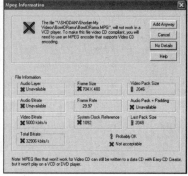

Figure 13.6

Of the two MPEG clips shown, only the one on the left (created using MPEG-1 encoding) can work with Video CD Creator. The video file outlined on the right is in MPEG-2 format, so the picky VCD Creator refuses to work with it.

In the File Information section of this image there are several components of your MPEG file that VCD Creator has analyzed. Any components that check out as okay are unmarked. However, there are two different icons that might appear should there be problems with some part of your file. A yellow exclamation point next to an item indicates that it will probably be okay, but is a little off the standard. A big, red X character next to an item indicates that it doesn't meet MPEG-1 guidelines and most likely will not be playable in a DVD player if you include it in the layout.

Don't Get Burned

Remember, from Chapter 12, that there are distinct differences between MPEG-1 and MPEG-2 video. VCD Creator cannot make use of MPEG-2, which is a Super Video CD and video DVD standard. If VCD Creator indicates one of your MPEG files does not meet its requirements, it could be that the file was encoded in MPEG-2. To use you'll need to use a video editing program to convert it to MPEG-1.

Click the Add button if the clip is okay and VCD Creator adds it to your layout. If you want to use a clip that does not meet the standards, click the Add Anyway button that takes the place of the Add button. Just don't say we didn't warn you! After you've added the clip, the Add New Play Item dialog box appears (see Figure 13.7).

Figure 13.7

Make sure to choose the correct output data format for use with your video display equipment.

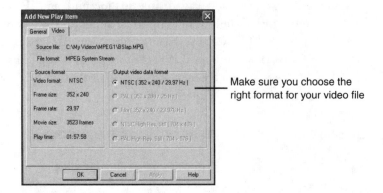

Make sure you choose the right format for your video file

As you can see, there are two tabs here. The General tab allows you to see a still image preview of the clip. The scroll bar underneath it allows you to see a still image from various points in the clip. The Video tab, shown here, gives you basic information about the clip. You must also select an output format, most likely NTSC (North America) or PAL (most of Europe). Click OK to close this dialog box and return to the main VCD Creator window.

You need only follow the same steps I just outlined to add all the clips you want recorded into the Layout pane.

Modifying and Playing Clips in the Layout Pane

Removing an item from the layout is as easy as either selecting it in the layout and then clicking the scissors icon on the toolbar or selecting Delete from the Edit menu. Either way, the program prompts you before it actually deletes the item from the layout. If you change your mind later, you can always put it back in again. Other options under the Edit menu enable you to cut, copy, and paste items. Sometimes you might want to use the same clip more than once in the layout. One way of doing so is to keep adding it over and over again. But you can save a little time and effort if you use Copy from the Edit menu and then use Paste to insert another copy of the particular clip in the layout. Remember that at this point, we're working with only the layout itself, not the actual files. Thus, editing a layout doesn't have to take a lot of time.

If you want to view a clip in the Layout pane, just right-click it and choose Play (or click the Playback menu and choose Selected Clip). This opens a small window containing the video and a second window with a series of VCR-style controls in it that you can use to control the playback (see Figure 13.8).

Figure 13.8

The MPEG Playback dialog box provides the controls you can use to play a sequence or an entire VCD layout.

This tool is only useful for watching the video. Still, it can help ease your mind that you have added the clips you want.

Saving and Loading the CD Layout

Now that you've gotten this far, it's a good idea to save the layout for future use. To save the layout you have created, use the Save or Save As option from the File menu. Using Save As enables you to specify the path and filename for the layout file. Use Save if you have previously saved this layout and are simply updating it.

When you want to open a saved layout, use the Open VCD Layout option from the File menu. You'll have to know where you saved the file, so keeping them all in one place is a good idea. When you open a saved layout, you can make changes to it and save it under the same name or a new name (using Save As).

Creating Video Sequences and VCD Menus

For VCD Creator to make a VCD, you must create a sequence in which the items in the layout will be played. You do this by selecting each clip in the Clips pane (on the left) and adding it to the Contents pane (on the right). You can create two kinds of sequences for your VCD. The first is a simple sequence in which all video clips are played in the order they are found in the particular sequence, from start to finish. The second method involves creating a menu that enables the viewer to select the clip to watch.

Creating a Simple Sequence

The Simple Sequence method plays all video clips in the layout sequence from start to end. For homemade videos that you have captured and want recorded to a VCD, this is most likely an appropriate choice.

To start the process of creating a sequence, click the Sequences tab in the Contents pane. Then ensure that the scroll box beneath the tabs is set to Start_Sequence (see Figure 13.3). Right now Start_Sequence is probably the only option in this box. As you add clips and create menus, this drop-down menu allows you to switch between them.

Now, to add a clip, simply drag it from the Clips pane back to Contents, in the area underneath Start_Sequence. The item should now appear in this pane (see Figure 13.9).

Figure 13.9

The VCD Creator enables you to specify the order of video clips in a simple sequence.

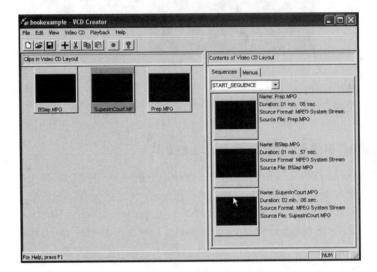

Continue dragging each clip, being sure to place them in the order you want them in the final playback of the VCD. Use the vertical scrollbar in either pane to get to clips that don't fit in the current view. If you change your mind about the order of the clips, simply use your mouse to drag them around in the Contents pane.

If you want to preview your basic sequence so you can see how well it all ties together, open the Playback menu and select VCD Layout.

Creating a Menu Sequence for the Viewer to Use

The VCD Creator program enables you to create simple, one-level menus the viewer can use to navigate between the clips on the VCD. The best way to think of these menus is like a chapter list on a DVD movie. On a DVD, this list enables you to advance to various sections of the movie by choosing which part (clip) of the movie you want to watch. Usually, these chapters won't all fit on the same *page*, so you can use your remote to scroll through more screens that contain more chapters. Although the method of control might vary based on the type of player you are using, a VCD menu works in much the same way.

Don't Get Burned

Although the comparison to a DVD chapter list makes it easier to understand a VCD menu, they don't work exactly the same. If you select a chapter on a DVD, the movie picks up from that point and plays through to the end. With a VCD, using the menu to play a clip will play only that individual clip. You can, however, group a set of clips under one menu selection if you want.

To some, it might seem like adding a menu is more trouble than it's worth, but adding a simple menu can be a good idea if you have a lot of video clips on the VCD and want them to be easily accessed. After all, you don't want to torture the viewer by making her watch a long string of video clips that she has seen before when a menu can jump right to the important stuff—then again, if it's your in-laws watching, maybe you do.

To create a VCD with a simple menu, you must first create a Start_Sequence sequence that will play each time the VCD is first played (as we did in the previous section). Once you have this sequence set, click the Menus tab in the Contents pane.

Arcane CD Speak

A **page** is where you put the menu items a user needs to advance to specific clips on the VCD. If necessary, you can use more than one page to apply to different groups of clips. After you've created a menu page, it appears on the Menus tab. You can right-click and select Properties to get to the Properties page for this menu page. Here, you can select how many times the background menu clip is played and the number of seconds between each play, if any.

There are two buttons on the Menus tab that you can use: New Page and Remove Page. To start the first page of a menu you must click the New Page button, which launches the Video CD Creator Wizard (see Figure 13.10). The first step in this wizard is to select a background for the menu page. You can choose one of the video clips from your layout or click the Add from file button to choose another (doing the latter adds that selected clip to the Layout pane).

Figure 13.10

The first dialog box asks you to select a file to be used for the menu background.

When you've made your selection, click the Next button. The next screen requires you to setup a menu page by deciding on the number of items that will be in the menu. In this figure we have entered the number 3. If, for example, you decided to enter the number 3 here, you would then create three play sequences, one for each selection. When the viewer is using this VCD, he will be able to enter a number (usually using a remote control) to select each menu choice. You can enter up to 99 menu selections, if needed!

Between Tracks

If you create more than one menu page, the viewer can use the left and right arrow keys on the controls of the VCD player to move through menu pages.

After selecting the number of menu items you want, click the Next button.

A dialog box now appears that enables you to see the menus associated with each clip and edit their names. Because these names aren't particularly descriptive, you can highlight each sequence and click the Edit button to change them (see Figure 13.11).

Figure 13.11

You can use the Edit button to change the text associated with a menu selection.

This sequence's name is being changed to Supes In Court

Edited sequence name

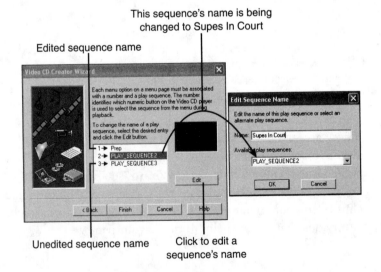

Unedited sequence name   Click to edit a sequence's name

When you are done, click the Finish button. You'll find yourself back in the VCD Creator window. Now, however, you will see your menu page on screen (see Figure 13.12).

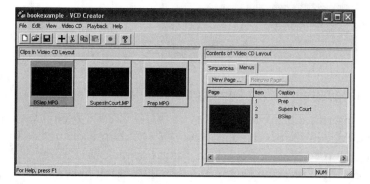

Figure 13.12

The Contents pane shows each page planned for your VCD and which clips are associated with it.

Recording a Video CD

When you're ready to create the VCD using the layout you have compiled, all that's left to do to kick off the recording process is click the button on the toolbar that has a large red dot on it.

However, before you start recording, you can use an option to check the contents of the CD layout to ensure that all the files can still be found. This is a good idea if you are using a saved layout, or one to which you have made a lot of changes. Select Validate Layout from the Video CD menu, and the program performs this quick examination.

If everything checks out okay, you are ready to record. You can either click the red button or select (from the Video CD menu) the option titled Create CD from Layout. Note that in this same menu you can create a disk image of the VCD on your hard disk. This option can be useful when making multiple copies of the same layout or if you're experiencing buffer-underrun problems as described in Chapter 21.

After you start the recording process, Video CD Creator begins processing all the clips in your layout (see Figure 13.13). Depending on the size and number of clips in your layout, this may take a few minutes. Shorter VCDs, though, should only take a few seconds.

Once this process is complete, the Record CD Setup dialog box appears. This dialog box is no different then the one we showed you in Chapters 7 and 10 for recording data and audio CDs with Easy CD Creator. For more information on the various choices here, see those chapters.

Figure 13.13

Video CD Creator is preparing clips for recording to disc.

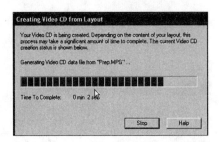

Click the Start Recording button to start burning the VCD.

If you haven't already inserted a blank recordable CD, VCD Creator prompts you to insert one. When you do, you see the standard Record CD Progress dialog box that shows the progress of the recording session. This dialog box looks and works the same as the one you get when recording audio and data discs using Easy CD Creator.

When the CD Created Successfully text appears, you'll know that the recording finished without incident. Take your new Video CD to the nearest compatible set-top DVD player and see how you did.

The Least You Need to Know

◆ Easy CD Creator includes two video-oriented applications: Video Impression and Video CD Creator. This chapter focuses on using Video CD Creator.

◆ If you want to create a video CD, you must have MPEG-1 files. These aren't the best quality video files available today, but they can fit a lot more video onto a lot less space.

◆ VCD Creator has a Clips pane where you choose which video clips to include in your layout and a Contents pane that lets you choose the order in which you want to burn those clips to a VCD.

◆ The VCD Creator program enables you to create menus to make playback on a set-top player easier for your viewers.

Chapter 14

Video Discs, Nero Style!

In This Chapter

- ♦ How to create a video CD or super video CD

- ♦ How to create a video DVD

- ♦ How to create a video CD or super video CD menu

- ♦ Why you need more than Nero to create a video DVD

While still somewhat on the frontiers of home computing, using your PC to put video on a disc that's playable in almost any set-top DVD player is becoming a reality. Nero Burning ROM provides three options for creating a video disc:

- ♦ **Video CD (VCD).** This disc uses the MPEG-1 video file format on an ordinary compact disc. It's compact but not much better than watching a home recorded VHS tape in quality (which is to say, passable but poor).

- ♦ **Super Video CD (SVCD).** This format puts higher quality MPEG-2 video files on a compact disc. Because every second of video requires more storage space when encoded in MPEG-2, as compared to MPEG-1, you can't store as much video on a CD as you could for a generic Video CD. However, what you manage to fit on there should look pretty good.

Cross Reference
For more information on the MPEG video standard and types of video discs, see Chapter 12.

♦ **Video DVD.** This is the equivalent of any DVD movie you'd pick up off the shelves of Best Buy or Circuit City. The file format is MPEG-2, but it's a bit more optimized, so it looks better than the video on a SVCD. Plus, a DVD-R/RW or +R/RW can hold seven times the amount of video!

I discuss creating each of these disc types in this chapter.

Setting Up a New Compilation

Like creating a data or audio disc, creating a video disc in Nero Burning ROM requires you to create a new compilation. When you open Nero (click Start, All Programs, ahead Nero, Nero-Burning Rom), if the New Compilation window doesn't open automatically, you can force the issue yourself by opening the File menu and selecting New.

When the New Compilation window opens you must first select the type of video disc you want to create (see Figure 14.1).

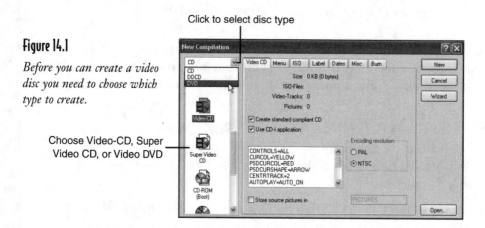

Click to select disc type

Figure 14.1

Before you can create a video disc you need to choose which type to create.

Choose Video-CD, Super Video CD, or Video DVD

Once you select the type of disc media you want to use, you need to select the type of disc. If you're creating a CD, choose between Video-CD and Super Video CD. If you want to create a video DVD, then choose DVD-Video.

Regardless of the type of media you're using, once you select from one of the video disc types you'll see, at least, the following tabs:

- ◆ ISO
- ◆ Label
- ◆ Dates
- ◆ Misc
- ◆ Burn

Because I already discussed the features found in these tabs in significant detail in the "The New Compilation Window Tabs" section in Chapter 8, I don't discuss that information here. There are, however, a couple new tabs to discuss. The following sections discuss these.

DVD-Only Tabs

If you're creating a DVD, you'll see a multisession tab. While I did discuss use of the multisession tab in Chapter 8, I recommend that you choose the No Multisession radio button and leave it at that. When creating a video DVD, it's doubtful you'll want to add more to it or that you'll end up replacing any existing files. Creating multisession DVDs should really be reserved for the realm of data backups.

VCD and SVCD-Only Tabs

Whether you're creating a VCD or SVCD, the New Compilation for these disc formats has two tabs that are unique from any other disc you might create (refer to Figure 14.1):

- ◆ Video CD
- ◆ Menu

In the next two sections, I break down both of these tabs.

The Video CD Tab

The Video CD tab includes information about the disc compilation (which you have yet to create), and a few options that can help control what types of players with which you want the disc to be compatible. The encoding resolution section allows you to choose between the two primary world standards in video broadcast resolutions. If you're in North America, stick with NTSC. If you are located in Europe, select the PAL radio button.

If you're creating a Video CD, Nero also includes a pair of check boxes that address compatibility issues: Create Standard Compliant CD and Use CD-I Application. Nero enables these options by default, and unless you know better, I suggest you leave them that way.

Don't Get Burned

Remember that different set-top DVD players and CD/DVD-ROM drives are not compatible with all disc formats, regardless of the options you select here. For a fairly comprehensive list of players and formats with which they've been tested, point your browser to www.vcdhelp.com/dvdplayers.php.

If you're creating a Super Video CD, you don't have access to these check boxes. Instead, you should see a Compatibility button. Clicking this button opens the Super Video CD Compatibility Options dialog box, shown in Figure 14.2.

There are two sections on this window: Videos directory and ENTRIES.SVD File Identification. Each has a pair of radio buttons that let you choose between the default standard SVCD options and an alternate encoding option. Again, unless you know differently or are having compatibility problems between the discs you create and your set-top player, I suggest you stick with the default.

Figure 14.2

Choosing between compatibility standards for a SVCD is only slightly less arcane than doing so on a VCD.

The Menu Tab

Creating a VCD or Super VCD gives you the option of having a menu system that lets you interact with the disc when using it in a set-top player (using your remote control). The menu tab for both types of discs is exactly the same (see Figure 14.3).

To enable this menu system (and I suggest that you do), put a check mark in the Enable menu check box. This enables several fields, which you can use to customize the look of your menus.

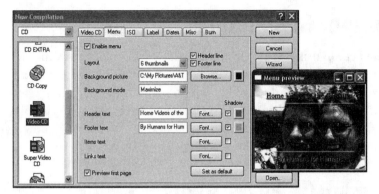

Figure 14.3

Creating custom menus for your VCD or SVCD is the only worthwhile way to go.

The easiest way to see how your changes to this tab affect your menu is to enable the Preview first page check box near the bottom of the screen. This opens up a small window like the Menu preview box that appears in Figure 14.3, which Nero updates as you make changes to your disc. Use the Layout scroll box to select the layout for the menu. You can choose to have a single, titled video per page, or slots for between 6 and 15 selectable thumbnails. When selected with your remote control, each of these thumbnails is attached to a single video segment (which you'll add to your compilation later in this chapter). Keep in mind that, for example, just because you choose the six Thumbnails option, you don't *have* to have six video segments. If you only had three, the final menu would only have three.

You can select a background picture for the menu system (really only useful if using a layout comprised of thumbnails) by clicking the Browse button. If you do so, use the Background mode scroll box to choose how to "frame" the picture. If you want it to fill the whole screen, for example, choose Scale And Fit.

If you want custom text (like a title or message) at the top or bottom of the menu screens, enable the Header line and Footer line check boxes and then type the text into the Header text and Footer text fields. If you want to customize the look of the text, click the Font button or, to add drop shadows behind the lettering, enable the Shadow check box and choose a shadow color by clicking the colored button next to the check box.

While there is no text field for Items text and Links text (which Nero assigns automatically based on your video compilation), you can use this tab customized the text Nero uses for them. This works no differently than customizing text for the Header text and Footer text fields.

Putting Video in Your Compilation

Once you've completed configuring your options in the New Compilation window, click the New button. This sends you to the main Nero interface and opens two different windows. One of these is the File Browser window (if this doesn't open, open the View menu and select New File Browser). If you know how to use the Windows File Explorer or My Computer, then you can use this window. The other window that opens depends on the type of disc you're creating (see the following table).

Windows Nero Opens Based on Disc Type Selected

Disc Type	Action
Video CD	Opens a window called Video
Super Video CD	Opens a window called SuperVideo
Video DVD	Opens a window called DVDVideo

Because the requirements for using the windows here change depending on whether your recordable media is a CD or DVD, use one of the next two sections, based on each media type, to create your compilation.

VCDs and SVCDs

While the window names vary slightly, the interface for creating a Video CD or Super Video CD is identical. As you can see in Figure 14.4, there are three parts to this window. Both halves of the upper pane list files and folders that contain VCD/SVCD-specific information that Nero generates automatically. You need only concern yourself with the lower half of this window, which lists the various video files included in your compilation.

Adding Video Files

To add video files to you compilation, as I've shown here, you need only locate them in your File Browser window and drag and drop them to the lower pane of the Video/SuperVideo window. As you drag each file (or group of files), Nero checks them to confirm that they conform to the correct specifications (MPEG-1 for VCD and MPEG-2 for SVCD).

If a file doesn't fit the exact standards Nero requires, you'll receive a message like the one shown in Figure 14.5.

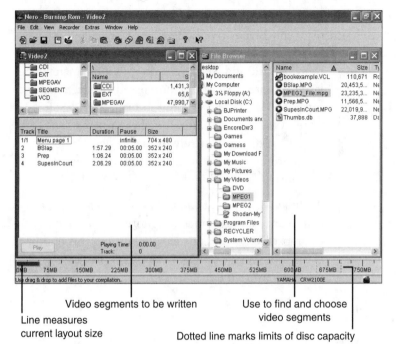

Figure 14.4

When dragging files to your disc compilation, always use the pane on the lower half of this window.

Video segments to be written

Line measures
current layout size

Use to find and choose
video segments

Dotted line marks limits of disc capacity

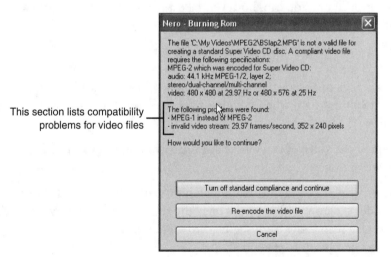

Figure 14.5

Nero found that this file was not compatible with the type of disc for which it was intended.

This section lists compatibility
problems for video files

If you're sure you're using an MPEG file, it's most likely that it is either one of the following:

◆ A SVCD or DVD-encoded MPEG-2 file being placed in a VCD compilation.

◆ A MPEG-1 or DVD-encoded MPEG-2 file being placed in a SVCD compilation.

In the case of the file being used in Figure 14.5, I tried to add an MPEG-1 file to a SVCD compilation. In this situation, you have two options: Click Cancel and use a third-party program to convert the file to an SVCD MPEG-2 file, or click Re-encode the video file and have Nero do it. Unfortunately, the latter requires that you've purchased and installed a separate MPEG encode plug-in from Ahead Software (www.ahead.de). I'm too cheap for that, so I used a program I already owned, called Ulead VideoStudio to convert the file (see Chapter 19 for more information on Ulead VideoStudio).

> **Between Tracks**
>
> If you need to convert video from one MPEG format to another and don't have your own third-party software to do so, your least expensive option is to purchase and download the Nero plug-in. Visit www.nero.com for more information on Nero's various plug-ins.

Technically, you could also click Turn off standard compliance and continue to ignore the problem, but the most likely consequence of choosing this option is that your VCD or SVCD wouldn't play in any set-top player you own.

Tweaking Your Compilation Files

After you've added compatible video files to your VCD or SVCD compilation, you're almost ready to get your burn on. You can, however, take a few seconds to perform a few customizations, if you want.

Based on the number of videos in your compilation and the layout you selected for your menu system, you'll see one or more Menu Page listings in your compilation. Double-clicking a menu page opens a window with a sample of the menu page. If you don't like it, you can always fix it when it comes time to record the disc. Click OK to close this window.

If you double-click one of the video files, you see a similar window, but this one has two tabs and a few more options.

The first tab, Attributes, displays basic information about the file's format, and allows you to set the duration for a pause, which occurs once the segment finishes playing. If you want the disc to play seamlessly from segment to segment, select zero. Otherwise, the default five-second option is as good as any.

On the Menu tab, shown in Figure 14.6, you can change the menu name for the video segment and the thumbnail image used to identify it.

To change the thumbnail image in this preview, drag the slider underneath it from side to side until you find the image you think fits the menu. Once you've made your choices, click OK to close the window. (This returns you to the main Nero window, as shown in Figure 14.4.)

Figure 14.6

Use this tab to choose the thumbnail image that appears on the menu for this video segment.

Drag slider to navigate through still frames of the video segment

Finally, you can preview or change the order of the videos on the disc. To change the ordering, just select a video and drag it up or down in the compilation. To preview it, click the Play button. This preview only works if Nero has the decoder plug-in necessary to play it. If you get an error here that doesn't mean there's anything wrong with the video file.

Next, we take a look at this process for creating a video DVD. If you're not interested in making one of these discs, skip ahead to the "Recording the Video Disc" section.

DVDs

Creating a video DVD compilation in Nero is both easier than making a VCD or SVCD and much more complex. It's easier because by the time you add files to the compilation, the menu system, preview thumbnails, etc., have already been chosen. All you have to do is drag the DVD files into the VIDEO_TS folder shown in Figure 14.7. The bad news is that it's all that easy because you have to use a different program to create these files.

Video DVD file construction operates a bit differently for VCDs and SVCDs and, unfortunately, Nero does not include the tools necessary to create a video DVD-compatible file system.

Cross Reference

For an example of creating a video DVD menu system, see Chapter 19.

Now, let's get to the good news. If you own a DVD+RW or -RW drive, then odds are you got just such a program with your drive. Of course, the question then becomes, why not use that program to write the DVD as well as just encode it? If you want to encode with your software and burn the disc with Nero, you can. But honestly, I've yet to think of a good reason to jump through that many hoops when you can do it all from within one program.

Figure 14.7

Once you have your video files created, you need only drag them into the VIDEO_TS folder to create your DVD.

Nero requires all video DVD files to be pre-recorded

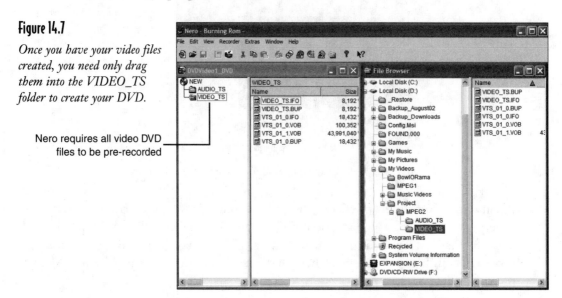

Once you've added your video DVD files to your compilation, you're ready to start burning discs.

Recording the Video Disc

Before recording your compilation to disc, it's a good idea to save it to your hard disk. You never know when you might need to duplicate it or make small changes to it (like changing a menu thumbnail or adding another video segment).

Don't Get Burned

When recording video to your hard disk, be sure to keep tabs on how much disk space you have and how much you're taking up. Video eats up space quick!

To save your compilation, click the floppy disk icon on the toolbar or click File, Save. This opens up a Save dialog box which you've likely seen a million times. Enter a name for you compilation and click Save. If you've already saved your compilation once and want to save it again under a new file name, choose File, Save As instead.

When you're ready to start recording, click the burning disc icon on the toolbar or select File, Write CD.

When you do, the Write CD window appears. Surprise! Aside from the fact that you can no longer change the type of disc you're recording to, this window is no different from the New Compilation window I discussed earlier in this chapter.

If you want to change any options here you can. If you do want to make changes, you'll most likely want to make them to the Menu tab (for VCDs and SVCDs). If you need help, refer to the "Setting Up a New Compilation" section earlier in this chapter. When you're ready, click the Write button to initiate the recording process.

The recording process could take just a minute or two or an hour or more depending on the speed of your drive, whether your disc media is recordable or rewritable, and whether you're creating a VCD/SVCD or video DVD on a +R/RW or -R/RW disc. When the disc is complete, you'll see a dialog box confirming the successful burn. Click OK to close this dialog box.

This returns you to the recording window where you have three options. Nero keeps a log of the entire recording process, which can be seen in the scrollable box near the top of the window. If you're having problems with successfully recording to disc, you can save or print this log for future reference and troubleshooting. Most likely you'll just want to press the Discard button to close the window.

Congratulations! You've got yourself a video disc!

> **Don't Get Burned**
>
> Sometimes certain parts of the recording process, like the final writing of the "lead out" on a video DVD can seem to take much longer than it should. Be patient. Such a hang-up could be an error, but it may just take Nero some extra time to complete a step.

The Least You Need to Know

◆ Most of the process for creating a VCD, SVCD, or video DVD in Nero is the same.

◆ Creating a menu system for your VCD or SVCD is the best way to inject your creativity into your project.

◆ Creating a video DVD requires that you first create the menu system and authoring files in a separate program.

◆ Remember that even though they both store video compressed in MPEG-2, SVCDs and video DVDs store video on the disc much differently.

Part 6

Picasso Was Overrated: Creating Great-Looking CD Labels and Jewel Case Inserts

There's an old saying in the consulting industry: appearance is everything. The same goes for your CDs and DVDs. Both Easy CD Creator and Nero Burning ROM (Chapters 16 and 17) come with applications that enable you to create fantastic CD labels and jewel case inserts. You can buy blank jewel case boxes at most electronics stores now, so you might as well dress them up a bit! Before you jump in, though, be sure to linger on Chapter 15, in which I explain the ins and outs of creating jewel case inserts and disc labels.

What You Need to Make Great Labels and Inserts

In This Chapter

- ◆ A quick look at several kinds of labels and inserts

- ◆ Do-it-yourself inserts!

- ◆ Do's and don'ts of making CD labels

The CD labels and jewel case inserts that come with most recordable discs are pretty plain and usually littered with manufacturer logos. As you'll find in this chapter, there's no need to subject your CD burns to such inartistic treatment. Roxio Easy CD Creator 5 Platinum and Nero Burning ROM come with utilities that allow you to print CD labels and jewel case inserts. Using these programs and the appropriate paper stock or pre-cut labels, you can print out customized disc labels and jewel case inserts to suit whatever project you have on your plate.

Because recordable DVD is still a hobby in its infancy, it's no surprise that tools for making custom inserts for the types of DVD cases that hold DVD movies are somewhat rare at this point. In fact, pretty much all recordable DVD discs ship in standard CD jewel cases. We do discuss

Arcane CD Speak

A **jewel case** is the standard case used to house and protect a typical compact disc (like the CD albums you purchase at any retail music outlet).

making inserts for DVD cases in Chapter 17, but because even that feature is limited and because Easy CD Creator does not support DVD-case label making at all, we'll stick to standard jewel case labels and inserts in this chapter. The good news is that because DVD discs are the same size as CDs, most of the tools discussed here for creating CD labels will also work with DVDs!

So Many Programs, So Many Labels

When any new device is created for use with a PC, you can be sure that a new market will open up for other products to support it. The recordable disc drive is no exception. Indeed, several companies have jumped in to provide supplies for you to use with your CD or DVD drive.

The most obvious example is the blank, recordable disc itself. These are made by many manufacturers, and their usefulness on your system will depend on myriad factors, such as your drive model and your particular media, as previously discussed in Chapters 1 and 2.

The other "expendables" you should think about are paper jewel case inserts and label stock. You can pick up these labels at any office supply store and most consumer electronics stores as well (like Best Buy and CompUSA). Some of the major brands include Farrow's Neato, Memorex, Stomper, and Avery. There are also new brand names and varieties coming into the market even as this book is being produced. The big advantage in using these products is that they generally include mechanisms for cleanly putting a label on a CD. The adhesive "glue" that all but permanently affixes a CD label to a CD is some serious stuff. If you don't line it up properly when attaching it to the CD, there's no swinging around for a second landing attempt. The applicator mechanisms that come with certain CD label kits allow you to easily affix CD labels correctly each and every time.

Depending on your budget, the number of labels you want to make, and whether or not you need an applicator mechanism, the cost of these packages can get pretty significant. There is another option, though, and we'll quickly dig into that before moving on to the next two chapters, which deal with the creation of the labels in the aforementioned programs. Why put the stock before the program? Because CD Label Creator (part of Easy CD Creator) and Cover Designer (part of Nero) both support just about any label/insert type you might want to use.

Card Stock and Jewel Case Inserts

Before you start worrying about which card stock or inserts to buy, it's important to understand the lingo used to describe each part of a CD label or insert. It may be basic, but these terms are used on most CD label packages to describe how many of each label or insert it contains. You do want to know what you're buying, right?

Basically, what you're dealing with are labels, which attach to the actual compact disc, and inserts, which go into a CD's jewel case. The label is, obviously, simple enough to grasp. But the inserts are broken down into a couple of subcategories, as follows:

- ◆ **The U-card.** Forms the bottom and spine of the jewel case.

- ◆ **Front/inside cover.** These are pretty self-explanatory. Hopefully, these are part of the same insert sheet. However, some labeling kits only provide inserts that fill the role of the front cover.

Figure 15.1 illustrates each of these, along with the orientation for applying a CD label, for the more visual folks among us.

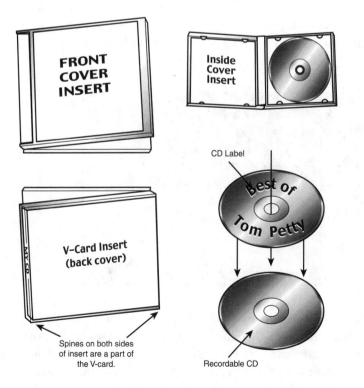

Figure 15.1

A look at the various parts of jewel case inserts and CD labels.

For those who don't want to get soaked paying for expensive brand-name inserts, you can use your CD label software to print to *card stock*, which can be found at any office supply store. It's usually near the stationery section. This kind of stock has many uses, but if you can find it in the 50 to 65 pound range, you've got about the same thing as what comes in the expensive packages CD label vendors try to sell you. Most card stock also comes in colors. If you are using a black-and-white printer instead of a color inkjet, this can spice up your inserts. Heck, color stock is useful even if you have a color printer because it could save you a ton of ink! After all, why soak white paper stock in red ink if you can just buy red paper to begin with?

> **Between Tracks**
>
> Many, if not most, of the major CD label products come with their own software, which you can use to print your custom labels. The usefulness of this software depends on the package, but generally CD Label Creator or Cover Designer are still your best options.

Besides cost, the trouble with most label and insert packages is that they don't come with enough jewel case inserts to match the number of CD disc labels you get with them. Who knows why they do this. I blame it on the secret society, led by Colonel Sanders and Big Foot, that runs the world. On top of that, some products only print to one side of the front jewel case insert. This is a drag when compared to brands like Stomper, which design their jewel case inserts so that you can print the front and inside covers on the same sheet of paper (see Figure 15.2).

Figure 15.2

Pre-scored inserts for a jewel case's front cover are generally found in two varieties. Printing these two inserts on the same sheet (and folding it in half) makes the insert thicker and much less likely to just slide out of the jewel case like the flatter, one-sided inserts often do.

Although you might not have any issues with spending a few extra dollars on brand-name labels, just remember that the only difference between card stock and prepackaged inserts is that card stock doesn't have the pre-scored lines that make taking it apart after you print it an easy job. Of course, recent studies suggest that a special pair of cutting instruments, called scissors, could actually serve this purpose!

Disc Label Do's and Don'ts

There are a few things you must keep in mind about CD labels and inserts. First, the label (top) side of a disc is actually closer to the data layer of the disc than the data layer is to the bottom of the disc. The bottom side, where the disc is read, has a protective layer between the surface and the data layer.

Because no such protection is on the label side where you are going to be sticking CD labels, you have to be very careful after you place the label. First, under no circumstances should you try to remove a label after you've stuck it onto a CD-R disc. You can damage the reflective surface and render the CD unusable.

Second, if you print with an inkjet printer, remember that water causes the printing to run. Don't leave discs with inkjet-printed labels lying around on the coffee table or anywhere else it might get wet!

If you intend to write information on the disc label with a pen, use one with a felt-tip (with water-based ink, not oil-based), like a Sharpie. Ball-point pens and others with harder tips can press clear through the label and scratch the data layer of the disc!

Don't Get Burned

If you are using an inkjet or other similar printer technology, you should probably give the label or inserts a little time to dry so you don't smear the ink when applying them. I recommend at least a half-hour.

You should also keep in mind that jewel cases are not exactly indestructible. Inserting a U-Card requires that you first pry up the plastic portion of the CD case that holds the CD in place. Although it's a simple process, it is very easy to snap off the pegs that hold it in place. This, of course, pretty much hoses any further use of the case. I find the easiest way to avoid this is by opening the jewel case and laying it on a flat surface. Then, use your fingernails to pry up the center portion of the holder that is located where the front and back sides of the jewel case join. It may not seem like rocket science, but don't cry to me when those cheap little plastic pegs start breaking!

When printing to precut inserts, it's also a good idea to print to a regular sheet of paper first. If you place the test page back to back with the labels page, you can make sure that the printer is printing inside the labels and not slipping off the edge. If it is off a bit, you'll need to use your CD label creation software to adjust how paper aligns with the printer.

The Least You Need to Know

- You can use pre-made labels, generic print stock, or even plain paper to create custom labels for your CD.

- Certain jewel case inserts only provide for the case's front cover, not the inside front cover.

- Be careful when attaching a label to a CD. Because of the powerful adhesive, you'll only get one chance. Use a CD applicator mechanism to ensure proper alignment every time.

Chapter 16

Making Killer Labels with Easy CD Creator CD Label Creator

In This Chapter

◆ Using CD Label Creator for audio CDs

◆ Using CD Label Creator for data discs

◆ Use custom backgrounds and themes to further enhance the look of your labels and inserts

After you've got your labels or paper stock, as discussed in Chapter 15, all you need is an easy way to print the right information on them. Enter Roxio's CD Label Creator. This program is an excellent one that does just about everything the other programs, which come with some brand-name labels, do. For most purposes I think you'll grow to like Roxio's CD Label Creator for its ease of use. It also has a huge advantage over some other programs I've looked at in that it can automatically look up and insert artist, title, and song names onto your labels using the layout you used to create the disc. That can save you a lot of typing!

Between Tracks

CD Label Creator cannot make DVD case inserts like those used for most DVD movies. However, since most recordable DVD media comes in jewel cases, the instructions provided in this chapter should still suit most of your label-making needs.

Between Tracks

After you successfully burn a new CD from Easy CD Creator, you can jump directly to the CD Label Creator. The Success dialog box that appears when the burn is done contains a button labeled CD Label Creator. If you click this button, you go directly from creating the CD to making the jewel box case and label for it.

In this chapter, we're going to look at how to use CD Label Creator to make both basic and more advanced disc labels and jewel case inserts. While the features included with CD Label Creator won't make your CDs burn faster or more reliably, they do allow you to give them a more professional look, or at least a snazzier one.

Using Roxio's CD Label Creator for Audio CDs

You can start up the CD Label Creator the same way you start up most other Roxio applications, through either the Project Selector or the Start menu. For the latter, click Start, Programs, Roxio Easy CD Creator 5, Applications, CD Label Creator. If you'd rather use the Project Selector, double-click its desktop icon, hover your mouse-pointer over the CD Label Creator button (lower-right corner), and then select the second CD Label Creator button, which then appears in the middle of the window.

Once you open CD Label Creator, you're brought to the main CD Label Creator screen shown in Figure 16.1.

A close look at the screen shows that it's not going to be a difficult program to operate. There is the usual menu at the top, starting with File and including standard menus, such as Edit and Help. Under this is a toolbar that can speed up many tasks. To the far left is a Page bar, which allows you to select which part of the disc label or jewel case insert you want to view (Front Cover, Inside Cover, etc.).

Most of the window space, however, is taken up by the drawing space where you can construct the printouts that can be used to line the back and front of a jewel case. Using this program, you can also print a label that can be applied, by one of several popular applicators, to the CD. Assuming that the Front Cover icon on the left of the window is selected, this drawing space shows an editing field outline in which you can insert the name of the artist of the CD. The field under it enables you to enter the title for the CD (see Figure 16.1). If your screen resolution is high enough, you may also be able to see the Inside Cover portion of the disc label, which you can access directly by clicking the Inside Cover icon on the Page bar to the left of the screen. Ignore that one for now, as we'll look at it in just a minute.

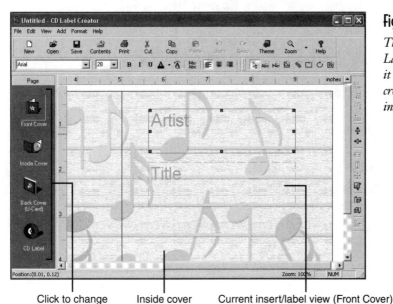

Figure 16.1

The main window of the CD Label Creator is modest, but it hides a wealth of tools for creating terrific labels and inserts.

Click to change   Inside cover   Current insert/label view (Front Cover)
insert/label view

Veterans of Easy CD Creator Deluxe 4.0 might remember a pesky little creature that looked like a dot with a face that would appear near the bottom of what was then called the Jewel Case Creator window (was actually a wizard). In a perfect world, this demon-spawn of Clippy (of Microsoft Office fame) would have provided users with valuable help information when needed. In practice, he just took up valuable screen real estate. Mercifully, Roxio has put this annoying little spell-meister to the sword so you won't have to waste valuable mouse clicks exorcising his scrawny butt from your screen.

So now that we have opened the program and offered a basic understanding of the interface, let's get to the real work of making some inserts and labels for your discs.

Adding Audio CD Information and Contents Automatically!

The best place to get started in making audio CD labels and inserts is to automatically have CD Label Creator add some tracks to your inserts. Since this requires a virtual palette for the program to work from, you'll need to make sure you've inserted an audio CD into your CD-ROM or CD-RW drive. CD Creator can get CD information in one of three ways:

♦ If you have an Internet connection and are making a label for a commercial music CD (or a duplicate of one), you can download the CD's information using the same online database described in Chapter 10.

♦ If you have downloaded the information for this particular CD previously (even if it was from within the main Easy CD Creator program), CD Label Maker has that data stored on your PC and can recall it upon command.

♦ Finally, if your CD has its track, artist, or title information encoded on it (including compilation CDs created with Easy CD Creator), CD Label Maker can read that information straight off your CD.

Between Tracks

Unlike Easy CD Creator, in which you must enable your automatic Internet connection for audio CD data downloads, if CD Label Creator wants to access the Internet, it will. By default, it doesn't ask you first, it just goes for it, even going so far as to initiate a modem connection (for those of you with dial-up Internet access).

If you want to have better control over this process, select the Edit menu and choose Preferences. The dialog box that appears contains several tabs; choose the one for Internet. The three check boxes here should look familiar to you if you've read Chapter 10 (refer to Figure 10.5). To prevent CD Label Creator from going to the Internet at all, make sure each check box is cleared (although this would defeat the purpose). To have CD Label Creator ask you nicely before connecting to the Internet, make sure the first two check boxes are enabled (Enable Audio CD Information Download and Prompt Me Before Attempting Internet Download).

If you don't know what information is required of the Access The Internet Using a Proxy Server check box, then you really don't need to worry about it at all or shouldn't be messing around with software toys at work. Just leave the box disabled.

You don't actually have to choose between these methods. CD Label Creator automatically goes with the simplest option. To let the program work its magic, click the Add menu and then select CD Contents. If you have not downloaded the disc's information yet, you'll next see a dialog box telling you that a music service is being contacted on the Internet to get the album information. This, of course, is why you need that Internet connection. Regardless of whether the information is coming from the web or is already stored on your hard drive, it should take just a few moments to complete the process.

Once CD Label Creator has the information it needs, it fills up your inserts and CD label views with that data. The CD I'm using for this example was identified properly as *Telling Stories* by Tracy Chapman. By default you should already be in a view that shows the CD insert's front cover. If you're not, go ahead and press the Front Cover button to display it. Because CD Label Creator uses that nice folded cover technique I mentioned in Chapter 15, it puts information about each song title and its length on the inside cover. Clicking the Inside Cover button on the window's left toolbar brings up this information (see Figure 16.2).

Figure 16.2

The inside portion of the folded jewel case cover lists each track, along with its total length.

CD Label Creator filled out this track information automatically

Now, if only doing your taxes could be that easy! All you had to do was click Add and then CD Contents, and instantly you've got yourself a jewel box cover.

If you click the icon labeled Back Cover, you'll find it looks similar to the inside cover (see Figure 16.3). Indeed, they are similar in that they both list the song titles and the play times. This back cover, which is also called the U-Card, has a subtle difference. On each side of the cover you'll see text written in a vertical mode. This portion of the printed card will be folded so that when you insert it into the back of the CD jewel case, it will show the song titles on the rear of the case, and the album artist and title on both spines.

Between Tracks

You may notice that there is a track called Data used in the example shown in Figure 16.3. This indicates the CD has a separate data track that can be accessed through a CD or DVD-ROM drive (or RW drive, for that matter). You can read more about discs containing both audio and data in Appendix C.

Figure 16.3

The U-card is where information for the back and sides of the jewel case comes from.

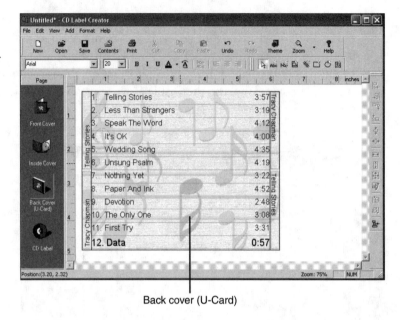

Back cover (U-Card)

The final button on this toolbar is for the CD label itself. As you can see in Figure 16.4, CD Label Creator places the album artist, title, and tracks on the CD label.

Figure 16.4

In addition to the case inserts, CD Label Creator lets you print labels for the CD, too.

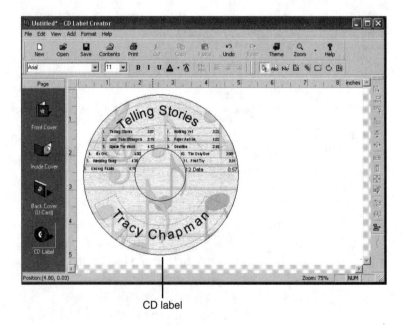

CD label

Don't Get Burned

If you want CD Label Creator to be able to identify compilation CDs you may have created with Easy CD Creator, then it's important to make sure you've both identified the individual tracks to be written and enabled the Write CD Text option on the Record CD Setup dialog box before burning the CD.

This is necessary because, after all, any compilation CD you create won't be listed in the Internet database! (Unless you're able to exert some considerable influence over the folks who maintain it.)

Entering Information the Hard Way: By Hand!

Unfortunately, it's not always possible to create all the components of the jewel case with just a few clicks. It can be a little more difficult if you're using an unidentified compilation CD or if the album is not found in the Internet database (a rare occurrence). I've personally tried a wide variety of commercial CDs and have yet to have one that wasn't found, but as many of us found out in high school chemistry, nothing is an exact science (a discovery for which I am still paying off the bill). If you do run into this problem, you'll have to enter the information manually.

The good news about typing in information yourself is that once you're done, you can save the label information, just like you saved Easy CD Creator layouts in previous chapters. This way, if you need to print a new copy or modify the inserts in some way, you can open it back up whenever you need to. To save the layout, just click the File menu and choose Save As. From here, you can give the layout file a name, clicking OK to save it on your hard disk.

Entering the Title and Artist

As you saw in Figure 16.1, CD Label Creator has two boxes, called *fields*, that appear by default on the jewel case insert's front cover. You can use these fields to enter information about the CD title and recording artist or group. You can select one of these fields by clicking it. After it's selected, the border around the field turns dark and several *handles* appear around it, which you can see in Figure 16.5.

Arcane CD Speak

Handles are little boxes that appear in each corner and halfway between each side of a selected field.

Figure 16.5

You can manually enter the information for the jewel case cover by typing it into the available fields.

Click and drag to move field

Handles

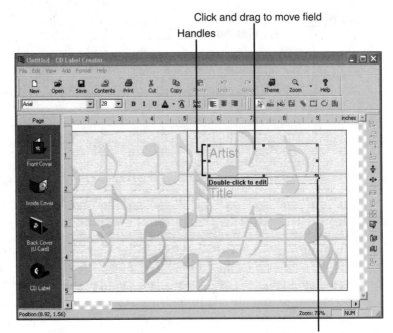

The double-arrow mouse icon appears when you hover over a handle

When you position your cursor over a handle, it turns into a double-arrow symbol. You can then press and hold down the mouse button while you drag that particular handle to change the size of the field. The position of the handle you click determines the direction in which you can move when resizing (horizontal, vertical, or diagonal).

Similar to a painting on a wall, you also can move a field to a different location on the cover. Just place your cursor inside the field (it turns into a crosshair), and then click and hold. Now you can drag the field to any part of the cover.

Obviously, you aren't going to jump through all these hoops unless there's information worth typing in the field. To add text to a field, just double-click it. This opens the selected field for editing via your keyboard.

Because the field is highlighted automatically, all you have to do is start typing in the appropriate information. As soon as the first key is pressed, the existing title disappears, replaced by whatever you're typing. You can change both fields as often as you want.

One nice feature about using the built-in templates CD Label Creator supplies is that certain fields are linked. For example, the CD title appears on the front cover, the edges of the U-card, and the CD label. Changing the title on the front cover also changes it on those fields.

Adding the Titles of Each Track

Adding the artist and title were easy—they were short and didn't take much time! The next thing you have to do can be the most tedious part.

Entering in each song title, in order, and, if you want, adding the play times for each song can take a bit of time, especially if you have a lot of tracks or type using the time-honored "hunt and peck" method. To add this information, click the Inside Cover icon on the left side of the CD Label Creator window to bring up that view. The view, like the rear end of a horse, isn't much. Because each track gets its own field and, at this point, CD Label Creator doesn't have a clue how many tracks are on your CD, the inside cover (and back cover) is blank.

Between Tracks

Keep in mind that if you don't care to know the length of a track, you don't have to enter anything for the duration. If you've put together a compilation from various CDs, you can even use this field to enter other information, such as an artist's name.

To start entering the track titles, click the Add menu at the top of the window and then select Track. In Figure 16.6, you can see that a new dialog box, titled Add New Track, appears. Here you can enter the track number (which always defaults to the next new track number), the track title, and the time, which refers to the total length of the track. That, of course, means minutes and seconds, so don't be a wonk and enter, "An Eternity," as the time for the Guns 'N' Roses song, "November Rain."

Note the Preferences button in Figure 16.6. This brings up the Preferences dialog box, which has several tabs that can help give you more control over your label designing experience. This is the same Preferences dialog box that pops up when you select Preferences from the main program's Edit menu. For now, don't worry about this feature. We will discuss the preferences you can set for the program in the following sections.

Entering information in this window is no different than any other generic Windows dialog box. You can move between the fields with a click from your mouse or use the Tab key to jump through them all in order. You can give the tracks titles you want, but generally speaking, naming a track Celine Dion's "My Heart Will Go On" when it's actually Tone Loc's "Funky Cold Medina," is only good for practical jokes.

When you've entered all the information you need for the first track, click the Add Track button and the track information appears on the main program window. The

Insert New Track dialog box does remain on the screen, though, incrementing the track number by one; you can continue to add tracks until you are done, in which case, click the Done button (note that the Done button replaces the Cancel button after you add your first track). When entering track information, notice that CD Label Creator sizes the text you enter according to the number of tracks you use. This helps ensure that everything fits on the label appropriately.

Figure 16.6

The Add New Track dialog box enables you to enter information for each track on the CD.

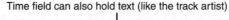
Time field can also hold text (like the track artist)

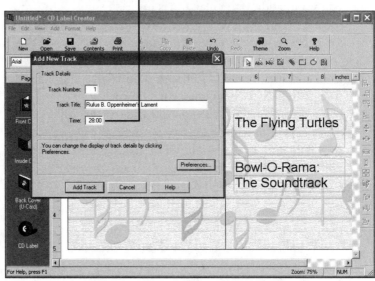

Making Data Disc Labels

Using CD Label Creator to make data disc labels isn't much different from making them for audio discs. The only key difference is that instead of working with track times, artists, and song titles, you're working with folders and their file contents.

Adding the Disc Contents

Adding the contents of a data disc to a jewel case insert can be an ominous task! It's not likely that you're going to store just two or three enormous files (unless you're creating artwork with high graphics

Between Tracks

If your current theme is designed for audio, when you add contents from a data CD, CD Label Creator asks you if you would like to switch to a data-oriented theme. Unless you've got other plans, choose Yes and select one from the list that appears.

You can find more information about themes and backgrounds in the later "Choosing Your Theme and Background" section.

resolutions or working for NASA). Instead, you're likely to store a large number of files, and probably folders, on any disc you record.

To add a data disc's contents to your inserts, click Add, CD Contents. If you have chosen a data theme (as explained in the next section), the program attempts to fill in the contents of the CD, as you can see in Figure 16.7, by simply listing the files and folder in the main directory on the disc (until it runs out of room).

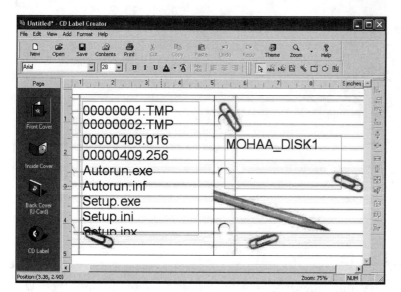

Figure 16.7

This CD actually contains the data for a game called Medal of Honor: Allied Assault. Because CD Label Creator can only generate disc information based on file names, you'd never know it based on the information shown here.

Since the Add Contents function inserts a label that was assigned to the disc when it was written, if anything, the information it generates will probably look rather bizarre, like a codename or locker combination, which isn't particularly useful. For a data CD insert it's often easier to just do away with a U-Card and just print the CD label and the front card piece with only the most basic information included. For that, all you need is a descriptive title. Choose Front Cover from the left toolbar; you see just a single field, similar to the one shown in Figure 16.8.

Between Tracks

If your data CD is part of a periodic backup of important information on your computer, you should include a date as part of the disc title.

Changing this field, as I have done in Figure 16.8, is no different than changing the title of an audio CD. If you double-click inside the field, the existing name becomes highlighted. Enter a useful new name, press Enter, and that's all she wrote.

Figure 16.8

The front view of a data CD shows only one field in which to place information.

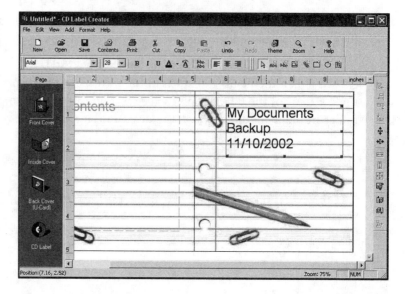

Should you run out of room entering the name or description for your disc, remember that you can resize the field by clicking it once to select it and then clicking and holding one of the handles to stretch or shrink it as necessary.

Editing Text on Jewel Case Inserts for Data CDs

As you saw in Figure 16.8, only one large field, by default, is on the front of the CD cover. When you choose CD Contents from the Add menu, the inside insert and the U-card insert automatically get a listing of the directories and files on the CD, space permitting. Only a single field, however, is used for this listing. This differs from the track listing produced for audio CDs which also had a field for track duration.

Cross Reference

To get more information on the controls for adding tracks, see the "Adding the Titles of Each Track" section earlier in this chapter.

You can easily edit this field any time you want. To replace the existing text, just double-click the field; the text in the field turns blue. You can press the Delete key to delete the text and then enter your own. Remember, in addition to using the handles to resize a field, you can move the entire field around on the page by placing your cursor inside it, holding down the left mouse button, and dragging it.

Using Add Tracks for the Data CD Cover

Oddly enough, you can also use the Add Tracks option from the Add menu when using a data CD jewel case theme. Because we covered using the Add Tracks process earlier in this chapter, we won't go over it again here. Using this capability, you can add a numbered list of items that describe the purpose of the CD, or even a list of the major programs or data files. Because the disc doesn't really contain any audio tracks, you can just leave the time field blank.

There is one pitfall to this method: It is mutually exclusive with the Add CD Contents method. If you've already used the Add CD Contents option, Add Track is no longer available. This rule also works in reverse. After you use the Add Track option, you can no longer click Add CD Contents.

Choosing Your Theme and Background

Up to this point, we've covered how to get the CD information onto the various pieces that make up the CD insert and CD label. One thing we've completely ignored is the background art that accompanies the jewel case parts. For those who find CD Label Creator's default background for labels to be about as pretty to look at as Linda Blair in *The Exorcist*, there is good news. These "background" elements can be changed to much more appealing options with just a few mouse clicks. In the following sections, we look at themes, backgrounds, and how to incorporate your own artwork into the cover.

Themes

With CD Label Creator, you get a small selection of *themes*. In the examples shown so far in this chapter, the musical notes background, meant for audio CDs, is called the Music (audio) theme. CD Label Creator comes with dozens of themes, both for audio and data CDs. We won't cover them all here, but instead just tell you how to change them. For those who regularly visit the Internet—and who doesn't nowadays—visit Roxio's site at www.roxio.com for frequent updates that enable you to download new themes.

When you click the Format menu in CD Label Creator and then select Change Theme, it brings up the Change Theme dialog box shown in Figure 16.9. On the right side is a preview of the selected theme, featuring samples of the folded front cover/inside card, the U-Card, and

> **Arcane CD Speak**
>
> Many Windows users are already familiar with the concept of **themes**, which let you customize the appearance and responsiveness of the user interface. In the case of Easy CD Creator, a theme involves giving your inserts and labels a special look. CD Label Creator includes a couple dozen themes ranging from Rock and Roll to Autumn.

Between Tracks

Because clicking OK with a theme selected changes your labels to that theme, be sure that it's the theme you want. If you're only browsing the themes for the moment and don't want to change, click Cancel instead.

the CD label. On the left side are titles of other themes that you can choose from (many of these themes are geared only for audio or data discs and are labeled as such). If you make a lot of copies, you might want to vary the themes a bit, so that all your discs don't look alike! To get an idea of what a different theme looks like, select its title. The Preview section of the window changes to show the new sample. Once you've found a theme you're happy with, just click OK.

Notice that a small check box is also near the bottom of this window called Set as default theme. If this box is checked when you click OK, any new labels you create will start out using the current theme.

Figure 16.9

You can change the theme for the jewel case art by selecting Format, Change Theme, and then choosing a new theme in the Change Theme dialog box.

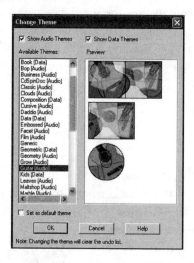

Don't Get Burned

Choosing a background color overrides whatever theme you are using. Therefore don't choose a color like blue and expect to be able to see the Guitar theme you selected earlier.

Backgrounds

This is similar to changing themes, but instead you can vary the background by selecting a picture or color. To open the Backgrounds dialog box, click the Format menu and select Change Background. If you click Select a Color from the box that comes up, you will see the familiar (to regular Windows users) dialog box that enables you to select a background color. Note that you'll need a color printer, such as an inkjet, for this to work properly. If it's only black and white, this selection is about as useful to you as a bowling ball in a game of Ping-Pong.

If you decide to change the background color, just click that color and then click OK. When choosing a background color, it's important to keep in mind the color of the text for your CD. Even the best eyes aren't going to pick up black text on a black background! We'll discuss changing text colors later in this chapter.

Adding Pictures

A niftier way of giving your CD Label Creator inserts and labels a suave look is to add images from your own collection of images.

 Between Tracks _____

For those who haven't worked much with graphics files, the various formats and types can seem a little overwhelming. With CD Label Creator, you have to worry about only two because they are the only ones the program supports: *bitmap* (files with a .bmp extension) and *JPEGs* (files with either a .jpg or .jpeg file extension). If you have a graphics file in one of these formats, then you can import that picture into your jewel case layout.

To select a graphics file as the background for your jewel case insert or label you must make sure you know where the file is stored on your hard disk. Usually, it's best to use one folder, such as My Documents or My Pictures.

To add a background picture, which can be used to cover the whole front cover, back insert, or label, use the following steps instead:

1. Click the Format menu, and select Change Background.

2. The Change Background dialog box that appears enables you to select a background color or a picture. Note the other options available in this dialog box allowing you to choose where the background is located. It can be placed on any part of the jewel case insert or CD label, and can even be spanned across the front cover and inside cover. Click Select a Picture.

3. A standard Open dialog box appears from which you can locate the directory and file that contains the picture you want to use. When you've made your selection, click the Open button.

4. You should now find yourself back in the Change Background dialog box. For the views you've selected, you'll see *thumbnails* of the picture you selected.

Arcane CD Speak

The term **thumbnail** is often used in graphics programs to refer to a miniature representation of a graphics file that can be previewed much more easily and quickly.

5. You can continue and select a different background picture for each of the major components of the jewel case and label. You do not have to use the same picture for each part of the package.

6. Click OK when you are satisfied with the picture(s) you've selected. The background picture(s) will now be displayed when you select those views in the main program (see Figure 16.10).

Figure 16.10

You can add pictures to be the background of part or all of the jewel case and label printout.

Image is spread across the front and inside covers

Since the themes provided with CD Label Creator will clearly not suit everyone's personal tastes, being able to use your own pictures for disc label and jewel case inserts is a nice feature to have!

Printing the Jewel Case Inserts and CD Labels

After you've used the CD Contents or the manual-entry method to finish your CD covers or label, you can print the results. If you thought adding CD content information was easy you'll find that actually printing labels and inserts is a breeze.

To get started, click the Print icon on the toolbar or select Print from the File menu. The Print dialog box pops up to enable you to make some changes before you print. In addition to selecting the printer (if you have more than one), there are some other options on this dialog box, shown in Figure 16.11, that you also need to pay close attention to.

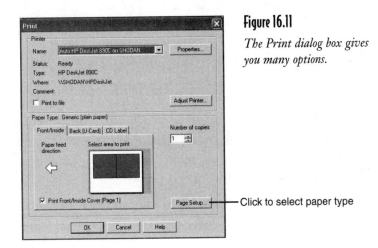

Figure 16.11

The Print dialog box gives you many options.

Click to select paper type

Next, you need to select which of the label types you want to print. Near the bottom of the Print window is a dialog area with three tabs, one for each label type (Front/ Inside, Back (U-Card) and CD Label). Each of these tabs has a check box on it that enables you to select the labels you want to print (or deselect those you don't). If you want to print just the front and inside covers, you can. If you want to print all the covers, but not the CD label, you can. If you want to become the leader of the free world … you're reading the wrong book.

The most important button on this dialog box is the Page Setup button. This opens the Page Setup dialog box where you can select the kind of stock you are printing with (see Figure 16.12). Like the Print dialog box, there are three tabs here. One for each type of label or insert you can print: Front/Inside, Back (U-Card), and CD Label. If you are using labels from one of the firms mentioned in Chapter 15 or from one of the myriad of others, this is where you make sure CD Label Creator knows it.

CAUTION

Don't Get Burned

Before you even think about starting the printing process, make sure you have the correct kind of paper or label stock in the printer first! For more information on label stock, check out Chapter 15.

Figure 16.12

The Page Setup dialog box enables you to select the kind of label or jewel case insert stock you are printing.

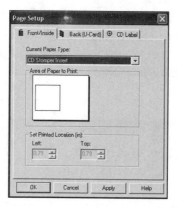

Clicking the drop-down box labeled Current Paper Type brings up the list of paper options you can choose from. CD Label Creator supports the majority of the big names and, if you go with my preferred method and use generic card stock, includes a generic output option.

After choosing the type of paper you're using for each of the labels, click the OK button on the Print dialog box to return to the print window.

After you've selected what to print and what you plan to print it on, you're finally ready to put an end to the insanity and print! Click the OK button at the bottom of the window and await the results.

Let's Talk About Preferences

Now that you've got a firm grasp on creating basic disc labels and jewel case inserts, it's time to take a look at how to customize CD Label Creator to your tastes, using the Preferences tool. To bring up the Preferences dialog box, select Preferences from the Edit menu in CD Label Creator (see Figure 16.13). You'll notice that this dialog box contains six tabs, each of which customizes certain aspects of CD Label Creator.

Figure 16.13

The Preferences dialog box contains tabs that let you control some aspects of the program.

The Front/Inside and Back (U-Card) Tabs

Under the first tab, named Front/Inside, there are two pairs of options. The first set consists of the Front/Inside Options, where you can select from two check boxes. The first, Print Front/Inside Cut and Fold Lines, tells CD Label Creator to print a thin set of lines along areas of the front and inside jewel case inserts for where to cut and fold the inserts. The second, Print Front/Inside Outline, prints a visible border around the inserts. Particularly for those without steady hands, the cut and fold lines can make cutting inserts out of nonperforated paper much easier.

The second pair of options is found under the Track Details section of the dialog box. Here you can control how much information about a track is printed on the inside cover. Specifically, you can disable the display and printing of track numbers and track durations (information not everyone finds necessary).

If you click over to the Back (U-Card) tab, you'll find the options available there are exactly the same as the ones in the Front/Inside tab.

The CD Label Tab

The information contained on the CD Label tab is very similar to what's found on the tabs controlling the various jewel case inserts. However, in addition to giving you control over cut and fold lines, solid borders and the display of track numbers and times, this dialog box lets you control whether to put tracks on the CD label (rather than just the artist/group and CD title). If you enable this check box, you can also choose to show track information in one or two columns (see Figure 16.14).

Figure 16.14

The CD Label tab gives you control over how disc labels are printed.

The Assistance, Internet, and Units Tabs

The tabs described in this section are all very basic. First of all, the Assistance tab lets you get some basic extra help from CD Label Creator. With this option enabled, any time you hover your mouse pointer over an object that requires you to double-click it to make edits, CD Label Creator causes a small pop-up message indicating just that.

The Internet tab is where you can control the download of information about a CD from an Internet source. We discussed this tab in the section, "Adding Audio CD Information and Contents Automatically!"

Finally, the Units tab enables you to specify the method used for measurement in CD jewel case layout. You can select inches or centimeters.

Close the Case (Jewel, That Is)

There are other tools included with CD Label Creator that allow you to further customize the look of your labels and inserts. They're not as robust as you'll find in a high profile, even higher-priced, graphics application, but they help make CD Label Creator an ideal utility for quickly and easily creating attractive CD labels and inserts. This is especially true if you're making a gift of a CD for a relative or significant other who doesn't know how easy it is. For you guys in the audience, you should pay particular attention. This sort of thing can break up the tedium of endless bouquets of flowers for every time you staple the family cat to the floor while laying carpet!

The Least You Need to Know

◆ Although it's not terribly powerful, using Roxio's CD Label Creator is an easy way to quickly create audio or data disc labels and inserts.

◆ You can use CD Label Creator's CD Contents option in the Add menu to automatically try to identify the names and lengths of tracks on your audio CD. If that doesn't work, you can use the Add Track option to enter them manually.

◆ CD Label Creator can do a lot more than just add song titles to your layout. It also allows you to choose custom background colors or themes to help enhance the look of your label and insert creations.

Chapter 17

Expressing Yourself with Nero Cover Designer

In This Chapter

◆ Find out what kinds of case inserts Nero Cover Designer can create

◆ Learn how to navigate the Nero Cover Designer interface so you can make labels and inserts for both data and audio discs

◆ See how to add information such as disc title, artist, track, and file and folder names using Nero's Document Data window

◆ Learn how to modify the formatting and placement of the fields on your inserts and labels

Like Easy CD Creator (ECDC), Nero Burning ROM includes a tool for making your own disc labels and case inserts, the Nero Cover Designer. This tool is a little more complex than the one included with ECDC, but then you can do a bit more with it.

To open Nero Cover Designer, click Start, All Programs, Ahead Nero, Nero Cover Designer. Then get ready to make some labels and inserts!

This chapter only covers the basics of creating labels and inserts with Nero Cover Designer. It is not intended to cover every control and option in the program.

Choosing Case and Data Types

When you open Nero Cover Designer, before you can get to the main interface, the New Document window opens (see Figure 17.1).

Figure 17.1

With Nero Cover Designer you're not restricted to creating inserts for your standard CD jewel cases.

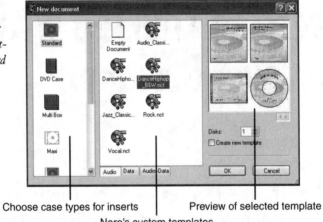

Choose case types for inserts   Preview of selected template

Nero's custom templates

As you can see, there's more to choose from here than just the theme or background of the case inserts. True, you can create conventional jewel case inserts, but you can also create inserts for: DVD cases, multi box, maxi, slim pack, mini CD, biz card, and rectangular biz card.

After you select one of these icons, the pane in the middle of the screen changes to reflect the pre-created templates associated with that case type. Unfortunately, as you'll soon notice, the only case type that has a true template is the standard jewel case. The others contain blank documents cut to the form factor of the case you select but containing no pre-created text or images.

Between Tracks

For more information on the types of CDs that are associated with some of these case formats, see Chapter 1.

Regardless of which type of case you create inserts for, there are three tabs to choose from based on the content of your created discs:

- Audio

- Data

- Audio+Data

Hopefully, these are self-explanatory. Unfortunately, if you want to create a prototypical video DVD case, you'll probably have to create your own template, by enabling the Create new template check box.

If you do select Standard from the left-hand pane you will notice various pre-designed templates. Click a template to select it. When you do, Nero displays a preview of that template's appearance on the right-hand pane. If you're creating labels for more than one disc, use the scroll arrows on the Disks field to select the appropriate number.

Between Tracks

Despite all conventional wisdom and the standards used in the primary Nero Burning ROM program, Nero Cover Designer likes to spell disc, with a "k." While this spelling is usually only applied to magnetic storage media (hard disks and floppies), Nero Cover Designer uses it for optical discs like CDs and DVDs. So when you see the term *disk* applied to the media types in this chapter, blame Nero and not this author or the book's copyeditor and proofreaders!

In this chapter, I focus on creating labels and inserts for a standard jewel case. The tools and processes described here, however, are no different when creating labels and inserts for any of the other case types. Click OK to open the template you selected and start designing.

Designing Inserts and Labels

When you've selected the type of inserts and labels you want to create, Nero opens the template you designated in its primary window (see Figure 17.2).

There are toolbars across the top and left side of the main window that allow you to control the interface and the contents of the selected insert or label displayed in the main window. Underneath the main window is a series of tabs. The tabs you see here depend on the type of case for which you're creating inserts and labels. Templates based on a standard jewel case have tabs for: Booklet (Front), Booklet (Rear), Inlay, and Disk. For a DVD, there are tabs for: Booklet, Insert, and Disk.

The number of Disk tabs that appear here depends on the number you choose when selecting a template. You can change this if you want, a subject that I address in the next section.

Figure 17.2

Don't expect to be wowed by the Nero Cover Designer interface. It does the job without being particularly pretty.

Click to open the Document Data Window

Select a tab to choose between label and insert views

The Document Data Window

As you can see from Figure 17.2, the template used for this standard jewel case is of the audio variety. When creating inserts based on an audio disc template there are at least three key pieces of information you're likely to include: the name of the disc, the artist(s), and the track list. Nero also includes a field for the year of the disc. You can, of course, use this field if you want, but I only find it useful in certain circumstances (depending on the theme/content of the disc).

Unlike using the CD Label Creator in ECDC, filling out the content of your labels and inserts is not done directly to the image in the main window. There are, however, format changes that can only be made here. When it comes to filling out content for the various fields, treat this window more like a preview. To insert or modify content for the included fields, click the Document Data icon on the toolbar. You can also click Document Data from the Data menu or select a field in the main window, and wait for a mini-toolbar containing the icon to appear (which you can click). In any case, the Document data window opens, as shown in Figure 17.3.

This window is broken in two halves. The left side contains a "tree" that breaks down the current layout of inserts and labels. It starts at the document level and then lists each disc in the layout and the type of data it's designed to hold (audio, data, or both).

The right side of the window provides various fields for adding information about the content of the disc. This specific field Nero displays here depends on what you've selected in the left pane. By default, the Document Data window selects Disk 1.

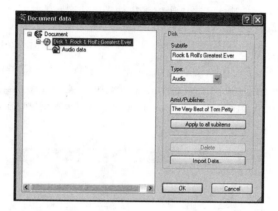

Figure 17.3

Use the Document data window to fill in information about your disc.

Entering Disc Data

When any disk is selected in the left pane of the Document Data window you see the fields, shown earlier, in Figure 17.3. These fields include the following:

- **Subtitle.** While the field says subtitle, this is the title for the disc. For example, if you were making a backup copy of the Counting Crows CD, *August and Everything After* for use in your car, then that would be the subtitle.

- **Type.** Regardless of whether you selected an Audio, Data, or Audio+Data layout at the templates screen, you can change the content format for any individual disc in your layout. Choose between these three formats.

- **Artist/Publisher.** This one should be self-explanatory. If it's a Counting Crows disc, for example, then that's what you would enter here.

There are also three buttons:

- **Apply to all subitems.** Adds the current text of the Artist/Publisher field to any disc beneath the one you've currently selected.

- **Delete.** This button can be used to delete any disc in the layout as long as it is not Disk 1.

- **Import Data.** You can automatically add information about a disc's contents by clicking Import Data with the disc inserted in one of your computer's disc drives. This replaces any information about the disc you might have already entered.

Let's begin by adding the disc title and artist information. For this example I'm going to create a Best of Tom Petty collection. Some might argue this to be a contradiction in terms, but hey, to each their own.

To add information about the actual contents of the disc, click the Audio data entry on the disc tree. If you set the disk type to Data, you'll see a File system data entry instead. If you chose Audio+Data for the disk type, you should see both entries.

When adding audio data you have two options: Add Track or Delete All. If you haven't included any tracks yet, this option is disabled. Click the Add Track button once for each track on your disc. Then, select each track and enter the information you want included for it (see Figure 17.4).

Figure 17.4

Entering track information manually can be a very time consuming process.

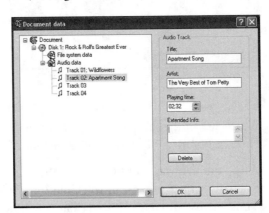

If you're creating an audio CD with more than one artist, you can actually enter an individual artist for each track on the disc. In that case, I recommend you replace the Artist field of your disc with the name of the compilation.

Between Tracks

You can change the order of tracks in an audio CD or the order of a file or folder listing in a data layout by selecting the track, file, or folder you want to move and dragging it up or down in the list.

If you're adding data disc information, the process is very similar. Instead, however, there are buttons for Add Files and Add Folder. The only editable field for files and folders is the Title field. Instead of information about the artist or length of the track, Nero shows you the "path" from which you located the file or folder and the size of its contents (including all files within an added folder).

Entering Document Data

Once you've added any audio or data information about each disc in your layout, you can also add information about the overall layout using the Document entry in the tree (see Figure 17.5).

Audio disc

Data disc

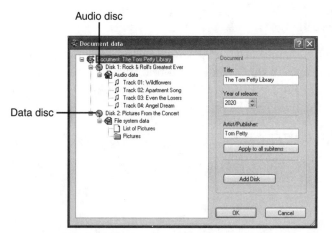

Figure 17.5

Use the Document entry of the Document data window to enter information applicable to the entire layout, no matter how many discs you've included.

Many of the fields shown here are similar in nature to those for the individual disc layouts. However, the usefulness of these fields depends on the layout you've chosen. Most audio CD templates, for example, don't include Document Title or Document Artist/Publisher information fields on the inserts or labels. So unless you add them to the layout, any information you enter here won't be used (see the next section). You can also use the controls for this tree entry to add a disk. Just click the Add Disk button.

CAUTION

Don't Get Burned _____

When you add a disc using the Document data window, the disc you add, for some reason, is completely blank (even after you add information using the disc's tree entry).

Regardless of which you may have chosen, Nero does not apply any template information to the new disc layout. So there's no fields and no background for the disc label.

While you can add fields yourself, and you can add pictures to use for a background, I've not been able to come up with any means of adding a template background. Because of this rather significant shortcoming, if you use any of Nero's templates then I suggest you be sure in advance of how many discs you intend to use.

If you want to remove an added disc, right-click it in the tree and choose delete. Once you've finished inputting information about your disc(s), click OK to close this window. If you deleted a disc from the layout while using this window, Nero Cover Designer asks that you confirm the deletion. Click Yes as long as you're sure of your choice.

Working With the Layout

When you return to the main Nero Cover Designer window after you've added information about the discs in the layout, you'll find that Nero has added that information to the display. In Figure 17.6, you can see the contents Nero has produced for the front and rear of the booklet, the inlay (U-card), and audio CD.

Figure 17.6

Based on the information I've provided so far, these are the results Nero Cover Designer generates.

As you can see, Nero does a fairly good job of fitting the information you give onto the inserts and labels. However, you can make changes to the layout if you want.

Moving and Resizing Fields

For example, if you think the front cover looks a little barren, you can move and enlarge the disc artist and subtitle fields. Just click a field once to select it. You should notice several handles appear around it (see Figure 17.7).

To change the size of a field, hover you mouse pointer over a handle, then click, hold and drag it in the direction your mouse cursor indicates (horizontal, vertical, diagonal). To move a field, click inside it, hold and drag it to its new location.

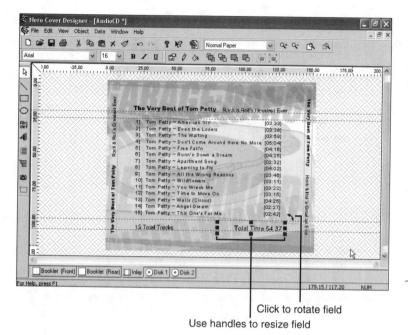

Figure 17.7

With the Total Time field selected, I can move, resize, or even rotate its contents.

Click to rotate field
Use handles to resize field

If you want to rotate the field, click, hold, and drag the curved double-arrow icon that appears over the handle on the upper-right corner of a selected field.

Changing Field Formatting and Links

In addition to moving fields around you can change the font, size, color, and orientation of the text. You can also change what piece of data a field is linked to. Earlier in this chapter, for example, I mentioned that in an audio disc template the Document fields in the Document data window weren't of much use because they don't appear in the default layout.

You can change that by either adding the fields or changing an existing field to point to them. To add a field, open the Object menu and select Insert, Field, and the name of the field you want added (Title, Artist, etc.).

Between Tracks

You can also add images to your layout by clicking the camera toolbar icon on the left of the screen. In the dialog box that appears, locate the file you want inserted and click Open. If you're working with a blank template, you can use pictures as your backgrounds. You can even save them as a new template by opening the File menu and choosing Save As Template.

To change the link for an existing field or the way the text is formatted inside it, you need to access its properties sheet by double-clicking it (see Figure 17.8).

Figure 17.8

The Properties sheet for a field gives you access to most of its formatting and linking options.

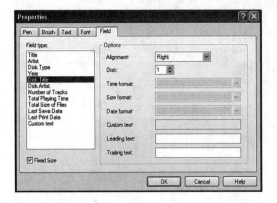

To change the link, choose a new one from the Field type pane. Use the Alignment scroll box to center, left, or right justify the text it contains. If you're modifying a field contained on a disc (and not the document) you can use the Disk scroll box to choose the disc for which you want to modify formatting. Finally, you can use the Leading text and Trailing text fields to include the information of your choosing in front of or after the text the field already contains.

Change to the Font tab to change the text style, formatting, and size.

On the Text tab you can enable the Bent check box to make the text curved (this requires some resizing of the text field to make the text legible). This option is designed for use on disc label fields, since your disc is curved. It can be used on inserts as well, though.

Between Tracks

If you've resized a field, you've probably noticed that Nero Cover Designer modifies the size of the text to fit within the field. If you disable the Fixed Size check box on the Properties window Nero lets the text go beyond the field's boundaries.

As they deal more with the design aspects of creating labels and inserts, I don't cover the Pen and Brush tabs in this chapter.

In Figure 17.9, you can see a front cover sample with text fields in which I've modified the text font and size and rotated one of the fields.

Once you're happy with the contents and layout of your inserts and disc labels you're ready to finish the job.

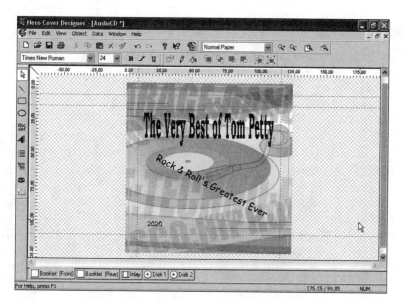

Figure 17.9

If I were creating this label for real and this were a full-color series, I would have added some color to help spice this up a little.

Printing Your Labels and Inserts

Printing your case inserts and labels is the goal you're always working toward when using Nero Cover Designer. Before initiating the print process, however, you need to take care of a few final details.

First, make sure you've configured Nero to print to the type of paper you plan to use for your labels and inserts. On the toolbar at the top of the Nero Cover Designer you should see a scroll box containing the currently selected paper type (probably Normal Paper). If this matches the type you're using, then you're nearly good to go. However, if it's not a match, open the scroll box and select one (see Figure 17.10).

Keep in mind when choosing a paper type that you must do so for each label and insert in your layout.

> **Cross Reference**
>
> For more information on paper stock and label application, see Chapter 15.

Once you've selected the right paper type, you should save your work. Open the File menu and select Save. Saving your layout guarantees that if something goes wrong you can always get it back later.

Once you're ready to print, either click the printer toolbar icon or open the File menu and select Print (see Figure 17.11). (You can also select Print Preview if you want a look at how the final results should appear.)

Figure 17.10

This scroll box contains a few dozen options from which you can choose. If yours isn't there, try to find a close approximation, or go with the Normal Paper option.

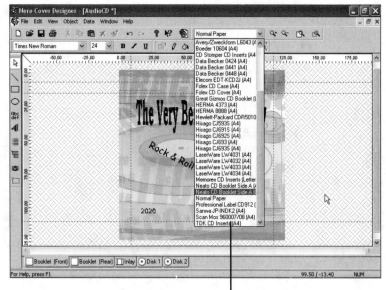

Use the drop-down menu to select a label and insert paper type

Figure 17.11

After all the hard work, you're now ready to print your disc labels and inserts.

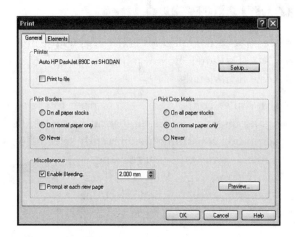

The Print dialog box has two tabs. Use the Elements tab to select which specific inserts and labels you want to print (you might not want to print them all, depending on your needs).

On the General tab shown here you can choose to print borders or crop marks. Borders give your labels and inserts a solid outline to cut around. However, if you just want guides for where to put those scissors (if your printing media isn't perforated), just enable the Crop Marks option.

In the Miscellaneous section of this dialog box put a check in the Enable Bleeding dialog box if you want the colors to "bleed" over the edge of the label or insert. This helps ensure that the entire label or insert is printed (since the process can be off by a few millimeters). You can customize the length of the bleed, but the 2 millimeter default that Nero assigns is a good place to start.

If you want the printing to pause between each page (so you can ready the right paper stock, for example), enable the Prompt At Each New Page check box.

Once you're ready, click the OK button to start printing. If all goes as planned, the work your printer churns out should more than justify the time invested in designing the labels and inserts. However, keep in mind that the quality of your output also depends on the quality of both your print media and the capabilities of your printer.

The Least You Need to Know

◆ Nero can create inserts for a variety of disc case types, including jewel cases and the style used for movies on DVD.

◆ Nero Cover Designer only includes swank templates for standard jewel case designs. For other case types you must work from a blank template.

◆ The Document data window is the primary interface that allows you to add information about the contents of you disc to your labels and inserts.

◆ You can customize the look of each field in your layout, including the ability to resize, move, rotate, and change the text font.

Part 7

Putting the Cherry on Top with More Great Tools and Software

Easy CD Creator and Nero Burning ROM are hardly the only kids on the block when it comes to recording great CDs and DVDs. First, Chapter 18 shows you the ins and outs of using MusicMatch Jukebox to record audio to your PC and create great audio CDs. If you want to turn your PC into a sound machine that can spit out great compilation CDs at the drop of a hat, then this one's for you. Chapter 19 goes the same route, but instead I show you how to use Ulead VideoStudio to capture, edit, and record video CDs, Super Video CDs and video DVDs. In Chapter 20, I show you how to preserve your precious family photos by using Roxio PhotoRelay to create digital photo albums that you can burn to disc and take with you wherever you go. Finally, for those of you at your wits' end because you turn out more coasters than killer discs, I offer some general troubleshooting guidelines in Chapter 21 that can hopefully get you back on track.

MusicMatch Jukebox: Making Your PC the Ultimate Jukebox

In This Chapter

♦ MusicMatch Jukebox is one of the best programs available for ripping, recording, and listening to music

♦ MusicMatch Jukebox has three core components: the Player windows, the Music Library window, and the Recorder Window

♦ Use the Music Library to create a compendium of all your MP3, MP3Pro, WMA, and WAV files

♦ In addition to ripping music from CDs, MusicMatch Jukebox can burn music files back to various CD and DVD formats

Throughout this book, we have used Easy CD Creator 5 Platinum and Nero Burning ROM 5.5, which are both great applications, all-inclusive programs. Of course, these aren't the only software programs available for creating CDs and DVDs. In just the last two years, there has been a boom in new recording software that can accomplish all your data and audio CD recording needs. There are other applications, though, that offer much more specialized services. Because we think it's one of the handiest tools for the digital audiophile, I've devoted this chapter to the use of MusicMatch Jukebox (MMJ) 7.2. For those who live to acquire, sort, and create tons of specialized discs for the road, it doesn't get much better than this program (even more so if you prefer to use your PC as a digital jukebox for all of your music).

Introducing MusicMatch Jukebox 7.2

For a few years now MusicMatch Jukebox has been an application you can use to find, rip, organize, burn, and play audio files of various formats. However, in MMJ 7.2, MusicMatch has added a few new features, including support for downloading to MP3 players, recording to the MP3 Pro format, and recording to DVDs.

> **Cross Reference**
>
> You'll find more information on the various audio file formats, like MP3 Pro, in Chapter 9.

To begin, MusicMatch Jukebox can work with the following file types:

- MP3 (and MP3 Pro) files

- Windows Media files

- Music CDs (CD-DA)

- WAV files

- Shoutcast

- Secure Music

- M3U files

> **Between Tracks**
>
> As MusicMatch Jukebox continues to evolve, it's become increasingly feature-rich. This chapter is only intended to cover the very basics and a few of its whiz-bang features. There's much more to the program than what we can cover in these pages.

You don't have to worry about the details of what these formats are (though you can always refer to Chapter 9). The point is that with this wide assortment of formats, you'll have no problem acquiring audio files from most sources. And several sources for music are out there—including your local discs, Internet radio, Internet sites, and so on.

The good news is you don't have to do much to get MMJ. You can download the latest demo version from the web at www.musicmatch.com. This demo version doesn't enable all the features MMJ has to offer, but you can register for and download the full version of this application. Currently you can do so with a year of free updates for $19.99. If you're willing to fork over the money (about $39.99), then you can get the lifetime subscription in which all future versions are yours at no extra charge. If you find that you do like using this program, the lifetime subscription is well worth the cost and it is updated frequently. Between the second and third editions of this book, MMJ has evolved from version 6.1 to 7.2!

Don't Get Burned

Note that this chapter is based on MusicMatch Jukebox 7.2. While other versions operate in a nearly identical manner, certain features, along with the overall look of the program, may be different in your version should it be older or even more recent.

Also, the status of Internet Radio broadcasts is in flux with copyright monopolists like the RIAA spoiling yet another good party. You may or may not have much luck finding an Internet Radio broadcast. See Chapter 3 for more information. Fortunately, while Internet Radio could go the way of the dodo (bird), MMJ's built-in radio service is still firing on all cylinders.

Getting to Know MusicMatch Jukebox

When you launch MusicMatch Jukebox (either from a desktop shortcut, system tray icon, or Start menu path) the program immediately opens into its default interface (see Figure 18.1). This is a slight departure from version 6.x, in which you had to first dismiss a small "Welcome" screen.

Player window

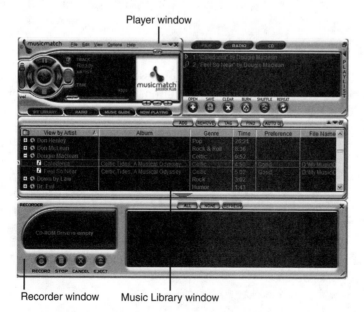

Figure 18.1

The main window for MusicMatch Jukebox enables you to perform many functions.

Recorder window   Music Library window

One important thing to note here is that the screen you see in Figure 18.1 is a compilation of four windows all scrunched together. It might look like one window here, but technically it's not. If you look carefully you can see the divisions between sections. If you want to move all three windows as a single unit, just click and drag on the title bar of the top window. Otherwise, you can click and drag the other two separately by using their respective title bars.

What you see when you launch MMJ depends on the default settings or how it was configured to look when last used. If you don't see all three windows when opening MusicMatch Jukebox, don't fret, these windows can be opened and closed individually. The top window is called the Player. It sports the typical universal audio controls for play, pause, stop, and so on. This is where you get information about the music track currently playing and what tracks are in your Playlist (which we'll cover in a bit). The Recorder window is the bottom window shown in Figure 18.1. Here you can record music from a disc to your hard drive. Finally, the window stuck in the middle of these two is the Music Library, which is where you can organize the music on your hard drive.

> **Between Tracks**
>
> To open the Recorder, you can click the button with the red Record dot on it. You can also take a shortcut to opening your music Library by clicking the My Library button. Both of these buttons appear on the Player window (see Figure 18.2 in the next section).

To open a missing Library or Recorder window you have a couple of options. You can use the View menu on the Player window and make sure both the My Library and Recorder options are enabled (a checkmark appears next to the option if it's enabled).

Controlling the Player Window

The Player window in MusicMatch Jukebox is more or less the Mission Control center for the entire program (see Figure 18.2). Its main function, of course, is to play music.

Figure 18.2

The Player window sports a variety of buttons and menus that provide control over all facets of MusicMatch.

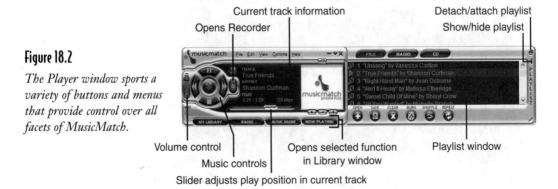

Current track information
Opens Recorder
Detach/attach playlist
Show/hide playlist
Volume control
Music controls
Opens selected function in Library window
Playlist window
Slider adjusts play position in current track

As you can see, the Player window is divided into two parts. On the left is the Player itself and on the right is the Playlist. The next two sections take a look at each.

The Player

Along the top of the Player is a series of menus which give you access to all of MMJ's functions. To the left of the window there are a series of CDlike controls. These operate pretty much as you'd expect, with buttons for stop, play, skip track, previous track, etc. With the scroll bar to the left of these controls you can set the volume. While this is all pretty straightforward, there are a few other controls here worth calling attention to.

First of all, in the center of the Player controls is a red dot, which is what you'll use to activate or close the Recorder window. Near that is information about the currently selected track, artist, duration, and recording quality. Beneath the track information is a horizontal slider that measures a track's progress. To skip ahead or backward in a track just drag the slider around to the approximate point in the song to which you want to listen. Finally there's a series of four buttons beneath the Player controls:

♦ **My Library.** This button brings up the Music Library, as it was shown in Figure 18.1 (the middle section). Your Music Library contains all the information you could possibly need regarding the audio tracks on your hard drive.

> **Cross Reference**
>
> For more information on Track Tags, see Chapter 9.

♦ **Radio.** This feature takes you online, allowing you to select from hundreds of Internet-based radio stations. If you work at home or are allowed free Internet reign where you work, this is a handy way to have free access to a variety of music that you may not have in your Library.

♦ **Music Guide.** The Music Guide takes you to the Music Match website, where you can catch up on their latest news and offerings.

♦ **Now Playing.** If you have an active Internet connection, the Now Playing guide shows information contained in an Internet database about the currently playing track (including information on the album to which it was recorded). If you're offline, it lists whatever information it has available from the track's tag.

Each of these buttons controls what appears in the middle MMJ window, which normally displays your Music Library. For the purposes of this chapter, we're going to stick to the Music Library, as discussed in the next section.

The Playlist

The Playlist portion of the Player window appears on the right of the Player controls. Although you can play individual songs from wherever you find them, MusicMatch Jukebox uses the concept of a playlist to organize audio files into groups. It can show the contents of a CD, the song currently playing over MusicMatch radio, or any combination of audio file contained in your Music Library. The three buttons along the top of the playlist control the functions to which you currently have access:

♦ **File.** The File button sets the playlist to show the most recent active collection of audio tracks you have selected from your Music Library (it may be empty if you've not used it before).

♦ **Radio.** Like the Radio button we discussed in the previous section, this opens up a web page with options for connecting to an Internet radio station. The difference is, this also opens a default station and starts playing right away.

♦ **CD.** If you have a music disc in your disc drive, this button sets the playlist so that it shows its contents.

You may have noticed that a series of buttons appears beneath the Playlist. These controls change (or disappear) depending on which of the three buttons we just discussed is selected. If you've enabled the Radio, you won't see any buttons. With File selected, however, you can choose from:

♦ **Open.** Choosing Open brings up the dialog box shown in Figure 18.3. From the Open Music dialog box you have access to music from a variety of sources on your computer. Using the buttons along the left side of the dialog box you can select music contained in: your Music Library, saved playlists, music on a disc, saved to your Windows desktop, or elsewhere on your computer. Regardless of which source you choose, once you've selected the tracks you want, they'll appear in your playlist.

♦ **Save.** Lets you save the current playlist so you can load it later using the Open button.

♦ **Clear.** Clears all tracks from the current playlist. This gives you a fresh start when creating a new playlist.

♦ **Burn.** Starts the process of recording your playlist to disc. We'll get more into this option later in the chapter.

♦ **Shuffle.** Plays the tracks in your playlist in a random order.

♦ **Repeat.** Causes the playlist to repeat play until stopped.

Select a button to access music from a specific source

Choose tracks or playlists here

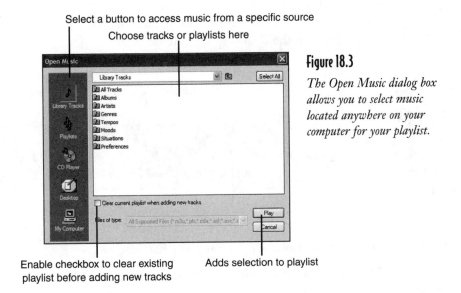

Figure 18.3

The Open Music dialog box allows you to select music located anywhere on your computer for your playlist.

Enable checkbox to clear existing playlist before adding new tracks

Adds selection to playlist

For CD you can select from:

- ◆ **Drive.** MMJ only searches for one drive when playing music from a disc. If you have more than one disc drive, using this button allows you to select the one from which to play music.

- ◆ **Shuffle.** Plays the CD's tracks in a random order.

- ◆ **Repeat.** Causes CD to play repeatedly until stopped.

Finally you can exert more control over the Playlist window using the two buttons on the window's right side. The arrow can be used to hide the playlist from view, or reveal it if it's already hidden. The "double-window" icon allows you to separate the Playlist from the player, giving you more control over how it's sized.

Getting Used to the Recorder

Now that we've got the Player window sorted out, let's step through the controls available on the Recorder window, which you can see in Figure 18.4.

As you can see, there are only a handful of controls you have to worry about here. In the small window to the left, you can see information about the CD currently in the drive set for recording. Once recording begins, this window indicates how much progress has been made and how quickly the tracks are being ripped. We're going to assume that you have a music CD in this drive, however, if the drive is empty or contains a data disc then the Recorder indicates as such.

Figure 18.4

The Recorder window shown here is currently ripping music tracks from a music CD to the computer's hard disk drive.

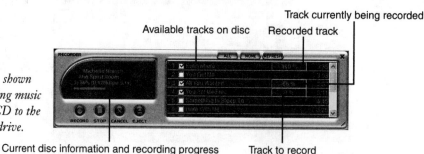

Available tracks on disc | Recorded track

Track currently being recorded

Current disc information and recording progress

Track to record

Beneath the small display window are four buttons:

- ◆ **Record.** Begins recording selected tracks from CD to your hard disk drive.

- ◆ **Stop.** Stops a recording in progress after it completes the current track it's ripping from the CD.

- ◆ **Cancel.** Immediately cancels the recording of a CD to your hard drive.

- ◆ **Eject.** Ejects the disc currently in the drive.

When a music CD is in the drive you're using to record, you'll see a listing of its tracks in the right side of the window. Accompanying each track is a check box, which you can use to select the tracks you want to record. To make the task of selecting tracks simpler you can use either the All or None buttons above this list. Along with these two buttons is a third button, labeled Refresh. If you've changed discs in your recording drive, you can use this button to refresh the contents that appear in the list.

Between Tracks _____

As with listening to a music CD with the Player window, you can rip music tracks using any available CD drive in your computer. To choose from the available drives, go to the Player window and click Options, Recorder, Source, and then the drive from which you want to record.

Also note from the list in the Source pane that you're not restricted to your disc drives as a source. If you have analog music input through your sound card or you want to record voice through a microphone, you can do so from here as well.

The MusicMatch Music Library

With the possible exception of the Player itself, the Music Library is the core of MusicMatch Jukebox. As you can see in Figure 18.5, this library contains a listing of all the music on your computer.

Click a field to sort Music Library by field catagory

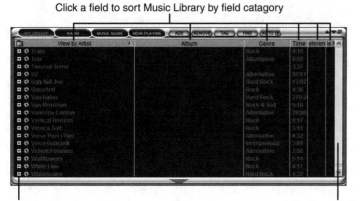

Figure 18.5

The Music Library turns your PC into a digital music jukebox.

Click +/– icon to expand/contract tree

Use to scroll through Music Library

Between Tracks _____

If you compare Figure 18.5 to the Media Library portion of Figure 18.1, you'll see that the buttons for My Library, Radio, Music Guide, and Now Playing have moved between the Player and Music Library windows. If the two windows are connected, these buttons appear on the Player. However, if you pull them apart, as was done when capturing Figure 18.5, the buttons shift to the Music Library window.

The controls on this window appear simple, but they belie a wealth of options that you have at your disposal. First, let's tackle the series of buttons at the top of the window:

- **Add.** Clicking this button opens the Add Tracks To Music Library dialog box (see Figure 18.6). With this button you can add tracks to your Music Library that already exist on your hard drive.

- **Delete.** This button removes a track from your Music Library. If you choose this option, the dialog box that appears also has a check box that, if enabled, removes the track from your hard drive as well.

Figure 18.6

With this dialog box you can choose audio files on your hard drive to include in your Music Library.

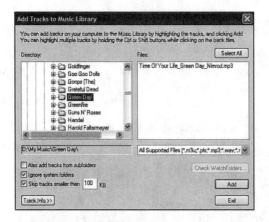

- ◆ **Tag.** Audio files, such as MP3s, have a track "tag" that can store information about the track, including the artist, album, and track names, genre, and more. Clicking this button allows you to edit a track's tag information.

- ◆ **Find.** If you start putting every track of every CD you own on your hard disk, you'll find that your Music Library gets pretty big, pretty darn fast. Use this button to search for a specific track in your library.

- ◆ **AutoDJ.** Can't decide what to listen to? Use the AutoDJ to have MusicMatch Jukebox create a playlist for you. You can choose the total running time of the playlist and have the AutoDJ filter music using track tag information, including song tempo, preference, and genre.

> **Between Tracks**
>
> The leftmost heading in the library is the key by which tracks are sorted. By default, this key is the artist or group. You can change this option by clicking the folder icon on the leftmost heading. This produces a list from which you can choose the criteria by which the entire list is sorted. Generally, I recommend sticking with the Artist option.

Once you have tracks in your Music Library they appear in the main part of the library's window. As you can see from the previous figure there are several headings that can be used to classify the music. The information for filling these headings comes from the track's tag. Like using Windows Explorer, you can click the + signs on the leftmost listing to expand the tree and see different tracks. By clicking on each of the library headings, you can sort the listing of tracks according to that header's category.

Putting MusicMatch Jukebox to Work

Now that we've gotten familiar with the MusicMatch Jukebox interface, it's time to start learning how to make all these different features and controls work for you.

In the following sections, we'll take a look at some of the main uses of MusicMatch, including building a playlist, recording CDs to your hard drive, and recording a playlist to CD. There are other ways in which you can make use of this program, but these are the most useful and most central to this book's theme, so let's get started.

Filling Your Music Library

Before you can record your songs to CD using MusicMatch Jukebox, you have to actually have them on your computer and in the Music Library. To acquire the audio files you want, you'll have to record them to your computer from CD. There are, of course, other sources of varying degrees of legality from which you can obtain audio files, but we'll focus on CD ripping here. Hopefully, if you have the CD, it means you legally purchased the music.

Extracting tracks from your CDs is easy using the Recorder window shown back in Figure 18.4. After ensuring you have an active Internet connection, just insert the audio CD into your disc drive. MMJ will then access the Internet and identify the CD's artist and track titles (it may find more than one match, in which case, you'll need to select the correct one). If the Recorder doesn't update its contents for a newly inserted disc, give the Refresh button a click. If that still doesn't work, make sure the Recorder is looking at the right disc drive, as discussed earlier in the "Getting Used to the Recorder" section.

Using the check boxes that appear with each track, select the individual tracks you want, or use the All button to select them all. Regardless of whether you are record-ing 2 tracks or 20, click the Record button on the left side of this dialog box when you're ready to start recording these files to your hard disk. The default location the Recorder uses for the files it extracts from your CD is C:\My Music. You can change this by opening the Options menu on the MMJ Player window and selecting Recorder, Settings. The Settings dialog box that pops up gives you the ability to configure many aspects of the Jukebox program.

Between Tracks

If you don't have an active Internet connection or if MMJ can't match the CD to a record in the Internet database, it will simply list the tracks as "Track 1," "Track 2," etc. You can click these tracks and manually name them if you want.

The options in this dialog box are pretty self-explanatory, and because we're more concerned right now with choosing where to store your music, look to the dialog box's upper-right corner and click the Tracks Directory button. This brings up yet another dialog box, which is shown in Figure 18.7.

Figure 18.7

You can change the directory the Recorder uses to store newly recorded songs.

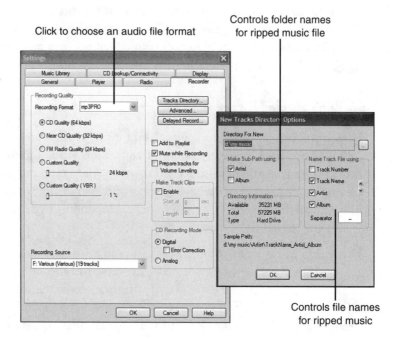

Click to choose an audio file format

Controls folder names for ripped music file

Controls file names for ripped music

In addition to letting you customize where to store music files, this dialog box also enables you to decide how to name the new files. You can change the default folder for new songs by clicking the Ellipse (...) button in the Directory For New field. Then navigate to the folder in which you want your music tracks stored. If, when you record new music to your hard disk, you want to have MusicMatch Jukebox automatically create new folders in your main music folder, based on the artist name or the album title (or both) then use the check boxes found in the Make Sub-Path Using section.

Note that when you use the sub-path options, you see that, at the bottom of this dialog box, the Sample Path field shows you what you've selected.

You can also see in this figure that you can further customize how music files are named and stored on your computer. For example, when you want to record a song from a CD, you can name the song in several ways:

◆ The number of the track as it appears on the CD (use the Track Number check box)

- The song title (use the Track Name check box)

- The artist's name (use the Artist check box)

- The album name (use the Album check box)

- Any combination of the above! (Select more than one check box)

For example, one of my favorite songs is "Right Here, Right Now" by Van Halen. This song appears on a couple of their CDs. If I wanted to name this song, I might want to use both the Artist and the Album check boxes, so I could look back and determine where it was obtained. Perhaps you are like me and sometimes buy a CD just for one song. In that case, you might just use the Album check box.

If you do use more than one of these check boxes, MusicMatch Jukebox names the file accordingly and places a separator character between each of your choices when it creates the filename. The Separator check box allows you to select any character you want to separate the names, although a hyphen, underscore, or space generally works the best in practice.

My recommendation is that you have MMJ create a folder for each artist whose songs you record to your hard disk, and then name the tracks according to: artistname_ songtitle_tracktitle.

Click OK when you've finished viewing or modifying information in this dialog box.

This brings you back to the Recorder tab in the Settings dialog box. To change the default recording format, click the Recording Format scroll box and select the type you prefer. To adjust the recording quality, select a radio button beneath the Recording Format field. The higher the quality, the better your music files sound. However, the higher the quality, the more space these files take up on your hard disk drive. When you're happy with your settings here, click OK to return to the main MusicMatch window.

> **Cross Reference**
>
> See Chapter 9 for more information on audio file formats and recording quality.

When you've selected the tracks you want to record and have made any adjustments you want on the Settings dialog box, just click the Record button to start the actual recording process. As each track is recorded, you'll see a progress bar slowly (or quickly depending on your hardware and patience) start marching toward 100 percent (see Figure 18.4). When it reaches that number, the check mark disappears from the track's check box and the Recorder moves on to the next track. When it's done, you'll find each of the tracks listed in your Music Library.

Generating Playlists

As we've already discussed, the two central themes around which this application runs are your music library and playlists. The library tells MusicMatch Jukebox which audio files are on your hard disk and where they are located. The playlist is nothing more than a collection of audio files from your library that you want played as a group. This is similar to a collection of tracks from a music CD. The idea of libraries and playlists is a standard feature you'll find in most good media software. Because you can use playlists to burn a disc, they pretty much make you the producer of your own CDs. You can generate playlists in a variety of ways. In the following sections we'll take a look at a couple of those ways.

Creating a Manual Playlist

A manual playlist is one in which you select individual songs or groups of songs. It might be time-consuming, but it does help ensure that you get only the songs you want. You do this by dragging the song from the Music Library window to the Playlist pane in the Player application (or right-click the track and choose Add Track[s] To Playlist). After you've selected all the songs you want for a particular playlist, just click the Save button in the Playlist pane. The Save Playlist dialog box pops up and enables you to give a name to the playlist so you'll be able to retrieve it at a later time.

To open a playlist after you've created it, just click Open. Then, in the Open Music dialog box, click the Playlists button and select the list you want to open.

You can delete songs from any playlist by simply clicking the song in the list and pressing the Delete key on your keyboard. If you want to reorder the playlist, click the song and drag it to a new location in the list. To make this change permanent, be sure you use the Save button to resave the list.

Using the AutoDJ to Create a Playlist

If you don't want to be tied into selecting each song for your playlist, MusicMatch Jukebox has an AutoDJ feature that can save you some time. To begin this process, click the AutoDJ button on the Music Library's toolbar. The dialog box shown in Figure 18.8 enables you to select the criteria that MMJ uses to select songs for the playlist. In Chapter 9, we discussed the concept of track tags. Not only do these tags store information about artist, song title, album name, etc., it can also store information like: genre type, mood, tempo, and more. For AutoDJ to work effectively, it needs this information!

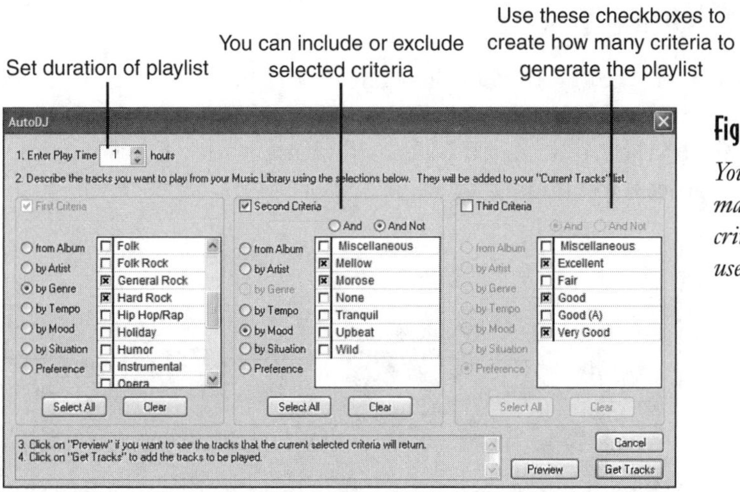

Use these checkboxes to
You can include or exclude   create how many criteria to
Set duration of playlist   selected criteria   generate the playlist

Figure 18.8

You can select music automatically by specifying the criteria the AutoDJ should use.

You can select tracks by artist name, album name, genre, and other categories. You can further subselect by breaking up your preferences into first, second, and third criteria.

To make these selections, first determine the number of criteria you want AutoDJ to use by enabling or disabling the appropriate check boxes (you can't disable the First Criteria section for what are, hopefully, obvious reasons). From here, select the First Criteria from options like Album, Artist, Mood, etc. Once making that selection you must actually choose how AutoDJ will select from the category. For example, if you choose by Preference, do you want to hear only songs you've classified as Excellent and Very Good? Do you want to hear only songs that you think are just Fair? Use the check boxes to make these selections and then do the same for the Second and Third Criteria.

When you're finished selecting criteria, click the Get Tracks button; the AutoDJ then makes selections for you and adds them to the current playlist window. You can then use the playlist to start playing the songs, or you can save the playlist and give it a name. You also can use the playlist to burn a CD.

Between Tracks

Certain criteria selections require you to select either an And or And Not option. The default is And which specifies that you want to include tracks that fit the selected criteria. And Not means that you actually want to filter those matching tracks out of the list.

Using Burner Plus to Record a CD

If you look at the player window, the buttons beneath the Playlist pane include one labeled Burn (you must have File selected). Click this button to start the recording process. This brings up the MusicMatch Burner Plus that gives you complete control over the recording process (see Figure 18.9).

Figure 18.9

The MusicMatch Burner in version 7.x of MusicMatch Jukebox provides much more sophisticated controls over the burn process than what was included in previous versions.

Controls for Burner Plus

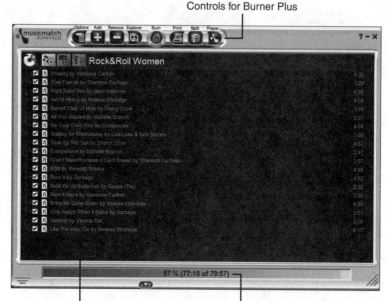

Tracks to be recorded   Length of recording versus disc capacity

When you first open Burner Plus, any tracks listed in the MMJ Playlist find their way into its main window. Using track tag information, Burner Plus lists each track title, its artist, and length, alongside a check box which you can use to remove or re-add a track to the recording list.

At the bottom of the window is an indicator that lets you know how much of the disc's capacity the current playlist will use up. If the number is more than 100 percent, then you need to remove as many tracks as it takes to go under that number. You could also use Burner Plus's SmartSplit feature, which we'll discuss in a moment. Beneath this indicator, however, is a small button that opens (and closes) an information window that shows you the current recording settings. This window is for informational purposes only.

Just above the track list are three buttons that allow you to choose what type of CD to record: music, MP3, or data. If the music systems you plan to play the disc in support MP3 file, you might want to record in the MP3 format. Depending on file quality, a CD can hold in the neighborhood of 130 tracks! For this example, though, we'll stick with a music CD.

Finally, at the top of the Burner Plus window is a line of several buttons:

- **Options.** Allows you to configure basic recording criteria, like disc type (music, MP3, and data), the drive to use for recording, speed of the burn, and more.

- **Add.** Allows you to add more tracks to the list.

- **Remove.** Removes the selected track(s) from the list.

- **Explorer.** Opens Windows Explorer, allowing you to browse your computer for audio files.

- **Burn.** Begins the disc recording process.

> **Between Tracks**
>
> To change the name of the disc from the default title Burner Plus assigns, right-click the title and select Rename Disc. Then just type the name directly into the Burner Plus interface.

- **Print.** Allows you to print a jewel case label. The jewel case creator included with MMJ can be best described as "basic." It works, but don't expect fine art!

- **Split.** If your recording list is too big for a single disc, use the SmartSplit feature. This causes Burner Plus to break up the list into two or more chunks that can then be recorded to multiple discs. Burner Plus ensures that none of the lists contains more disc than can fit onto the selected media type (74-minute CD, 80-minute CD, 4.7GB DVD, etc.).

- **Player.** Returns the main MusicMatch Jukebox interface to the front of the screen (if it wasn't there already). This does not close Burner Plus.

From these buttons, I've left one important option left unexplained. It's explained in the next section.

Burner Plus Settings

Click the Options button and select Settings from the menu that appears. This brings up the Burner Plus Options window, which sports several tabs, only two of which are we interested in for this chapter. Those tabs are:

- **General.** Unless you want to change how Burner Plus looks, ignore the Appearance section of this tab. Instead, focus on the Preferences section (see Figure 18.10). Use the Media Size scroll box to choose the type of disc you want to record to. You can choose from: 5, 21, 74, and 80-minute CDs, 1.3GB DD

CDs, and 3.9 and 4.7GB DVDs. The Disc Type at Startup field allows you to select the default mode for Burner Plus when you start it (audio, MP3, or data).

Figure 18.10

Use the General tab of the Burner Plus Options window to select what type of disc to which you want to record. Select the Media Type scroll box to alter the type of disc to which you intend to record.

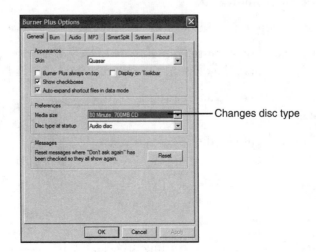

Changes disc type

◆ **Burn**. In the Drive section (see Figure 18.11), use the Burn tab to choose which drive and at what speed you want to use to record to a disc (you can only select a drive and speed valid with your computer's hardware). Under Burn Mode, choose whether you want to test a burn before writing. If you've used your disc recorder to successfully burn a disc already, you should be safe in choosing the Write Only option.

Figure 18.11

The options on the Burn tab let you select the type and speed of disc recorder you use and whether you want to do a test burn before recording the disc.

The remaining tabs: Audio, MP3, SmartSplit, System, and About contain options that allow more advanced users tailor the recording process to their needs. If you're just getting your feet wet, you needn't worry about them. (This is an *Idiot's Guide*, after all!) Click OK (or Cancel) to return to the main Burner Plus window.

Burning the Disc

When you're finally ready to get the show on the road, click the Burn button. MusicMatch Burner Plus immediately begins processing the play list. If you've elected to have Burner Plus balance the volume across tracks, it will start with that process. If you've set Burner Plus to first burn tracks to a single temporary file (called an image file) on your hard disk (a more reliable burn) you'll next see it start creating that file. Finally, Burner Plus will begin recording your disc. Regardless of the stage, the screen you see looks like the one shown in Figure 18.12.

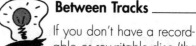

Between Tracks _____

If you don't have a recordable or rewritable disc (that is not closed) in your disc drive, Burner Plus will produce an error that you must insert a blank disc.

Current track information

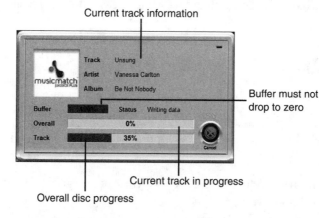

Buffer must not drop to zero

Current track in progress

Overall disc progress

Figure 18.12

MusicMatch Burner Plus makes recording music to a CD or DVD a snap!

When complete, the screen shown in Figure 18.13 indicates whether or not it was a successful burn. Hopefully, and most likely, all has gone well.

From this screen you have two options: return to Burner Plus or create another copy of the disc. Click the button for the option of your choice. When you're done, close Burner Plus and enjoy the fruits of your efforts!

Between Tracks _____

If you're having problems creating a successful burn, have a look at Chapter 21.

Figure 18.13

When Burner Plus indicates the recording completed successfully, you'll have a new disc loaded with music for your listening pleasure.

A Perfect Match?

Whether MusicMatch Jukebox is worth the price of admission or effort to download really depends on your own needs. Certainly many Windows users would prefer to use the Media Player application, which comes free with Windows. There are also other downloadable programs like WinAmp that draw rave reviews. However, I will say that I've used many an application for stockpiling my MP3s and none of them has held a candle to MusicMatch Jukebox when factoring in ease of use, appealing interface, features, and overall quality.

The Least You Need to Know

◆ MusicMatch Jukebox is available as a free demo program from www.music-match.com. However, without the full version, certain key features are disabled.

◆ Use the Player window to control songs being played and to view and edit the playlist.

◆ Use the Music Library window to generate playlists and organize the music tracks on your hard disk drive.

◆ Use the Recorder window for ripping music CDs to your hard disk drive.

◆ Use Burner Plus to record music to your CDs and DVDs.

Chapter 19

Ulead VideoStudio: Making Your PC the Ultimate Movie Factory

In This Chapter

♦ An introduction to the world of Ulead VideoStudio

♦ Capturing video with Ulead VideoStudio

♦ Basic editing with Ulead VideoStudio

♦ Authoring a Video CD, Super Video CD, or video DVD with Ulead VideoStudio

As this book is about creating both CDs and DVDs, I almost feel like my DVD audience is getting shortchanged, being tied to a pair of applications in Easy CD Creator and Nero Burning ROM that can't get you from beginning to end if what you want most to do with your DVD drive is record video. Roxio, in this regard, is a joke, and while Nero does a terrific job of recording your video DVD files to disc, it can't do anything in terms of converting MPEG-2 files to the video DVD format that you can record.

Unfortunately, with the DVD recording market in its infancy, there's only so much you can do when it comes to recording video. Most DVD drives come with their own utilities for authoring a DVD, but most I've seen can't adequately get you from capturing to authoring using a single piece of software (although I do like the SonicDVD authoring software that comes with HP's DVD Writer 200i).

Cross Reference

For more information on video file formats, like MPEG, see Chapter 12.

Arcane CD Speak

A **pro-sumer** application is one that is geared towards average home users but is of high enough quality to produce output that is *nearly* on par with some professional-grade products.

Odds are, the best beginning-to-end application you'll get (short of buying a $100+ application off the shelf) will come with a video capture device (should you choose to buy one).

There are a lot of these applications to choose from. Certainly, if you have the money, a *pro-sumer* application like Adobe's Premiere is tough to beat. Premiere even comes with some of the pricier video capture devices you can buy. However, we can't all plunk down $700 to $2,000 for a nice video capture package. I've found that many consumer-level packages offer either MGI Videowave or Ulead VideoStudio. For this chapter, I've chosen to focus on the latter. Though even if you're using a different program, you can still learn basic capture, editing, and authoring concepts from this chapter.

All About Ulead VideoStudio

Ulead Video Studio is commonly packaged with moderately priced video capture devices (think the $100-$200 range). It's a little finicky and limited in its abilities, but if you want to capture, edit, and author a Video CD (VCD), Super Video CD (SVCD), or video DVD, it's a good, relatively inexpensive tool. You can even obta in a 30-day trial version from their website (www.ulead.com).

Between Tracks

While VideoStudio has tools that let you perform such functions as adding a new audio track, putting text over an image, etc., this chapter focuses exclusively on capturing, basic editing, and authoring of video. For a more detailed explanation of the editing process and how to do it, you need a book dedicated to the subject. There are a ton out there. One specific to digital video that I'd recommend is *The Five Essential Steps in Digital Video* by Denise Ohio.

This chapter is based on Ulead Video Studio Version 6SE DVD. There are other (probably older) versions out there, but in terms of overall usage, you shouldn't find this one to be too different from what you have at home (although DVD authoring support may be limited in older or demo versions).

Using VideoStudio you can capture video from a capture device, perform basic editing functions, and record that video to disc. The rest of this chapter breaks the program down along those lines. The first step, though, is to get it opened up. Click Start, All Programs, Ulead VideoStudio 6, Ulead Video Studio 6SE DVD. When VideoStudio opens, you'll notice a series of tabs along the top of the screen (see Figure 19.1). These tabs allow you to proceed through the video creation process, practically step by step. By default, VideoStudio opens to the Start tab shown in Figure 19.1.

Selected tab Video preview window and controls

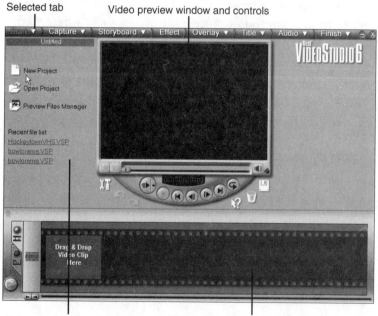

Figure 19.1

From the Start tab you can create new projects or load in existing ones that you haven't yet finished.

Options in this area changed   Video storyboard and timeline area
based on selected tab

While there are variations in the interface between the various tabs in VideoStudio, they all have the same basic layout, which you'll need to get to know to make effective use of the program.

Dominating the middle of the window is a preview screen that shows you the video as you capture it or play it back. Underneath the video display is a Tracking tool. This tool allows you to manipulate various tracks, including: video, audio, and title (think film credits).

On the right side of the video display, on every tab but the Start tab, is the Library tool. The Library in VideoStudio isn't much different from a Music Library in MusicMatch Jukebox or Easy CD Creator. This one comes with a few preset categories for video, still images, and colors. Using the provided scroll box you can choose among the various library types or gain access to the Library Manager option, which allows you to create new folder categories. To the right of the scroll box is a folder button that allows you to add existing videos, images, and so on, to the currently selected Library folder.

The left side of the VideoStudio interface changes based on the tab function you've selected. When VideoStudio opens, you should find yourself at the Start tab. If, however, it goes directly to the capture screen, click the Start tab to go there.

The controls on this tab allow you to create and load VideoStudio projects. Think of a project like a disc layout in Easy CD Creator. It doesn't actually contain the video you intend to create, edit, or record, but it does store information about where your video files are and what editing changes you've made to it.

To get things started, click the New Project button. This opens the New Project dialog box. In this dialog box you can choose the directory you want to work in (this is also the location where your project files are stored) and the type of video you want to create and with which you want to work (see Figure 19.2).

Figure 19.2

Make sure you choose the right video format for the project you want to create.

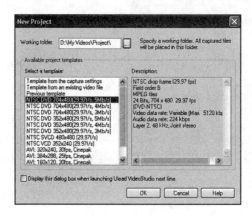

Assuming that your end goal is to author a VCD, SVCD, or video DVD, the selection you make boils down to:

- **NTSC DVD.** There are several options that affect overall quality here. A resolution of 704×480 is much crisper than 352×480. The lower the Mb/s (megabits of data recorded for one second of video) the more likely the video is to appear blocky or pixellated.

◆ **NTSC SVCD.** This kind of disc is for those that want to create near DVD quality video, but want to put it on a recordable CD. (Don't expect to fit more than 30 minutes of video on the disc.)

◆ **NTSC VCD.** Those looking to record more than 30 minutes of video to a compact disc should go with the VCD option. It's not as pretty, but it works.

Regardless of which type of disc you want to create, these settings are all about quality versus file size. The better the quality, the bigger the files. A 30-minute video recorded at the highest quality VideoStudio offers takes up more than 1GB (gigabyte) of disk space. As long as you have the hard disk space that's fine. But if you don't have the disk real estate, plan on making low-quality or very short projects.

For this chapter I focus on creating a video DVD of the highest visual quality. However, no matter what type of video you intend to work with here, the steps after this point are largely the same. So just make your selection in the New Project dialog box and click OK.

Arcane CD Speak

NTSC refers to the National Television Standards Committee, which is the standard format in which North American programming is broadcast.

Capturing Video

As soon as you choose a new video format VideoStudio takes you to the Capture tab. Fortunately, this is not just a clever nickname for the tab. This is, indeed, where you capture your video (see Figure 19.3).

The controls on the Capture screen include the following:

◆ **Capture Video.** Starts the video capture process. Be sure to have your video source playing before you press this button. While capturing video, this button changes to read Stop Capture.

◆ **Capture Image.** This allows you to capture a single frame of video, rather than a long stream.

◆ **Duration.** This indicator lets you know how much video you've captured in terms of time.

◆ **Format.** This scroll box allows you to change your video capture file format between MPEG, AVI, and DV (Digital Video).

◆ **Driver.** If you have more than one video capture device connected to your system, this scroll box lets you choose which one you want to use.

Figure 19.3

USB Instant is the name of the video capture device that VideoStudio is accessing to obtain a video feed into this PC.

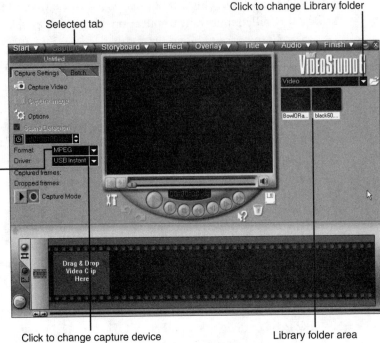

Selected tab

Click to change Library folder

Format to use for captured video

Click to change capture device

Library folder area

◆ **Capture/Dropped Frames.** These indicators let you know how many frames of video VideoStudio has captured (roughly 30 frames per second of video) and how many have been dropped (frames that were missed during capture). Although an isolated dropped frame is not of much consequence, if this number consistently climbs, your captured video will probably appear very choppy on playback.

◆ **Capture/Playback Buttons.** These buttons change the mode of VideoStudio between capturing new video and playing back captured video.

The first thing you should do on this screen is ensure that your capture driver is properly selected and is receiving a signal. Start playing your video source (I'm assuming you're using a VCR or similar device). After a few seconds, you should be able to see the video (and hear any accompanying audio) in the video display. When you're ready to capture, press the Capture Video button (see Figure 19.4).

Cross Reference

For more information on video file formats, see Chapter 12.

Records duration of capture process

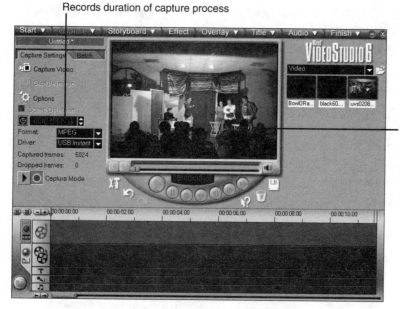

Figure 19.4

5024 frames captured and not one dropped. Woo-hoo!

Video being captured

It usually takes VideoStudio a few seconds to read and adequately monitor the video in the preview window. Once it gets going, though, you should see a smooth stream of video cross your screen, while the Duration and Frames Captured meters start ticking away (you should also be able to hear any audio included on the source video).

When you decide you've had enough, click the Capture Video button again. It takes VideoStudio another few seconds to catch on that you've actually clicked a button, but as soon as it gets done processing the last of the video it places it in a new file on your hard drive and in your Video Library (under a file name with the letters "uvs" followed by a few numbers; not very descriptive).

Yes, it's just that easy! Once, you've got the video capture it's time to hit the editing room.

Basic Video Editing

The various editing tools included with VideoStudio are spread out across the Story-board, Effect, Overlay, Title, and Audio tabs. As mentioned earlier in the chapter, we're going to stick to just some basic editing, so give the Storyboard tab a click.

Between Tracks _____

If you don't want to edit the video you've captured, you can skip over this material on using the basic editing tools. You can go right to the "Putting Video on a Disc" section, which covers using the Finish tab.

Those expecting to be wowed at the differences between the Capture and Storyboard tabs are going to be underwhelmed. It's the same interface, except that the capture controls have been replaced with two readouts that monitor "in" and "out" points.

There are two modes to the Storyboard tab: Storyboard and Timeline. You can choose between them using the buttons indicated in Figure 19.5. Click the Storyboard Mode button. If you're going to work from freshly captured video, VideoStudio should have already dropped the segment into the Storyboard view. If it hasn't, or if you're working from video you captured previously, select your captured video clip from the Video Library section and drag it down to the Storyboard area. Once the clip's icon appears in the storyboard area, use the Video Library to drag it there again, so that two clips are in the Storyboard (don't worry, I'll soon explain why).

Figure 19.5

If you haven't seen the film Bowl-O-Rama (shown here), then odds are you weren't in Steve Lipkin's film production course at Western Michigan University in 1997. Tough break.

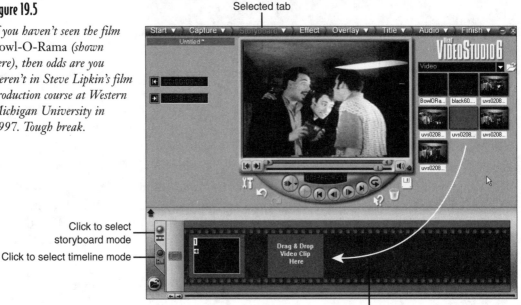

Selected tab

Click to select storyboard mode

Click to select timeline mode

Drag and drop library videos to add to the storyboard

How to Edit

The important thing to understand about using the storyboard in VideoStudio is that you're basically creating a series of clips. You're not so much editing the video content as you are choosing "in" and "out" points in the video for each clip. Each clip can have only one in point and only one out point. When you set these points, you're basically choosing a sub segment of the entire video stream that you want shown when that clip plays. When you watch the completed video, each clip in the project plays seamlessly from one to the next, creating a complete video.

For example, say you've videotaped a Nick at Night rerun of *Cheers* that you want to put on DVD. You've captured that video, that's the first step. But before you put it on disc, you want to edit out all the commercials. So for every commercial break in the program, you'd need to drag a complete segment of the program. If there were two commercial breaks then you would want three instances, as follows:

- ♦ **Clip 1.** This clip covers the ground between the beginning of the program (in) and the first commercial break (out).

- ♦ **Clip 2.** This clip picks up at the end of the first commercial break (in) and ends at the beginning of the second break (out).

- ♦ **Clip 3.** This final clip picks up from the end of the second commercial break (in) and runs through to the end of the program (out).

While this is sort of a "neat and tidy" example of the editing process, that's really all there is to it. If you've got home movies of your baby and you want to get rid of the part where he hurls on your significant other you'd apply the same techniques to cut around it (you can always put the "spewage" back in when you make your director's cut).

Navigating the Video

Okay, so you've got your clips in the Storyboard and you want to start editing. Well, you can't set your first in point until you know how to use the VideoStudio interface to navigate to it.

The first step is to choose the segment with which you want to work. Take your mouse on a stroll to the Storyboard section of the interface and give the segment a single click. Then move the pointer to the left and click the Switch to Timeline Mode button (see Figure 19.6).

In Timeline Mode, instead of seeing each segment of a Storyboard, you see a stream of images from an individual segment. Above the series of images are time indexes that mark where, in hours, minutes, and seconds, that image appears in the video (so the very first frame would be 00:00:00).

Between Tracks ____

If you have more than one segment in your story-board, they will all appear (end-to-end) in your Time-line. Despite being able to see the entire project, the edits you make are still made to just one segment at a time.

Figure 19.6

Use the Timeline Mode when scanning for in and out points of a video clip.

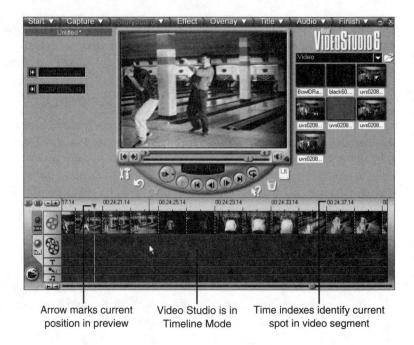

Arrow marks current position in preview

Video Studio is in Timeline Mode

Time indexes identify current spot in video segment

Underneath the timeline is a slider bar that allows you to move forward and backward, very quickly, along the timeline.

To the left of these time indexes are four buttons that control them. Starting from the left, they are as follows:

- **Zoom To.** Clicking this button brings up a menu of time ranges that control how much of the clip you want to see at one time in the timeline. The times range from a $1/6$ of a second to one minute; you can also set it to a series of single frames, or to view the entire clip. So if you were to choose one second, each time index in the timeline would be exactly one second apart.

- **Fit Project In Window.** This reduces the time index breaks to the point where the entire segment fits on the screen.

- **Zoom Out.** Increases the range of time between breaks so that you see more of the segment on screen than is currently visible.

- **Zoom In.** Reduces the scope of breaks in the timeline so that you can focus in on smaller piece of the segment.

If you click the Fit Project In Window button, so that you can see the entire segment in the Timeline, you should at some point see a blue arrow (pointing down) above the series of still images. You can click on and drag this arrow left and right along the timeline. As you do, the point at which the arrow is currently pointing becomes the image shown in the video preview window. Depending on the length of the segment and the length of time between breaks in the timeline, this can be a very imprecise way of finding an in or out point. (This arrow becomes more useful later when I cover previewing your video.) Fortunately, there's a more precise way to find the exact frame you want.

The controls in the Timeline are great for getting to a general area of a long clip. However, when you're editing, you'll probably want to get down to the exact frame. This is achievable using the video controls just underneath the video preview window.

There are two sliders just beneath the video image. The first we'll worry about when we get to setting in and out points. The second operates similarly to the blue arrow in the Timelines; it lets you quickly navigate to a general area of the video segment. Beneath those sliders are several buttons.

The functions of these buttons should be fairly clear to those who've used a VCR. The two on the left with right-pointing arrows play the clip from the selected point. The next four buttons, in this order, move the preview point: to the beginning of the segment, back one frame, forward one frame, to the end of the segment. The final button, Repeat, is a toggle that replays an edited segment over and over again until you stop it (you do, of course, have to hit play first).

The frame-by-frame tools are great for really fine-tuning your in and out points, but wouldn't it be nice if you could physically enter time codes to move the editing point to a specific location without all this dragging of sliders and such? Fortunately, the digital time code in the middle of all these buttons isn't just about looks. If you click any of the numbers between the colons you can enter a specific time in the segment you want to see. The 00:00:00.00 format works in: hours, minutes, seconds, frames. Because there are just 30 frames of video per second, the last entry in this code only goes from 00 to 29, rather than 60.

Setting In and Out Points

Now that you've mastered the control in the Timeline interface it's time to actually set an in and out point for your video segment. The first thing you need to do is make sure VideoStudio is in an Editing mode.

Whether you are in Timeline or Storyboard view, VideoStudio has two modes that you can work in: Editing mode and Preview mode. The Preview mode (like the one shown in Figure 19.6) lets you set in and out points for watching a "preview" of the video. This is something I'll discuss in more detail in the next section. The Editing mode is the one you need to be in to make your edits.

To enter Editing mode, click on any of the still images in the Timeline (if you're in Storyboard view, click the image of one of the segments). If they weren't there already, you should see some new controls appear to the left of the video preview window (see Figure 19.7).

The three time displays show the length of the clip, the current in point, and the current out point. There are some other controls beneath them that you need not worry about for basic editing (though you may find a use for the audio fade in/out buttons underneath the time displays). Finally, underneath all the junk are two buttons: Reset and Apply. Right now these should be grayed out (i.e., unusable).

Figure 19.7

This four-minute clip has edit points set to start at approximately six and a half minutes into the segment and end at 10:24.

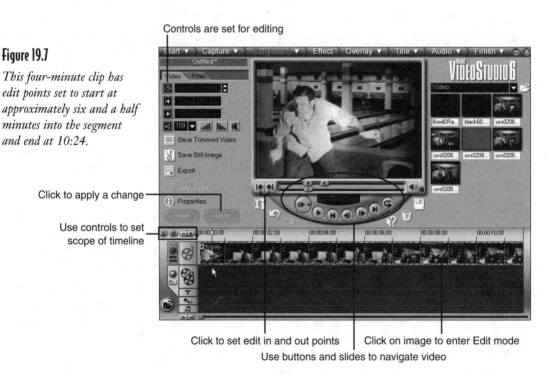

Controls are set for editing

Click to apply a change

Use controls to set scope of timeline

Click to set edit in and out points   Click on image to enter Edit mode

Use buttons and slides to navigate video

To set an in point, navigate to the point in the segment where you want the clip to start. Once you've located it, press F3 on your keyboard (or click the Mark In button on the lower left of the video preview window). Once you've set an in point, you'll notice that the Reset and Apply buttons are suddenly enabled. Click Reset if you've made a mistake and want to reset the point from scratch. Click Apply to set the current in point in stone for this clip.

When you click Apply, you'll notice that the timeline begins wherever you set the in point at. Now it's time to set an out point. Navigate through the video segment until you find the spot at which you want the clip to end. When you find a likely spot, set the out point by pressing F4 on your keyboard. If you're happy with the result, click Apply. The clip in your timeline will now begin and end according to your in and out points.

Return to the Storyboard view and follow the same steps to set up clips for each entry. When you're done, you'll have successfully edited your very own video project.

Between Tracks

Technically you can edit segments into clips from the Storyboard view, using just the tools on the video preview window. I think the Timeline view makes the process easier.

Previewing Your Project

While you could throw caution to the wind, fly in the face of death, and perform several other cliché actions, you'll generally want to preview both your edits and your entire project before writing it to a disc only to find out that you ended clip 2 at 15:32 instead of 14:32.

Back in the "Navigating the Video" section, I mentioned that the arrow in the Timeline view would come back into play. Well, as they say, the time is now. (Who "they" are, I have no idea.)

Using this arrow you can set a different sort of in and out points, although these have nothing at all to do with editing video. Instead they allow you to choose a preview "window" in which you can watch a clip from the in point through to the out point. As when editing a segment, use the F3 and F4 keys to mark the in and out points.

Don't Get Burned

When setting these preview points, make sure that you are in Preview mode. In this mode only the In and Out time markers should be visible on the left of the video preview window. If you see the other buttons, like Reset and Apply, then you are in Editing mode and could ruin your existing edits!

Once set, hold down the Shift key on your keyboard and click either of the Play buttons on the video preview window. Your project will then play from your in point all the way through to your out point (see Figure 19.8).

You may notice a bit of a hitch in the video when it plays. This is normal and shouldn't indicate a problem with the final video output. What you're really looking for here is to make sure that clips are edited the way you want and that they flow smoothly (content-wise) from one to the next.

Figure 19.8

Can you believe Arnold beat this guy out for the lead role in The Terminator?

Indicates video preview in and out points

Sets video preview in and out points

Saving Your Project

It's just about time to author your video disc, but before you go too far, you should save your project to disc. This doesn't create any new video. Rather it just saves information about what video files you're working with and what edits you want made to those files.

To save your project, click the floppy disk icon underneath the video preview window.

> **Don't Get Burned** _____
>
> If you save your project for later use, make sure you don't move your source video files around (or change their file names). If you do, VideoStudio will be unable to find them!
>
> You can, however, re-link a video file to VideoStudio. Open your project and select your video file from your library. When it says it can't find the file, choose to Relink it. In the dialog box that appears, find the file's current location and select it.

Putting Video on a Disc

Now, mercifully, it's time for the last step. Putting your video on a disc; in this case, a DVD. The first thing you need to do is click the Finish tab in VideoStudio (see Figure 19.9).

Selected tab

Figure 19.9

The final phase in the process, recording to disc!

At this point your project should be good to go. If you're not sure, click the Project Playback button, which plays your video from beginning to end according to the various edits you've made to the original material.

You can also click the Create Video File button to create a new video file on your hard drive that contains the results of your project (use the down arrow to select a format). Keep in mind, though, that when you create the disc VideoStudio will force you to first save your work to a video file so it's not strictly necessary to use this button (unless all you want is the video file).

Once you're satisfied, you can click the button for creating a video DVD, a Video CD, or a Super Video CD. For this example, I'll click DVD. VideoStudio asks you to choose a location to save your project in a video file format consistent with the type of disc you want to create.

When you choose a location, VideoStudio begins "rendering" the project. You probably noticed that your video quality during the whole capture and editing process wasn't always the best. That's a sacrifice made so that you can quickly scan through and edit your video. The rendering process Video Studio executes goes through your project and creates a high quality version of your video, which is what you'll see when your watch the recorded disc. Be ready, the longer your video, the longer this process takes. An hour and a half DVD could take a *very* long time! (A lot depends on how much system memory you have and the speed of your computer's processor.)

Once the rendering process is complete you'll see the Start screen for the Ulead DVD Plug-in (see Figure 19.10).

Figure 19.10

Welcome to the start of burning a video DVD!

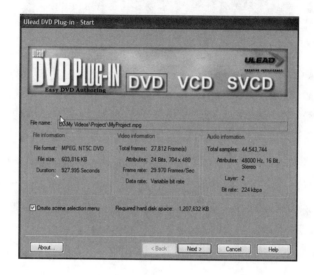

The only thing you need to do on this screen is click Next. There is a check box, which is enabled by default, that allows you to create a menu system for the disc. If you don't want to create a menu system, disable the check box and click Next. For this example I'll keep it enabled.

The Add Scene window pops up next. This window allows you to use a preview window interface (not unlike the one in the main VideoStudio application), which you can use to select a frame from your video to add as a chapter. If you broke your project down into a series of clips, then the DVD Plug-in will already have provided chapter menus based on the first frame in each clip. You can add to or remove chapter breaks from this list using Add and Remove buttons that appear between the preview window and the list of chapters. Click Next to continue.

On the Select Menu Template that pops up next you can choose a menu background from several templates (use the Project Template scroll box). If you have a different image that you want to use, click the Background button (see Figure 19.11).

Once you've chosen a template, click Next.

The next window, Playback Simulation, allows you to simulate how the video disc will actually operate using a simulated remote control and a small "TV" window. Use your mouse to click various buttons on the remote, which is not much different from a remote for a set-top DVD player, to navigate the disc menu and play its video clips. Click Next to continue.

Click to change background template

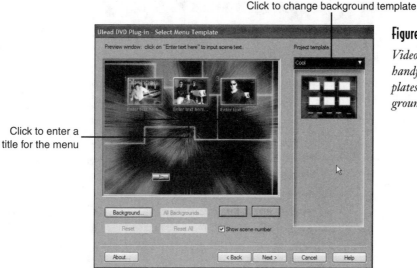

Figure 19.11

VideoStudio provides a small handful of worthwhile templates for use as a background on your video disc.

Click to enter a title for the menu

Finally, it's time to initiate the disc creation process. In the Determine Output Options Settings window you can choose a temporary folder for VideoStudio to use when creating files for your video disc (see Figure 19.12). You can also choose your disc recorder (if you have more than one) and the recording speed. Unless you know what you're changing, go with the default settings and click Next.

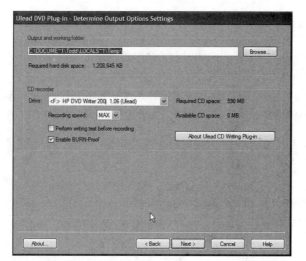

Figure 19.12

Just stick with the default options on this screen (unless you think you know better).

When the Finish window opens, you have only to click the Create DVD (or VCD or SVCD, as the case may be) button. This kicks off the disc creation process, as shown in Figure 19.13.

Figure 19.13

If the video is a large one, creating the DVD can take a while. Generally +R/RW discs burn faster than discs of the -R/RW family.

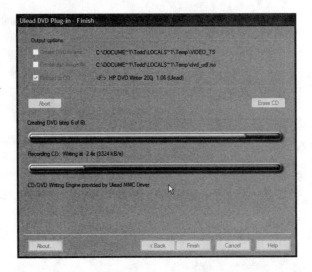

When the burn is complete you'll get a small success or failure message. I've yet to see a DVD burn fail, and I don't imagine you'll have any problems (so long as you don't interrupt the process on purpose).

Once your video disc is complete, you can play it in any compatible player. For a list of DVD players and the types of discs with which they are compatible (ranging from VCD to -R/RW to +R/RW), visit www.vcdhelp.com/dvdplayers.php.

The Least You Need to Know

♦ Ulead VideoStudio is a popular, but not powerful video editing application that comes for free with some video capture devices.

♦ When capturing video you should use MPEG-1 standards for Video CDs and MPEG-2 standards for Super Video CDs and video DVDs.

♦ Editing a video file requires creating a storyboard of video segments and using in and out points to edit the segments into just the clips containing the video you want.

♦ VideoStudio is capable of creating a simple but attractive menu system on your video discs to aid in using them on set-top players.

Making Digital Photo Albums with Roxio PhotoRelay

In This Chapter

♦ Using PhotoRelay to create digital photo albums

♦ Adding audio to individual pictures in your photo album

♦ Creating an album of pictures that you can then send to friends and family via e-mail

♦ Burning your photo album to CD using PhotoRelay

Most people I talk to who have CD burners use them to make copies of CDs they already own or to store important files on CD for long-term storage. However, a lot of other fun programs are out there that you can use with your burner, which you might not have ever thought about. For example, you already know, if you've read this book from the beginning, that you can take all your graphic files—family photos and stuff like that—and store them on a CD. However, when you want to go back and use them, you must go through all the trouble of finding specific pictures and cranking up some graphic editor to look at them. After all, these picture files, when viewed in My Computer or File Explorer, don't look different from any other data file you might store on the disc.

Virtual Photo Albums to the Rescue!

If you have lots of disk space on your computer, you can use PhotoRelay to create photo albums that can hold both photographs and audio files that play when you view the photo or album.

Between Tracks

This chapter focuses only on acquiring photos with PhotoRelay and the tools that allow you to burn them to a disc. It does not cover PhotoRelay's Web and Email functions.

PhotoRelay can be used sort of like a word processor—you can start creating the album, and when you get bored, you can save it. Later, you can come back and add more to the album or delete stuff that you've changed your mind about. In contrast to a real photo album, however, you won't run out of space for your pictures (unless your hard drive fills up). You can also burn the album to CD when you have finished fine-tuning your project so that you don't have to waste that valuable real estate on your hard drive.

However, you must create the album before you can create the CD, so let's start with creating an album first. To open PhotoRelay, start the Roxio Project Selector and hover your mouse over Make a photo or video CD (see Figure 20.1).

From this menu, choose Photo Album. Now it's time to get to the real work!

Figure 20.1

The Roxio Project Selector makes quick work of launching PhotoRelay.

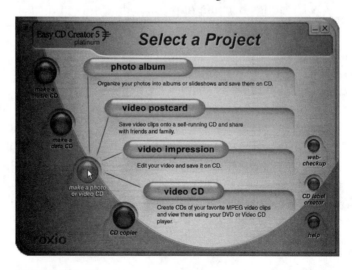

Working with PhotoRelay

When you start PhotoRelay from the Project Selector, a window like the one shown in Figure 20.2 pops up. From here, you are ready to create a new photo album. By default, when you open the PhotoRelay application, a small dialog box also opens letting you know about the two icons (Add and Acquire) that you use to add photos or videos to your album. Just click OK to continue.

Album Picture area   Photo Relay toolbar

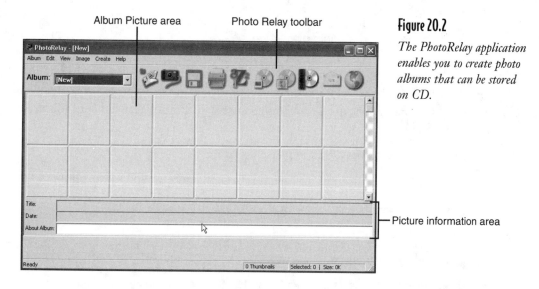

Figure 20.2

The PhotoRelay application enables you to create photo albums that can be stored on CD.

Picture information area

The PhotoRelay interface is organized into three main areas:

- **The PhotoRelay Toolbar.** Gives you access to all the primary PhotoRelay controls.

- **The Picture Area.** This is the area that shows you *thumbnails* of all the images in your album.

- **The Info Area.** This area displays information about your album and whichever image you have selected in it (you must enter this information manually).

Note that the Album field in the toolbar says New. You can use the pull-down menu for this field to open any albums you've already created. By default there is a "Photos" album that contains several basic pictures already included when you install PhotoRelay. You probably won't have much use for this one.

Arcane CD Speak

When you need to see several pictures on the computer screen at the same time, such as when working with PhotoRelay, it's impossible to display them all in their full-size format. This isn't just because of limited screen space, but because a large number of picture files takes up a lot of memory, too, which slows down your computer. A **thumbnail** is basically just a miniaturized version of a picture that takes up less screen space and considerably less memory. Although it has much less detail than the actual picture, it makes it easier for you to keep track of your work when dealing with many pictures, such as, say, in a photo album, maybe?

In addition to the Album field, there are several icons on the PhotoRelay toolbar. Each of these icons represents a tool you can use with PhotoRelay. These tools are as follows (from left to right):

- **Add.** Adds files to the album you are creating.

- **Acquire.** Use your scanner to "acquire" a new photo to add to the album.

- **Save.** Enables you to save your work on the current active album.

- **Print.** Prints all or part of an album.

- **Sort.** Sorts your images.

- **MakeSlideShow.** Creates a picture slide show that you can play on any Windows 95 or newer system.

- **MakeWebAlbum.** Allows you to record a web album to disc. When used in a PC-based disk drive, it opens up its web browser to view the album.

- **MakePostCard.** Creates a Video "Postcard" that you can play back on any Windows compatible computer.

- **SendMail.** Embeds a picture in an e-mail message using your default e-mail program. As it falls well outside the scope of this book, I don't cover the SendMail feature in this chapter.

- **PhotoIsland.** This button connects to an online website (www.photoisland.com), where you can sign up for storage space that you can use to upload and download your pictures to and from the web. As it falls well outside the scope of this book, I don't cover the PhotoIsland feature in this chapter.

Before you can get into actually creating photo CDs, you need to first learn how to build a photo album.

Adding and Removing Photographs from the Album

To add a picture to an album, click the Add tool—the first icon in the toolbar after the Album field. The Add to Album dialog box appears and enables you to select the disk and directory that contains the photographs with which you want to work.

To select an image for the album, just double-click it in the dialog box or click once to highlight it and then click the Open button. A thumbnail for the picture is created and presented on the application window. In Figure 20.3, you see PhotoRelay with an assortment of images ready for recording.

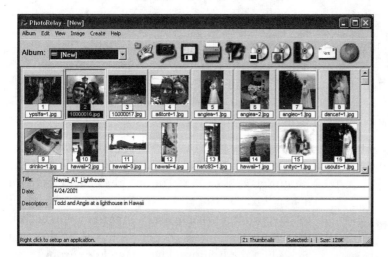

Figure 20.3

Thumbnails appear on the PhotoRelay window for each picture you select.

To add a photo from an external device, like a scanner, click the Acquire button on the toolbar. This brings up a dialog box that lets you choose from the available sources. In this example, I've chosen my scanner (see Figure 20.4). Once you scan an image, PhotoRelay automatically adds it to the current album.

Whether adding from your hard disk, external scanner, or some other device, your album will continue to fill up. As you continue to add photographs to the album, you can use the scrollbar on the right side of the program to run through the album's contents.

Don't Get Burned

Unfortunately, Photo-Relay does not let you choose where to save scanned pictures. If you want to copy a scanned picture from the default folder to the one you actually use, select the image in your album and choose Copy Image(s) To.

Figure 20.4

Here, I'm scanning an image of myself and a friend dressed as Jay and Silent Bob at a Halloween party. For the record, those are tarragon leaves in the bag.

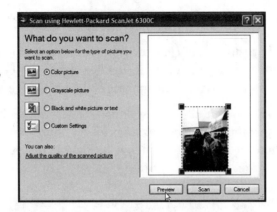

Note that three fields are at the bottom of the PhotoRelay main window: Title, Date, and Description (refer back to Figure 20.3). (If you have no image selected, the Description field is replaced with an About Album field.) You can fill in these fields for each picture as you add it. Or later you can go back and click any picture to change this information.

Removing an image is just as simple as adding it to the album. Just right-click the image and select Delete from the menu that appears. When you select this option, PhotoRelay asks you to confirm the deletion. On this dialog box, you can also choose to remove the picture from your hard drive in addition to removing it from the album (this means it's gone forever). To do so, put a check in the Remove The Image Files From Disk check box. Once you're ready to proceed, click OK.

Between Tracks

If you double-click an image in your photo album it opens it up in a separate window (see Figure 20.5). This window includes some very basic editing tools that allow you to adjust things like color contrast and brightness.

Don't Get Burned

Unlike the rest of the Easy CD Creator audio-related applications, PhotoRelay has not added support for WMA audio files. The only audio formats you can use are MP3 and WAV.

Adding Audio to a Photo

You can easily add an audio clip to any picture or to the whole album. If you add an audio clip to an individual picture, that audio clip gets played when the picture is displayed, such as in a slide show.

Simply select the picture on the workspace area and, on the Image menu, select Audio, Attach Audio. You are prompted to locate the file using the typical Open dialog box you see everywhere in Windows programs. Find and select the file; then just click Open and you're done. Once you've attached Audio a tiny musical note icon appears on the upper-right corner of the picture in your Photo Album. To preview the audio associated with a picture you can click the Image menu and select Audio, Play Attached Audio. A small audio player control box appears on the screen as shown in Figure 20.5.

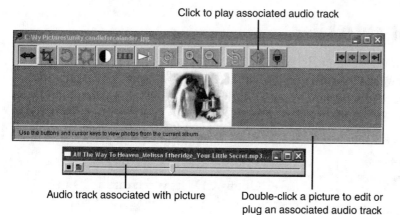

Click to play associated audio track

Audio track associated with picture

Double-click a picture to edit or plug an associated audio track

Figure 20.5

Here we have a wedding picture that plays "All the Way to Heaven" by Melissa Etheridge. All together now ... Awwwwwww.

Finally, if you decide you'd rather not have audio associated with a picture, you can choose to remove the attachment by clicking the Image menu and selecting Audio, Detach Audio.

Don't Get Burned

Note that saving the album *doesn't save all the photographic image files you've selected.* It just saves the thumbnail that was created of the photo and other information you might have entered into the album, such as the title. When you recall an album to look through or to edit, the original files should still be present (in the same drive locations) if you want to burn the CD. Just remember that until you do burn the CD, don't touch any of the photographs you've selected for the album! Even moving them to a new folder on your hard disk makes it so your album can't locate them.

You can tell if PhotoRelay has a problem locating an image when you reopen the album. It indicates this by putting the universal symbol, the red circle with a line through it, at the upper-left edge of the thumbnail.

Saving the Photo Album

You can save a photo album at any time during your work by clicking the Save tool (the floppy disk icon on the toolbar). You can also select Save Album from the Album menu. Either method brings up a small dialog box that enables you to give a filename to the album. After you've saved it, the "New" text in the Album field is replaced with this album's title.

You must save the album to disk before PhotoRelay will let you record it to disc!

Burning an Album to CD

When you've gotten together an album of photographs, and perhaps some audio to go with it, that you want to put to disc, all you need to do is decide which kind of photo CD you want to create. As mentioned earlier, your choices include:

> **Between Tracks**
>
> You can simply select the Add All button if you want all the pictures in your album on the CD, rather than select them one at a time.

◆ **SlideShow CD** shows the images in the order you decide and autoruns when inserted on a computer that supports that option.

◆ **WebAlbum CD** lets you create a CD that enables you to view thumbnails of your album in a web browser.

In the following sections, we'll take a look at both of these methods.

Creating a Slide Show

After you click the MakeSlideShow button, a dialog box titled Select File pops up and prompts you to select the images from the album that will be recorded onto the CD. You can pick and choose using the Add or Remove buttons.

After you've selected what you need, click Next to continue.

The next dialog box (shown in Figure 20.6) is titled Audio Options.

The Audio Options dialog box enables you to choose from:

◆ **No Audio.** Select that no audio be used on the CD.

◆ **Play Attached Audio Files.** Any image with an audio file associated with it will play that song when you view the image in a slide show. If you don't choose this option, the slide show will not play the audio file.

◆ **Play Single Audio File.** This option enables you to play one audio file over the course of the entire slide show, and the slide show is timed to fit within it. Of course, as you can see in Figure 20.6, you must select the audio file you want to add using the Browse button if you use this option.

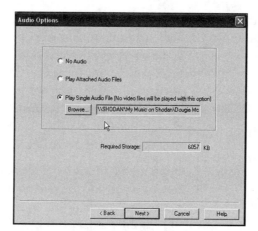

Figure 20.6

You can select how audio files are used when creating a slide show.

Before clicking the Next button to keep going, do be sure to glance at the Required Storage field to make sure it doesn't exceed the size of your disc (that would require a heck of a lot of photos, or some very large ones). Once you're satisfied, click Next.

If you've selected audio, it might take a few seconds or even a minute or two before the next dialog box pops up (see Figure 20.7). This dialog box, titled Select Destination, enables you to copy the slide show to disc or to your hard disk (if you want to further edit it).

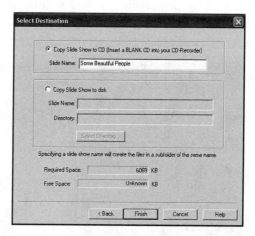

Figure 20.7

You can select to burn the CD or to store the slide show in a hard disk location.

If you choose to first try out your slide show by storing it on the hard disk, you can also use the Directory field to tell PhotoRelay where you want it to place the files. If you are ready to burn a disc, then you also can specify a name.

Because this book is about burning discs, we'll go with the burn to disc option. Click the Finish button to leave this wizard and set up for the recording.

The Record CD Setup dialog box that you're used to seeing (assuming you've read up on any of the other Easy CD Creator programs) then pops up and enables you to make changes to several options. See Chapter 7 for the skinny about using this dialog box's more advanced features. For our purposes, leave Track-at-Once selected in the Record Options section and choose Finalize the CD. To start the CD burning process, click the Start Recording button.

> **Between Tracks**
>
> If Windows Autorun doesn't automatically read your disk drive, open the disc in My Computer and double-click the application file in the folder on the disc (the folder is given the name you chose, as in Figure 20.7).

If you haven't inserted a blank CD-R into the recorder yet, you are prompted to do so. The CD Creation Process dialog box shows you the progress of creating the CD.

Again, if you've used Easy CD Creator, you're used to this dialog box. It shows you which step the program is currently working on in the creation process. When the CD has been successfully completed, it tells you so and gives you the option to create a CD label or jewel case insert using the CD Label Creator program.

To use your new disc, just reinsert it in your disk drive. Windows Autorun should immediately read it and start playing the slide show.

When the album plays, you'll see an image like the one shown in Figure 20.8. (If you assigned any music to the show or individual pictures, those also play.) The show plays out automatically, but you can use the buttons (rewind, play, pause, and fast forward) on the lower right to exert greater control over the presentation.

Figure 20.8

We've now reached the father-daughter portion of our presentation.

Creating a Web Album

Making a web album involves recording your photo album to a disc that, when used in someone's PC, allows people to view the album using their web browser (Internet Explorer, Navigator, etc.). If the computer supports the autorun feature, your browser pops up automatically and enables you to select from the thumbnails to see the full image.

To create a web album, select its tool from the PhotoRelay window. The next dialog box that appears is the same as for the slide show, asking you to choose the images you want to appear in the web album CD. Make your selections and click Next. This takes you to the Layout dialog box, shown in Figure 20.9.

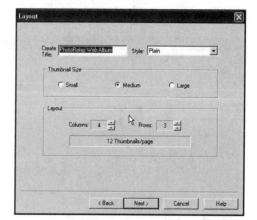

Figure 20.9

You can customize the layout of a web album using the Layout dialog box.

In this dialog box, you can select the size the thumbnails will be on a web page (small, medium, or large) and the number of rows and columns for the display. Based on your selections, PhotoRelay tells you the number of thumbnails that appear on a page when it is displayed. You also can use this dialog box to give your web album a title. Click the Next button when you are ready to continue.

Another dialog box asks you to select details you want to have displayed with each thumbnail. These include the title, date, and description of the image. Remember those three fields you had the option of entering information for each photo on the main PhotoRelay album window? This is where the web album gets that information. Options are also available for including the picture's filename and file size. You can use check boxes to select which of these to display.

After you click Next, the Select Destination dialog box, which we saw back in Figure 20.7, appears and lets you choose to burn your web album to a CD or to a directory on the hard disk. Make your selection and click, finally, Finish!

Once again, CD burners get the CD Creation Setup dialog box. Select to finalize the CD unless you plan to add more albums to the CD. Click the Start Recording button, making sure you have a recordable CD already inserted in your disc burner.

The CD Creation Process dialog box will keep you company and show you the steps being taken to create the CD, along with the number of files and tracks that have been written. When the CD is finished, you'll see the usual dialog box confirming your successful recording of a CD.

To use your new web album, just reinsert it in your disc drive. Windows Autorun should immediately read the disc and open your album in your web browser. If it doesn't, open the disc in My Computer and double-click the application file in the folder on the disc (the folder is given the name you chose, as in Figure 20.7). When the main album page opens, you'll see an image like the one shown in Figure 20.10.

Figure 20.10

Sending a disc-based PhotoRelay web album to distant friends and family is a heck of a lot easier (and cheaper) than sending your physical photo album!

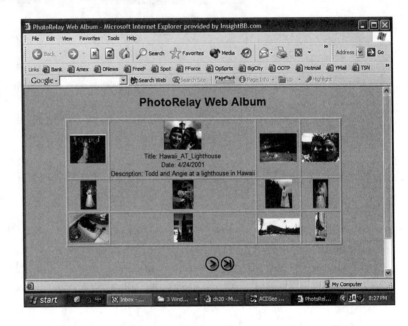

You can click any thumbnail to open the larger picture. If there are more pictures than can fit on a single page, then you'll see buttons underneath the assorted thumbnail images that you can use to navigate from page to page.

The Least You Need to Know

- ◆ You can use PhotoRelay to store pictures on your hard disk and then to burn to disc.

- ◆ You can use the Slide Show function to create a disc containing a slide show of your album. You can even have music play during the presentation.

- ◆ You can use PhotoRelay to create a web album that can be viewed using a web browser.

Chapter 21

Troubleshooting Disc Recording: A One-Way Ticket Out of Coaster City

In This Chapter

◆ Nothing's perfect in a changing world, especially CD-recording technology!

◆ If there's a problem, always check your source first

◆ If your source is okay, check the discs you are recording to

◆ Is your software and hardware up to date?

◆ Check your vendor's site for help specific to your products

Are you ready to throw your computer out a window, recordable drive and all? Okay, but make sure the window is, in fact, open … or you can look to this chapter for a fix to your problem. Before you begin to troubleshoot, remember that any technology is always prone to problems and the recordable drive market is still a relatively young one (especially with regards to DVD). With luck, and the use of this wonderful book, you are going to succeed.

Before I set you up for disappointment, though, understand that the contents of this chapter are just guidelines that hit on some of the more common problems you might encounter. A comprehensive discussion on fixing all but the most obscure problems would take an entire book, not just a single chapter!

The good news is that the problems I do discuss here are the common ones. So if you can't burn a disc and are turning out more coasters than an amusement park, then this should be your first stop. If you can't find help here, it may be time to contact the tech support department for your recording drive or software.

General Guidelines

No matter how good the technology, there are always going to be gremlins working themselves into the machinery here and there. In a field such as CD recording, where there are standards but in which many companies produce equipment of varying capabilities, you can expect even more gremlins.

Fortunately, a lot of these gremlins can be slain rather easily. When it comes time to troubleshoot, it's best to rule out the basics first.

Check the Recordable Disc

Not all recordable discs, be they CD or DVD, are made equal. Different dyes and metal alloys are used in various brands. Some might work better on your drive than others. Some might not work at all. As drive technology continues to improve, and as manufacturers keep working at getting the perfect media, these kinds of problems will go away. But I wouldn't hold my breath for that happening any time soon. The most important factor here is just to make sure you get discs rated to burn at a speed equivalent to what your CD-RW drive is capable of.

Don't Get Burned

Even though they're probably new, you should also make sure that your discs are clean and not all scratched up. If your recorder's laser can't focus through a nasty scratch then there's no chance of recording to the disc successfully.

If you've used your current brand of disc successfully in the past, that may not mean as much as you think it should. Recordable disc distributors, in an effort to get the best deal, are continually switching to different manufacturers to provide them with their discs. That means you could have recorded successfully a hundred times with Memorex discs and then find that the next hundred bomb out every single time.

Be aware of the compatibility and differences between different media types. Recordable (R) and

Rewritable (RW) discs are functionally different, which accounts for why RW discs are considerably less compatible with a wide variety of drives and players than R. For more information on CD discs and drives, flip back to Chapter 1. For DVD disc and drive information, take a gander at Chapter 2.

And let's not forget DVD. With two main, completely incompatible formats, that whole market is a throwback to the VHS versus Betamax days. If your drive uses +R/RW discs, then don't stick a -R/RW disc in it! Not only that, the first generation of DVD+RW drives weren't even compatible with +R discs. If you bought a new drive after June 2002, it's less likely you would have one of these drives, but don't rule the possibility out if you can't write to a +R disc.

Check the Source

Whether you are making a simple copy of a disc or are undertaking a more complex project, such as creating a video DVD, the first rule of thumb should always be to start with a good source.

If you're copying a CD or DVD directly, keep in mind that the source may have copy-protection built-in (all commercial DVDs do, as do a small number of audio discs).

If you're making an audio disc with music from an analog source, don't be surprised if the sound quality is spotty. Use the cleaning options that Roxio SoundStream provides to help clean it up a little, but don't expect miracles.

I mentioned this for your target disc in the previous section and it's even more true here: make sure your disc is clean. If your source disc has more scratches than a guy in a room full of cats and one bag of Meow-Mix, then don't expect it to copy well. If you're desperate, try copying it to your hard drive first; you could also try one of those disc "cleaning" tools found at most consumer electronics stores.

Drive and PC Limitations

If you're copying disc to disc and experiencing buffer underruns, then your hardware may not be able to transfer data between both your drives fast enough. There's a good reason for this, but it would require an overhead and laser pointer to explain, so just trust me on this one. Try recording the source disc to an image file on your hard drive first. Then record the image to your target.

Also make sure that you've closed all other programs. Some disc drives and disc burning software packages don't share your PC's resources well with others. Closing down a few applications, and giving your recording software and drive free reign can make a measurable difference in successfully recording a disc. Make sure you also shut down any programs running in the background (out of sight and not visible on your task bar).

> **Between Tracks**
>
> Although they don't all appear here, the easiest way to disable a background program is to look at the list of icons in your system tray (next to the clock on your desktop). Right-click each of these icons; you should see an option for closing or disabling them. Doing so prevents them from running and taking up resources that your CD-burning program might want to use.
>
> You can also press Ctrl+Alt+Delete on your keyboard to bring up the Windows Task Manager. From here you can select any of the listed tasks and click the End Task button. Just make sure you don't try to shutdown the program Explorer, though, or you'll crash Windows!

If your recordable drive doesn't have buffer-underrun protection then you have to expect a buffer underrun or two. If it becomes the rule rather than the exception you should consider buying a newer drive that prevents buffer underruns. CD-RW drives are getting cheaper practically every week. With the right rebates you should be able to find one for less than $100!

Finally, an often over-looked component in your PC is the power supply unit (PSU). This is the unit in which your PC power cord plugs in. It's responsible for delivering a clean power signal to every component inside your PC. If it's underpowered or being overtaxed by too much internal hardware you can expect problems when burning a CD. If, for example, you receive constant *Power Calibration Errors* before the recording process even gets started, then it's a good sign your PSU isn't cutting it. The PSU can be upgraded, but make sure that it not only has adequate wattage (300W or better) but is a quality unit from a reputable manufacturer. I buy any PSU I need from PC Power and Cooling (www.pcpowerandcooling.com).

Can't Read a Successfully Recorded Disc

One frequent problem I see occur is when someone creates a disc and then takes it to a friend's place, only to have him or her complain that it doesn't do anything in another player. When using recordable media, remember that older players (be they CD or DVD) and older computer CD and DVD-ROM drives might not be able to read your discs. Even CD-Rs aren't guaranteed to be compatible with everything.

It really becomes a hit-or-miss thing, because people tend to keep a working machine, such as a CD player, around until it breaks, which can be a very long time. Just about all the newer, and many of the older, audio players can read CD-R discs, and many of the latest ones can read CD-RW and even discs recorded with MP3s! Older DVD players get even more spotty. Some will read +R and -R, but not +RW and -RW. Some can read -R/RW, but not +R/RW. There's no easy way to tell just from looking at a player. Fortunately, for you DVD writing nuts out there, you can point your web browser to www.vcdhelp.com/dvdplayers.php. This page contains a compatibility list of virtually every DVD player on the market.

Another thing to remember is that if you use multiple sessions on a disc, then usually the last session is the one that's readable by a PC-based drive, by default. To change sessions you'll need a product such as Roxio Session Selector (click Start, All Programs, Roxio Easy CD Creator 5, Applications, Session Selector). If you've recorded a disc with both audio and data, remember that a set-top or car CD player reads the first session first. If you put data in the first session the only noise you'll hear from your stereo is the kind that blows out both your ears and your speakers.

Other Common Problems

Remember that although specific standards exist for the way data and audio are recorded onto disc, there are many manufacturers and each might come up with a different method of creating a CD burner or a CD reader. Little differences between manufacturers can be significant problems for some people. For example, some people like using the 80-minute CD-R media instead of the standard 74-minute discs. Suppose you want to use these discs and find that your software says no way, can't use them. Well, that could be a software or hardware problem. You could try upgrading your software to a version that does allow 80-minute recording, but still find out that your CD burner has a built-in 74-minute limit (not that common anymore)! If you leave your computer unattended while you burn a disc, make sure you disable any power saving features or screen savers. These, obviously, take away from system resources your PC needs to record a disc. Believe it or not, even if your PC is going crazy managing a disc to disc copy, a screen saver timer won't recognize that you're

Between Tracks

To disable power management or a screensaver, right-click the Windows desktop, choose Properties from the menu, and then click the Screen Saver tab in the dialog box that pops up. Here, you can turn off your screensaver and access any of the power management functions (which work a little differently depending on your flavor of Windows and computer hardware).

actually doing something. Only inputs from your mouse or keyboard suspend the timer unless you manually disable these features.

In the following sections, we'll look at some of the more common problems and some ways you can fix them.

Buffer Underruns: The Ultimate Coaster Creators

When we were looking at creating or copying CDs in previous chapters, we saw that Easy CD Creator and Nero have a progress dialog box that keeps you posted on the status of the CD burn that is in progress. The reason I mention this dialog box is that it has a field that shows you the amount of data available in your drive's write buffer. Because the laser burner has to receive a constant stream of data telling it how to make burns through the dye layer of a blank disc, problems occur if an interruption of data occurs. For this reason, a buffer in the computer's memory is created to store part of the data stream. If the hard disk from which the file is coming is partially fragmented, there might be milliseconds here and there that are wasted while the disc heads look for the next block of data. During this seek time, the buffer is supplying data to the laser. If the CD burner looks to the buffer for data and nothing is there, you'll get more use from your disc by setting a cold drink on it than you would trying to put data on it.

So a buffer underrun, as you can see, is a serious problem. Watch the buffer indicator on the recording dialog box closely and be sure it stays near 100 percent. If it drops a bit, you should be okay, but you might start to see problems if the buffer consistently drops below the 75 percent mark (depending on the total buffer size). If you have a newer computer and a drive with some form of buffer underrun prevention technology, you probably won't have any problems with buffer underruns.

Some other buffer-underrun prevention tips include:

- Stop using the computer for anything else while the CD is burning. Don't use up the computer's resources while it's trying to keep that buffer full!

- If you're burning a disc on your work network or you have a home network, then for goodness sakes don't use a network drive as your source! The network is gazillions of times slower than accessing your hard drive.

- If necessary, defragment your hard disk drive. If you are copying CD to CD, this won't help. But if you are copying WAV, MP3, or image files to your CD burner, a defragmented disk reads much more quickly, keeping that buffer full. (Click Start, All Programs, Accessories, System Tools, Disk Defragmenter.)

- Check for viruses on your system! If you're on the Internet and you don't have a virus checker, you're just waiting around for trouble! A virus can hide in the background, unnoticed, using up valuable system resources.

- Burn your disc at a slower speed. Writing at 32× doesn't mean squat if the result becomes a drink coaster. Back your drive down to 8× or slower. If it works, try bumping up the speed a notch on each following burn until you've hit your sweet spot.

- Turn off any background processes that might be running (as described in the previous section).

Pops and Clicks That Weren't on the Source

Sometimes the actual burning process produces pops and clicks in the output CD you create that sound as if you were recording from an FM radio station that was too far out of range. This can be due to many causes, such as a bad WAV file to begin with. If you extract audio CD-DA tracks to WAV files, be sure to listen to them using Sound-Stream, the Windows Media Player, or some other applicable program before you record to a blank CD. If these turn out to be the problem, try extracting the WAV files at a slower rate or try recording them using a different CD-ROM drive (for this, you could even record from your CD-RW drive).

This problem can also occur when copying from a CD-ROM drive to your CD recorder. If your CD-ROM drive is an older one, and it passes the digital audio extraction test to see if it can extract data at a fast enough rate to keep the recorder supplied, problems can still occur if you have a source CD that has minor errors on it. You might not be able to detect these sounds when you play the CD, but when the track is being extracted and the data is being sent to the recorder, these problems can become magnified. To find out whether this is the cause, try using your CD burner itself as the source, copying the CD image to a disk image file, and then burn the CD from that image. If this doesn't work, try cleaning the CD to eliminate the possibility of minor errors caused by a dirty disc.

> **Between Tracks**
>
> You might think that recording at the fastest rated speed of your recorder drive might be the best thing. Unfortunately, that's not true. If you find it doesn't work well at the highest rate, then back down. Even though it takes a lot longer, almost everything works at slower speeds like 4× through 8×.

Finally, consider the possibility that, if you're getting the music from a commercial CD, that it has been encoded with copy protection. Some of the primary copy protection schemes the music industry is endeavoring to deploy kill the quality of the audio if it's recorded to your PC.

The CD Recorder Drive Wants a Bigger Disc!

Sometimes we bite off more than we can chew! The same goes when trying to record more data to a disc than your disc can hold. (Weren't you watching the indicator at the bottom of the application window that tracked your time?)

Sometimes, however, it's because you've attempted to copy a commercial CD to a 74-minute disc that was actually created at a length greater than 74 minutes. I've run into several of these *overburned* CDs myself during the copying process. CD-burning fans of Frank Sinatra surely know what I'm talking about.

The solution? If your drive works with them, go out and buy some 80-minute blank CDs and try using those. Blank CD media also can be found in 90- and 99-minute formats, but compatibility with those formats can get pretty spotty. Regardless, if a higher capacity disc doesn't quench your drive's hunger for space, then nothing will.

Finally, while I hate to point out the obvious, remove some of the data from your recording layout so that you're no longer over the capacity limit.

I Used Audio Cleaning Options to Reduce Noise, and I Get a Dull Sound!

Options that allow you to "clean out" pops, hisses, and scratches from recorded audio must be taken with a grain of salt. Although they do work, they're not the most perfect tools you could use to do this. And remember, when filling in a pop or a click in the record, the sound has to come from somewhere. When you take away some of the bad, you also take away some of the good.

Cleaning and pop-removal tools should be used on WAV files on your hard disk so you can preview the output before committing it to a CD-R blank. I've found that when I've recorded some old LPs to CD, it actually doesn't sound that bad to have an occasional noise distortion here and there. To us old-timers, songs recorded with pops, hisses, and scratches is what nature intended! Besides, it brings back memories.

If you use the cleaning tool to its extreme value, which might be necessary for a record from the early part of this century, you get a very dull output. Experiment! However, light applications of this tool seem to improve some records significantly. Try it at your leisure, pretending you're cutting your latest album and trying to get that groovy *sound*, man! Can you dig it?

Another option is to try a more sophisticated sound-editing program. Many are available; just check your local computer store and look for product reviews in magazines and on the web.

Keep Your Software and Hardware Current

In the changing scene of technology that disc recording is, you should always check with your vendor(s) on a regular basis (or, more accurately, their websites). If you are a hobbyist and are having great results from your computer and the applications you are using to make discs, then just employ the time-honored, "if it ain't broke don't fix it," strategy and call it a day. However, as new patches are issued for operating systems, such as Windows, and new devices are created and brought to market, the possibility always exists that, to get your parts all working together in unison, you'll need to download something from somebody.

The first place to start is your software vendor. Publishers like Roxio (ECDC) and Ahead (Nero) are usually pretty consistent about issuing updates and patches that fix bugs and increase their program's compatibility with different hardware setups. (Though sometimes, these patches break more features than they fix.) Next, check your recordable drive's manufacturer website. Disc recorders often receive what are called *firmware* updates. Sometimes these updates fix bugs, sometimes they improve compatibility with certain media formats and software products. Whether or not such an update will solve whatever problem you're having is a shot in the dark. Still, it's better than nothing!

Arcane CD Speak

Firmware is a software code, which usually is stored in a device's memory. This code can be used to modify the operation of the hardware without having to actually change the hardware! In other words, firmware is the code that runs on the card or drive you've attached to or installed in your computer, but it's stored in a special kind of memory on the card or adapter, not the computer's memory.

Other Resources

Okay, so tracking down the easy stuff hasn't solved your problems. As long as your Internet connection works, you're not out of options yet! Try visiting:

- **support.roxio.com.** This site provides support for the Easy CD Creator software, but the posters on their support forum (think message board) are often more than willing to help out with any recording problem you might have.

- **www.ahead.de/en/index.html#c1002822798638.** This link goes straight to the Support FAQ for Nero Burning ROM. Ahead Software doesn't provide a forum for posters to help support each other, but if your problem is in Nero, then this is better than nothing.

- **www.vcdhelp.com.** If you're trying to burn a video disc of any kind (CD or DVD), this it the site for you. It's loaded with troubleshooting advice, access to utilities, and more information than most any site on the web.

- **homepages.nildram.co.uk/~abcomp/lp-cdr.htm.** This isn't a huge troubleshooting reference site or anything. But if you need help copying an LP to a CD then this is the place for you!

- **www.cdrinfo.com.** This is just a great site for news related to disc recording, covering both CDs and DVDs. It also has a wealth of articles on media formats, drives, and making successful recordings. It's well worth a notch in your Internet Favorites list.

The Least You Need to Know

- Go slow if you have problems recording. Use a speed in the 4× to 8× range for difficult discs or recorders.

- Clean up your sources before you record! A smudged or scratched CD isn't going to copy without a little luck.

- In addition to recording at a slower speed, if you're having buffer-underrun or other recording problems, make sure you're recording first to an image file on your hard drive, before recording information to a disc.

- Update your software frequently by visiting the home pages of software vendors. The same goes for hardware vendors who might have to issue new driver software as operating systems continue to evolve.

Appendix A

Installing Roxio
Easy CD Creator

Installing Roxio Easy CD Creator 5 Platinum is a somewhat time-consuming but mostly painless process. This appendix provides an overview of the Easy CD Creator (ECDC), its installation, and how to bring it up to date.

Getting to Know Easy CD Creator 5.0 Platinum

Before you first install Easy CD Creator 5, you should double-check to make sure your computer meets its hardware requirements. Obviously, you must have a recordable drive installed, but you should also make sure it's a supported drive. Easy CD Creator supports a lot of recordable drives, but not necessarily all of them. Roxio maintains a compatibility list at www.roxio.com/en/jhtml/cdrdatabase/database.jhtml (see Figure A.1). Use the scroll boxes on this page to choose your drive's make and model, and then click the Go button. You'll then see a web page letting you know if your drive works with Easy CD Creator.

Figure A.1

Enter your drive's make and model in Roxio's Recorder Support web page to determine if your recorder works with Easy CD Creator.

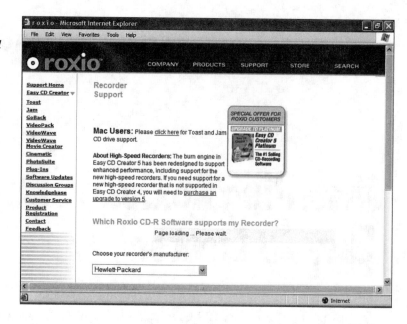

Between Tracks

This appendix assumes you're installing Easy CD Creator 5.0 Platinum. If you've recently purchased Easy CD Creator your CD may already have version 5.3 or a newer version.

Between Tracks

If you're using a version of Easy CD Creator that bears the name Adaptec instead of Roxio, you need not worry. Roxio was a spin-off of Adaptec in 2000, but is part of the same big happy family. Outside of changes between the 4.x and 5.x versions, Easy CD Creator operates the same whether your title screen bears the Adaptec or Roxio name.

Once you've established that your recorder is compatible with ECDC you should make sure the rest of your PC is up to snuff. Your computer should meet these requirements:

◆ A 200MHz or better Intel Pentium, AMD K6, or equivalent processor. Most any PC purchase new in the last four years meets this requirement.

◆ A modern version of Windows, like 9x/Me/NT4/2000 or the version that was used to create this book: Windows XP.

◆ 32MB of system memory, but 64MB is a more preferable sweet spot. As cheap as RAM is these days, if you don't have at least 128MB you should consider an upgrade.

◆ At least 205MB of free space on your hard disk.

◆ Windows-compatible audio built into your PC's motherboard or on an audio card (virtually any PC that meets the previously described specs should have this).

While in this "wonderful new millennium" (or so marketing folks tell us) most PCs should have no trouble meeting these requirements, if you're unsure about your system there's an easy way to check.

Right-click the My Computer on the Windows desktop (may only be in the Start menu in Windows XP) and choose Properties. The screen that appears shows your PC's Windows version, amount of System RAM, and processor type. If you see Pentium II, III, or 4, Athlon, or Athlon XP then you can stop fretting over system requirements right now.

To check your available hard disk space, open My Computer and select your hard drive. The left side of the My Computer window should show both the total space on your hard disk and how much of it is free space. (If it doesn't, right-click the drive and choose Properties.)

Whenever you install a new program, especially a disc authoring program like Nero, you should take a couple of precautions before you start copying all those files.

1. Back up any critical files and data (including e-mail). I have found the book *PC Fear Factor*, by Alan Luber to be very useful in this regard. It contains excellent and easy-to-follow information on backing up your data.

2. If you use Windows Me or XP, create a System Restore point. Click Start, (All) Programs, Accessories, System Tools, System Restore. Select Create Restore Point, give the restore point a description you'll understand if seen later, and click the Create button. By creating this restore point, if the installation causes system instability, you can always restore your PC to the point just prior to installation (though any installed files will still be on your hard disk).

3. If you use a firewall or virus checker (like Norton AntiVirus), you should disable them. While unlikely, it is possible these programs could interfere with an application's install. Be sure to disconnect from the Internet if you do this as you would otherwise leave your PC vulnerable to hackers and viruses. As soon as the installation is complete, re-enable your firewall or antivirus program.

4. Close any open applications. While also unlikely, they could interfere with Nero's installation.

Once you've jumped through these hoops, you're ready to install!

Starting the Easy CD Creator Installer

Before you install Easy CD Creator, first exit all other programs you may be running, just in case one of them doesn't play nice with the other kiddies (disable any antivirus programs you may be running). Once you insert the Easy CD Creator CD, Windows should immediately recognize it and ask you if you'd like to, "install the product now." There are buttons for Yes and No. Presumably, you're going to click Yes, in which case Easy CD Creator runs various checks on your system (verifying drive space and requirements) before launching its InstallShield Wizard, which makes installation a breeze. Click Next to continue.

Between Tracks

If you find that the installation menu does not pop up automatically when you insert the installation CD, you might not have your computer set to use the Autorun feature. In that case, open My Computer and double-click the icon for your disc drive. Depending on your flavor of Windows, this will either launch the Autorun process described previously or open up a listing of files on the CD. If it's the latter, look for a file named "Setup," and double-click it.

This being the modern age of legalisms and technical gobbledy-gook, the first thing you'll have to endure is agreeing to Roxio's licensing "agreement." This "agreement" basically tells you all the things they don't want you to do with your software (and is found in any software package you install). Some choice. Either you agree to its terms or take the software back to your local software retailer, who's likely to not accept a return of opened software, for a refund. Assuming you're willing to agree to the license (or willing to pretend to), click the radio button next to the option for I Accept The Terms In The License Agreement and click Next.

The next screen asks for your name, organization, and CD key. The last of these helps ensure you're not running someone else's copy of the software (see Figure A.2).

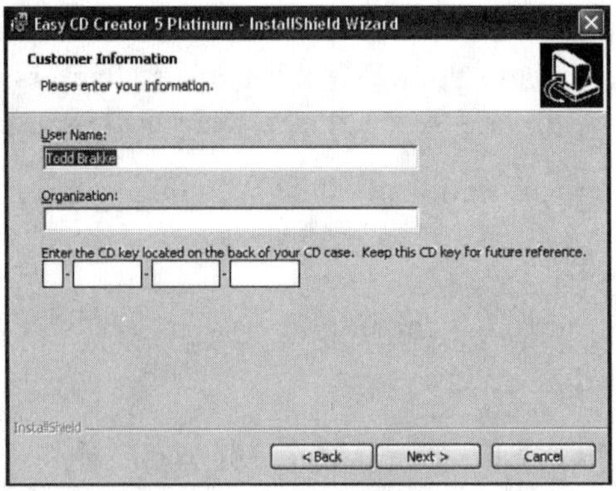

Figure A.2

Roxio tries to ensure its software isn't being pirated through the use of a CD key that you must enter before the program can install.

While you can ignore the Organization field, you must enter your name and the CD key number, which is located on the back of the CD's packaging. When ready, click Next.

The next dialog box asks you what kind of setup you'd prefer to use. If you want to keep it clean and simple, select Complete and click Next. However, for reasons which we'll soon explain, you're better off selecting Custom, which allows you to control which Easy CD Creator programs are installed on your computer (see Figure A.3).

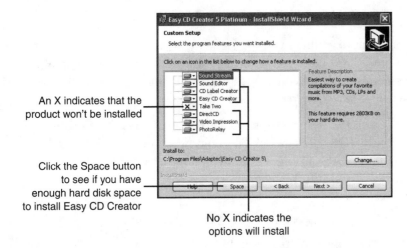

An X indicates that the product won't be installed

Click the Space button to see if you have enough hard disk space to install Easy CD Creator

No X indicates the options will install

Figure A.3

Make sure you disable Take Two before you install a program that could turn your hard drive into an expensive paperweight.

The list of programs for the Platinum edition consists of:

- ◆ **SoundStream.** For creating compilations of music from various sources like MP3s, WAV files, and even LPs. SoundStream is covered in Chapter 10.

- ◆ **Sound Editor.** Allows you to edit audio files encoded in the WAV format. As it strays a bit far from the topic at hand, I don't cover Sound Editor in this book.

- ◆ **CD Label Creator.** Allows you to create killer CD and jewel case labels. CD Label Creator is covered in Chapter 16.

- ◆ **Easy CD Creator.** As the name suggests, this is the core Easy CD Creator 5 Platinum application. Use it to create audio and data CDs from scratch. Making audio and data CDs with Easy CD Creator is covered in Chapter 5.

CAUTION **Don't Get Burned**

Make sure, when entering the CD key, also called the TSID (Technical Support Identification) number, that you enter exactly what is shown on the label. Even one incorrect digit will prevent Easy CD Creator from installing.

CAUTION

Don't Get Burned

The shipping version of Easy CD Creator 5 has a horrid problem that Windows 2000 Professional users must take note of. If running Windows 2000 Professional with certain removable-drives, the Take Two software in Easy CD Creator, ironically designed for backing up data, can seriously and irrecoverably corrupt information on your hard drive. Roxio did release a patch to fix this, however, subsequent patches removed Take Two entirely.

◆ **Take Two.** A program that allows you to back up your hard drive's data. As of version 5.1, this program is no longer a part of Easy CD Creator. Roxio could never make this utility work in Windows 2000 and XP and has apparently given up for the time being. I strongly recommend that you not install this program.

If you get to this point and are unsure as to whether you have room on your hard disk to install the Easy CD Creator Platinum programs you've selected, click the Space button on this dialog box and you'll see a screen that breaks down your available hard drives, how much space is required, and how much you have available.

◆ **DirectCD.** This is a packet writing tool that lets you write files to your disc drive from Windows Explorer or My Computer, just as you would when moving files around on your hard drive. Packet writing is discussed in Chapter 6, while DirectCD is covered in Chapter 7.

◆ **Video Impression.** Lets you Spielberg and Lucas wanna-bes edit and burn video to CD. Video Impression is covered in Chapter 13.

◆ **PhotoRelay.** Gives you the ability to store digital pictures in virtual photo albums and burn them to CD so you can amaze (or bore) your friends and family with pictures from your vacation to Aunt Millie's house in North Dakota. PhotoRelay is covered in Chapter 20.

By default, all of these programs are installed in a Complete or Custom setup. However, if you left-click the icon next to the program you don't want installed, you can click the red "X" on the shortcut menu that appears (you should do this for Take Two). If you change your mind later, bring up the menu again and click This Feature Will Be Installed on Local Hard Drive.

Finally, if you prefer to control the locations to which programs like Easy CD Creator are installed, click the Change button on this dialog box and choose a new folder. Once satisfied with your selections, click Next to continue and Easy CD

Creator will ask you to confirm that you're ready to begin installing its applications. In case you haven't already guessed, click Install.

Finishing the Installation

Once you click Install, Easy CD Creator finally begins the installation process shown in Figure A.4. At this point it should only take a couple of minutes to install.

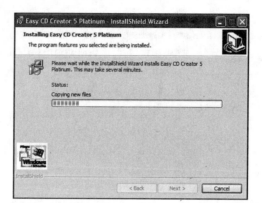

Figure A.4

After a whole lot of mouse clicks, Easy CD Creator finally begins installing.

![lightbulb icon] **Between Tracks** _____

Like many other programs, Roxio commits a sin that's sure to annoy any users who put their computer's performance over convenient launching of applications. In this case, it puts background programs for the Project Selector and DirectCD functions in your system tray.

You can rid yourself of these icons, and others like them, in several ways. The easiest way is to click Start, Run, type msconfig and click OK. This opens the Windows System Configuration Utility. Click the Selective Startup radio button and then select the Startup tab. Here you'll see a list of all the programs that load when Windows starts.

To prevent these two programs from loading on startup, remove the checkmarks from the options for AdaptecDirectCD and CreateCD50. While doing so does mean you'll have to launch these programs manually when you do want to use them, I think most people prefer to have the choice.

You'll have to reboot to make this change take effect. When you do, Windows will display a message that you've started up using a Selective Startup mode. Just let it know that all is well with the world and close the window.

Once installation is complete, yet another dialog box opens to let you know. Click Finish and you'll get one final gotcha, as you must now restart your computer so that certain files can load properly during your computer's boot process. If you're not ready, you can click No and reboot later, but it's better to take the time to do so now, so click Yes.

When your computer reboots, it will automatically open the Easy CD Creator Project Selector (see Figure A.5 in the next section).

Finishing Touches: Using Web-Checkup

Once you have Easy CD Creator installed, you have one more extremely important task to accomplish: making sure ECDC is up to date.

No program is bug free and so software publishers are frequently called on to release patches that fix broken features and other problems. Easy CD Creator is no exception. In fact, if you've installed ECDC 5.0 and want to burn DVDs using ECDC you have to upgrade to at least version 5.1.

Between Tracks

Easy CD Creator 5.1 only supports DVD burning to the -R/RW format, not +R/RW. For support for the latter of these two, you must download and install at least ECDC 5.3.

The easiest way to check for updates in Easy CD Creator is to open the Project Selector; click Start, Programs, Roxio Easy CD Creator 5, Project Selector. Most of the options in the Project Selector are covered in other chapters throughout this book, however, there is one to take note of: web-checkup (see Figure A.5).

Figure A.5

Use the Roxio Project Selector to launch Easy CD Creator programs and to update the product with web-checkup.

To use web-checkup, ensure that your PC is connected to the Internet and then click the web-checkup button on the Project Selector. When you do, it opens your default web browser (such as Internet Explorer or Netscape Navigator) to the update portion of Roxio's website.

This page has some basic instructions for how to update your product. The long and short of it is that you must click the link on this page that matches your software (most likely the entry that reads Easy CD Creator Version 5). When you do, a list of available updates appears (see Figure A.6).

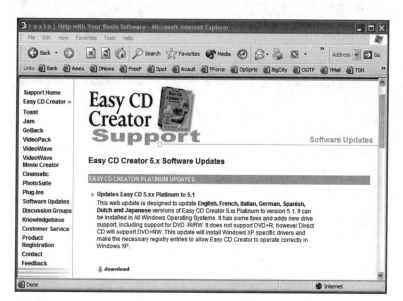

Figure A.6

This update, available at Roxio's website, downloads a file that updates Easy CD Creator 5.0 to Easy CD Creator 5.1.

Between Tracks

Since Easy CD Creator is technically a suite of several software products, the page shown here will list updates for each program. The most important ones apply specifically to Easy CD Creator, but you might also find updates for Video Impressions, Photo Relay, or other applications. You should download those updates that apply to the Easy CD Creator products you use. For the sake of this appendix, we'll focus on the main ECDC update (to version 5.1).

Click the download link for the update that will bring your version of ECDC up to date. Because ECDC is available in multiple languages, the next web page you see instructs you to select the one applicable to you. Next you are presented with a screen letting you know what we've all suspected for years: the Take-Two backup utility doesn't work. This page let's you know that your update will force you to uninstall Take Two if it is installed already. Click Yes to continue.

Because privacy no longer means anything in this country and because nothing in life is ever easy, Roxio now requires you to register to download product updates. Boo

Roxio. Boooo. If you've already registered you need only provide your login and password. If you have not, click the "First Time? Become a New Member!" link (see Figure A.7). It's funny how they make it sound like you have a choice.

Figure A.7

Why is it that so many software publishers these days think they have a right to your personal information just so you can download the functionality you should have received on the retail CD in the first place?

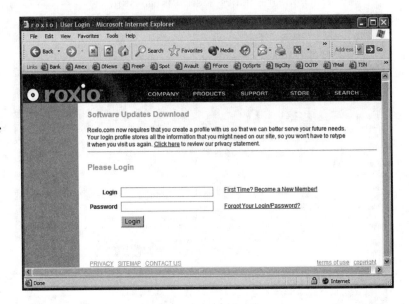

In any case, once you've registered and logged in, you're finally presented with a link that lets you <gasp!> download a file. Click this link and, on the File Download dialog box that appears, choose Save. Select a location, and once the download is complete (it will probably be very large) choose to Open the file.

This, finally, starts the update (see Figure A.8). Click Install to get things going.

Figure A.8

Compared to actually getting a patch downloaded, installation of an ECDC update is a snap!

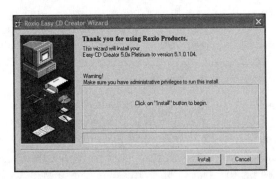

Once the update is installed, you'll probably be asked to reboot your system. You should go ahead and get this out of the way. When Windows comes back up, you can continue downloading any other available updates or start burning discs with your new installation of Easy CD Creator!

Installing Nero Burning ROM

This appendix covers the installation of Nero Burning ROM 5.5 from Ahead Software. While the steps necessary to install any Windows application are largely the same, there's always a unique hurdle or two in any software installation program and Nero is no different in this regard.

Before You Install

Before you install Nero, it's always a good idea to double-check to make sure your computer meets its system requirements (obviously, you need a drive capable of recording to at least CD-R or CD-RW media). In the case of Nero 5.5 you need to have at least:

♦ An Intel Pentium 133MHz processor or better (if you have at least an Intel Pentium II, Celeron, or AMD K6, Athlon, or Duron processor, then you're very much in the clear).

♦ A modern version of Windows. This includes Windows 95, 98, Me, NT4, 2000, and XP.

♦ 16MB of system memory. Really, though, you should have no less than 64MB on any modern system (256MB is preferable).

♦ At least 25MB of free space on your hard disk. To check available disk space, open My Computer in Windows, right click your hard drive (Local Disk C:) and select Properties. If the Free Space field shows a number in the gigabytes (GB) range, you have plenty of space.

Cross Reference

For a general overview of the Nero 5.5 software, flip back to the Introduction section of this book. We introduce both Easy CD Creator 5 and Nero 5.5 there.

Between Tracks

If you are in the market for a new PC, we recommend you consider a quality system from a vendor like Dell or Gateway. If money is no object, point your web browsers to the website of Falcon Northwest (www.falcon-nw.com). When it comes to quality, support, and performance, they have no equal.

If your computer falls short of these requirements, don't kid yourself, it's time for a new PC. It's been five years since Pentium-class PCs were the norm and if this profile fits your PC, then you'll be hard-pressed to find any recent software that can run adequately on your machine. They say time waits for no man, and that's especially true in the computing world.

Once you've established that your PC lives up to these rather pathetic hardware requirements you should check to see if Ahead Software has verified your disc recorder's compatibility with Nero. Just point your web browser to www.nero.com/en/content2/recorder.html. If Nero should change this link for some reason, just go to www.nero.com, select Nero Burning ROM and click the Supported Recorders link at the bottom of the page. This link takes you to a page with a table full of disc recorder manufacturers. Select the manufacturer for your drive and you are taken to a new page with a table of supported drive models for your drive's manufacturer (see Figure B.1).

Figure B.1

The Ahead Software Supported Recorders page lets you ensure your disc recorder is compatible with Nero Burning ROM software.

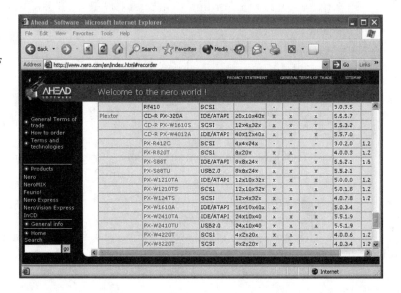

Once you've verified that your drive is compatible with Nero and that your PC meets its system requirements, there's just a couple more house-cleaning procedures you should take before installing Nero.

Don't Get Burned

If your disc recorder isn't listed at the Nero website, it doesn't mean your drive won't work with Nero. There's every probability that it will function without hiccup or error. However, if Ahead Software hasn't verified compatibility with your recorder, it's still a roll of the dice. If you come up snake eyes you'll have to return Nero for a refund or replace your recorder with one that is supported.

Whenever you install a new program, especially a disc authoring program like Nero, you should take a couple of precautions before you start copying all those files.

1. Back up any critical files and data (including e-mail). I have found the book *PC Fear Factor*, by Alan Luber to be a very useful reference in this regard. It contains excellent and easy-to-follow information on backing up your data.

2. If you use Windows Me or XP, create a System Restore point. Click Start, (All) Programs, Accessories, System Tools, System Restore. Select Create Restore Point, give the restore point a description you'll understand if seen later, and click the Create button. By creating this restore point, if the installation causes system instability, you can always restore your PC to the point just prior to installation (though any installed files will still be on your hard disk).

3. If you use a firewall or virus checker (like Norton AntiVirus), you should disable them. While unlikely, it is possible these programs could interfere with an application's install. Be sure to disconnect from the Internet if you do this as you would otherwise leave your PC vulnerable to hackers and viruses. As soon as the installation is complete, re-enable your firewall or antivirus program.

4. Close any open applications. While also unlikely, they could interfere with Nero's installation.

Once you've jumped through these hoops, you're ready to install!

Installing Nero Burning ROM 5.5

Once you're ready to install Nero, put the disc in the drive. If enabled, Windows Autorun should immediately recognize the disc and begin the installation wizard.

Between Tracks _____

If Autorun is not enabled on your PC, open My Computer. Right click the drive in which you inserted the Nero CD-ROM, and choose Explore. Double-click the Setup icon that appears in this Window to initiate installation.

When the install wizard begins you'll see a screen like the one shown in Figure B.2.

Figure B.2

The Ahead Installer lets you choose which Nero Burning ROM applications you want to install.

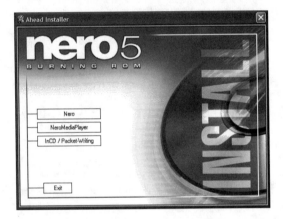

As you can see from this figure, Nero Burning ROM comes with a couple of different applications that you can install separately. The next three sections take a look at the installation process for each of these applications.

Nero

From the screen shown in Figure B.2, select Nero. This launches the Nero Burning ROM Installation Wizard. Click Next and use the following steps to set up and install Nero:

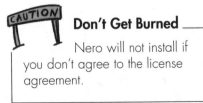

Don't Get Burned _____

Nero will not install if you don't agree to the license agreement.

1. When you click Next from the first Wizard screen Nero presents you with an End User License Agreement. Read it, don't read it, it's entirely up to you. However, if you wish to know what rights Nero gives you as a user of the software, you should take the time to look it over. Select the I Accept the Terms of the License Agreement option and click Next.

2. Nero then asks you for your customer information. Input your name and product serial number. You should find your serial number on the inside front cover of the jewel case for your Nero CD-ROM. Click Next to continue.

3. The Setup Type screen allows you to choose how Nero installs. You can choose from Typical, Compact, or Custom installations, though we're going to assume you're going with the Typical install. Select Typical and click Next.

4. At this point Nero is ready to install. Click Next when the Ready to Install the Program screen appears.

5. Nero then starts copying files to your computer. When the process is complete you're presented with a screen that lets you know the process has completed successfully (see Figure B.3). Click Finish to close the installer.

Between Tracks _____

By default Nero installs into the Program Files folder on your main hard disk drive. If you want to change this location, you should choose a Custom Installation.

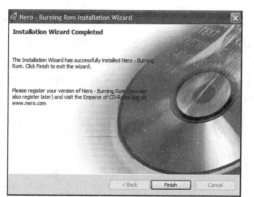

Figure B.3

At this point you can either begin using Nero or install one of the other Nero applications.

Nero Media Player

If you want to install Nero Media Player, you should eject and reinsert the Nero CD-ROM to reactivate the Autorun setup program. On the screen that appears (refer to Figure B.2), select Nero Media Player and use the following steps to install the program:

1. The first screen you see when installing Nero Media Player is the basic welcome to the wonderful wizard screen that we've all seen and been nauseated by before. Click Next.

2. As when installing Nero, you must once again agree to an End User License Agreement. Select the I Accept the Terms of the License Agreement option and click Next.

3. On the Customer Information screen, you need to enter your name and company (not required). If you want to install Nero Media Player to a location other than the one listed in the Install To field, click the Change button and choose a new location. Click Next when you're ready to move on.

4. When you click Next in Step 3, the NeroMediaPlayer Installation Wizard starts copying files to your hard drive. When complete, you're greeted with a screen similar to the one shown in Figure B.3. However, on this screen the wizard requests that you reboot your PC before continuing. To reboot, click the Reboot button. To reboot later, click the Finish button to close the wizard.

With Nero Media Player installed, all that's left is to install InCD, Nero's packet-writing software that lets you write files to a disc like you would to a hard drive.

InCD / Packet-Writing

If you want to install InCD / Packet-Writing software, you should eject and reinsert the Nero CD-ROM to reactivate the Autorun setup program. On the screen that appears (refer to Figure B.2), select InCD / Packet Writing and use the following steps to install the program:

1. The first screen of the InCD Installation Wizard is the usual blasé window welcoming you to the product. Are you getting tired of this drill yet? Click Next to continue.

2. As when installing Nero and Nero Media Player, you must, yet again, agree to an End User License Agreement. Really, wasn't once enough? Select the I Accept the Terms of the License Agreement option and click Next.

3. The Customer Information screen that appears next is a virtual twin to the one shown for Nero Media Player. Enter your name and company (not required) and if you so desire, click the Change button to select a custom install location. Click Next.

4. At this point, the wizard starts copying over the necessary InCD files to enable packet writing on your computer. When it's complete you'll see another of those whacky Install Completed Successfully screens. As with Nero Media Player, the installer wants you to reboot your PC. You can either do so by clicking the Reboot button on this window or you can reboot later and just click Finish.

With Nero and all its components installed successfully, you might think you're ready to enter the pearly gates of disc recording heaven. If so, you'd be wrong. No program ships error free, so now it's time to make sure your version of Nero is as up to date as possible.

Finishing Touches: Keeping Nero Up to Date

Like most applications, when Nero was initially released it wasn't flawless. This is no fault of Ahead Software. No program as complex as Nero is ever perfect. But good software publishers do their best, even after the product hits the shelves, to keep improving their software and make it as error-free as possible.

At the time of this writing, Nero 5.5 was the most up-to-date version of Nero Burning ROM available off-the-shelf. However, that doesn't mean the disc in the box is the most recent version. A quick visit to the Nero home page (www.nero.com) shows that there have been a couple updates since my Nero 5.5 disc slid inside its trusty cardboard home. On the main Nero page is a section called Recent Updates, in which there is a listing for "Nero v 5.5.9.0." Depending on the frequency of further updates and when you're reading this, you'll probably see a higher number. Regardless, click the most recent update to Nero.

Don't Get Burned

Ahead Software has put the name Nero in a couple of different software packages, including Nero Express, Nero-MIX, etc. Be sure you select an update applicable to Nero Burning ROM!

When you choose a specific update to install, you're taken to a new web page that allows you to choose a location from which to download the update (see Figure B.4). Technically, any location should do, but you're probably best off selecting a flag of the local color.

Once you select a download link, Windows opens the File Download dialog box. Click the Save button and select a download location.

Once you've selected a folder to which you want to download the update, click the Save button. Windows should then start downloading the file. This may take just a minute or 15 minutes or more. It all depends on the speed of your Internet connection and the size of the update.

When complete, Windows asks if you want to: open the file, open the folder to which you downloaded it, or take no further action by clicking the Cancel button. Assuming you want to immediately install the patch, click Open. This opens up a welcome of the type you've probably seen many times before.

Figure B.4

When you hover the mouse pointer over one of the patch file links, the Nero website opens a small window showing approximate download time.

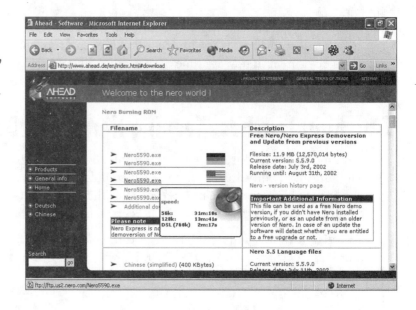

From here click Next, and use the following steps to apply the update:

Between Tracks

If you want to see a list of the fixes in a Nero product update, click the Nero—Version History Page link on the updates page (see Figure B.4).

Between Tracks

I've found it's best to create a My Downloads folder inside My Documents. I use this folder to store any files I download, making them easy to find.

1. Nero displays a window allowing you to choose whether you want to update your current version of Nero to the one included in the patch you downloaded or if you want to remove Nero from your PC (the latter option may be grayed out). Choose Update and click Next.

2. As when installing Nero itself, you must again agree to an End User License Agreement. It is possible when applying these updates for Ahead Software to change the terms of the agreement, so you may want to look this over. In any case, select I Accept All Terms of the Preceding License Agreement and click Next.

3. Nero will start copying the patch files over your existing installation. When complete you'll see a congratulatory window letting you know all went as planned. Click Finish.

Once you click Finish, the wizard exits and you're ready to start burning discs with your freshly installed, freshly updated copy of Nero Burning ROM!

Optical Recording Potpourri

I know most readers have purchased this book simply because they want a better understanding of how to use disc recording products like Easy CD Creator and Nero. I'd also like to think, however, that some of you have a genuine interest in how all this mumbo-jumbo geek stuff actually works. In this appendix I've included a loose collection of information detailing some of the more technical aspects of recording to CDs and DVDs. This is by no means a comprehensive look at how these discs operate, but if you're looking for a quick primer, this is the place to find it!

The Colorful Books of CD Standards

While those of us who grew up with phonograph records and black-and-white televisions never thought of the complicated technologies that were to come, we thought much less about standards. That is, until the famous VHS/BetaMax wars came along! Surely, some of you remember going to a video store and having to choose between the VHS and BetaMax sections? How horribly expensive Beta's death must have been for those who thought it would win out over VHS. More recently, what was a fledgling DVD industry had to overcome the early challenge of the pay-per-play DivX format, of which Circuit City had been the main proponent. In the here and now, however, there is still a nasty battle brewing over recordable and rewritable DVD standards. The +/- war, as it's sure to be known, is pitting the DVD Forum's DVD-R and DVD-RW against the DVD+RW Alliance's DVD+R and DVD+RW formats, with no clear winner in sight.

Fortunately, compact disc manufacturers were wise enough to avoid ugly scenarios like these by creating standards for the various kinds of CDs you use today. This appendix provides a brief overview of the books that define the standards that apply to your CD-burning lifestyle, all of which are known by the color of their covers. So if you're ever in a conversation with some cyber-geek and someone mentions the Orange Book or the White Book, you'll have some idea of what he's talking about.

Cross Reference

For more information on the recordable DVD format wars, see Chapter 2.

Between Tracks

My aim here is really just to give you a basic idea of what these standards represent, you're not going to come out of this appendix a scholar in the field. In fact, you might find that some of the numbers and specifications I'm bandying about are just way over your head. Don't worry about it—this is strictly an FYI for those who want a few more tidbits about the various CD specifics. That's why this is just an appendix!

For more information on the contents of these specification documents, just call up your "local" international manufacturer and ask for a copy … and expect a big bill! These aren't like Internet standards, which are developed by standards organizations comprised mostly of volunteers. These are the hard facts from the companies who developed the technology.

For this discussion, I focus on the "book" specifications that were written to define how certain types of discs should be created. Each book is used to define a different purpose for the compact disc, and each is identified by the color of the cover of the book.

The Red Book—the Audio CD Format

In 1982, Philips and Sony released the "Red Book," which set forth the specifications for creating audio CDs (also called CD-DAs). This is the CD with which most people are familiar. This type of CD uses an error-correction scheme called *CIRC*. When using Easy CD Creator, you can choose to record MP3 files in addition to the CD-DA tracks you can find on a Red Book CD. The program, however, converts the MP3 file to a WAV file, which is almost exactly the same as the Red Book CD-DA method. Either way, you won't be able to tell the difference.

The Yellow Book–the CD-ROM Format

This standard was released in 1983. As you can probably figure out, the term CD-ROM stands for "compact disc read-only memory." In other words, you can only read from it, not write to it. It would be years before we'd see the birth of a recordable CD.

The CD-ROM disc is the same size as a CD-DA disc, 120mm. However, the method used for storing data on the disc is much different, which is why the two formats are incompatible.

The Green Book–Interactive Multimedia Format

Just as computer manufacturers realized that an immense amount of data could be stored on a CD-ROM, companies specializing in multimedia came to the same conclusion. Thus the interactive multimedia (CD-I) format was released in 1987 to enable video, audio, and other files to be stored on a CD-ROM and to be used in special interactive devices or in a standard computer.

This kind of disc is usually found in those self-repeating product demonstrators found on kiosks in shopping malls. Its capability to allow the user to interact with a program and incorporate multimedia features makes it ideal for this purpose.

The Orange Book (Parts I, II, and III)–CD-Recordable

This kind of CD differed in its development from the others in that it was the first "recordable" CD. Actually, two kinds of CDs are defined in this book—called CD-WO (CD write once), which is now called CD-R, and CD-MO (CD magneto optical), which is usually found in high-end installations such as large computer rooms. These standards, which form Parts I and II, were released in 1990.

Part III of the Orange Book was released in 1995. It takes the CD-R concept and adds the capability to erase and re-record on a CD-ROM. The actual CD-R and CD-RW (which started out being called CD-erasable or CD-E) discs are, however, not manufactured in the same manner, and the reflection of the laser light is different on the two discs. If you have a recent model of a CD-ROM disc drive, it should be able to read CD-RW discs on the CD-ROM drive, but many older models cannot. CD-RW drives are now the industry standard (you'd be hard-pressed to find a CD-R-only drive anymore) and are backward-compatible with most other compact disc formats, so you will most likely be able to read any kind of CD on a CD-RW drive.

The White Book—the Video CD

This standard was defined in 1993 by Philips, Sony, and JVC to enable storing about 70 minutes of video on a CD-ROM. It was based partly on a karaoke CD that JVC had developed earlier. This was version 1.1 of the White Book. In version 2.0, released in 1994, Philips, JVC, and Matsushita developed a more versatile version of the video CD that could be used for standard video content, as well as provide support for interactive applications.

The drive used to read these kinds of discs is called CD-ROM/XA. The *XA* in this disc's name stands for *extended architecture*. This kind of disc is an extension of the Yellow Book standards and enables several kinds of data to be stored on the same disc, including the following:

- Audio
- Video
- Computer data
- Compressed audio

You will usually need a player capable of reading each of these formats (like a typical CD-ROM drive) to read a disc that is of the CD-ROM/XA type.

The Blue Book—CD-Extra

The CD-Extra format was released in 1996 and has been known by other names, such as CD-Plus and Enhanced CD. It contains multisessions, each of which can contain various kinds of data. For example, most audio CD players can recognize only the first session, and the music recorded there will play just as if the CD were of the CD-DA variety. However, a second session could be added to contain computer data. Because most audio CDs usually contain only 50 to 60 minutes of music, a second session could be added that could store a few hundred megabytes of computer applications or data. When played in an ordinary audio player, you would hear the music. When played in a computer, you would listen to the musical selections *or* play with the multimedia applications stored in the second session.

Between Tracks

A new method for writing data to recordable CDs is now finally beginning to emerge. CD-MRW, also known as Mount Rainier, makes it possible to write data to a CD without special packet-writing software. For more information on Mount Rainier, check out Chapter 1.

Packet Writing Formats (Sorry, No Color)

In many cases, you either copy an entire CD or at least select data from·several sources and write a CD-R disc during one session. A technology called *packet writing* enables you to write in much smaller increments to a disc over time. Two standards have been developed for packet writing. The CD-RFS format is a Sony-developed format, whereas the CD-UDF format is a more standard format for packet writing.

How Optical Discs Work

Optical discs like CDs and DVDs have something in common with the phonographic records of yesteryear: They are manufactured products that store information. As a matter of fact, although phonographic records use analog recording methods and optical discs use digital recording methods, they have a whole lot in common.

For example, one important aspect that phonographic records and optical discs share is the way the actual tracks of data are laid out on the media. This is in stark contrast to how data is laid out in the more common magnetic components of your PC, like a floppy or hard disk drive. In a typical magnetic hard disk (or floppy disk, for that matter), the data is laid out in a set of concentric rings. That is, circles within circles, as you can see in Figure C.1.

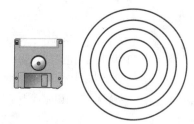

Figure C.1

Ordinary computer hard disks store data on separate tracks that are not connected. The closer to the middle of the disk, the shorter the track.

Each of these circular tracks is divided into sectors, which means the closer you get to the outside of the hard disk, the more sectors of data you can place on a track because a greater surface area exists to hold more sectors.

Optical discs do not use this method. Instead, similar to a phonographic record, a continuous spiral track is used, as shown in Figure C.2.

However, even though both use this spiral method for tracking, phonographic records are played by starting at the outer portion of the spiral and then following the spiral inward to the center of the record. Optical discs are played in just the opposite manner, by starting where the spiral begins in the center of the CD and continuing to the outermost portion of the disc.

Figure C.2

Optical discs, like phono-graphic records, use one long, continuous, spiral track to record data, unlike a com-puter's hard disk.

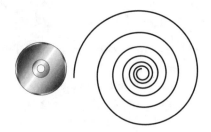

If you were to take the spiral track of a CD and stretch it out into one long line, it would go on for about three miles. Now that's a lot of room to record data! And to think a single layer DVD stores more than seven times the amount of information of a generic CD!

It's All About Pits and Lands

Computers, no matter how complex they appear to be, are really just sophisticated electronic adding machines. While I sit here and type this appendix on my computer, the actual background processes going on inside the computer involve moving around a bunch of 0s and 1s. At first glance, there doesn't seem to be much you can do when using just 0s and 1s, does there? The truth, however, is that you can digitize music and create a CD using 0s and 1s. You can compute the trajectory and flight path to send a rocket to the moon and back. In fact, 0s and 1s, or the binary numerical sys-tem, can actually be used to do a whole lot of things.

Between Tracks

The last few millimeters at the edge of the CD or DVD are generally not used. In addition, many disc manu-facturers deliberately do not use the entire capacity of an optical disc. By leaving a few minutes unused, a small area exists at the outer edge of the disc that contains no audio or data. This is done for two rea-sons. First, this makes it easier to control the quality of the disc. Second, it gives the end user a little leeway when handling the edges of a disc.

So to put music—or data, or whatever—on a CD or DVD, a method of recording 0s and 1s and reading them back again must exist. When your favorite CD or DVD is playing, what is really going on behind the scenes is that a laser beam (very tightly focused) is pointed at the CD and, depending on the amount of light that is reflected back, 0s and 1s are detected. The changes in the reflectivity of this light are caused by a series of pits and lands in the surface of the disc.

Although it might seem that the most logical way to record 0s and 1s on a CD is to have a pit represent a 1 and a land represent 0, that is not the case. As a matter of fact, even magnetic media, such as your computer's hard drive, doesn't use such a simple method. Instead, 0s and 1s are encoded by detecting the *change* from a pit to a land, and vice versa. As long as the surface of the disc remains constant, the reader records a stream of 0s; however, when the CD reader detects a change from a pit to a land, it interprets this as a 1 bit. The same is true when a change is detected from a land to a pit. It doesn't matter which direction the state change takes. It just matters that a change occurs at all. Figure C.3 shows this a little more clearly.

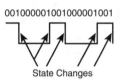
001000001001000001001

State Changes

Figure C.3

The encoding scheme encodes 1s as a state of transition, no matter which direction.

As you can see from Figure 2.3, every time the laser detects a change from one to the other (pit/land), it assumes that a binary bit with a value of 1 has been detected. Everything else is interpreted as a 0 bit.

Speed Kills

It should become quickly obvious that, for this scheme of pits and lands to work, *the laser must read the spiral track at a constant speed*—timing is very important when reading CDs.

Now, as any phonograph audiophile knows, on a phonographic record, the closer to the center of the record that the stylus gets, the faster it travels in the groove of the record. Or, more precisely, the more surface area of the record passes beneath the needle during a particular amount of time. If this *were* the case with a compact disc, this state change from pit to land would not work. No method would exist to detect the number of 0s if the area being covered by the laser was continuously becoming slower as the CD was read from the center to the edge. To remedy the situation, the CD reader actually increases the rotation speed as it approaches the outer edge of the disc. Thus, a constant speed is always being maintained so the state changes that the laser experiences can be accurate.

The Murky Waters of Multiple Sessions, TAO, SAO, and DAO

As you've probably already found out (or soon will), burning optical discs isn't always a straightforward process. Many times, you might want to add more data to a disc you've already burned to once (with extra space left over). Or, you might want to put music and data on the same disc. This is done by writing multiple sessions to a disc. A *multisession* CD is one that groups tracks together into *sessions*. Each session has its own table of contents and is essentially a mini-CD on a CD.

Sessions are basically just collections of tracks written in a single pass of the laser. A CD can be burned using several methods. One of them is the *track-at-once* (*TAO*) method, which allows you to write one track at a time, pausing in between. Note, however, using this method requires a two-second gap between each track for synchronization purposes. TAO offers more flexibility when you are putting together an audio CD because you can record a few songs and then add a few more later, closing the CD when you are ready to play it. However, if you don't want those mandatory two-second gaps, you need another method for recording the CD, such as session-at-once (SAO) or disc-at-once (DAO).

The *session-at-once* (*SAO*) method enables you to add groups of tracks that can, on the appropriate player, be read before the CD is closed. Once you've decided not to add more sessions (or you just run out of space), you can close the CD so that it plays in a wider variety of players. The SAO method avoids the mandatory two-second gap between each track. This does not, however, remove any silence that might be inherent in the actual start or finish of the track itself.

Finally there's the *disc-at-once* (*DAO*) method, which writes the entire disc in one session and closes it, so it can be read in a wider variety of CD-ROM drives and, for music CDs, most home CD audio players. Like SAO, this method does not enforce a mandatory two-second gap between tracks.

Between Tracks

One thing you should note when using multiple sessions on a CD is that there is an overhead cost to bear. Each session is like its own CD to the reader and has a lead-in and a run-out track. This overhead is about 20MB for the first track and 13MB for the remaining sessions you add. For an audio CD, this translates into losing about nine minutes worth of space for each session. For even an 80-minute CD, that's a lot of time to lose!

How Sessions Work

Because each session is kind of its own disc, when inserting a multisession data CD-R in a CD-ROM drive, for example, the drive must pick a session to read first. Most drives first read the last session written to the disc, the idea being that if you use the same disc to back up the same data several times, the last session contains the most up-to-date information. In this case, reading the last session first makes the most sense. However, you might be recording some tracks now and some later and need access to all sessions on the disc.

Fortunately, you can tell your optical drive which session you want to read (how depends on your software). Of course, this won't overcome the fact that you won't be able to play all sessions on an ordinary audio player. But, if you use the CD-R to back up important data, or if you use it for music and play it back on your computer, using multiple sessions can be very helpful.

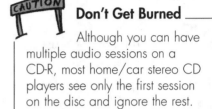

Don't Get Burned

Although you can have multiple audio sessions on a CD-R, most home/car stereo CD players see only the first session on the disc and ignore the rest.

Multisession Discs with Data and Audio

Today, the term *multimedia*, when it comes to computers, generally means a presentation that includes both audio and video, under the control of computer programs. Some are interactive and some are not. To burn a multimedia presentation onto a CD—in other words, using audio and data—usually requires burning a CD with multiple sessions. The two standard methods for doing so are called CD-extra and mixed-mode.

CD-Extra CDs

A CD-extra disc has two sessions—one to hold data and one to hold audio files. Because the first session holds the CD-DA (digital audio) tracks, you can play this kind of CD in your ordinary CD audio player to listen to just the music. The second session is written using the CD-ROM/XA data CD format. To use the programs or other data stored in the second session, you need a computer with an optical drive that supports multisessions. Don't worry about it, though, because most new drives do.

Because this is a multisession disc, the last session is activated and used by the optical drive first. Programs and data found in this session can be used with the audio session to present a multimedia presentation to the viewer. Although you won't see the packaging saying so, several CDs in your local CD shop were created using the CD-extra method. Do you have any music CDs that also include "CD-ROM" features? Odds are those are done using CD-extra.

Mixed-Mode CDs

Unlike CD-extra, a mixed-mode CD is technically not a multisession CD. I've included it here because ... well ... it just works better, okay? Instead, the audio and data are put into one single session. The first track contains the data. It also instructs your CD-ROM drive how to read the audio (CD-DA) tracks that come next. This first track can be in either the CD-ROM format or CD-ROM/XA.

Don't Get Burned

One caveat of a mixed-mode CD is that if you put it in an older audio player (or a cheaper new one), it might attempt to play the first track with disastrous results! Like what, you ask? How about frying your speakers with a shrill siren call that could wake up Elvis? In other words, don't try this at home.

The important thing to remember about recording mixed-mode versus CD-extra discs is that one method uses a single session on the CD, whereas the other method uses two sessions. Of these types of CDs, the CD-extra is generally more popular because of its capability to be used in any ordinary CD player without incident. On the other hand, if there's no chance that you're going to put the disc in a standard CD player, then you might prefer a mixed-mode CD that allows you access to all data on the disc without having to switch between multiple sessions.

Need More Input?

If all this hasn't satisfied your need for information about how CDs and DVDs work, there are more resources you can check out. On the web check out:

- ◆ **DVD+RW Alliance.** Located at www.dvdrw.com, this is the official home page of the supporters of the DVD+RW and DVD+R formats.

- ◆ **DVD Forum.** Located at www.dvdforum.com, this is the official camp of DVD-RW and DVD-R supporters.

- ◆ **CD-RW.org.** Located at www.cd-rw.org, this site is dedicated to all things CD-R and CD-RW related. They also provide several links to other exceptional optical recording sites.

If you still prefer the feel of a good book in your hand (who wouldn't?) and don't mind an extra 1,400 pages of information on your PC's other core components, check out *Upgrading and Repairing PCs, 14th Edition,* by Scott Mueller. This tome of all things PC includes more than 100 pages on the various optical disc formats and how they work.

Index